H O W   T O
PREPARE, STAGE,
& DELIVER
WINNING
PRESENTATIONS

NEW AND UPDATED EDITION

HOW TO PREPARE, STAGE, & DELIVER WINNING PRESENTATIONS

NEW AND UPDATED EDITION

THOMAS LEECH

amacom
American Management Association

New York • Atlanta • Boston • Chicago • Kansas City • San Francisco • Washington, D.C.
Brussels • Toronto • Mexico City

This publication is designed to provide accurate and authoritative
information in regard to the subject matter covered. It is sold with the
understanding that the publisher is not engaged in rendering legal,
accounting, or other professional service. If legal advice or other
expert assistance is required, the services of a competent professional
person should be sought.

Library of Congress Cataloging-in-Publication Data

Leech, Thomas.
    How to prepare, stage, and deliver winning presentations / Thomas
Leech.—2nd ed.
      p. cm.
    Includes bibliographical references and index.
    ISBN 0-8144-7813-1
    1. Business presentations.   I. Title.
HF5718.22.L43   1993
658.4'52—dc20   92-29518
                                         CIP

Printing number

10 9

Contents

Preface to the Second Edition

Over a decade has passed since *Winning Presentations* was first published. During that time it received high praise from many corners, including various Top 10 and Top 50 book lists; was chosen as an incentive for major corporate promotions; and received kind words from many people who found it useful to their business and personal needs.

The second edition retains the basic *Winning Presentations* approach to developing presentations and the fundamental principles of oral and visual communication. Since many people said they liked the book's design concepts, those have been retained, with many more illustrations in keeping with a basic presentations premise that a picture can be worth 1,000 words.

What has changed significantly over the past decade is the technology of presentations, which now use computer-generated visuals, LCD projection systems, wireless control devices, multimedia, and videoconferences (though the venerable black-and-white viewgraph is still the staple of the conference room). This technology has made it much easier to develop presentations and has brought the ability to produce quality visual aids out of the realm of graphic art departments and into desktop computers.

In this edition I've addressed many of the issues related to these new technologies. This is not a detailed how-to book about using specific, and constantly changing, computer software or hardware. It does provide many tips and cautions that can lead to better understanding and use of these technologies by presenters and those who help put presentations together.

Several thank-you's are in order: to Genigraphics' Judy Kremsdorf and Kathi Gabriel-Karen for providing many of the illustrations; to WordPerfect Corporation, IBM, and Claris Corporation for computer graphics software; to the many people who shared their feedback, support, and presentations wisdom; and to my associate and wife, Leslie, for pointers, proofing, prodding, and patience.

* * * Part I * * *
Presentations:
An Overview

✱ ✱ ✱ 1 ✱ ✱ ✱

The Role of Presentations in Business Today

KEY POINTS OF THIS CHAPTER

✱ Presentations are an integral part of business; how well they are done can have a major impact on business and personal success.

✱ Brilliance without the capability to communicate it is worth little in any enterprise.

✱ People spend years developing knowledge and skills of their professional specialty yet expend almost no effort studying how to communicate them.

✱ Leaders in many fields rank presentation skills as a top need and lament the quality of the skills they actually find.

"You can have brilliant ideas, but if you can't get them across, your brains won't get you anywhere." So says Lee Iacocca, chief executive officer of Chrysler Corporation. "I've known a lot of engineers with terrific ideas who had trouble explaining them to other people. It's always a shame when a guy with great talent can't tell the board or a committee what's in his head."[1]

In the world of business today—private industry, government agencies, the military, small businesses, and independent consultants—everybody seems to be giving oral presentations. Whatever their specialty or level in the organization, nearly all professionals find that presentations come with the job. It is a rare individual who can conduct his or her career communicating with only test tubes or computers. As business becomes increasingly complex, the need to communicate those complexities in concise terms that a broad audience can understand becomes more critical. One of the major tools for doing this is the oral presentation.

Top executives, program managers, engineers, bankers, architects, trainers, union leaders, politicians—all frequently find themselves facing audiences and selling their ideas through face-to-face presentations. These can be as simple as an informal talk to a half-dozen colleagues, using a few handmade viewgraphs, or as complex as a fully developed presentation using a hundred computer-generated slides and involving a dozen speakers.

What exactly is a presentation? Is it the same as a speech? Not entirely. A presentation differs from a formal speech in three main respects:

1. It is almost always given extemporaneously—prepared in outline form and spoken from aids or notes—rather than fully written and delivered word for word, as speeches may be.
2. It often involves visual aids; many formal speeches do not.
3. It is frequently given before an audience that is highly participative—asking questions and engaging in dialogue. For most *speeches*, the audience listens and perhaps asks questions later.

PRESENTATIONS PLAY A POWERFUL ROLE

People have been giving presentations with visual aids since time began. Cave dwellers supplemented their tales with wall paintings; the Egyptians probably got progress reports on the pyramids' construction via hieroglyphics; and Moses relayed the rules of life with the Ten Commandments.

Today's world sees presentations as playing key roles in opening doors, winning and sustaining business, and communicating with management and colleagues. Here are some specific roles:

- *Aiding in the pursuit of new business:* A company pursuing a competitive bid from government agencies or larger prime contractors, a civic economic development committee convincing industry to relocate, an advertising agency going after a new client.
- *Getting backing for growth or image:* An entrepreneur needing start-up money from venture capitalists, an expanding company floating a new financing program, the company president addressing the Chamber of Commerce.
- *Reporting status of ongoing projects to customers or management:* Design reviews, subcontract management allocations, production readiness, often involving many presenters from various disciplines.
- *Helping management stay informed for astute decision making:* Status of employee morale, budget reviews, requests for new equipment, go-ahead to pursue a new business line.
- *Keeping employees involved, informed, and current:* Product improvement team reports, new employee orientation, changes to procedures, training seminars.
- *Communicating between peers:* Industry trade shows, professional society annual conferences, management club meetings, technical symposiums.
- *Enhancing personal careers:* One of the highest-visibility methods of alerting others to your capability is giving presentations and speeches.

COMPUTER TECHNOLOGY FOR BETTER PRESENTATIONS—MAYBE

This is an exciting era for presentations practitioners. Advances in computer technology over the past decade have been so enormous that today's presenters get faster turnaround, better graphics, and a wider array of presentation types than they did just a decade ago in the form of color slides, headline-size type, clip art, and instant graphics of complex financial data. These types of presentations used to require artists, manual calculations, tedious paste-ups, and expensive machinery. Today's presenters get these swiftly from small office computers, graphics software, laser printers, and slide services. They benefit by turning out better presentations faster; their audience benefits from receiving better-quality products in a more timely manner. Getting on board today's presentations technology pays off.

The many high-tech options available have changed the nature of meetings themselves by tying the computer directly to output devices. Liquid-crystal displays eliminate slides and allow on-the-spot changes; videoconferencing allows groups to communicate from completely different locations; multimedia brings Hollywood to the conference room without Hollywood budgets.

Yet in this high-tech world, many companies still rely on black-and-white viewgraphs, personally delivered for the vast bulk of their presentations. Many computer-generated visuals are still hard to read, or they obscure, rather than clarify, a point. It is still the presenters themselves—the executives, engineers, or sales reps—who must come through with the knowledge, credibility, and persuasiveness to win over audiences.

High-tech computer tools are only as good as the wisdom and skill of those who use them. Computer experts have long known the acronym GIGO: Garbage In, Garbage Out. (A difference is that today's garbage out is much prettier than in the past.) Having the tools and the ability to use them properly *may* lead to better presentations, yet *without the fundamentals of public speaking and its related specialties, those tools are of marginal value.* As in carpentry, football, and romance, the best results come from having the tools, knowledge base, developed skills, and (don't forget this one) teamwork.

PRESENTATION SKILLS COMPLEMENT PROFESSIONAL SKILLS

In a 1980 survey of business leaders, 62 percent said the ability to write well was very important to their jobs. *Ninety percent said the ability to speak well was very important.*[2]

"Presentations are critically important to a wide spectrum of business endeavors," said Les McCraw, Jr., CEO of Fluor Corporation. "In our business, it's one of the critical elements. As we present ourselves, our company and our capabilities, we have to do so in as positive a light, clear and articulate as we can."[3]

The most brilliant idea is worth little until it is expressed. How well it is expressed can be as significant to its acceptance and implementation as the idea itself. A person can carry around terrific insights, knowledge, and analytical capability, but none of these abilities do him or her, the organization, or the world any good until it is communicated—fundamentally through writing or speaking.

The focus of this book is on the speaking avenue. Professionals might prefer to be left alone to communicate with the toys of their trade, but the day always comes when communication with superiors, peers, customers, or the public is necessary. For many people, oral communication is a continuous requirement, and for some, formal presentations are a daily or weekly occurrence.

Those who want to be heard and effect change recognize that professional skills go hand in hand with communication skills. And they work on both areas, expanding knowledge and capabilities.

Michael Bayer has been a top official in many agencies in Washington, D.C. Presentations in his business are life or death to ideas: "Here you are marketing to people overwhelmed with ideas. A bad presentation means the idea never connects, and in D.C. you rarely get a second chance."[4]

A presentation is an opportunity to take thirty minutes or several hours to talk about ideas to a group of important people. During that time, and possibly only then, you have their attention focused. This opportunity should not be taken lightly; a second chance may never come. Nevertheless, many people do treat the presentation lightly. They spend months working on a task but spend one day on the presentation of it. Yet the communication may be critical. How often can you get top management or customers to read a 200-page report? If you do a good job of presenting, executives may become inclined to read it or have staff dig into it. If no one reads it or listens to what it is about, what good is it?

"Presentation skills have to rate way close to the top in the modern business environment," said Arthur Toupin, vice-chairman, retired, of the Bank of America. "There is practically nothing in our business that does not involve communication, written or oral. Everything we do is communication, from the teller to the president of the bank. If there is anything more important than communication skills, particularly in the service industries, it's hard to think of it."[5]

WINNING PRESENTATIONS CAN BOOST CAREERS

Presentations are essential to the achievement of the goals of the enterprise and an extremely important avenue for career advancement. Few other activities have the potential for attention—favorable or otherwise—as do presentations. A person can toil unnoticed for years in the bureaucracies of large organizations. He or she can give one presentation to the right audience and suddenly be in the limelight. Want some examples? You've already heard from a couple of them.

■ *Lee Iacocca, once a shy introvert (hard to believe, isn't it?) who realized that not being able to speak well was going to hold him back. He determined to correct that with training and practice, and it became a major factor in his success and being a highly visible spokesperson for his company, American industry, and the Statue of Liberty restoration drive.*

■ *Les McCraw, Jr., CEO of Fluor Corporation, who, as a DuPont program manager, gave such an enthusiastic speech about the good work done by subcontractor Daniel*

Construction that Daniel's president made him a job offer. McCraw eventually rose to the top of Fluor (which had bought Daniel).[6]

 ■ *The governor who became Vice-President of the United States because of a superb keynote speech at the Republican convention. Wrong guess if you thought of Ronald Reagan, because it was Spiro Agnew, who became Richard Nixon's running mate in 1968. The decision makers were so dazzled they picked him without investigating him—a big mistake, as he later had to resign from office for malfeasance as governor.*[7]

A presentation is a public performance, equivalent to being under the spotlight on stage. It's hard not to be noticed in that setting. If you present ideas in an articulate manner and show you can think well on your feet, that will be noticed. If you ramble and rattle the change in your pocket, so will that.

A presentation is your opportunity to shine or blow it. I have seen careers take quantum jumps as a result of good performance in presentations and receive severe setbacks for poor performances.

Grant Hansen is a retired corporate top executive. He said,

> A comment was once made to me that careers are made or broken in ten minutes in the boardroom. One person may have that kind of opportunity and come across superbly. Another, who may be a brilliant scientist, comes across poorly. Comes the time for management to pick a person for promotion, they may well pick the one who came across well. The person who doesn't recognize this and train for it is missing something.[8]

A study was made to determine how executives, professional-society leaders, and university professors viewed the relative importance of the different topics studied at college.[9] The survey covered the field of engineering, but the results apply to many other fields as well. The most important capability for civil and electrical engineers, according to nearly 500 respondents, was the communication skills—writing and speaking. All the typical technical skills were ranked below communication skills in importance.

TODAY'S PRESENTERS—A MIXED BAG

The other part of the above survey asked the question: How good are the recent graduates in each of these capabilities? Fifty-nine percent were rated inferior, and graduates were rated higher on all other capabilities than for their communication skills. "The most astonishing finding of the survey," said the authors, "is that respondents overwhelmingly stressed the ability to communicate as most important, yet rated recent graduates—who will eventually take over as the leaders of our profession—very deficient in this attribute."

Every organization has outstanding presenters, whose technical or administrative skills are matched by their presentation skills. Much of the material in this book comes from the observations and experiences of many of these top presenters. In my experience, most of the people who rise to the top in organizations do so because they have demonstrated expertise in their specialties, plus they have good communication skills, particularly oral skills.

As a presentations consultant and as an audience member, I have seen many professionals whose presentation skills are extremely poor. I have sat through high-level corporate presentations where the visual aids could not be read, where presenters mumbled their words, where the message defied understanding, where equipment failed to work.

Sloppy presentations are not restricted to corporations. I've sat through them at important symposiums sponsored by professional societies and major universities. I've listened to nationally recognized authorities do terrible jobs of presenting. I've sat through incomprehensible presentations by civil servants. I've even experienced a few wretched performances as the presenter (early in my career, of course).

My observations are widely shared. Eric Herz, general manager of the Institute of Electrical and Electronics Engineers, the world's largest professional society, said, "I go to hear lots of presentations and get really bored. I feel like walking out, and often do. I don't see how other people can have the patience and politeness to sit there and endure that."[10]

From the vice chief of staff of the U.S. Air Force: "I am increasingly concerned about the quality of presentations. They need streamlining. A large number of presenters talk at great length from busy and unreadable charts on issues that are not germane to the subject."[11]

In "Executives Can't Communicate," Robert Levinson, vice-president and group executive of American Standard, Inc., said: "I have come to a shocking conclusion about the American executive. He talks too much, expresses himself poorly, and has an uncanny ability for evading the point. . . . It is astonishing how many otherwise able executives lack either the tools or the techniques for delivering their messages briefly, yet comprehensively."[12]

PRESENTATION SKILLS TAKE WORK—AND IT'S WORTH IT

People invest plenty to master their specialties. The typical professional has one or several degrees, reads trade journals weekly, participates regularly in professional societies, and continues to stay current.

How much time and effort do these same professionals put forth to develop their communication skills? On the basis of years of asking that question of many people in business and government, I suggest that the answer is, "very little." Beyond required, and generally hated, courses in English and speech as college freshmen, most have learned how to present by presenting. A few join Toastmasters or attend seminars. Some become outstanding presenters; many more don't.

Developing proficiency in oral communications does not occur automatically. The ability to speak may have come much as did walking and breathing, but speaking well to groups is another matter. Learning to organize thoughts and present them so people will listen and understand, determining what will win people over to your point of view, using visual and other nonverbal channels as well as the oral channel, developing sensitivity to what turns listeners on or off—these things may be assimilated by life experience, but to acquire a deeper knowledge of them requires serious attention.

Few things are more satisfying and confidence building than to experience important people intently listening to you as you go through your analysis and present your recommendations. Increased capability in oral communications serves a person well in many areas beyond presentations. Meetings, training, committees, personnel coaching and appraisal, leadership in professional societies, political or civic activities—all extensively involve oral skills. A person proficient in those skills is a valuable asset.

IN SUMMARY: PRESENTATIONS COME WITH THE TERRITORY

If you are a professional, you are probably fully aware that giving presentations comes with the job. If you are preparing for or are early in such a career, be aware that knowledge of your specialty is not enough. If you can't communicate it, how much is it worth? Developing this other important facet—oral communication skills—requires special attention. The investment can have ample rewards in terms of business and career success.

In case you need a bit more motivation, consider these words from Gilbert and Sullivan:

If you wish in the world to advance,
And your merits you're bound to enhance,
You must stir it and stump it,
And blow your own trumpet,
Or, trust me, you haven't a chance.

* * * 2 * * *

The Fundamental Fifteen: What Top People Say Are the Keys to Presentation Success

KEY POINTS OF THIS CHAPTER

* While much goes into planning, preparing, and giving business presentations, fifteen concepts stand out as fundamental.
* A speaker who applies the Fundamental Fifteen is well on the way to a successful presentation.

You are about to be exposed to several hundred pages describing the how-to's of winning presentations. If you feel overwhelmed as you read on, return to this chapter. Here is a boiled-down set of core principles (summarized in Figure 2-1), culled from my experience and the observations of many of the country's most active speakers and receivers of business presentations.[1]

1. *Be prepared.* "What causes speakers to fail? Absolutely—lack of preparation," said professional speaker and seminar leader Jane Handly. An article about the new CEO of a major electronics firm noted that he expects people to be ready when they walk into the conference room. He's known for ending the presentation on the first overhead transparency if he senses the speaker is not prepared.[2] Moral: Be _____.

2. *Believe that what you have to say is important.* Ashleigh Groce, senior vice-president of Leo Burnett, Inc., advertising, told of seeing back-to-back presentations about advertising successes:

> Such a difference. One case was so eloquently related, the speaker bubbled up from pride in her work and spoke with a true passion. The others had just as good a case, but they read from a script, and didn't demonstrate they believed in the work. We came away feeling the first was a better story, when the opposite was the case.

Figure 2-1. Back to basics—fifteen fundamentals to keep in mind.

1. Be prepared.
2. Believe what you have to say is important. It is!
3. Know your purpose, and make sure it fits reality.
4. Identify the fundamental message and key points.
5. Know your audience; speak to issues of concern to them.
6. For a busy audience, summarize at the start.
7. Win over your audience, stir with relevant reinforcement.
8. Make sure visuals are punchy and readable.
9. Pay attention to details when making arrangements.
10. Test your presentation, and always dry-run it.
11. Make the presentation a performance; keep the audience interested.
12. Be flexible; adjust the presentation as the situation changes.
13. Be ready for questions (also means being a good listener).
14. Keep your perspective; enjoy the presentation.
15. Remember: You're selling.

Friedrich Hegel wrote in his *Philosophy of History*, "We may affirm absolutely that nothing great in the world has been accomplished without passion."

3. *Know your own purpose in speaking and make sure it fits reality.* In all the pressure and furor of getting ready for a presentation, presenters may lose sight of their objective. Three questions help keep that focus in mind:

"What do I want to get out of this?"
"Is what I'm after feasible and appropriate?"
"Am I getting what I came for?"

4. *Identify the fundamental message and key points you want to get across.* "Many times people don't recognize what the key issue is. A lot of people avoid explicitly stating the point—they don't ever say why they're at the podium," said Eric Herz, executive director and general manager of the Institute of Electrical and Electronics Engineers. "I don't like to have to guess which of these things are important to the speaker and which are just being mentioned for completeness or opposition. Some people present eighteen facts, and they know three or four are more important, but they don't distinguish. I like for a speaker to help me understand."

What makes a speaker fail? "Not relating to the principal issues involved," stated Arthur V. Toupin, vice-chairman of the board, retired, of the Bank of America. "Talking, giving lots of background that is irrelevant to the audience. They don't get to the point, or by the time they do, people are unhappy with them because they've been waiting to deal with the issues and not getting there."

5. *Know your audience. Address issues of importance to them at a level they can understand.* The primary question in the minds of all audience members listening

is, "What is this going to do for me?" Yet commonly presenters discourse at length about topics of minor interest to a particular audience. Knowing and satisfactorily addressing audience priority needs is at the heart of successful attention and persuasion (see Figure 2-2).

The importance of tailoring the presentation at the proper level has been noted often—and the failure to do that is a nearly across-the-board lament. Jim Elms has been a top official in the government and an adviser to top corporation executives:

> As a governmental official, the thing I appreciated most was a presentation aimed at my level and where I was really learning something—where the material presented helped me understand better what the person was saying. The presenters who would fail would be the ones who would come in and give me all kinds of technical details and forget to tell me what the hell they were trying to tell me.

6. *Give a time-pressed audience an introductory capsule summary of your presentation (as appropriate).* A preview lets busy listeners know early on the essence of the message to come. "A person that can make a splendid summary of an issue right up front is an extremely valuable person," said Arthur Toupin. "He should state what action is sought—that is the most important part—and make sure that all the major issues are covered in a brief and succinct fashion so that the decision makers can get their arms around the problem in a hurry."

Brook Byers, general partner in the venture capital firm Kleiner, Perkins, Caulfield & Byers, constantly is on the receiving end of presentations. He advises

Figure 2-2. Words you don't want to hear.

Source: Genigraphics.

people seeking capital to "open with a bold, sweeping, almost controversial opening statement that immediately captures the goal, the expected accomplishment—for example, 'We're starting this new company . . . we expect it to be profitable in the sixth year . . . and we'll go on to be in the top ten in the [biomedical] industry.' "

7. *Win over your audience with solid, relevant reinforcement.* "Where's the beef?" means decision makers are looking for solid substance to back up claims. The power of a well-chosen example has been demonstrated many times in business, politics, and religion. My own experience in helping companies win contracts has shown repeatedly that credibility and confidence are often gained as much by the speakers drawing from personal, relevant experiences as from detailed studies and statistics.

8. *Make sure visual aids are readable, well focused, and make a clear point.* (See Figure 2-3.) "The most universal complaint people have in presentations is they can't read the damn charts," said Jim Elms. "It's so fundamental, yet we keep violating it all over the place. The other universal criticism is that people put too much on the viewgraph. The viewgraph may have seventeen lines on it because it was originally made to be shown in a very small room to four people. Now, with no changes, it's being shown to an audience of a hundred."

"It's astounding how many people still use overheads with a ton of information on them" lamented Department of Energy executive Michael Bayer. "I'm constantly appalled that the highest technology items are often attempted to be sold with the most brain-damaged, obsolete techniques imaginable!"

9. *Take care of the mechanics—or they'll take care of you.* Failure to follow this

Figure 2-3. Make sure visuals are readable and easy to follow, unlike this one.

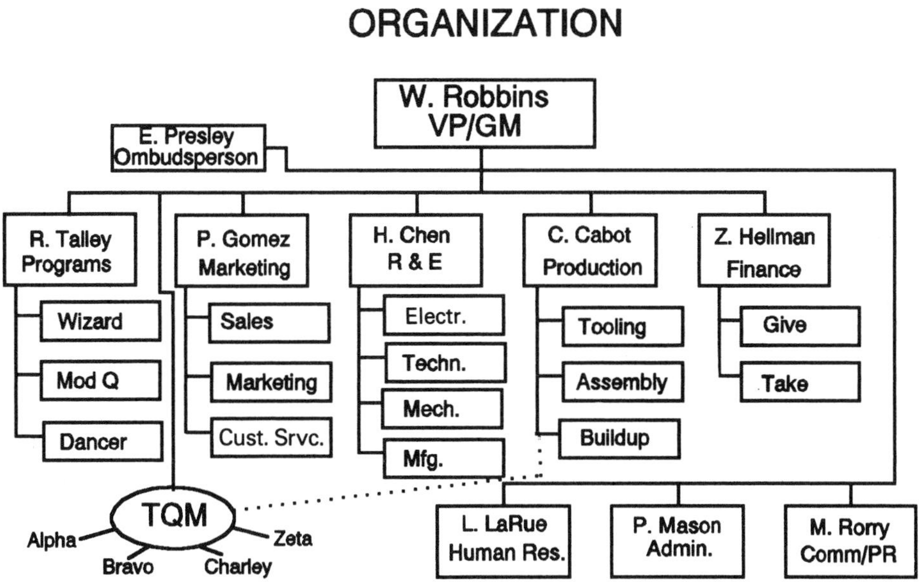

ORGANIZATION

simple axiom has been the grief of many presenters who tried to wing it and forgot the perverse nature of Murphy's Law—"Whatever can go wrong, will—and Leech's Variant—"especially right before or at the most critical part of the presentation."

Professional speaker and business executive Somers White has spoken to audiences in all fifty states and on all continents except Antarctica. According to him, "It's very important to get there ahead of time. Most speakers don't get there early enough. They don't check out the rooms, lighting, sound system, or audiovisual equipment." He's a firm believer in not only heading off problems, but being ready when they occur. "I was speaking at a hotel when the lights went off. I shouted 'I'll be up in one minute' and hooked in my own cordless mike and sound system. I asked the audience if I should continue, they said yes, and I spoke to them in the dark for another hour."

10. *Test your presentation before delivery and keep on practicing.* Rarely does a person get to be good at something without practice. This is especially pertinent to the business of standing up to speak before a group. Even skilled presenters benefit by dry runs of their presentations, and they get rusty if they don't keep their skills exercised.

Phil Joanou, president of Dailey & Associates, a leading advertising agency, gives or directs many presentations to potential or acquired clients. He says for him and for others that the way to become a good speaker is through diligent preparation and lots of practice. "To learn to catch a ball better, you catch a lot of balls. The more I practice, the better I am. Lots of people have the misconception that this is easy stuff. The best presenter I've ever seen is our creative director, and he really works at it just like the rest of us. When some fellow workers commented on how he had a gift for speaking, this is what he said, 'Gift, my ass! I've been working three nights on this pitch. These clowns think this just happens. Bull. You sweat!' "

11. *Put on a show.* "Every time you speak, you should realize you are putting on a performance," said Wes Magnuson, former national president of the National Management Association and a speaker of considerable experience. "It has to be interesting, and exciting; otherwise the audience will soon tire of it."

It is hard to get across a message to someone who is not listening. Communications consultant Gloria Goforth specializes in training executives to listen. She calls a presentation "industrial showmanship" and says that the success of a presentation rests on the extent to which the audience finds the speaker entertaining. "If you're all tensed up or bored, you won't hear a word the speaker is saying. So a bit of entertainment by the speaker frees the listener's minds so they can receive information."

12. *Be flexible; adjust your presentation to fit a changing situation and audience needs.* Grant Hansen noted the importance of adjusting to changing needs:

> My experience is that about 90 percent of people preparing presentations can't adapt if anything changes in circumstances. If a presenter has a sixty-minute presentation with a hundred viewgraphs and it gets cut to fifteen minutes, his usual approach is to talk as fast

as he can to cover all the material. As a result, the message gets completely lost. If there is one lesson I've learned, it is that presentations must be tailored to the situation, and the presenter must be flexible.

Eric Herz provides another example from an important presentation early in his career to an Air Force audience:

> We had developed a data processing facility with both company and government money. We felt it was necessary for the Air Force to come up with more money. I was all primed to make that request. Unfortunately, the project officers from the Air Force and our company had been having a knock-down, drag-out argument before I arrived, and here I was supposed to make a sale in this environment. I went through my material, and they weren't about to believe any of it. I had exhausted my resources and finally told them I was frustrated by my own inability to present the material in a way that could have any meaning to them. I said I absolutely know that this money was vitally needed and that I was terribly sorry I didn't know how to convince them. The top colonel looked at me and said, "If that's how you feel about it, you'll get the money."

13. *Be ready for material that is not in the presentation.* The ability of the speaker to handle audience comments or questions is often more critical than the ability to make the formal presentation. "It's a very bad situation to get a question you're not prepared to answer, particularly if it's in your field," said Arthur Toupin. "It's devastating not to be able to answer something about which you are the presumed expert and which you should be expected to know. That destroys your credibility. A good presenter has to be anticipating the thoughts of the audience and be prepared for things he doesn't plan to bring up, because they're likely to be asked. This is terribly important for a presenter."

Financial executive Brook Byers noted the importance of backup visual support: "Comes the question and the speaker reaches into the briefcase and has the perfect overhead transparency. Having that shows they've anticipated the question. It can be more impressive than forty or fifty slides."

14. *Keep your perspective. Let yourself come through and even enjoy the presentation a little bit.* Audiences relate well to speakers who are genuine, enjoy what they're doing, aren't uptight with fear about everything that can go wrong. Ashleigh Groce notes, "You have to enjoy making presentations. The key is really knowing your subject matter so you can be more extemporaneous and conversational versus stilted. You can make sidebar comments and add color to the presentation. The first few times you present may not be much fun, but you can learn to enjoy it."

15. *And remember: You're selling.* This pointer was not included in the first edition, perhaps because it's so obvious. Yet it kept surfacing as I watched many presenters approach presentations or deliver them as if it were business as usual,

except that contracts, budgets, and decisions were often riding on those presentations. As part of training seminars, I often invite top executives to address the troops about how they saw presentations. Consistently I heard them say: "Above all, keep this in mind: When you're up before that audience, you're selling!" What are you selling? Yourself and your credibility above all—then your organization, your information, and your proposition.

IN SUMMARY: THE BASIC STUFF WILL SERVE YOU WELL

Perhaps the most famous presentation of the past decade was a military briefing by General Norman Schwarzkopf. His presentation to the international press and television audience described how the United Nations forces achieved military success against Iraq during the Gulf War. Using poster charts, "Stormin' Norman" personified in action many of the Fundamental Fifteen: clear organization, good visual aids, energy and passion, superb question-and-answer capability. (Surprisingly, he said he did not do a dry run; he'd honed his skills so well over the years that for him it was just another briefing.) This briefing caught international attention, became a hot-seller in video stores, and led to the general's being touted as a candidate for political office and achieving a lecture circuit value of $25,000 a speech.

✳ ✳ ✳ 3 ✳ ✳ ✳
Becoming a Winning Presenter

KEY POINTS OF THIS CHAPTER

✳ Presentations are so crucial to business and personal success that developing presentation skills is an important personal investment.

✳ For those willing to pursue them, many avenues exist for enhancing skills.

✳ Stage fright is real, can be a serious detriment, and can be brought to manageable levels.

✳ Managers play a major role in helping others achieve better capabilities.

In Chapter 2 you read about the fundamentals of preparing and delivering presentations. How well the Fundamental Fifteen can be applied will differ widely depending on many factors: willingness to try, existing presentations capability, anxiety level, resources available, and work environment. This chapter shows how you can improve your presentations capabilities and ensuing success, heading toward the objectives realized by the speaker in Figure 3-1.

ENHANCING PRESENTATION SKILLS AND KNOWLEDGE

Where Are You Now?

Presentations capabilities range widely, from outstanding to dreadful. Some people never test these capabilities because they avoid presentations entirely; maybe they don't like doing them, maybe they've had bad experiences, or perhaps their pulse rate skyrockets at the mere thought.

A starting place for improvement is to do a realistic check of your capability. How successful have you been in the conference room or on the podium?

To find out your capability, do a postspeaking assessment yourself. Having yourself audio- or videotaped and reviewing the tape later provides helpful insights, if sometimes a dreadful jolt. Discuss with your supervisors how they see your skills and needs. Get some friends to sit in on a dry run or actual presentation as observers and give their feedback.

Figure 3-1.   The objective.

"Good presentation, Hotchkiss."

Source: The Wall Street Journal. Reprinted with permission of Cartoon Features Syndicate.

Where Would You Like to Be?

Project ahead a bit to what you'd like to accomplish on the job or for your personal interests. Would being a better presenter help you achieve that new position or enable you to be a more effective contributor? It almost always does. I've heard from many people who got a desirable job as project leader or executive, in large part because they became better presenters, or who were able to influence city councils or be a leader in an organization because their presentation skills made them so effective.

Perhaps you're already a good presenter, and you have a message you'd like to share with a broader audience. Or maybe you'd like to be more influential on a larger scale than your workplace. Your goal may be running for office, becoming a professional speaker, conducting university workshops, or starting your own company. Consider the level of presentation capability that will help you achieve those goals.

Commit to a Long-Term Plan to Improve

Since you've got this far, you've already made a major commitment. Keep it going. One way is to write down your plan, with specific objectives and milestones. Your supervisor can help by providing opportunities and guidance.

Get Started—Start Speaking More, and Better

A core part of sharpening any skill is doing it. You know that learning to swim or play tennis takes practice. So does speaking, a mixture of performance, on-your-feet thinking, interacting with people, self-talk, and skill development. It is especially important to speak often, get helpful feedback, and grow. You'll get rusty if you don't speak for six months. Here are specific ways to get that exposure and keep tuned up.

- *Join Toastmasters.* I often ask audiences how many of them are past or current Toastmasters and am generally dismayed at how few hands go up. Toastmasters is the most effective program I know of to help people quickly advance their speaking skills. It can bring about major change, not only in speaking but in a more assertive, open style that is helpful in meetings and personal relationships. When I was a Toastmaster during the 1960s, people would come to our club for the first time with limited skills and severe stage fright. After a few meetings, you could see the obvious improvement and would hear the comment, "Why didn't I do this twenty years ago!" Toastmasters Clubs are found throughout the world and can be located through telephone books or at their national office in Mission Viejo, California. A counterpart organization is International Training in Communication, formerly Toastmistress, with chapters worldwide and national office in Anaheim, California.

- *Take on a leadership role* in your professional association, management club, or personal interest group. In this role, you'll usually run meetings, introduce people, and give reports, all opportunities to try out your speaking skills.

- *Look for extra speaking opportunities in the workplace.* Offer to give a five-minute status report at a group meeting. Submit a proposal to deliver a paper at a professional conference. Talk to your training department or local college about teaching a class in your specialty.

- *Volunteer for a speakers' bureau* for a favorite cause.

- *Above all, apply winning presentation concepts* to all your normal work situations. Get feedback, and keep growing.

Keep Adding to Your Presentations Knowledge

Practicing is important. So is knowing what to practice or correct. And so is mastering the principles, processes, and tools. Some tips:

- *Watch and learn from good speakers, and poor ones.* Make every presentation—at work, in church, at club meetings, or from television speakers—a learning opportunity. Determine precisely what techniques make one person a spellbinder and another a bore.

- *Go back to the classroom.* Toastmasters is not just a practicing opportunity; it applies specific speaking principles. Companies invest in in-house or public seminars because they can bring about major skill boosts in a short time. College classes are an excellent and often low-cost way to learn about presentations and develop skills.

- *Learn about available tools and resources.* Presenters need to know about computer graphics programs and other ways to apply technology. Find out what help is available to get materials produced, either within the organization or through service bureaus.

WHAT ABOUT STAGE FRIGHT?

If you are one of those people who have been ducking presentations because you fear speaking before groups, you're far from alone (Figure 3-2). In one survey, researchers at Purdue University found that fear of public speaking was among the top ten fears (out of a list of 131).[1]

In the "knew it all along" category is the study done by Cedars-Sinai Medical Center, which found that many *mental* conditions can trigger the *physical* condition of heart stress. *The worst of all was asking people to give five-minute talks about their personal faults and bad habits to two observers.* Moral: Choose a different subject for starters.[2]

Philip Zimbardo, an authority on shyness, asked a number of students what made them shy. The worst situation, selected by 71 percent of the students, was where the person was the focus of attention before a large group, such as when giving a speech.[3]

Six Misconceptions That Stifle Presenters

1. *You have to have a God-given talent to be a good speaker* (and I don't have it). This is the myth that good speakers are born, not made. Who hasn't heard the

Figure 3-2. Nervous? Who, me?

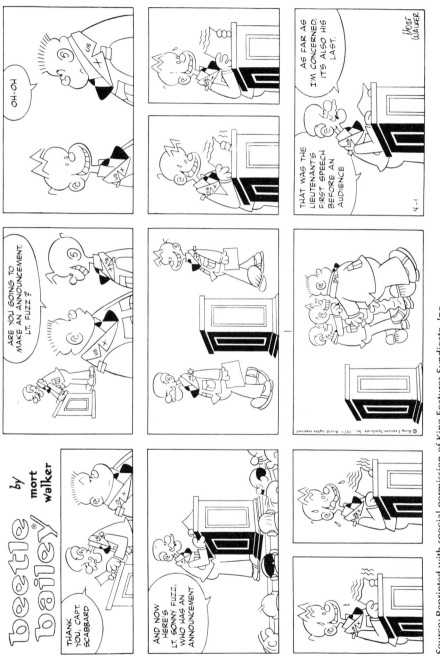

powerful voice and speaking style of James Earl Jones? God-given talent, you probably conclude. Yes, but Jones had to help a little. His teenage years were spent writing notes to teachers and chums instead of talking because he was a stutterer. "Whenever visitors came to the house," he recalls, "I was in terror of having to say hello." Fortunately, for his benefit and that of his many fans, Jones had a high school teacher who encouraged him to recite poetry, and he was able to do it fluently. That started him on the road to becoming the acclaimed actor he now is.[4]

2. *It was a lot easier for them* (they probably never had stage fright like mine). Lee Iacocca, chairman of Chrysler Corporation, is probably the most widely known business speaker in the country. In his autobiography, he tells about learning to speak by joining his high school debating team. "At first I was scared to death. I had butterflies in my stomach—and to this day I still get a little nervous before giving a speech. But the experience of being on the debating team was crucial. You can have brilliant ideas, but if you can't get them across, your brains won't get you anywhere." Even with that background, Iacocca avoided speaking during his first few years on the job, describing himself as "an introvert, a shrinking violet." Yes, Lee Iacocca. He broke that pattern when the company sent a group to a public speaking course. The rest is history.[5]

Eric Herz, general manager of the Institute of Electrical and Electronics Engineers (IEEE), was not always a good speaker. "My first presentation was in college. I had to address the student body and tell them how the newspaper was doing. It was pure hell, awful. I got to be a decent speaker by joining the IEEE. I organized a new chapter in my area and stood up at the first meeting to introduce the speaker. My knees were shaking a bit, but I was wearing long pants, so nobody saw them. As I gave more and more presentations at IEEE, and at work, it became easier and easier."[6]

3. *Good speakers don't have to work at it* (the way I do).

4. *The experienced people don't get nervous anymore* (and I do, so I must not be meant for this stuff).

Jane Handly has appeared before hundreds of audiences as a professional speaker and motivator but still has anxiety. "It comes and goes at the weirdest times. I feel like I'm going to hyperventilate and going to faint. Once in mid-speech, my foot cramped. 'Good grief,' I said, 'What is this?' Two keys: First, absolutely prepare well to head off the problem. Second, when it hits, I've learned to desensitize myself. I slow down, breathe normally, and focus on one or two people so I don't feel the dizziness of a big crowd. Within thirty seconds, it passes."[7]

As for stage fright, many grizzled veterans of public appearances of all types never completely get over it. Would you believe someone as confident as James Cagney used to get so nervous in live performances in vaudeville that he would throw up before every show? "They had a bucket at each entrance. I'd dance my head off, then go out and . . ."[8] Country singer Faron Young has long been a star and still trembles before every show. "And that's good," he said. "As Lionel Barrymore said, 'Show me a nervous actor and I'll show you a good actor.' "[9]

Many speakers admit to having butterflies in the stomach before they go on. One veteran observed that the main difference over his early speaking was that now the butterflies flew in formation.

5. *I could never be a good speaker* (so there's no sense trying).

6. *I've tried all that and it didn't work* (so it's futile).

These are the two most devastating misconceptions—number 5 prevents action, and number 6 represents resignation to failure. The most important step is to break the mold that says "I can't do it." This is the hardest one as well.

Dr. Wayne Dyer in *Your Erroneous Zones* described the "I'm" circle.[10] This is a vicious circle of logic that goes on in the heads of people who don't ever get around to doing things because they just can't do them. Figure 3-3 illustrates how it works to prevent people from breaking out of the mold of presentation avoidance. It starts at point 1, with the self-talker saying, "I'm no good at giving presentations," and ends back at the same place.

Before you turn down the next opportunity to give a presentation, look at whether you've talked yourself out of it through your own "I'm" circle. If so, break the loop at stop number 4, because the truth is you really can, if you choose to do so. Yes, there are risks . . . and rewards. The biggest reward of all is the self-respect that comes when you try a little bit, and it works, and you try a bit more, and soon you are doing exactly what you said you could never learn to do.

Novice speakers often get discouraged when they don't sound like Lee Iacocca on the first try. So they say, "I was right all along. I'll never be a decent presenter."

Wendell Johnson in *People in Quandaries* introduced a concept that pertains to this possibility. He called it the IFD disease.[11] Here's how that works: Joe Eager-Beaver decides to become a good presenter. He's seen Billy Graham on television, so that's his model (I—Idealization). He tackles his first couple of

Figure 3-3. The "I'm" circle stops many presenters before they get started.

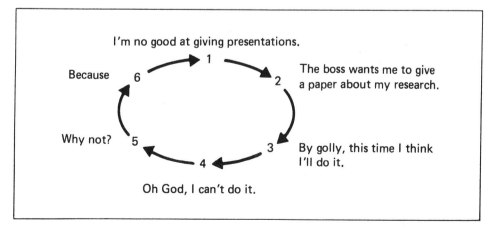

speaking opportunities, only he stumbles and gets frustrated (F—Frustration). He's feeling low and concludes he was stupid for even trying (D—Demoralization), so he says, "Never again."

With the IFD disease, people shoot too high too soon. They expect miracles, and those are rare. If you set out on a campaign to improve your speaking skills, be realistic about your program. If the IFD pattern starts to develop, put a healthy dose of realism into your expectations, and resist the urge to give up.

Breaking the Hold of Apprehension—A Dozen Tips

So how does a person who has let an excessive fear of speaking interfere too long with his or her success break the pattern? First, commit yourself to doing it. Then do an inventory of situations where you don't speak up and consider how productive those are for your organization and yourself. Apprehension stifles people in many situations besides presentations. It can deter people from asking questions, making valuable input during discussions, assuming leadership in organizations, even showing up at events that might expose them to uncomfortable speaking situations.

Look at the rewards that come with speaking up: increased participation and influence, the good feeling that comes from having your ideas and opinions listened to, increased ability to organize and express your thoughts, growth from exposure to new people and situations, and improvement in relationships because each party knows better where the other stands. I have seen many examples where a change in pattern has brought dramatic career moves, increased self-esteem, and a lot more fun.

Speaking success is also self-feeding. Each success makes the next step easier, particularly if positive feedback goes with the successes and excessive self-flagellation is avoided with the flops.

If you have severe apprehension or a speech impediment, seek expert help. Self-help attempts to change may be met with setbacks and leave you worse off than before you started. A professional can help prevent this and probably speed up the process.

Here are a dozen specific steps to help overcome apprehension:

1. *Start small.* Don't bite off a top-level customer briefing for starters.

2. *Add on progressively.* I start my college classes with simple exercises, provide a bit more of "how to," ask for a more demanding task, and continue to increase the level of sophistication. It works. A beginning step might be to sit up at the conference table during meetings rather than blending in with the paintings on the wall. Then you might start asking questions, volunteer opinions, help a colleague with a presentation, and give a short informational briefing to a few peers.

3. *Start with a message of importance to you.*

4. *Know your material and prepare well, using proven techniques.*

5. *Speak often, as much as you can, in all forms.* It gets easier the more you do it.

6. *Practice, test, be prepared for contingencies.* Uncertainties and problems that surprisingly pop up are real confidence sappers.

7. *Know the territory.* Strange environments and people can heighten reluctance to speak.

8. *Visualize and assume success.* It has been well demonstrated that doing something successfully in your head has a positive effect on actually doing it.

9. *Talk one-to-one with the friendly faces.* Forget the crowd and speak to one person. Would you be nervous if only the two of you were talking? Not likely. Now move on to a different person. Look for the smiling, responsive faces—they increase well-being. As your confidence grows, work on the dour ones.

10. *Focus on the message, not what they might be thinking about you.* Tell yourself, "What an egotist I am, to think they give a tinker's damn about the color of suit I'm wearing or whether I'm speaking perfect English. Get on with it." Really get into the subject and truly work to communicate your ideas and information to them. (Zimbardo notes that 85 percent of shy people say they are excessively preoccupied with themselves.[12])

11. *Perform activities that lessen inhibitions about speaking.* Play charades; read Dr. Seuss and Shakespeare aloud, and ham it up outrageously; spout off opinions in discussions; write letters to the editor; initiate conversations; speak to strangers; let the child in you come out.

12. *Give yourself lots of reasons to feel good about yourself.* Since reticence is strongly influenced by how you feel about yourself, a high evaluation of your self-worth is important. One of the best ways to improve self-esteem is by overcoming obstacles and achieving successes; this often occurs for people who tackle and overcome fear of speaking.

THE MANAGER'S ROLE AS SPEECH COACH

For over two decades, I've conducted hundreds of in-house Winning Presentations training seminars. A constant lament from participants is that they think this is all good stuff, but . . .

"The boss doesn't believe in it."
"We're so swamped that we never get any time to prepare."
"The person who really ought to be here is our VP. He makes the worst presentations in the company."

As most training specialists have learned, people's skill growth depends heavily on the support they get from their bosses. In seminars, we make extra efforts to get the "bosses" on board the process, with executive overview sessions, feedback to management, and specific suggestions to supervisors for them to become departmental presentations coaches.

"Not another job for me!" I can hear the wail. "That's all I need, along with the other thousand things I have to do every day. And besides, I don't know enough to be a speech coach."

As it turns out, becoming a reasonably respectable resident speech coach isn't necessarily complicated or burdensome. Those who place a high value on presentations and get involved in their development, as coaches and catalysts, see those efforts bringing about significantly improved results in the conference room and in the capabilities of their staff.

Here's how one manager seized the opportunity and made a difference. He came into an organization that was faced with marketing its services more seriously than before because of competition. The organization's technical capability was excellent, but its presentation and marketing skills were weak. (Sound familiar?) The division vice-president called the department's presentation skills "about the worst in the division."

The manager took as one of his most essential duties the role of presentations coach. He began by emphasizing to all hands the important part presentations played in getting top management's support and customers' contract dollars. He started reviewing presentations and sending most back for major surgery. He provided training and safe opportunities to speak in departmental meetings. And he made sure his own presentations applied good techniques. The results? This department now has the best presentations in the division. Was it worth the manager's time? Contract wins have increased significantly.

That example provides many of the keys to being an effective presentations coach:

- *Check it out.* Start by looking at the effect of presentations on your department's success and team members' effectiveness. How does your department stack up with peer groups or competitors? Are poor presentations costing you money? How efficiently are presentations prepared?

- *Commit and communicate.* Seriously take on the challenge to improve presentations quality. Let your employees know your expectations, reasons for increased emphasis, and plans for action. Insist on professionalism in communication as in doing the rest of the job.

- *Provide an environment of presentations excellence.* Do your own presentations display poor organization, cluttered visuals, and slumber-creating delivery? "Do as I do" is a stronger force than "do as I say." Apply the power of positive reinforcement by calling attention to those who have made good presentations and letting others know you expect better next time.

- *Make production and quality easier.* People often don't know what resources—graphics, software, video gear—are available or how to tap them.

- *Be there for review and support.* One of the miserable experiences many people speak of is being assigned to a presentation and being given little information or guidance. The "stuckee" flounders, goes off in too many directions, loses sleep, and comes up with a product that gets lacerated when the bosses finally take time to see it, usually during a dry run. "Gee, thanks for the help. But where were you when I needed you last week?" might be heard among the presenter's mutterings as he or she staggers out of the conference room. Your help can be invaluable at several steps along the way: initial directions, review of planning and strategy, outline and content reviews, practice sessions, actual event, and postmeeting feedback and pats on the back.

■ *Help your team members grow.* Four keys to strengthening employees' presentations skills are within the coach's area of influence:

1. *Motivation.* Clearly convey the importance of presentations to the person's effectiveness and departmental success, and make this a part of career growth discussions.
2. *Training.* Provide opportunities for in-house training programs and encourage the staff to take advantage of outside programs, such as Toastmasters or college classes.
3. *Practice.* Include short presentations in departmental meetings, promote professional papers, and delegate presentations to employees.
4. *Feedback.* Let presenters know how they're doing and what skills to keep working on.

■ *Be a good listener during presentations.* This is the hardest one of all.

IN SUMMARY: WHY NOT ADD TO YOUR PRESENTATIONS CAPABILITY?

Many people work hard to master the knowledge and skills of their profession. Developing the capability to present that expertise and their ideas in the best light is a valuable investment. Presentations growth comes from a determination to do it, followed by a program of knowledge sharpening and skill development through practice. Severe apprehension can be reduced to manageable levels by starting small and working up.

Tom Wolfe, in *The Right Stuff,* wrote about the seven Project Mercury astronauts, who were often called upon to "say a few words" to industry and civic groups during the early days of the manned space program. While some of the astronauts enjoyed speaking before groups, Gus Grissom disliked it intensely. In spite of that, one of the most powerful speeches of the whole program was given by Grissom. Here is the way it happened, as Wolfe wrote it:

> Gus Grissom was out in San Diego in the Convair plant where they were working on the Atlas rocket and Gus was as uneasy at this stuff as [astronaut Gordon] Cooper was. Asking Gus to "just say a few words" was like handing him a knife and asking him to open a main vein. But hundreds of workers are gathered in the main auditorium of the Convair plant to see Gus and the other six [astronauts], and they're beaming at them, and the Convair brass say a few words and then the astronauts are supposed to say a few words, and all at once Gus realizes it's his turn to say something, and he is petrified. He opens his mouth and out come the words: "Well . . . do good work!" It's an ironic remark, implying: ". . . because it's my ass that'll be sitting on your freaking rocket." But the workers started cheering like mad. They started cheering as if they had just heard the most moving and inspiring message of their lives: Do Good Work! After all, it's

Little Gus's ass on top of our rocket! They stood there for an eternity and cheered their brains out while Gus gazed blankly upon them from the Pope's balcony. Not only that, the workers—the workers, not the management but the workers!—had a flag company make up a huge banner, and they strung it up high in the main work bay, and it said: DO GOOD WORK.[13]

I have a special fondness for that story because I was an aerospace engineer fresh out of college and working on that program and on the scene the day Gus gave that little speech. That DO GOOD WORK slogan became the credo for the General Dynamics employees building those Atlas rockets. Signs, posters, stickers, newsletters all carried the slogan as a reminder to everybody of what was at stake. It is still spoken of fondly by those who were there and still in the business.

Gus's success illustrates that all the tips and rules are worth little in comparison to the right person having the right words at the right time—"the right stuff," as Wolfe already put it.

✳ ✳ ✳ 4 ✳ ✳ ✳

Introduction to the Systems Approach

KEY POINTS OF THIS CHAPTER

✳ The development of any new product typically follows a progression of steps from planning through completion.

✳ By contrast, development of presentations is often done in a haphazard, hit-or-miss manner. The results generally show it.

✳ The *systems approach* applies a proven process to presentations leading to better and more efficiently developed presentations.

✳ In preparing presentations, much time and effort are often wasted by going down the wrong path. Changes cost more the later they occur. Thinking ahead can help alleviate these common problems.

✳ Successful presentations result from intelligent and thorough attention to all elements. There are no guaranteed tips to success.

The aces in any field know what they are doing and why and how. Executives, financial analysts, and scientists have this characteristic in common with tennis professionals and Olympics stars. They achieve results by applying proven techniques to whatever problem they tackle.

Roughly the same sequence of events occurs in producing any product, whether it is an automobile, a can opener, or a software system. You don't start to build a new automobile before you design one, and you don't start to design one before you figure out if one seems needed and what kind.

One of the key factors that distinguishes the cool, efficient professional who gets results from the duffers who stumble around and rarely get anything done well is this knowledge of process. When given a tough problem, the duffer often doesn't know where to start. The professional knows precisely where to start and what has to be done to get to the desired result.

Now a strange thing happens to many of those same professionals—executives, financial wizards, and scientists—when they are asked to prepare *presentations* about their specialties. They forget all the wisdom that separated them from the amateurs—the proved, rigorous approach—and instead tackle the presentation in a haphazard, casual manner. Modern businesswoman Cathy demonstrates that approach in Figure 4-1.

This is how that works. "Schmidt, I want you to give a status presentation on the Model Q engine next week to the VP," says the program director. Schmidt goes to the file cabinet and pulls out a folder containing the visuals from last month's Model Q presentation, takes some drawings down to the repro room, and reduces them to fit on 8½ by 11-inch pages. He jumps on the computer and bangs out five more charts, adding some pizazz with computer clip art, Old English Script, and five colors. (Schmidt loves this new technology; he could spend hours on it, and does.)

Schmidt finally gets all his materials assembled, but there's no time for a dry run (he rarely does one anyway), so he heads to the VP's office. Except the secretary says the meeting is in the factory. Oops. Over he goes and slinks into the room, only to see the overhead projector is gone (and it was right there yesterday!). The VP stops the show on Schmidt's agenda chart: "What's this junk? I wanted production plans, not design plans. Who's up next?"

As executed, this presentation will yield a totally unsatisfactory, embarrassing result. If Schmidt and his program team had produced the Model Q engine following the same procedures as for his presentation, the engine would have been as big a disaster as Schmidt's presentation.

THE SYSTEMS APPROACH: BORROWING PROVEN METHODOLOGY

The same proven procedure professionals use in tackling any project can be applied beneficially to the development of presentations. This methodical, step-by-step approach can lead to better presentations, produced more efficiently. As adapted, what I refer to as the systems approach to presentations is shown in Figure 4-2.

Seven Steps in the Systems Approach

1. *Plan.* This is the market analysis, fundamental thinking-through phase, asking, "What do I want to get out of this presentation? How might that best be done?" The audience is identified, its interests examined, and themes and strategies developed.
2. *Organize.* This develops the framework, the skeleton of the package. The key ideas are identified and arranged in a clear, concise, and convincing manner.
3. *Support.* This adds the meat to the organizational skeleton. Material is developed to back up, illustrate, and clarify the positions and claims set forth. Visuals aids are shaped into punchy, effective tools of communication.
4. *Stage.* The goal is to head off the relentless power of Murphy's Law: whatever can go wrong, will. Leaving nothing to chance, the presenter identifies facilities, equipment, and schedules. Before heading off to the actual event, the wise presenter tests the product.

Figure 4-1. Cathy meets a presentations assignment in her own way.

Figure 4-2.   The systems approach to winning presentations means more gain with less pain.

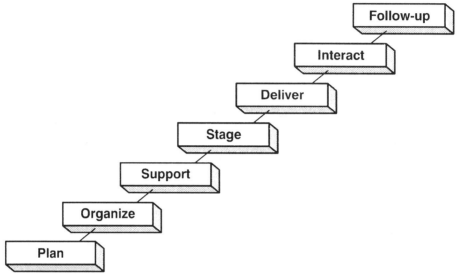

Source: Genigraphics.

5. *Deliver.* This is the moment of truth. The curtain is up; it is time to produce. Now real listeners are sitting there taking real notes, asking real questions, and taking real naps. This is the presenter's show: to speak with conviction and power to achieve what he or she came to do, to make points or lose them, to adapt to changing conditions.

6. *Interact.* Presentations rarely have a passive audience, especially when it is made up of customers or upper management, so the speaker must have the ability to handle the questions and answers (Q&A). The audience is an integral part of the presentation; their ability and style of coaching or challenging speakers plays a big role in meeting success.

7. *Follow up.* All is not over when the product is delivered. Now is the time to tally up the scorecard, take care of the loose ends, and apply the lessons learned toward a better job with less wasted effort the next time.

NO FAST-FOOD ROUTE TO PRESENTATION SUCCESS

I am asked by presenters, "Give me a few pointers so I'll be sure to do a good job." The following exchange typically ensues:

"When is the actual presentation?"
"Tomorrow."
"Are you going to be able to make any changes if I point them out to you?"
"Well, not in the visuals, but maybe in some of the other areas—like how I stand and can I be heard well enough."

How much of an improvement do you think a helping hand would be able to make under those conditions? The organization may be impossible, the visuals unreadable, the basic strategy completely off—any of which is probable disaster. And yet none of those can be changed.

The ability to help someone with a presentation depends greatly on when help is called in. The best time is during the formative stages of planning and organizing. A small suggestion here can get the presentation directed toward a better path before the detailed work begins. Many presenters lack knowledge of how to create effective visual aids or other support, so this phase can often benefit from astute coaching. Later, the dry run offers a coach many opportunities to help save the presentation.

Rarely will one or two tips cure a poor presentation or poor presenter. Perhaps because most people can talk, everyone assumes it's only a thin line between duffer and star. The systems approach concept and the Fundamental Fifteen presented in Chapter 2 should have dispelled the idea that there is a fast-food route to good presentations. There is a route, but it may not be fast. The route is careful, intelligent attention to all the parts that go into determining the success or failure of a presentation.

For providing confidence to a presenter, nothing beats knowing that the material is sound, that all arrangements have been carefully made and contingencies considered, that all parts have been proofed and refined, that the territory is known and well planned for. This is the best way I know for changing that fearful, queasy feeling to one that almost says, "Let me at 'em! I'm going to be great!"

THE SYSTEMS APPROACH MAKES SENSE (AND CENTS)

What most people want as they tackle a presentation is to be able to develop a winner with as little hassle as possible. Making presentations is not the prime line of work for most people.

Consistently I have seen presenters who follow the systems approach or something resembling it turn out effective presentations, not without the hard work but in a fairly predictable and trouble-free manner. I have seen many presentations that followed the haphazard approach with disastrous results: extensive revisions, many false starts, much scrapped work, and still marginal success with the customer.

"But I don't have time to go through all that stuff. It would make sense if this were a major presentation and all I had to do was work on it. It's all I can do to get everything done as it is." This is a standard wail I hear from presenters when the systems approach is proposed. This usually occurs when they are in the middle of putting together presentations. They've been gathering data for two weeks, their visuals are in final form, and much of what they've been doing is worthless. The usual reason is inadequate analysis and planning at the start, resulting in a lot of wasted effort. The final test—the actual presentation—often fails because of the many inadequacies at each step of the way. Dressing for success and flashy techniques rarely can overcome a third-rate product.

The question to be asked is, "Can I afford *not* to follow the systems approach or a reasonable facsimile of it?" Time constraints are certainly a reality, which makes it even more important to ensure that effort is well directed. Time spent asking the important questions at the start and then planning before doing is time well spent. For a quick turnaround presentation, this may allow only five minutes. For a major effort, it may take a week. The key point is to give each step intelligent consideration within the time available before tackling the next one.

In developing a presentation, costs increase and flexibility decreases with each succeeding step along the way. It's easy and costs little to change direction at the start. A procedure that leads to fewer false starts and last-minute changes has distinct advantages over one characterized by a panic, start-stop mode of operation. Some of the characteristics of a haphazard approach and a systems approach are shown in Figure 4-3.

Jack Dean, Aerojet proposal development manager, applies a systematic approach to proposal and presentations development. He described an event that reinforced his philosophy and made some more believers in the process:

> We were bidding to a prime contractor for a major proposal for an engine system and up against two other competitors. We turned in the written proposal and were asked to make an oral presentation. We applied the same disciplines to develop the presentation content and then put our speakers through a rigorous exercise of dry runs. We also made models, which we kept covered until the most dramatic moment in the presentation. The presentation went well to both the review board and the prime's top management. We were told they would review it, take it to management, and that we could expect a decision within a week.

Figure 4-3. A systems approach uses resources better and gets better results.

Characteristics of Presentation Development	Haphazard Approach	Systems Approach
Priority	Afterthought	Integrated
Focus of early effort	Visual aids	Analysis and planning
Material generated	Voluminous, scattered	Selective, pertinent
Top-management involvement	Late in cycle	Throughout
Nature of rework	Panic, overtime	Touch-up
Presenter's confidence	Shaky	Assured
Bottom lines		
Cost to produce	Overruns estimate	Close to estimate
Effectiveness	Often marginal	Often on target

We headed home. When our program head went into his office, he found a message waiting on his machine, from the prime. It said they were so impressed with the presentation, they made a decision on the spot and awarded us the contract. The program manager was dumbfounded as we knew it was a close competition.[1]

Now for a story from a department head of a different organization presenting a sad result from *not* doing it the right way:

This was a program review on an existing contract. We were awfully busy and felt we were in good shape on the program, so we didn't spend much time getting ready. No dry runs, for example. We got into the presentation, and the customer tore us apart. It was clear we were not prepared for this meeting. One measure of our success can be seen in the number of action items we carried away. Typically we get 25. This time we got 300. It's going to take us months to take care of them all. What a painful way to get reminded of the importance of preparing well.

IN SUMMARY: THE SYSTEMS APPROACH PAYS

Effective presentations result from careful and sensible attention to each preparation step. A haphazard, hit-or-miss approach commonly leads to massive last-minute changes or flops—and sometimes both. Following the systems approach can achieve a better product and better use of preparation resources.

✳ ✳ ✳ Part II ✳ ✳ ✳

The Systems Approach to Presentations

* * * 5 * * *

Plan

KEY POINTS OF THIS CHAPTER

* Planning is an important investment in time; good initial planning helps ensure that preparation is wisely directed.
* The approach selected in planning may be the most critical factor in presentation success or failure.
* Understanding clearly the goal of the presentation is the starting point.
* Knowledge of the audience and the occasion is fundamental in establishing presentation approach and strategy.

A manager on an important new electronics system was asked to tell a group of visiting Explorer Scouts about the program. He pulled two dozen visuals used for working meetings, went into great detail about technical aspects, and spoke of FLMs and MOKFLTPAC. He was enthusiastic, knowledgeable, and totally ineffective, since his audience was lost for about forty-four of his forty-five minutes.

During the 1960s, one of the big three television networks gave a presentation to several potential sponsors for a new series, "12 O'Clock High," based on experiences of Allied bomber pilots in World War II. Volkswagen was one of the prime client targets. Perhaps you can see some potential difficulties in that matchup. The network led off with drama, rolling the opening scenes of the film, which showed terrific shots of American bombers unloading their payloads and blasting the targets below. Within two minutes a German-accented voice—the Volkswagen representative—was heard muttering, "There goes our factory in Stuttgart." Shortly thereafter, the network team packed up its film and silently left the room.[1]

Grant Hansen, a retired executive, recalled the commencement address at his college graduation, shortly after World War II, when many of the graduates were war veterans. "The speaker had given the same speech for years. He told us about this great milestone—graduation—we had just achieved, and that soon we would be arriving at other milestones—our first jobs, then getting married, and soon having children. I looked up and down the row and saw all these war veterans, seated with their wives and kids behind them, and thought this speaker hadn't done his homework very well. I had myself been divorced and remarried."[2]

Many speakers are sincere in their desires to impart a message and put forth great effort in preparation, but all their efforts are for naught because they are misdirected. The foundation is faulty because of failure to consider adequately or correctly the audience part of the communication process.

Planning addresses the strategic part of presentation development versus tactics. It is doing the market research and analysis, needs assessment, and thinking. This is where the basic questions are asked: "Who is going to be in the audience?" "How can we get them to accept our ideas?" "Do we even want to give a presentation?"

The effective presenters almost always have a good sensitivity for planning. They understand it is a wise investment.

I have worked with presenters who were well along in preparation. They'd spent two weeks agonizing over organization, gathering data, making computer runs, and creating visuals and yet responded with blank stares when asked: "What do you want to achieve? What is your audience concerned about?" Too often this meant two weeks' work down the drain, because the basic questions were not asked or given enough of the right kind of attention *before* all that work started.

Several steps are involved in the planning process. Those outlined in Figure 5-1 suggest a neat, sequential process, and it may be for simple presentations. But for major ones, such as competitive marketing presentations by a team of speakers, the planning process can be involved and highly iterative. Once the plan is set, further development may surface new information or suggest better approaches, causing a reassessment of the original planning decisions. Key concepts from this chapter are shown in Figure 5-2.

SET GROUND RULES

Before racing off to order a hundred slides by Monday morning, gather, list, and clarify certain basic information. Ask questions now to head off wasted effort and dollars. These fall roughly into three categories: the five W's, audience or customer requirements, and detailed guidelines.

Figure 5-1. Planning examines several interrelated factors to develop a sound approach.

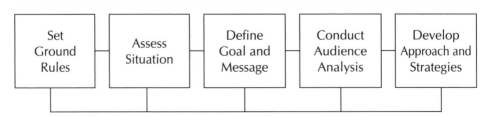

Figure 5-2. Apply these tips for effective planning.

- Establish requirements, constraints, and budget.
- Define your own objectives and the fundamental message you want to get across.
- Identify key members of the audience. Assess effects of their capabilities, knowledge levels, interests, and attitudes on the presentation.
- Set the presentation at a level appropriate for the audience.
- Be aware of individual and group needs and pressures, as well as organizational ones.
- Provide a message that will be of interest and value to the audience.
- Identify benefits your proposal offers the listeners.
- Be sensitive to immediate needs that may override long-term ones.
- Match your approach to where the customer is on the program decision sequence.
- Identify anything you must (or must not) say or do.
- Consider audience attitudes in planning your approach.
- If you have a lemon in your package, see if you can convert it to lemonade.
- Account for what an audience typically must go through mentally to do what you ask.
- Keep rechecking planning assumptions and decisions through all phases of the presentation. Be an ever-listening speaker.

The Five W's

These are the old who, what, when, why, where questions, such as:

- *Audience.* Who makes up the audience? Identify the organization, number of participants, and key individuals.
- *Subject of specific area of interest.* What do they want to hear about? What specific topic do they want to focus on? This may be only loosely defined for some presentations but tightly targeted for others.
- *Event and occasion.* Is this tied in with something else, such as a group of visiting dignitaries or the annual meeting?
- *Function.* What is this presentation intended to do? How does it fit into the broader scheme?
- *Date and time.* Is it tomorrow or next week? What time of day? Different considerations will be in order depending on whether the talk takes place first thing in the morning, over lunch, late in the afternoon, or after dinner. How firm are the date and time?
- *Location.* Here, there, or elsewhere? Is the room already set, or is one to be scheduled? What kind of place is it?
- *Speaker(s).* Who is actually giving the presentation? This may not be the person preparing the presentation. Will several presenters be involved?

Audience or Customer Requirements

For many presentations, the audience will explicitly request that certain items be addressed or procedures followed:

- For contract competitions, the customers may state the topics they want covered.
- Audiences may state or may need to be asked what *criteria* they will use to evaluate competing presentations. This can be potential customers, such as source selection boards; internal management reviewing research projects for future funding; or judges for speech contests. They may even have set evaluation forms; what's on those forms?
- Presenters may be given a list of *questions*.

It is vital that these be known, understood properly and clarified if needed, and integrated into the presentation. A presenter who doesn't heed this request will be deemed nonresponsive.

Detailed Guidelines

This gets into the operational, nitty-gritty stuff that is important to know from the start:

- *Type and length* of presentation (formal or informal).
- *Format and medium* (demonstrations, viewgraphs, slides).
- *Nature of meeting interaction* (audience questions during or after, many likely or few).
- *Operational constraints* (related to event, program, location, shipping, travel).
- *Budget and priority.*
- *Available help* (resources and people, decision makers, reviewers, presentations support, content contributors).
- *Anything else* to be aware of.

ASSESS SITUATION

After three days of campaign speeches, floor battles, and ballots at the 1988 Democratic convention, the delegates had selected Michael Dukakis as their presidential candidate. The plum assignment of introducing Dukakis to the gathered delegates and the nationwide television audience was given to Arkansas governor William Clinton. He was asked to speak for fifteen minutes.

What situation did he face? What was the environment or mood in the convention hall? What would happen any time he said "Michael Dukakis walks on water!" or "The other party [President Reagan's Republicans] has messed up the country!" Did he really have fifteen minutes?

The governor began his introduction, and true to form, the audience responded fervently each time he praised his side and disparaged the other. He continued on and further on into his speech. As it became clear that he was going well beyond the appropriate time, the initial cheers gave way to cries of "Hook!" The signal lights switched from green to yellow to red to flashing red, but Clinton kept plowing ahead. Even a whisper from the chairperson to wrap it up went unheeded until Clinton had read all *eighteen pages* of his script and fifty-three minutes had elapsed. By now the mood in the hall had turned ugly, and TV audiences across the country had probably given up on seeing Dukakis and switched to the wrestling matches.[3]

Failing to size up the situation properly led to a poor outcome and at least a temporary setback (and lesson learned, the hard way) to Governor Clinton's own political ambitions.

Designer engineer Jonathan Boardman was on the scene when another presenter was more successful at tailoring his talk to the situation. "I and the other employees of Short Brothers Aircraft Company in Belfast were on hand for the rollout of the first C23 cargo aircraft. Many politicians and military officers had gathered for the ceremony, with a speakers' platform, a military band, and a huge American flag across the stage. Several dignitaries spoke to the invited guests. Then a top U.S. general took the microphone and said, 'I'm not going to address you people. You didn't do anything.' He turned away from the invited guests and walked over to face the workforce. Then he said, 'I'm going to address you people. You did all the work and you're the ones we're counting on to continue doing good quality work.' He gave his speech entirely to us. We loved it and cheered mightily. We were all really pleased and talked about it for weeks afterward."[4]

Here's another example. A human resources manager was to be one of many speakers at a three-day management retreat. His slot was at 4 P.M. on day 2. His job was to renew interest in the employee suggestion program, not a high-interest topic. We reviewed his planned presentation and found it to be dry, information heavy, and weighty with busy charts. The review team predicted severe Slumbersville and headed him back to the drawing board. He came back with a totally transformed presentation: a much snappier opening, simpler content, punchier visuals, and a more spirited delivery. His presentation was one of the best of the conference.

Knowing the meeting environment or circumstances surrounding the event can help a presenter do the right thing or avoid doing the wrong one. Probably every experienced speaker has realized upon leaving the podium that he or she has just done something stupid. Several questions are worth asking to avoid problems:

■ Does the occasion have any special requirements that may be peripheral to the presentation? For example, protocol can define rigorously specific procedures or rituals that must be observed.

■ Is there anything I must absolutely not forget to say or do? You can talk wonderfully for an hour and then blow the whole situation by neglecting some required statement or task. Senator John Glenn campaigned in New Hampshire for the 1984 presidential campaign. Many supporters had flown in from his state of Ohio to help. At a meeting of supporters, Glenn thanked the Ohio people profusely but said little about all his New Hampshire supporters. They were not pleased.[5] I, too, once thanked only part of a committee. Did I hear about that!

■ Is there anything I must clearly avoid? President Jimmy Carter found out the answer to this one on a visit to Mexico, when he jokingly noted he had a touch of Montezuma's revenge. This was a nerve ending for his audience and cast a shadow on the whole trip.

■ Is there a vital issue—something the audience specifically wants to hear about? If the audience is hungry for news about the new contract, failing to mention it can leave them dissatisfied. Even saying "I can't say anything about that contract yet" is generally better than skipping the subject entirely.

■ Is anything else occurring that is likely to affect my presentation? If the presentation is after a two-hour hospitality period, your audience may not be in a proper mood to assimilate a forty-five-minute talk on the needs of higher education. I watched a famed speaker do exactly that at a national conference. The only people listening after the first five minutes were the emcee, the speaker's spouse, and me, taking notes incredulously. Everybody else had faded.

■ Is anyone else involved that I should know about? If you are scheduled to follow Don Rickles (or vice-versa), you may want to reschedule.

■ Is the present audience the real audience? An example where this is not the case is a televised talk. Focusing on the immediate audience may prove deterimental to communicating with the real audience—the television audience. During the 1960 presidential debates, Richard Nixon was credited with winning the debate inside the television studio; John Kennedy won it where it counted, in the homes of millions of viewers.

Situation analysis is not something done once and forgotten. Events may occur right before or during the meeting that can seriously affect attendees' spirit or attention. I was conducting a seminar the morning the space shuttle *Challenger* blew up during launch. The company was a shuttle subcontractor. As we watched the event on television, I knew the relaxed, learning mood was no longer there and suspended the planned activity.

DEFINE GOAL AND MESSAGE

What is the speaker's purpose? What does he or she hope to achieve? What message does he or she wish to get across? This is the *raison d'être*, the basic object, of the presentation, and yet it is frequently not clearly understood or unrealistic. Gerald Phillips and Jerome Zolten call this the critical step in speech preparation: "Figuring out exactly what you want to communicate to your audience. Whether spoken or written, formal or informal, the fate of a message depends on two things: the ability of the communicator to isolate his purpose clearly, and the ability to coordinate personal resources to achieve his purpose."[6] Three steps are involved: defining the (1) basic purpose, (2) end product, and (3) main message or theme (see Figure 5-3).

Basic Purpose

This is likely to fall into one of four categories:

Figure 5-3. Define the goal and the message—an example.

Basic purpose: To persuade.

End product: To obtain the vice-president's approval of our facilities proposal.

Main message: We should build the new facility because it is the most cost-effective remedy for our overcrowded condition.

---

1. *To persuade (or convince).* Marketing presentations almost always are of this type, as are presentations seeking approval and support for new programs or facilities or ideas.
2. *To inform (or explain).* A professional paper, an orientation to a new product or procedure, a classroom lecture, and a status report are examples of presentations whose primary purpose is to inform.
3. *To inspire.* This is regarded by many authorities as a subset of persuasion. Its primary purpose is to fire up or move the troops, with Knute Rockne's "Win one for the Gipper!" and General Patton's address to his troops as classic examples.
4. *To entertain or preside.* Welcoming new employees, presiding at a retirement or change of command, contributing at a "roast" are in this category.

Frequently presenters either lose sight of their purpose or have not thought through clearly enough what their purpose should be. The result is often an inappropriate presentation or a confused audience. While overlap among these four categories often occurs, it is still worthwhile to know into which of them the presentation purpose primarily falls. Organization and type of material may differ significantly if the purpose is to inform instead of to persuade or to entertain.

End Product

What is the goal of this presentation? How will you know you've succeeded? This is what the *end product, specific purpose, or presentation objective* specifies. It may seem simple and obvious, but it is frequently absent or vague. The end product is the outcome you desire from your audience in specific terms that help you know, not guess, if you succeeded. It is what they will do, believe, and know.

Writing down your end product helps clarify and focus your presentation. Here are some criteria to help you do that:

■ *Is it achievable?* Getting the audience to give blood to the blood bank is a worthy objective, but how likely is success if the audience is composed of hemophiliacs? If you need approval of a $50,000 budget item and the principal listener can approve only $10,000, you need to rethink your plan.

■ *Is it a present or ultimate objective* (or is it achievable now?)? Ask an eager marketer what the objective is, and the answer may be, "To win the contract, of course!" Is that likely to occur as a result of this specific presentation? "Well, not really. We have a long way to go before that can occur." Then what *is* possible with this presentation? "We'd like to get them to put us on the bidders' list."

■ *Is it measurable?* When you ask yourself or the boss asks, "Was it a winner?" a well-defined end product gives you a *yes* or *no*. "How do you know that?" may be met with silence unless it's measurable. "Get four sign-ups" is measurable; "sell the idea" may or may not be. This criterion may not fit all objectives, however.

■ *Is it sound business?* "I convinced them to invest," said the salesperson from Investments-R-Us. "They're putting all their money into no-load mutual funds." Nice job, except IRU isn't in that business and won't make any money themselves.

Now for some specific end products. A helpful way to write these is to state, "As a result of my presentation, the audience will _____," and fill in the blank. Some examples are shown in Figure 5-4.

Main Message

An essential part of this stage of planning is to determine the main message. To do this, assume you can say only one sentence to your audience. What would it be? This may seem trivial and obvious. Let me assure that it is not. Many presenters are vague about their main messages or their purpose in speaking.

Where this occurs in the planning process depends on the situation. Sometimes you may know early on what the nature of your core message is. At other times you may not have a good grasp on it until you dig deeper into planning. We'll refine the main theme later in the chapter.

Distinguish between the "subject" and the main message. A frequent comment by presenters when they're asked to state their main message is: "Well, I'm talking about safety." That's the *subject*, not the message. The *message* would be perhaps, "Knowing and following safety procedures saves lives," or "Wear your safety glasses at all times when operating machinery."

Why is identifying a main message so important? For one thing, it may be the wrong message for the audience or not the best one for the presenter's purpose. Writing it down as a complete sentence serves as an early check on where this presentation is going. For another, having a clear main message will help ensure that it gets said, emphatically and often. Finally, the main message is the focal point for all other parts of the presentation. Nothing should be included or generated if it does not support or tie directly to that single statement. If the main message is poorly stated or faulty, the efforts to follow will be misdirected to a large degree.

Beveridge and Velton apply this concept to proposals: "A good proposal opens with a message. It closes with a message. And in between you keep socking home the message. . . . You dare not start any proposal effort without knowing just what your message will be."[7] This advice is equally valid for presentations.

Figure 5-4. Make sure you know your objective.

Specific Purpose	To Achieve	End Product: The Audience Will:
Persuade	Action or attitude change	Approve $10,000 for new computer Write Congress and ask support of bill 200 Buy off on the estimate
Inform	Change in audience knowledge or ability (behavioral objective)	Know three main problem areas of program (upper management) Complete new form correctly in ten minutes Understand seven steps to winning presentations
Inspire	Emotional impact, enthusiasm	Be eager to do a great job on new promotion (sales force) Be aroused for the final push (proposal team)
Entertain or preside	Warm feeling suitable for the occasion	Give Charley an appreciative and jolly send-off for his retirement Greet the new leader with respect and warmth

Another way to think about the main message is to ask, "What is the main theme, idea, or point I want the audience to take away with them?" Gerald Phillips and Jerome Zolten, in *Structuring Speech,* call this the "residual message—the idea that breaks through the resistance, that stays in the listener's mind when everything else is forgotten."[8]

In addition to writing out the main message or theme, it is helpful to identify the three or four main points of the main message. A practical way of uncovering those is to assume you are writing the summary visual aid for your talk, and that it is all you will be able to show the audience. What would you put on it? These preliminary points may be changed during the design phase as the presentation structure takes shape, but they provide useful early clarity and guidance. Here are some examples of a main theme and main points backing it up:

Wear your safety glasses at all times when operating machinery (main theme to persuade).

- Several serious accidents have occurred recently.
- Safety glasses could have prevented the injuries.
- It only makes sense to wear them when operating machinery.

XBC Corporation has three major product lines (main theme to inform).

- We make and sell food products.
- We supply medical products.
- We design and build shopping centers.

CONDUCT AUDIENCE ANALYSIS

In the audience were a dozen high-level, extremely knowledgeable people. The speaker was describing the procedures used for financial analysis and resource allocation. Said one attendee: "It was awful. The speaker went into every detail of every procedure and covered the full background of how each system evolved. No one cared, but he never caught on. We kept waiting for him to get to the heart of it, but he was enamored with all this history and background. If you asked him a simple question, he went off again into every minute detail. I couldn't wait to get out of there."

Earlier I referred to the nomination of Michael Dukakis as the Democratic presidential candidate for the 1988 election. At one campaign stop, Dukakis addressed a group of factory workers. Because one of his major campaign themes was the accelerating rate that American companies were being bought up by foreign interests, he asked the group how they'd like it if their children had to work for companies owned by foreigners. Want to guess who owned the factory where he was speaking? Fiat, the Italian automaker.[9]

These are two presenters who failed to ask some basic questions about their audiences.

Audience analysis is a crucial and often neglected part of presentation development. The audience is the principal cog in the whole presentation, its target, the reason for its very existence.

Audience analysis can encompass many parts and levels, including psychological drives, learning theory, and resistance to change. To boil all that down to something manageable, we're going to look at five composite audience characteristics (see Figure 5-5).

- What are they *capable* of doing?
- What do they already *know?*
- What are their needs and *interests?*
- What are their *attitudes* toward my proposition, my organization, me?
- What is their meeting or listening *style?*

What baggage—impressions, experiences, and agendas—do listeners bring to a presentation, and how did they come by it? "The most fundamental rule for successful persuasion," said Henry Boettinger in *Moving Mountains,* is to "start where *they* are, not where you are. In order to start where an audience is, you must know something about them. Their familiarity with the subject, their present attitudes toward it, past views on similar subjects, what they are anxious about, limitations on their actions, and their goals in life all contribute to what they call their position."[10]

Figure 5-5. Audience analysis attempts to discover what "baggage" each principal listener will bring to the conference room.

WHAT BAGGAGE DO THEY BRING?

The Ever-Listening Speaker

Audience analysis is not a one-shot activity but continues throughout all phases of preparation and during the presentation itself. This continuous sensitivity to the audience results in a "listening speaker," a term coined by Paul Holtzman: "The listening speaker, throughout his preparation, engages in an imagined transaction with his audience-image. He tests ideas and materials and ways of stating them to see if they evoke the desired responses. On the basis of his tests, he organizes or programs his ideas and materials and his ways of stating them. Then, while in the actual speaking situation, he continues to test for response and continues the process of seeking causes for the desired effects."[11]

The Many-Faceted Audience

Assessing audience characteristics is complicated by the heterogeneous nature of many business audiences. In one group may be the company controller, the quality director, and a human resources manager. How do you tailor a message to fit all these people?

A fundamental question to be asked is: Does this group contain key or primary listeners at whom the talk is mainly aimed? For a talk to a professional society, probably all listeners are roughly equivalent in importance. For a marketing presentation or program review, one or several listeners generally carry the greatest clout. In that case, thorough audience analysis should be done for each primary listener.

Occasionally speakers concentrate exclusively on those individuals they determine to be the key decision makers. They prepare a talk with only the leaders in mind and during the talk direct the message almost entirely to those few people. This can be a serious mistake, as other so-called lesser individuals may be more influential than is assumed and may be irritated at receiving cavalier treatment.

Here is what consultant Jim Elms says on this subject:

> Suppose I had an audience of eighty people and am sure that ten people in the front row have 99 percent of the power and that the others are there because it's something to do. Don't give your pitch to eighty people; give it to the smallest audience. On the other hand, the ones in the back row may have more to do with it than you think. They can tell the general your proposal is all screwed up technically and that he shouldn't have anything to do with it. Especially when you give him viewgraphs he can't read and he's had his mind about 51 percent decided to give the business to your competitor. All he needed was some reason to quit listening—and you gave it to him. If those in the back row come in and say the presentation by XYZ Company (your competitor) was satisfactory, but they haven't the foggiest idea what those guys from ABC Company (yours) were talking about, you've sure had an ineffective presentation.[12]

For other persuasion situations, every member of the audience may be key. A typical proposal review team comprises members from many specialties, levels, and areas of responsibility, and each member has a vote. Within the bounds of practicality, an audience analysis should be done for each member. The approach to the presentation may be to give the full audience a general summary (often called an executive overview) and then give a series of talks for various specialties, with a clear agenda so members can come and go and still hear the main part of their interests. If a single presentation is all that is possible, the presentation becomes a composite, not for one audience but for several at once. Knowing what to cover or omit and what to condense or expand so that critical needs of most listeners are met is not easy, but it's essential.

Audience Capability

This may seem to be so obvious as not to need special attention. Yet many speakers do not adequately define the action they expect to achieve and, consequently, do not match that action against the audience's ability to achieve it. Gaining a favorable attitude toward your goal is nonproductive without the power to implement it.

At the core of presentation planning is making sure you are speaking to the right audience. Identifying the decision makers or influencers is the first task. Getting them to listen to your presentation is the second. If you can't do that, further work on the planned presentation is worthless, and you need to redefine the objective of the presentation or rethink the whole approach.

Audience Knowledge

"The most effective presentations are those that take into account the knowledge of the audience," said Bank of America retired vice-chairman of the board Arthur Toupin. "The biggest mistake is the failure to understand that the audience is not normally as expert as the presenter. To presume that the audience knows all the jargon of the presenter's trade is a presumption in which one cannot indulge. Perhaps the single most important thing in making a presentation is understanding by the presenter of the degree of knowledge and interest by the principal audience members. My own observation is that very few people who make presentations understand that. It is unusual to find a person making a special effort to allow his audience to understand what he's talking about."[13]

Correctly gauging the knowledge level of the audience is a constant problem in business, with highly diverse audience members and many presentations for a specific program. How much do they know? How much background should I go into? Can I assume they know all the program terminology? These are serious questions that need to be asked and for which answers are often hard to come by.

"People don't do much homework regarding the sophistication of audiences," notes Brook Byers, principal partner of Kleiner, Perkins, Caulfield, Byers. "They usually underestimate the level—for example, all of our partners have backgrounds in managing technology. You want to present at or slightly above the knowledge level of people in the room."[14] Knowing that level in advance can be a problem. Byers says, "If I don't know, the first thing when I get the floor is to ask, 'What level of technical detail should I go to?' " If audience members can't understand your language, don't relate to your references, or can't follow your line of discussion, it is highly unlikely that they will grasp your message. On rare occasions they may go away impressed at the knowledge you seem to have, but more often they will be baffled and irritated. The standard comment is, "I don't know what he said. It was over my head." (See Figure 5-6.)

A heavily tutorial message or one that aims at an elementary level can alienate an audience. Also, erroneously assuming a low level of audience expertise may find one unprepared for questions or attacks from highly competent opponents.

Figure 5-6. Set your presentation at such a level that the audience can understand it. And remember, your listeners may not tell you that they don't have the slightest idea of what you're talking about.

"The worst thing you can do to a top executive is to make him or her uncomfortable," said consultant Jim Elms. "One way to do that is to say, 'Of course, you understand so and so,' or to go into all kinds of detail. The listener has two choices: to say, 'Aw, I don't know what he's talking about, but I'm sure not going to admit it,' or to say, 'No, I don't understand.' *Do not make an important listener go through that decision.* Darn few people will stop you and say that you're over their heads.

"On the other hand, you don't want to say, 'Now, sir, you're a general, so obviously you don't understand $F = ma$. What that means is, if you push on something, it will accelerate.' If you want to make a mistake, make it a *little* more technical than what you think the guy will understand. Then he's flattered."[15]

Audience Interests and Needs

Hand in hand with determining the audience's level of knowledge about the subject is identifying what aspects of the subject the audience might be interested in hearing about. This is generally more difficult to assess than the knowledge level and more critical to presentation success.

An equally important reason for exploring audience interest and concern is that these provide the principal avenues for reaching and moving an audience. The heart of successful persuasion is showing people that adopting your proposition will serve them well.

At a success seminar, a dozen top speakers offered inspiration and ideas. They were flamboyant, told great stories, and employed sensational visual effects. One speaker opened his talk by flatly stating he had none of those—he was not a spectacular speaker. What he did have was a message that hit home with his audience and powerful credentials to verify that his words were worth heeding. He was the most spell-binding speaker of all. Audience members hung on his every word and feverishly scribbled notes to capture as much of his message as they could. They also cleaned out the supply of books he offered for sale afterward.

Advertising executive Phil Joanou says:

> Too many presenters go in with their own self-interest as their main talking point, that is, to tell you how wonderful they and their product, service, personnel, etc. are. They're not thinking about how they can help the customer. The first thing I do is to find out what my company can do for the customer, to really try to find out what his needs are and even to help identify those which the customer may not know clearly. Then I try to put the proposal in terms of how we can help the customer.[16]

Needs Analysis—Business. Locating the organization's most pressing single need, or group of needs, is critical to success. General Motors may solicit bids to supply a new axle. Supplier A comes in with a durable, low-cost design that is immediately available. Looks like a sure winner, to company A. Company B has done its homework better and proposes a design that costs more and is less durable than company A's design but weighs six pounds less. That increases mileage by a half-mile per gallon. GM buys company B's design because better mileage, not durability or cost, is its most pressing need.

Identification of customer organizational or contractual needs is reasonably straightforward. Establishing the *priority* of those needs is extremely tricky. Knowing your customer well and sounding out ideas in informal discussions is paramount. One of the values of presentations is that they give you an opportunity to test if you have guessed right and are emphasizing the right points. If the real customer "hot buttons" are identified early enough in the marketing program, later efforts, such as formal proposals, can reflect these.

Beveridge and Velton cited an example of two competing contractors stressing different priority needs. One was right.

> In an important fighter aircraft competition, one fellow said, "A hot fighter, which incidentally can do the fleet air defense role quite admirably." The other fellow said, "Performs the fleet air defense role very admirably with essentially no compromise as a fighter." It is unlikely that the planes were all that different. But one competitor saw the customer as mostly wanting a fighter and always addressed his proposal toward the fighter first, the fleet air defense role second. The other fellow seemed to be subtly accenting preserving the plane as a (missile) carrier, while pointing out that you still could get a good fighter. When the smoke cleared, the accent on hot fighter carried the day.[17]

Knowing the organization's *current* focus of activity for a sequential program is vital to receiving an attentive hearing instead of a curt, "Quit wasting our time. Come back when you've got something we can use." Failing to be on the customer's wavelength is what leads to the classic turnoff, "Don't call us—we'll call you."

Consultant James Elms told of reviewing a client's presentation about to go to a government-agency audience. The presentation was to discuss development of a concept the agency was funding:

> We said over and over—make the pitch as follows: you already have the contract; you know a specific problem has yet to be solved; now go off and figure how to do that and tell them about that. Do not keep selling. *Please believe me—there is nothing to sell!* The decision has been made to do it. The only question is how. Later we can once again put on the sales pitch, when the center is fully convinced but they're not sure how to sell it to Washington. Then you can give them some ideas as to how to do that.[18]

The winning supplier who sensed that General Motors' present situation dictated a primary need for increased mileage over such staples as cost and durability understood the concept of immediate needs. In the face of a current pressing problem, an organization might be responsive to an appeal that normally would be low on its priority list.

Individual needs are subject to the same changeability. A change in job or charter, an emergency at home or work, a dragged-out meeting can all cause people suddenly to lose interest in a topic they would normally respond well to. When John F. Kennedy was shot, interest in almost any other subject dropped for several days.

Frequently, shifts in need can be identified well before the presentation—early enough so that appropriate changes in the approach can be made. Other changes may be so recent that only last-minute adjustments are possible.

It is a rare situation that appealing to a single need will be successful. Audiences are made up of many individuals, each with his or her own internal set of hot buttons. Each individual has multiple needs, some stronger than others, but several possibly related to your topic or proposition. The successful speaker will address the several audience needs that seem most pertinent.

Needs Analysis—Personal. In late 1991 Houston contractor Brown & Root won a major contract for a multibillion dollar resort in Japan. The president of the firm developing the resort said he wanted a U.S. prime contract for partly personal reasons. A U.S. military officer had been kind to his older brother during the occupation of Japan after World War II.[19]

This and the fighter aircraft example suggest that another set of needs may be at work: the personal needs that individual listeners carry within them. These deal with such mundane matters as personal prestige, recognition, opportunity, excitement, advancement, and money. These needs almost never get put into writing. They may not ever be spoken or be recognized as existing. Yet they are powerful baggage that each listener has brought to the conference room.

From *Strategic Selling* by Miller and Heiman:

> . . . the reason that people really buy is only indirectly related to product or service performance. That's why we don't focus on the product. Instead, we show you how to use your product knowledge to give each of your buyers personal reasons for buying. You can't just meet their business needs. You have to serve their individual, subjective needs as well.[20]

Jim Dollard, president of Management Analysis Company, is often involved in new business presentations. "When you are presenting to an evaluation board, it's important to remember those gut level issues which may not be in the evaluation criteria or on a list. A friend used to say, *'There are the issues and then there are the real issues.*[21]'" Dollard offered some possibilities:

- A suspicion that some of the key players may not be truly available.
- Political issues, such as what would be good for the procuring agency or some of the decision makers.
- Having a foreign team member. It may be acceptable on the surface but at the gut level may be troubling to the board reviewer.

The following illustrates these two types of audience needs:

Business Needs	*Personal Needs*
• Cost	• Political
• Schedule	• Power
• Performance	• Personalities
• Quality	• Past
• Support	• Culture

Audience Attitudes

Having given careful thought to all the considerations thus far discussed, the presenter should have a reasonably good picture of the audience. Glimmers of an important audience characteristic—attitude toward the subject, proposition, speaker, or organization—may have already been seen. Understanding the audience's predispositions on these matters is vital to establishing the presentation approach.

Attitudes can vary from totally enthusiastic and supportive to uncommitted-but-willing-to-listen to tomato throwers. (See Figure 5-7.) Complicating the process is the fact that all of them may be in the same audience. Speaker style, arguments and order of presentation, degree of support, and recommendations all are influenced by audience attitudes.

Ferreting those out may be difficult. People may not be willing to state

Figure 5-7.   Are they with you? Neutral? Against you? Your approach differs for each audience attitude.

Source: Genigraphics.

publicly the attitudes they hold. A decision may have been reached but may not yet be ready for release. Showing bias either for or against may not be appropriate. Listeners may hold down their own preferences in favor of those of higher-level listeners or group influences. People also may not be aware of the attitudes they hold.

Group Influences. Identification of group influences that will affect the responsiveness and actions of individuals is essential. Holtzman describes those as factors that do not generally account for success but can be the source of failure or of boomerang effects.[22] Groups themselves have interests and values that they hold dear, and ignoring or flaunting them is a likely source of trouble that may override all the other wondrous features of your case. A presenter hoping to win Army support for a program spoke with great admiration about how well the Marines had managed a similar program. He shot himself down in spite of a good proposal. Praising the Marines is not the way to win friends in the Army, he now knows.

How heavily individuals are influenced by the group depends on how firmly the individual is wedded to the group's values and how strongly the presenter's ideas touch or affect those pertinent values. A member of the Chamber of Commerce who strongly supports the Chamber is not likely to go for a proposal that runs counter to the Chamber's philosophy and positions. If the individual is loosely linked to the Chamber, he may be receptive to such ideas, especially if he belongs to other organizations that are more important to him and whose philosophy is compatible with the presenter's ideas. Clearly this information is of great importance to the presenter.

Individual Backgrounds. Tied closely to listeners' values and needs are the experiences, training, and environment to which they have been exposed. Awareness of these can offer valuable insight into what they are concerned about, what they might focus on, what they are prejudiced for or against, what level of discussion they are comfortable with, and what style of operation they are likely to employ.

A presenter from XYZ Company spoke to an audience from a company considering XYZ for a subcontract. To provide credibility for his cause, he spoke in glowing terms about several contracts XYZ had undertaken in earlier years. An executive in the audience had been assigned to monitor one of those programs, and for him it had been a wretched experience. He reacted derisively to the speaker's comment and blasted the speaker several other times thereafter. No one had told the presenter (or, better stated, he had not found out) that the executive had had such a negative experience with the program. Inadvertently he had opened the legendary Pandora's box, much to his regret.

Cultural and Generation Gaps. A common error in assessing needs and attitudes of listeners is to assume that they see things the same way as the presenter and that they will respond to appeals in the same manner as the presenter—that is, to equate the speaker's way with the "logical" and "reasonable" way. A speaker who is disappointed because her terrific ideas have been rejected may have fallen victim to a cultural or generation gap. She may then question the intelligence or ambition of her audience as she puzzles over her lack of success: "Those people just don't know what's good for them. I just don't understand people like that."

When presenter and audience come from considerably different backgrounds—nationality, age, income, race, religion—the possibility of badly misgauging the audience is high. Locating or understanding the "different strokes for different folks" is tricky but vital.

A personnel director spoke to a group of recent hires from disadvantaged backgrounds. His purpose was to inform them of all the assistance the company would give them for further education, specifically courses leading to four-year college degrees, "a great program that I know you'll want to take advantage of, because a college degree, as you know, can open many doors to you." He had no takers, because in their worlds, a college degree meant little.

Audience Style

An article about the new president of a large electronics firm said he expected presenters to be prepared. On numerous occasions he shut off the overhead projector on the first viewgraph if he felt the speaker wasn't prepared. That was the end of the presentation.

Knowing how receivers behave or like to get information is crucial to communicating successfully with that person. Some people are information sponges; others go on overload after the third statistic. Note the differences between Presidents Carter and Reagan. Would you present the same to both of them? (Managing these differences will be addressed in Chapter 7.)

The key style is the *receiver's,* not the presenter's. A common mistake is the presenter's speaking in his or her own style. Consider the problem if a detail-loving engineer presents detail to a vice-president who is more of a big-picture person. The Golden Rule—do unto others as you would have them do unto you—is bad advice for speakers. Better is: *Do unto others as they would like to be done unto*—what author Jim Cathcart calls the Platinum Rule.[23]

Formalizing Audience Analysis

It is helpful to compile the various pertinent factors about a given audience into a form for easy perusal. Figure 5-8 can be used for this purpose. When completed, it provides an overall picture of your audience.

DEVELOP THE APPROACH AND STRATEGIES

Now that you've gathered all that useful information, what will you do with it? All the factors analyzed must be deliberately weighed to determine how best to plan and shape the presentation. Many preliminary judgments will have been

Figure 5-8. Summarize audience analyses for a big-picture review of winning approach.

Key Listeners	Capability/ Influence	Knowledge Level	Interests/ Concerns	Attitudes	Listener Style
1.					
2.					
3.					
Composite Audience					
Indicated Approach					

made during the course of data gathering and analysis. Now is the time to review these and revise them as indicated by all the information at hand. Here are some suggestions for developing specific strategies for success.

Adapt to Audience Knowledge

Tailoring the presentation to the audience's knowledge level can operate in two ways: (1) if the topic and level of discussion are not already determined, you can aim it at the level the audience can understand; (2) if a certain level of detail or complexity must be covered, the audience has to be given adequate background. For either case, care must be taken to ensure that the audience can follow the talk adequately. Suggestions for doing that for three levels of audience familiarity with the subject are summarized in Figure 5-9.

Assess Audience Attitude and Interest Level

Combining both of these important audience characteristics offers valuable insights not obvious from a separate consideration. Each of the following presenters planned his talks carefully, yet each was totally unsuccessful.

Figure 5-9. Adjust your approach to fit audience knowledge.

Knowledge level	Suggested approach
Low	Be realistic about objective and points that can be covered. Stress use over how something is done. Lay the groundwork—background, basics—carefully without insulting your listeners. Speak lay English, avoid acronyms and jargon. Use stories, analogies, relevant examples; big picture versus detail; keep visuals simple, punchy, and pictorial. Build in checkpoints. Restate, summarize, and promote questions.
Medium	Set the level slightly above audience level. Be ready to shift into more detail. Give a big-picture overview. Check, by asking if necessary, if what you're covering is useful to them. Clarify and interpret information. Use jargon with awareness; explain acronyms the first time used if necessary.
High	Check your assumptions, especially if you have a mixed audience or one you don't know. Move through the groundwork quickly. Supply ample and detailed information, but cull to provide the most pertinent. Use trade terminology, but be alert for signs of uncertainty.

■ A military recruiter visited a high-school senior class to try to interest the students in a military career. The speaker gave a totally factual, dry presentation. Result: Most of the listeners went to sleep or wrote notes to each other.

■ A task force from division Alpha of a large corporation was assigned to investigate why sister division Bravo had botched a large contract. The presenters were from the Alpha task force; the audience consisted of Bravo managers, who were not particularly pleased about Alpha's assignment. The Alpha speakers immediately set about showing how much smarter they were than Bravo had been. The speakers were aloof, gave abrupt answers, and deferred most questions. Result: The audience, initially cautious, became hostile toward the presenters, challenging them vigorously. It soon became a shouting match.

■ At a political gathering, the keynote speaker gave a highly informative presentation, presented the pros and cons of the issues, stepped through all the key points to prove his case—that the other party was incompetent. Result: An initially enthusiastic crowd soon settled down and then ignored the speaker. The end was met with polite applause, mostly in appreciation that he had stopped beating the dead horse.

The presenters could have averted these dismal outcomes by examining their planned approaches on an audience interest/attitude graph (Figure 5-10). This graph and the related strategies provide a quick look at approaches likely to be successful or unsuccessful.

Figure 5-10.   The audience attitude/interest graph provides a basis for first-cut strategies.

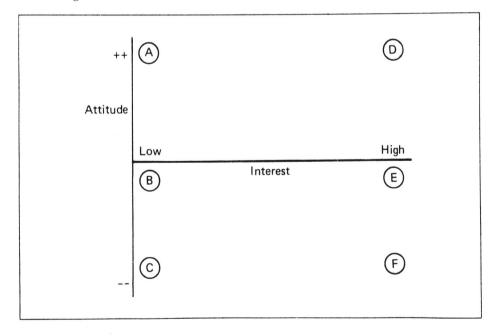

Before reading further, size up each of the above three examples by locating them based on their audience's interest and attitude.

Now check the accuracy of your placements for the three situations: the senior class was position B; Bravo division was F; the political audience D. In each case the presenter applied the wrong strategy, with poor results. What could each have done? Figure 5-11 sums up general strategies for each of the six positions noted on the matrix.

Target Audience Priority Needs

"Ninety-nine percent of business plans fail to attract money because they are written from the owner's point of view rather than the investors'," said Bruce Blechman, president of the Capital Institute.[24]

A fundamental axiom in presentations is that the messages must be focused on the needs and interests of the *audience*, not the presenter. An extremely

Figure 5-11. The attitude-interest matrix quickly shows basic strategies.

	Low interest	High interest
Positive attitude	They're pleasant but lethargic, convinced but not moving. Address value to them; visualize results and benefits with emotion. Make action easy and immediate.	They're sold, so don't bother with elaborate proofs or motivation. Go light on information, and heavy on catchy themes, color, and emotion. Move toward specific action.
Neutral	Get them to listen. Here's the place for a punchy dog-and-pony show, delivered with spirit. Get them into it quickly—mentally or physically. Get on their wavelength and tuned in. Then convert them.	Prove your case clearly and thoroughly. Show benefits and have facts well backed. Be prepared to discuss all options and defend your positions. Stress logic over emotion.
Opposed or hostile	Assess why they're so hostile and what you can do to rectify the situation or at least show you are aware of that. Try a challenge, unusual approach, or self-effacing humor to lighten them up and maybe get them to listen.	Approach carefully. Set modest objectives. Look for common concerns or positions. Show you understand and respect their position. Stay cool and firm but *not* arrogant.

common cause for the demise of presentations is failure to consider that critical factor and to tailor the presentation accordingly. Several concepts can help direct that focus to where it needs to be.

Rank Audience Needs—Business and Personal. If you are not addressing audience key issues, the audience will be only mildly interested in your presentation. If you have accurately determined what issues are most pressing or foremost in their problem-solving/decision-making process and you address those issues, they will be attentive. Whether you win them over depends on how you address those issues.

Suppose you've identified the major issues:

Unranked Major Issues

Business	*Personal/Subsurface*
Reduction of inventory	Under fire from boss
Early delivery date, with confidence	Political "who controls"
Improved product quality	Competition is reviewer's cousin

Further probing reveals that three issues are most pertinent and should be given priority treatment in the presentation:

Ranked Priority Needs

1. Political struggle
2. Confidence in delivery date
3. Improved product quality

Fill the Need Better Than the Competition. By matching each of these identified priority needs with your solutions, you are stating "why our proposal is best." Addressing the personal issue (political power struggle) may need to be done subtly or even privately. What are your approaches to ensuring delivery date confidence and a high-quality product? If you've got the most credible answers to all these versus the audience's other options, you probably will win out.

Stress Benefits, Not Features. This is the old axiom: "Sell the sizzle, not the steak." A computer manufacturer may have a terrific product, an upgraded design, and a fine service network, none of which by themselves mean anything to a customer. This is a very important point: Don't emphasize how wonderful your product is but what it can do for the specific people who are listening to you. Talking about features is a common mistake and generally leads to yawns and the predictable question: "O.K., I believe you have the greatest product since sliced bread. Now, what is it going to do for *me*?" (See Figure 5-12.)

The astute presenter switches the order of discussion to the benefit first and foremost that his or her great features bring about:

Figure 5-12. Focus on their concerns—more on what *they'll* get and less on how *you'll* get there.

"Our Model Q will save you 35 percent over your present system [*benefit*] through improved design and production innovations [*features*]."

"Downtime is less than that with Brand X [*benefit*] because of our large service network [*feature*]."

"Double the jobs can be run compared to your present system [*benefit*] because of our expanded memory and new microcircuitry [*features*]."

The customer's primary interest is going to be the benefits to him; features are secondary.

Stress Results Over Process. Technically oriented people frequently lose their audiences because they spend too much time talking about how something was done. Busy listeners rarely have the luxury of listening to all the analyses, trials and errors, and statistical methods used, and most of them don't care anyway. What they do care about is the "what" and the "so what"—the results, implications, and significance.

Adjust to Current Needs. Joan Smithfield has prepared a terrific forty-slide presentation for a top-level military audience, meeting for an all-day conference. Her talk is scheduled for 2 P.M. At 5:30 she finally gets the word: "You're on."

Joan gives her full presentation, failing to notice that most of her listeners, having fidgeted for ten to fifteen minutes, were no longer around to see those lovely visuals.

What happened to Joan has happened to many other presenters who have failed to sense the mood of the audience. The group that would have sat intently for an hour at 2 P.M. was exhausted by 5:30. Their immediate needs—a quick summary and then relief—had superseded their long-term needs—to receive information and arguments contained in Joan's oral/visual report.

Dig Deeper into Audience Attitudes

Your audience analysis may have revealed that the group or certain key listeners are likely to have some reservations about your proposition. Here are some strategies for winning these people over.

Know What's Behind Their Positions. The degree of knowledge held by an audience can make a difference in how it should be approached. This is particularly worth exploring for the group that has not committed itself or has chosen to stay neutral.

People in a high-knowledge-level group have made a conscious decision to stay neutral. They know the arguments in favor or against and remain unmoved. Clevenger suggests that a long-term campaign will probably be required.[25] Willingness to debate all sides of the issues objectively and to patiently back up arguments is needed. The presenter can work to strengthen favorable points and weaken barriers, as long as no high-pressure campaign is used.

The low-knowledge-level group has not explored the issues, probably because this is not a topic of great concern to these people. The first task is to convince them that it is an important topic. The presenter can then make the case without much concern for other options, being ready to counter the obvious objections and do it with a reasonable dash of enthusiasm. Conversion may be possible in one shot, and action or commitment should be obtained while the receivers are sold. "Just sign on the dotted line." Because they know little about the subject, they are susceptible to counterarguments, so a bit of insurance, raising and shooting down the opposing arguments they are likely to hear, is often wise.

Rank Potential Objections. List the possible topics the audience may have concerns about and rate these as to highest importance to the listeners. This seemingly simple exercise is often treated lightly or ignored by presenters. Often they're so wrapped up in their work or so sold on the obvious brilliance of the concept that they can't think of any possible reason anyone would question what they're proposing or reporting.

Do not take this exercise lightly. These may be fetishes, high-risk areas, or parts of your proposition you've done a mediocre job of explaining. If a key listener is an expert on aerodynamics or had a previous negative experience with titanium and you're proposing a titanium airfoil, be ready to answer detailed questions. If you have good answers, surfacing and addressing these issues can be beneficial (and potentially crucial) to your cause. Failing to anticipate this can leave you with the proverbial egg on your face.

Develop Counters for Each Major Objection. There may be some legitimate black marks or "lemons" on your record. If they're likely to be a major point of concern for the listener, you can't ignore them, much as you would like to. Look for ways to make lemonade from the lemon—that is, turn the negative into a positive. One company did this with a manufacturing disaster it had on its record. It was bidding to get a new contract in the same product area. What to do about the lemon? The company finally chose to face it head on and acknowledge that it had real difficulty with the earlier contract. "But," the company said, "we learned a great deal from that job, and we have made the changes necessary to do it right now. We've made our mistakes and learned from them." Unspoken was the hint that the main competitor, who had no experience of that type, was still learning and probably would run into the same problems, on the customer's money.

Refine the Message

Earlier we developed the concept of the theme and main points. In practice, the theme may not become clear until after audience analysis. Or the "obvious" theme may be seen on further review as not the best one, especially for persuasive presentations. Fine-tuning the theme takes into consideration the audience "hot buttons," such as priority needs and potential objections, and your strongest attributes, which enable you to meet those needs better than the audience's other options. The theme thus captures the essence of the overt selling message (addressing personal needs may require a subtle approach). Some examples:

- Increased productivity achieved through better computer graphics capability
- System VI—Proven turnkey approach for assured delivery
- There's no fat in our system, so there's none in our prices (UPS ad slogan)

This is a good time to review not only the main theme but also the main points you identified back in the "define goal and message" stage and crystallize these into a set of core messages.

Lay Out a Realistic Operational Plan

The culmination of planning is to provide a basis for making smart decisions about how to proceed with this presentation. Here are some of those decisions you will make.

- *Should a presentation be made?* If so, when, where, and to whom? Test the assumption that a formal group presentation is needed; often an informal, one-to-one discussion will be better. Perhaps a series of presentations is needed because of different targets and themes.

- *What media should be used?* The purpose, situation, environment, audience, and budget affect media selection. A viewgraph presentation may be fine for a conference room but not workable on the factory floor. Flipcharts may work well for an audience of twenty but flop with one of two hundred. A full color slide show may be terrific, but what about budget and changeability?
- *What's the slant of the message?* A soft-sell or no-sell approach may be wiser than a strongly partisan one. The extent of background and motivational material needed differs widely for different audiences.
- *What type and depth of supporting material is suggested or readily available?* For some audiences, fewer numbers and more stories or humor may be indicated.
- *Who will, or should be, the speakers?* How should they dress and act? Does this call for a conservative business style or a more casual approach?
- *What else needs to be considered besides the presentation itself?* Hospitality, field trips, separate meetings, and distributions of materials should all be considered early.

Schedule Key Events

The final step in laying out the plan is to establish how all this work will get done. What specific steps will it take to get the presentation developed? When must these be done and in what sequence to meet the delivery date while making efficient use of available resources and staying within budget? For a one-person presentation of modest priority and due in two days, this plan may have only a few items. For a major presentation involving many speakers and support staff, the plan can be highly detailed. Whatever the level of presentation, it pays to lay out a milestone schedule—for example:

Event	*Target Date*
Kickoff meeting with team	_____
Plan details reviewed	_____
Outlines and storyboards done	_____
Visual aids/graphics ready	_____
Rehearsal	_____
Travel	_____
Delivery day	_____

Review

Before charging further down the presentations development road, it's a good idea to bounce your analysis off someone else. An astute observer, such as your boss, someone more familiar with the audience and situation, or even a colleague can review your analysis from a perspective different from yours. A brief review (or sometimes not so brief, for major presentations) can provide insights you are missing, add information, and steer the presentation in a wiser direction.

IN SUMMARY: PLANNING IS A SOUND INVESTMENT

This is the most important chapter in this book, and the most important activity you will do as you develop your presentation. The analyses and decisions made in planning set the direction and focus of all other phases to follow. Wise upfront thinking leads to good resource use and a successful presentation. The trails of many poor presentations and inefficient uses of resources often lead all the way back to slipshod or faulty planning.

PLANNING APPENDIX: A DEEPER LOOK

The key elements of planning a presentation have been addressed in this chapter. For those wishing to delve deeper, several topics are discussed further here.

More on Needs Analysis: Targeting the Right Decision Point

Particularly in persuasive presentations, it's important to know just where listeners are in terms of the decision sequence. This information helps you focus your attention and keeps you from wasting energy on areas not of interest to the audience. Figure 5-13 illustrates this.[26] Strategies for each level are discussed below.

■ *Needs recognized.* An unsolicited proposal often is submitted by a contractor with a concept that may fill a need the customer has not identified. Much of the presentation/proposal has to address the need the presenter perceives as existing for the listener. It does little good to focus on the great features of the new concept until the listener has been shown the need. Getting immediate acceptance of the presenter's proposal may be too ambitious, so the purpose may be to open doors to further dialogue or to initiate a reading of the presenter's proposals.

■ *Problem defined.* If this is the position of the listener, the presenter's approach depends on whether he or she has the same problem definition as the listener. If the presenter agrees with the listener's viewpoint, the approach may be to reinforce that viewpoint and go on to discuss the plan to resolution. If the presenter feels that a good case can be made for a different problem statement, the task will be to convince the listener of the validity of that viewpoint. Unless that is achieved, the presenter's ideas for addressing the problem will be futile.

■ *Alternatives identified.* This is a common dialogue point between customer and contractor. If the customer is open to alternatives, the presenter has a free hand to propose one or more approaches. If the customer seems to have fixed onto two or three alternatives and the presenter wants to enter another for consideration, the task is to persuade the listener to consider the added option. Another question is to ask: Has the listener failed to see your alternative, or has he or she seen it and already recognized it?

Figure 5-13. The presenter's focus depends on the audience's position in the decision/program life sequence.

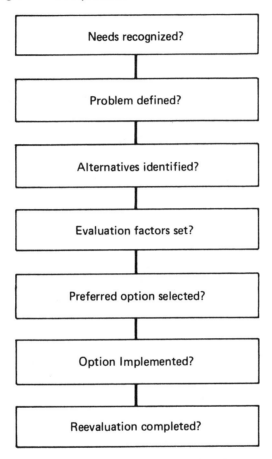

• *Evaluation factors set.* The assumptions, ground rules, procedures, and evaluation criteria are often subjects of discussion as new programs evolve. These also can be critical in determining how your concept will stack up against the others. Your effort then may be to show the listeners why certain criteria are preferable to others.

• *Preferred option selected.* This is not a desirable place to find yourself in a discussion with the customer, unless yours is the option selected. If that is the case, the customer may need further backing for the selection. He or she may need to convince a high-level agency of the wisdom of the choice (a common occurrence between government centers and Washington). If you disagree with the option selected, your task is to persuade the listener to reopen the competition, and your arguments can operate at any of the previous spots in the decision sequence. Probably the bulk of such arguments focuses on the evaluation factors, though other positions, such as failure to consider a given alternative, may be the focus of the case. Often the decision is no decision, in which case your task may be to provide the customer with a strong enough case to change the decision to a go-ahead for your concept, to revise evaluation criteria, or to give him or her added support so he or she justify a decision your way.

■ *Options implemented.* If your concept has lost, you may not find yourself presenting to a customer in this position. On the other hand, all may not be lost. Is there a follow-on contract with open competition? Is the program early enough in development that the customer is still receptive to new ideas? Are there offshoots of the main contract that might be available? Is the winner doing a poor job? All these offer avenues for further dialogue after the decision is made.

■ *Reevaluation completed.* A common and fertile dialogue point, this is a stop-and-assess time before the next phase of the program is initiated, which itself may repeat the previous sequence or may pick up partly along the way. "Is it a new ballgame?" and "Can I still play?" are leading questions.

More on Understanding Individual Needs

The two different categories of audience needs—business and personal—were noted earlier as a key part of audience analysis. Personal needs often operate at a subsurface level, making them easy to miss.

One way of assessing these is through Maslow's hierarchy of needs.[27] (See Figure 5-14.) The key to reaching and moving a person is to find out the level with which he or she is primarily concerned. If your attention is given to a level either below or above the one at which the individual is operating, you are not addressing the need to which he or she will respond. A person operating at the ego/esteem level, for example, theoretically is little concerned about social, safety/security, and physiological needs, because all those needs (lower on the order) are taken care of. Thus, an appeal based on fitting into the group better (social) or getting more to eat (physiological) will receive little attention by that person, but stressing the increased recognition or leadership position (ego/esteem) possible through your proposal will be listened to. Whether you then move the person to accept your ideas or to act in the direction you desire depends on how strong those needs are, how believable your case is, and how well it meets those needs. Locating the correct level of interest is no guarantee for success, but talking at the wrong level generally ensures failure.

Lower-level needs certainly should not be ignored. According to Maslow's theory, if a lower-level need is threatened or becomes shaky, it becomes the overriding need. If accepting your proposition strengthens the listener's lower-level needs or if not accepting it may lead to weakening of those needs, it may be fruitful to address that.

Suppose your presentation is to persuade a group of smokers to quit smoking, and you determine that three types of smokers (on Maslow's needs hierarchy) make up the audience:

1. *Physiologically concerned.* These people are sensitive to the need for good health but apparently haven't been adequately convinced that smoking

Figure 5-14. The hierarchy of needs offers insight into listeners' personal areas of response.

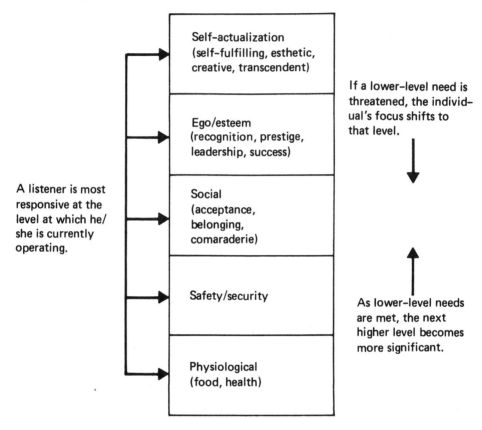

is unhealthy. A factual presentation, or new findings, well substantiated, may have some success.

2. *Socially oriented.* Health is secondary to this group. People in this category want to be part of the gang, so if smoking is "in," they're likely to do it. Facts about cancer rates mean little, but if smoking can be seen to have strong enough social liabilities, they may respond.

3. *Ego oriented.* The slogan for this group is: "I am the master of my fate. I can do anything." Facts and social arguments are worthless for these people. But pointing out that nicotine seems to be the master, not they, may challenge them to straighten out that situation.

Considering Audience Reaction Patterns

One of the essential and most difficult tasks is getting the right people to show up for the presentation. When they do, they bring as baggage all the expectations, prejudices, opinions, and concerns previously discussed. These will be exercised, validated, and reshaped according to what happens during the presentation.

Your listeners typically will go through five basic stages as they buy or turn down your proposition. This internalization process can be viewed as a set of concentric circles (Figure 5-15). The receiver starts at the outer circle and, with certain expectations, is not likely to move to the next inner circle until he or she feels satisfied that the present level has been sufficiently exercised.

A great deal of research has been done in each of these areas to find out what works and doesn't work. Here are some of the key findings.

Step 1—listening. If an audience is not listening to what you are saying or not looking at what you are showing, all the brilliant ideas you have and the marvelous facts you present are for naught. They might as well be spoken to the wind. The fundamental task is to catch the attention of the audience and keep it throughout the talk. Many presenters overlook this basic truth. They adopt the philosophy that the facts will speak for themselves and that anything except a dry, low-key approach to the audience is not warranted.

People *listen* to a speaker who:

- Is enthusiastic, believes in his or her message, and wants others to hear about it.
- Speaks on a subject of importance to them and gives them something of value in a language they can readily understand.
- Arrives with credentials that they respect or that intrigue them and dresses and behaves in a way that is in keeping with their expectations.
- Makes them feel comfortable and puts them in an enjoyable mood.

Figure 5-15. The circles portray how a receiver processes the sender's or presenter's message. In general, a circle won't be activated unless the ones surrounding it have been satisfactorily addressed.

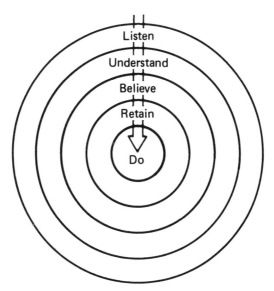

- Livens the talk with punchy visuals, interesting anecdotes, and a bit of hamminess in voice, expression, and movement.
- Recognizes when it's time to take a break.

Step 2—understanding. Listeners are more likely to *understand* a presentation that:

- Is clearly organized, with a definite theme, major points that stand out, and plenty of road signs to mark the way.
- Presents material in digestible amounts, at a suitable level, and in a clear language, with plenty of sink-in time and repetition where needed.
- Explains and interprets material, not just presents it.
- Identifies key and difficult points by highlighting, repeating, and vocally emphasizing them.
- Illustrates points by visual aids, examples, analogies, demonstrations, or hands-on activities.
- Encourages and responds to feedback for checking comprehension.

Step 3—accepting or believing. People are more likely to *accept* a speaker's proposition when all, some, or a single one of the following are present:

- The speaker is judged personally competent and trustworthy (Aristotle called it ethos) or likable; the speaker or her or his organization has a proven record that bears directly on the proposition.
- They were leaning in that direction in the first place, or organizations or people they value support it.
- It seems valid because of the reasoning and substantiation offered, competitive viewpoints make a weaker case, and major objections have been satisfactorily addressed.

Step 4—retaining. This is only partly applicable *during* the presentation; it more basically occurs (or doesn't) *afterward.* If people are expected to do or recall something later, they must remember certain information at that time to some degree of accuracy. People are more likely to *retain* the essence of a message for many of the same reasons they will understand it.

Step 5—doing. People are more likely to *act* favorably on the speaker's proposition when most of the following conditions are present:

- They are asked to do it, it is feasible and not too much trouble or too big a step beyond their normal action range, or they were inclined to do it in the first place.
- They like and believe in the presenter or have had previous positive experiences with her or his organization.
- The course of action proposed by the speaker meets their major needs better than other options; the potential benefits satisfactorily outweigh

the risks, which are at acceptable levels, or probable effects from *not* doing it are unpalatable.
- The speaker's proposal is compatible with the goals of the group or valued individuals.
- Their ideas are incorporated into the proposition.
- Their fears have been allayed by test drives or other participation.

*** 6 ***

Organize

KEY POINTS OF THIS CHAPTER

* How well a presentation is organized has a major impact on its success.
* The organization of a presentation is like the foundation of a house: it makes sense to spend some time on it before putting up the walls.
* A cookbook formula, based on Introduction, Body, and Summary, greatly aids the organizational process.
* Tools, such as outlines and storyboards, can expedite the organizing process, especially with the help of computers.

Audiences tend to be tolerant. They can put up with many characteristics of speakers that are normally regarded as weaknesses in public speaking. Unusual dress, poor grammar, "funny" accents, even loosely backed propositions may be readily tolerated or overlooked by listeners. One of only a few things that can cause them to become downright hostile to the speaker is poor organization.

Leslie McCraw, Jr., CEO of Fluor Corporation, said better organization is first on his top three needs list (with visuals and delivery): "So often the delivery is more memorable than the content. It's a real challenge to make sure the organization is simple enough and easily enough followed so that what is said isn't lost in the shuffle—so the audience can take away some of the key points."[1]

The effectiveness of the message can be significantly increased by clear, logical organization. This not only is intuitively obvious; it has been demonstrated by behavioral studies in which audience members' receptiveness to ideas was measurably increased by organized ideas as compared with random presentation of the same ideas.[2]

Organization offers a powerful way to keep the attention of the audience focused. One of the most memorable speeches in recent times was Dr. Martin Luther King's "I have a dream!" speech before a quarter-million people at a rally in Washington, D.C., in 1963. King used this repeated theme dramatically with powerful results: "I have a dream that one day this nation will rise up and live out the true meaning of its creeds. . . . I have a dream that one day on the red hills of Georgia. . . . I have a dream that one day every valley shall be exalted."

Careful attention to organization was paid by another political speaker centuries earlier in Shakespeare's *Julius Caesar*. Brutus, fresh from putting a knife into Caesar, had just spoken to the alarmed Roman mob and convinced them that the assassination was admirable. He turned the platform over to Mark Antony, who was supposed to say much the same thing. Antony's true intent was to convince the mob of exactly the opposite viewpoint: that Brutus was a traitor who ought to be punished for this heinous crime. By presenting his ideas in an order that allowed him to conceal his true opinion until after he had conditioned the mob to hear it, Antony was able to reverse the mob from the position it had so enthusiastically applauded only minutes earlier. It should not be comforting to know that his organizational method is the same one used in many advertisements on television today.

Consider the organizing phase as a disciplining program, in which you take a jumble of ideas, cull out minor or weak points, and set down the ones that are most vital and valuable—the ones that capture the essence of what you are trying to say. Our minds and files are cluttered with far more material on our specialties than we can or should present in the time allotted to this audience. Next, the organizing process puts some order and priority into that teeming mass of raw material so that the message can be readily digested in the time allocated.

Organizing ideas into the arrangement that best presents the message is not easy, but it can be aided by considering some fundamental principles, which are often not recognized, and applying well-proved techniques. These are summarized in Figure 6-1.

Principles for Sound Organization

■ *A presentation is different from a written report.* Being subjected to boring, seemingly endless presentations is a common lament of audiences. Too many people develop presentations that resemble technical or financial reports— thorough to minute detail, carefully rigorous in development, nothing pertinent left out. The trouble with this approach is that it won't work with busy audiences lacking the luxury and ability to absorb all that information. Figure 6-2 illustrates these differences.

■ *Presentations illuminate the essential.* Presentations seldom cover the whole territory; they cover the key issues that will do the job to the audience's satisfaction and in the specific time allowed.

■ *Simplicity is utmost.* In a world of complexity, achieving simplicity may seem an impossible task. Yet it is vital in presenting to people with possibly mixed backgrounds and in an environment loaded with hazards to communication. Structuring it so a fourth grader can track it is not a bad policy.

■ *Less may be more.* The tendency is strong to want to tell all: to go into detail about all eight benefits, to spell out the entire chronology of the program, to itemize a complete résumé when asked about qualifications. This is fine for the written document but not for presentations. Do three priority topics well, and hold back on the other five. Government executive Michael Bayer said: "The first-pass, door-opener presentation has got to be simple. Most are far too

Figure 6-1. Key how-to's for organizing a presentation.

- Keep focus on audience needs and design accordingly.
- Establish a single-sentence overall theme.
- Identify the three to four essential ideas to establish the key segments you will discuss.
- Design the talk as comprising three parts—introduction, body, and summary.
- Open with a "zinger"—catch their attention.
- For most business presentations, tell 'em up front what's coming.
- Often, making a few background comments to get everybody "up to speed" is time well spent.
- In refining the body design, write all key points and subpoints as complete, simple sentences. This clarifies ideas and aids testing for logical connection of ideas.
- Several factors influence order of topic presentation, including audience interest, importance of material, and time allowed.
- Have a concise summary; writing it first is a useful way to get at the fundamental ideas you want to present.
- Don't write out a presentation; write an outline instead.
- For visual-aid presentations, use a storyboard to match the oral and visual elements and develop visual concepts.

detailed. We're usually overwhelmed with information, as presenters ignore the fact that we've probably already been subjected to eight hours of presentations today. Most do a good job with a second presentation where detail is O.K., except they constantly do that on the first presentation."[3]

■ *A journalist's approach may win points.* Executive Grant Hansen has observed that many technical people make poor presentations because they apply the scientific methods they learned in college to presentations. These then resemble mystery novels, where you don't find out the butler did it until the last page. A better way, he suggests, is to use a journalistic approach, which sums up the key points at the start, "So a busy person can read as far as he's interested in or has time for." His suggestion applies equally to nontechnical presenters.

■ *Change is likely, so plan for it.* Noting that the rules often change, Hansen also suggested that people develop and be ready with two presentations: "The thirty-minute presentation you were asked to give and the ten-minute presentation you'll be allowed to give." (Take it one step further and be prepared with the one-minute or elevator speech—the one you give to the vice-president as the two of you ride down the elevator as he or she is racing to the airport.)

■ *Audiences like road maps.* They appreciate and need periodic guideposts to be clear about the route being taken and the territory already covered. Direction or transition statements are like road signs; they let the audience know what's coming and give assurance that progress is being made.

■ *The audience, not the speaker, is paramount.* An audience of financial specialists were gathered to hear about a new software package. For the first forty minutes of the forty-five-minute presentation, they heard the sales rep cover all

Figure 6-2. Written reports tell the whole story; presentations illuminate the essential.

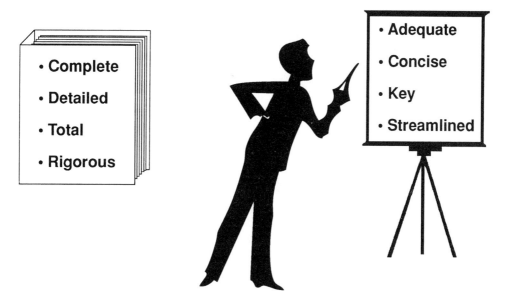

- Complete
- Detailed
- Total
- Rigorous

- Adequate
- Concise
- Key
- Streamlined

sorts of information about his company, its facilities and many operations, the organization chart, the elegant analytical architecture that went into the software—information of apparent great importance to the speaker but of ho-hum interest for the audience. What did they want to hear about to help them decide whether to buy the product? "What will it do for me?" They didn't hear it—and they didn't buy. If the speaker had shifted focus to a more strongly audience-centered organization, success might have been achieved. (See Figure 6-3)

With that foundation of core principles, here are specific techniques that can help develop a sound set of ideas that are concise, clear, cohesive, and convincing.

Practical Tips for Sound Organization

■ *Check the clock, process, and other ground rules.* How long is the presentation supposed to be? What specifically has been requested or specified? Is this likely to be a silent audience, or will it be highly interactive? These questions should have been addressed in planning but are often overlooked.

■ *Set a realistic presentation scope.* Knowing the expected time is thirty minutes, that plenty of questions are likely, or that audience feedback about your ideas is vital to the topic, coverage, and method. Said Michael Bayer: "Too many people don't factor in open space. Almost everyone wants to talk, and no one wants to listen. They walk away and don't know if they got their point across or what information they need to continue."[4]

■ *Capture the essence of the talk in one complete statement.* That is the same message discussed in planning: the single statement you would make if that's all

Figure 6-3. Many presentations fail because they are speaker rather than audience centered.

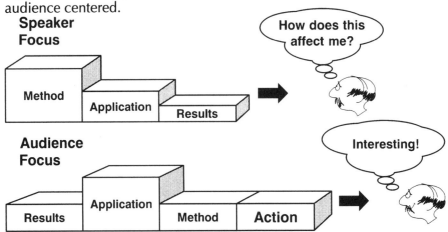

Source: Genigraphics.

you could say. All ideas and support material are directed toward supporting that single theme, which may be as simple as "Buy our product" or "Our new Model M Computer is ready for delivery." Make it a simple declarative statement.

- *Boil down the dozen or so ideas you'd like to talk about to the three or four you must talk about.* This gets to the real essence of the message and zeroes in on the most effective points that can be presented in the time allotted. If you can get three clear ideas across, that's about as much as an audience can absorb. Depending on time, more topics may be workable, but carefully examine your points for possible combinations to tighten the structure.

Suppose your task is to persuade the operations vice-president to approve the purchase of a $5 million milling machine. You list all the benefits: faster turnaround, increased capability, reduced labor costs, fewer errors. You've done analyses to prove each point and need about five minutes to cover each, so you ask for a thirty-minute presentation. He gives you ten. Do you (1) cut the detail, (2) cut the number of points to cover, (3) arrive with a thirty-minute presentation anyway?

- *Put the key points on one page as your summary chart.* Consider this set of key messages as a summary of your entire presentation and make this the first visual aid you prepare. Modify as needed, but keep it highly visible as you continue to develop the presentation.

- *Write out these core ideas as full statements.* This sounds simple, but it's often hard to do. Writing these out in full forces typical idea fragments to be crystallized into clearer points and sometimes cutting concepts because they're not clear.

For example, here's a basic presentation structure in *topic* form:

Main message: How great the Model M is.
Key points: Cost, service, and features

Fleshing out the ideas into *full sentences* leads to this set:

Main message: Buying the Model M is a wise investment for your company.
Key points:
1. Our model is cheaper than that of our competitors.
2. Downtime is reduced with our extensive service network.
3. Faster speed increases production.

The second set is much clearer than the first. Both speaker and receiver understand clearly just what message the presenter intends to get across. Use this technique of writing out full sentences whenever you find yourself struggling to get your ideas to coalesce.

■ *Make sure that main points truly support your main theme.* Are they relevant or germane to the theme? Does the basic idea set make sense? This is one of three tests, adapted from Samovar and Mills, to establish whether the basic idea set is cohesive.[5] To check for relevance, review this set:

Main message: The Model M computer is economical.
Key points:
1. Initial cost is low.
2. Maintenance.
3. It's a pretty blue color.

What does the third point have to do with the theme of economy? Eliminate it or change the theme (and fix point 2 as well, since it's not clear).

Consider this one:

Main message: Vitamins and minerals are needed by the body.
Key points:
1. Protein does this.
2. Vitamins do that.
3. Minerals do something else.

And the astute reader exclaims, "Huh? Where'd that first point come from?" It may be valid, but it is not part of what the speaker says is the message.

As a simple check of relevance, for presentations whose purpose is to persuade, place the word "because" between the main message and each of the main points. Try that for the first example above—the Model M is economical—and you can immediately see the lack of sense of the irrelevant idea contained in point 3. For a presentation whose purpose is to inform, place the words "for example" between the main message and each of the main points and observe whether it makes sense. Do this with the second set about vitamins and minerals.

■ *Are the main points truly independent?* Often ideas put forth as key points are completely relevant to the main message but seem to overlap. Two points may be covering much the same type of ground. Consider this example:

Main message: Buy the Model M computer.
(because)
Key points:
1. Overall costs are low.
2. Maintenance cost is low.
3. Performance is better.

Again, all points meet the "because" test and are thus relevant to the main message. However, since overall costs include maintenance costs, point 2 is a subpoint of key point 1. It fails the independence test.

▪ *Do the points do the job?* All the previous tests may be successfully passed, yet the set of ideas may still have a fatal flaw. Unless the topics presented *adequately* cover the subject, the audience is unlikely to feel satisfied. For example, to prove the readiness of a new aircraft, discussing the structural, propulsion, and hydraulic systems and ignoring the fire control (or other systems) may be unacceptable to the audience.

The criteria for adequacy are a matter for personal judgment and must take into account time constraints and uncertainties about audience makeup and interest. A ten-minute top-level briefing will have a different adequacy criterion from a one-hour presentation to a specialized group.

▪ *Prioritize topics.* Examine adequacy from two perspectives: the presenter's and the audience's. The listeners may have certain topics they specifically want addressed and some they don't care about. The presenter may feel specific topics must be covered to prove or demonstrate the case. Listing topics by priority can sort these out—for example:

Must	*Maybe*	*Slim Chance*
Total sales	Sales by product line	Market share
	Sales by geographic area	Competitor sales
Sales trend	Trends by division	Competitor trends

▪ *Develop primary and backup materials.* Once you've settled on the primary, workable topics, don't discard the secondary ones. Remember the value of flexibility and the interactive nature of presentations. One common technique for contingency insurance is to be ready with a dozen backup charts to supplement, if needed, the ten primary charts. If detail is requested, having a backup chart can get that information across quickly and leaves a strong nonverbal message of a prepared speaker.

▪ *Continue to follow these same concepts as the remaining details of the presentation are added.* Each key point becomes an entirely new main theme. Subpoints can then be tested for their relevance, independence, and adequacy.

THE STANDARD PRESENTATION FORMULA

Most business presentations follow the same organizational design, which is the old "tell 'em" formula: Tell 'em what you're going to tell 'em; tell 'em; tell 'em what you told 'em. This is a straightforward approach, with the audience knowing upfront what the presentation is about and where it's headed, and with few surprises. It follows another simple organization formula put forth more than fifty years ago in the classic *Public Speaking as Listeners Like It* by Richard Borden:[6]

Ho hum. (Light a fire to overcome apathy.)
Why bring that up? (Build a bridge to the heart of listeners' interests.)
For instance. (Get down to cases with specifics that make your point.)
So what? (Ask for action.)

Introduction: Get Them on Board

D. P. Burkitt is his name. He's an English doctor who specializes in fiber, and he certainly knows how to grab an audience.

"How many of you," he once asked an audience at a medical meeting after a flowery introduction, "are sufficiently concerned about your wife's health to check a weekly stool specimen?"

Nobody stirred. Nobody dared.[7]

The introduction is the most important part of the presentation and one often shortchanged by speakers. Often the presentation is won or lost in the first minute, or its direction may be completely shifted depending on how the speaker handles this phase. This is when attention is focused on the speaker, the stage is set, and the audience is conditioned to being receptive to all that will follow. Giving casual treatment to this phase or even ignoring it is like starting a car in third gear—you need to go through first and second gears first.

The effective presenter moves deliberately but swiftly through the introduction to get to the heart of the matter, the body. It is important that each of the introductory tasks be consciously examined and addressed appropriately—that means given enough attention to be useful *and no more.* A five-minute presentation requires a much more concise introduction than a thirty-minute one. As a rule of thumb, the introduction should take no more than about 10 percent of the talk.

The items set out in Figure 6-4 are the key elements of an introduction. All items may not necessarily apply to every presentation.

1. *Establish rapport.* This item deals with the audience-speaker relationship. It may consist of comments about the occasion, the group, or the community to show that the speaker has some sensitivity to or kinship with the group. If appropriate and not done by someone else, the speaker should identify herself and enough of her background to establish credibility.

Another important consideration is what the audience may be needing at this moment. Veteran presenter Wes Magnuson has often found himself standing up to speak after sitting for a long spell while other speakers preceded him. "It feels so good to stand up and stretch and I'm standing there straightening my pants behind the podium where they can't see me and I realize the audience would probably dearly love the opportunity to stand up and stretch for a minute too. So I invite 'em to do that. Goes over very well."[8]

2. *Catch attention.* Almost any presentation can benefit greatly from a snapper opening—a "grabber" or a "hook." Consider the difference between these two opening statements:

Figure 6-4.   What order and parts of the introduction's key elements will be used depends on the presentation.

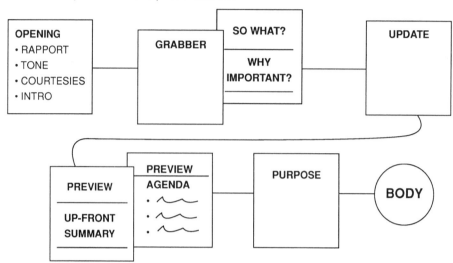

> "My subject today is printed circuit boards. We use these in many of our electronic packages and they're pretty expensive. I'm going to talk about three facets of this problem. . . . [*Dull, dreary*]"
>
> "[*Presenter holds up a printed circuit board.*] How many of you know what this is? It's a printed circuit board from our Q10 robot. How much do you think it costs? $500. What if I told you of a way we could produce this same board for $3? [*a grabber*]"

One of the most attention-getting introductions I've seen was delivered by a deputy sheriff. While making his opening comments, he deliberately pulled two rubber gloves onto his hands. At precisely the right moment, he reached into a box and pulled out a grimy Hell's Angel motorcycle gang jacket and gingerly held it up for all to see. As he introduced more of the topic—violence among gangs—he pulled brass knuckles, chains, leaded belts, and other dangerous paraphernalia out of the box. He had our attention, and he never lost it.

That is the key concept: To overcome that "Ho-hum" tendency, you must first get the audience to listen to you. A presenter has a wide array of options from which to choose a punchy opener:

- *An illustration or story.* A presentation on safety started with a story about a fellow employee and how an accident would have cost him an eye if he hadn't been wearing safety glasses. The story can be equally effective as a hypothetical illustration. A relevant humorous story often works well as an opener.
- *An analogy.* Writer Barney Oldfield opened his presentation to a group of fellow writers with this statement: "An occasion such as this resembles the

predicament of Zsa Zsa Gabor's latest husband on their wedding night. He knows what's expected of him, but what can he do that's different?"[9]

- *A dramatic demonstration.* The sheriff's Hell's Angel gadgetry is an example of a riveting opener. A program manager wanted to instill a positive spirit among the project team making an advanced system for the F-14 fighter aircraft. He had placed a portable stereo system at the front of the conference room. To open his presentation, he flipped the switch, and out boomed the music from the movie *Top Gun*, a recent hot movie. "How many of you recognize this music? Do you recall the plane that Tom Cruise flew? The F-14." From there he bridged into their role on that same plane.
- *A testimonial or quotation.* One speaker opened a presentation about quality with a pithy quote from *In Search of Excellence.*
- *A troubling statistic.* The circuit board presenter opened with this.
- *A strong opinion or interesting observation.* A proposal leader began his motivational talk this way: "Folks, at the rate we're going, we haven't the slightest chance of winning this proposal." From there he went into what the team had to do to win.
- *A rhetorical question.* Another tack the proposal leader might take is: "What will it take to win this proposal? That's a critical question for this team, and that is what I want to talk about."
- *Reference to the occasion or group, a recent event, comments of previous speakers, or preceding activities.* (They may be tied to establishing rapport.) For example, "Yesterday the president of this company proposed a major policy change that will affect all of us."

3. *Provide motivation.* This is a vital step that tells the listeners why the information to follow will be of interest to them. It answers the fundamental and unspoken question, "Why should I listen to you? What am I going to get out of this?" or, "Why bring that up?" It is a simple task, yet many speakers fail to do it. Many times I have seen listeners never get into the talk or soon drift away because the presenter failed to spell out the importance of the presentation to the listeners.

The motivation step also provides a bridge into the topic. The speaker on safety who opened with the story about the worker who almost lost an eye, might continue with: "So what? you might ask. The next almost-lost eye might be yours, if you ignore the safety procedures. That's what I'm here to talk about."

4. *Background: Bring them up to speed.* This is often helpful to your audience. They may be tracking a half-dozen programs like yours, and a quick update, perhaps with a visual aid, will be appreciated—for example: "This report covers the Amiga program. Our customer is the city of Chicago, contract value is $6 million, first delivery is June 1 . . ." or "At our last meeting, you asked us to prepare a cost comparison of three options. We've done that and are here today with that report."

5. *Preview the message with a concise summary.* "Tell 'em what you're going to

tell 'em." Many executives stress the importance of this upfront summary. A rule of thumb is that the higher the audience level is, the stronger is the need for the preview. "Make sure all the major issues are covered in a brief and succinct fashion so the decision makers can get their arms around the problem in a hurry," said Arthur Toupin, vice-chairman, retired, of the Bank of America. He gave this example: " 'I want to spend $10 million to do this [for example, build this type of building for this purpose on such and such a street, all in one sentence].' What is it you want? Then why is it a good idea? Also point out any problems; don't leave any bombshells for later discovery."[10]

For presentations seeking financial backing, Brook Byers, principal partner of the venture capital firm Kleiner, Perkins, Caulfield, Byers, advises: "Open with the strongest thing you have to say. Senior people are busy, and you have about two or three minutes to capture their attention. Open with a bold, sweeping, almost controversial statement, such as what goal or accomplishment you expect."[11]

An exception to a straightforward upfront summary is when your proposition is facing a hostile reception.

6. *Further tell 'em: the agenda.* Standard in most presentations is the agenda chart, which lists the topics to be covered, the speakers for team presentations and information about the process ahead.

"I don't like to be left dangling as to where this presentation is going," said general manager of the Institute of Electrical and Electronics Engineers Eric Herz. "I might be tempted to ask a question on chart two that you're probably going to answer on chart six. I'm an impatient listener. If you tell me what you're going to talk about, I'll probably hold off my questions."[12]

7. *Clarify the purpose.* Let the audience know early the reason for the presentation: "At the conclusion of my presentation, I will be asking for your approval to purchase this new system." People listen with different ears if they know something is expected of them at the end. As it is good practice to state the reason for a meeting, it makes sense to state the purpose early. An exception is when doing that may kill off success, as when the audience's starting position is negative (as in Mark Antony's speech after Caesar's assassination, in which he was careful to not state his true purpose at the start).

Body: Present the Main Sections

In the body, the presenter states each key point, amplifies with subpoints, and provides material to support or illustrate the points (Figure 6-5).

General Organizing Methods. Speakers have long used organizing formulas to lay out their thoughts in a clear and often dramatic manner. Here are some examples:

Enumeration	"Five factors . . .
	"Point 1. Point 2. Point 3."
Enumeration combined with alliteration	"Five C's of Marketing"
	"Four P's of Winning Presentations"

Figure 6-5. In the body, lay out key main topic segments in the best order.

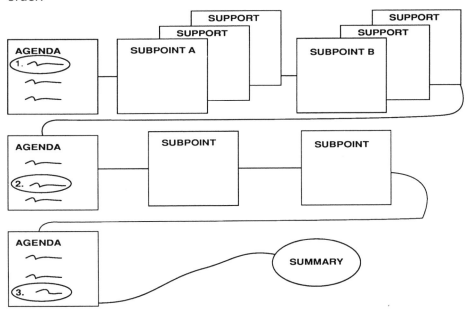

Repeated theme	"I have a dream that . . . I have a dream . . ."
	"Ike brought prosperity and so will [our current hero]. . . . He brought peace [and so will] . . ."
Plays on popular themes	"The Good, the Bad, and the Ugly"

Specific Organizational Patterns. A variety of idea arrangements are possible (see Figure 6-6). Which is best for a given presentation depends on the nature of the subject, the purpose of the presentation, the time allotted, and the audience orientation.

A proposal to acquire a new facility might be best presented by first describing the need and showing what's wrong with the existing facility; then presenting options to correct the problems identified; presenting the pros and cons of the various options and the rationale for selecting the proposed facility; and finally giving the proposed plan of action to implement the proposed solution. This *problem–solution arrangement* is extremely common in business, particularly when the purpose is to obtain approval for a specific course of action.

An orientation program describing the features of a new product might best be organized by product system, component, or function: "Today we will be looking at three main systems of our new airplane: the airframe, the propulsion system, and avionics." Arrangement by *subject characteristics* is frequently used in informative presentations.

A presentation to the investment community might have these modules: sales, earnings, assets, liabilities, net worth. Presentations given to a professional

Figure 6-6.   The common organization patterns are applied here to a
military/civil aircraft.

Pattern	Application Examples	Organizational Sections (Typical Key Points)
By subject affiliation Nature, features	Product description, system readiness review	Propulsion Electrical Hydraulic
Process/operation (may be chrono-logical as well)	Manufacturing se-quence, mission briefing	Fabrication Subassembly Assembly
Discipline	Total program review	Financial Engineering Production
Characteristics, qualities	Marketing presentation	Performance Cost Safety
By professional standard	Financial review	Sales Earnings Financial analysis
By time (chronology) or sequence	Program history, sequence of events	Phase A study (1993–1994) Full-scale development (1995–1999) Production (2000–)
By location	Supplier review, organizational responsibilities	Engine—Michigan Guidance—New York Air frame—California
By logical development	Change proposal, fail-ure analysis, new-con-cept introduction, motivational talk	Problem Probable causes (solution) Comparative assessments (effects) Selected solution Implementation

group often are expected to follow certain *standards* associated with that group.
A presentation often uses different organizational patterns for the separate
sections, such as for this example:

> *Main message:*   The Gizmo Program is generally on course.
> *Key points:*   1. Financial picture is good.
>   a. Sales projections look good.
>   b. Earnings expected to track well.

2. System design is well along.
    a. Structure meeting key milestones.
    b. Engine system earlier problems resolved.

The first subpoint set follows a professional standard pattern; the second is subject nature pattern.

■ *Achieving pattern logic and clarity.* The importance of proper linkages between themes and main points has been discussed. These should be kept in mind as the full presentation structure develops. Two applications of those tests for relevance, independence, and adequacy are illustrative.

The first is *mixing apples and oranges.* For a program review of an aircraft program, a "features" pattern was chosen, with the key topics of propulsion, electronics, hydraulics, and cost. The problem here is that cost is not a feature in the same sense as the other three. This imbalance was resolved in the following manner:

Main message: These are characteristics of the 757.
Key points: 1. These are the features.
                A. This is the propulsion system.
                B. This is the electrical system.
                C. This is the hydraulic system.
             2. This is what it costs.

The second application is *topic pollution.* Suppose the system review had these four topics: propulsion, engine, electronics, and hydraulics. "Engine" is part of "Propulsion," so should be placed as a subpoint.

■ *Limiting items to seven or fewer.* People can absorb only a limited amount of material and can more easily grasp and retain points if they are presented in small bites. The high-end number has been experimentally shown to be about seven. Any listing above seven will be in trouble.[13] A list (points, arguments, specific examples, topics) that is organized into logical groups of threes or fours will be picked up much better than a list of a dozen. If the items are then verbally enumerated or visually shown, they will be even easier to follow: "We have three arguments to present. The first is . . ."

■ *Looking for common bonds.* Not spotting and grouping the common elements is an extremely common weakness in presentations. An easy and fruitful activity is to look at lists and search for the common bonds. Here's an example:

radishes	*animals*
chickens	chickens
iron	horses
plastic	sheep
strawberries	*vegetables*
horses	radishes
diamonds	wheat

rice	strawberries
wheat	rice
sheep	*minerals*
	iron
	diamonds
	plastic

The list on the left looks shorter; the list on the right is clearer.

■ *Keeping the clinkers out.* Once you set a phrasing style, keep all equivalent-level points in that same style. Another way of stating this is to keep all parallel points consistent with one another. Here's an example of inconsistency:

Main message: Our new computer-controlled machine will save you money.
Key points: 1. It reduces maintenance costs.
                  2. It reduces material costs.
                  3. Labor hours are cut.

The third point deviates from the pattern set up by the first two.

Inconsistencies or changes from an established pattern are generally easy to spot and frequently found in main points, subpoints, and visual aids. They are generally not harmful to the basic logic, and the question is often asked, "Why bother with them?"

The answer is that observers often equate style inconsistencies with sloppy thinking and inadequate homework on the part of the presenter—which are generally correct assumptions. Pattern changes create questions in the minds of the listeners, such as, "Hmm, now why is it worded that way?" or "Am I missing something? Why doesn't the last item follow the same pattern as the others?"

For a new military procurement in the billion-dollar class, one of the competitors had assembled several high-level inside and outside consultants to review the contractor's presentation, which was to accompany its written proposal. During a dry run of one of the presentations the following interchange occurred:

Consultant A: I would clean up those charts. You are not consistent with your terminology in too many places.

Consultant B: Remember the words of Emerson: "A foolish consistency is the hobgoblin of little minds."

Consultant C: And absolutely necessary when talking to generals!

Organizational Clueing Devices. Remember the value of road maps. Since the body is the bulk of the presentation and may involve complex material, it is often helpful to the audience to receive frequent direction signals. Here are some ways you can do this:

■ *Moving agendas.* Repeat the original agenda chart, with the upcoming topic highlighted.

■ *Clear spoken lists and transitions.* "With that background let's now look at my first major topic . . . Which brings us to my second topic . . . And in conclusion . . ." Transition statements provide direction and regain attention. They're useful at major break points: between introduction and body, between main body sections, between body and summary and beyond. They're also useful as lead-ins to visuals or demonstrations.

■ *Mini-summaries.* These are capsule versions of the most recent key points—for example: "We've examined the new manufacturing plan with its three features: computer-controlled milling, an advanced production control system, and a modularized assembly technique. Now let's look at how this affects our personnel requirements."

■ *Orientation devices.* Visual aids can be designed with their own directional clues. Reduce an overview flowchart, copy it onto successive charts, and highlight the block being discussed. Use colors to code a series of block diagrams, sketches, or word charts.

Factors Influencing Order. Several factors can influence the order in which material is best presented.

■ *Audience interest.* The most common problem is spending far too much time on material of secondary interest to the audience. If the key listeners are primarily interested in sales projections or financing arrangements, leading off with a lengthy description of the product or how it was developed will quickly lead to fidgety, or departing, listeners.

■ *Audience knowledge.* Another mistake is going directly into detailed informational material, such as how something works, when addressing an audience that has only mild interest in and limited knowledge of the subject. Instead, speakers in such situations should emphasize motivational material, applications, and benefits.

■ *Audience attitude.* Problems often occur with audiences that are wary of the speaker's proposition. For example, if a community group is gathered to hear a company spokesperson explain a proposal to put a new chemicals plant in their city, talking about only the positives and ignoring the potential negatives will probably do little to overcome resistance.

■ *Controversial nature.* Some points may be easily accepted; others may generate controversy. If the controversial points are presented first, audience interruptions may prevent the other points from being heard fairly or at all.

■ *Importance.* Since presentations often do not go according to plan because of interruptions or changes in schedule, it often is wise to present the most important ideas first. If time runs out, the main material has been covered.

■ *Time constraints and consumption.* If ten minutes is all the time available, skip the background and get to the heart of the matter quickly. If two topics have the same degree of importance and controversy, and if one takes fifteen minutes to cover, the other only five, present the shorter topic first.

■ *Relationship.* Complex ideas are often more easily grasped by first explaining the more fundamental concepts. To explain the football play system to a group of novices, it may be best to start with, "First let's look at the different types of players. This is a back . . . this is a lineman . . ." On the other hand, it may be more effective to go the other way: first present the whole, and then work down to the basic parts.

Another form of relationship to consider is that of items at the same level. In describing the systems of an airplane, is it easier to explain the propulsion system if the structural system has been discussed first? Often it is.

■ *Logical progression.* Development of material may proceed *from* the main proposition—"X is true for these reasons: A, B, and C"—or *toward* it—"Our studies show A, B, and C, leading us to conclude that X is true." The first is called *deductive* reasoning, the second, *inductive.*

If your audience is likely to take issue with your conclusion, it may be wise to move toward it rather than from it. For example, arguing in favor of gun control to gun enthusiasts and starting with the statement (your proposition) "Handguns are a menace and should be banned" would probably make for a short but stimulating presentation. Building toward it might give you a better hearing and enable you to establish agreement on some points, if not the whole proposition.

The latter approach would be inductive. You attempt to gain agreement or acceptance on several pieces of evidence or argument, and keep building the case until you have shown that enough evidence exists (you hope) to gain acceptance for the proposition. For example:

> "We are having quality problems in the shop [*prove it*]."
> "Maintenance on our equipment is costly [*show the data*]."
> "Production rates have been declining [*show the trends*]."
>   All this shows that:
> *Proposition:* "We need to replace our machinery."

Deductive reasoning starts with an accepted generalization:

> "We need to replace our machinery with a better-quality, lower-cost, and
>   faster machine."
> "The Brand X Mod-95 is such a machine."
> "We should replace our machinery with the Mod-95."

The Summary: Tell 'em What You Told 'em and Ask for the Action

The most important parts of a presentation are the comments to begin and those to wrap up. The summary gives you one more opportunity, and the final one, to hammer home the key parts of your message and to make sure the basic ideas are conveyed.

Writing the summary is one of the most important activities in shaping a presentation. I have seen vague and rambling presentations come into focus by the simple expedient of asking the presenters to write out summaries. This forces the presenter to identify the true essence of what she or he wants to get across, and it applies a fundamental principle of learning: that restatement is often essential.

A concise summary also provides flexibility during a presentation as time is shortened or some points take longer than planned. The presenter can cut material and still make sure the audience hears all the key points. Without a summary, this flexibility is lost. If points are skipped during the body, they may be skipped forever.

It is important that the summary be given proper treatment. Do what you must with the body—omit detail, cut charts, skip material—but *do not shortchange your summary.* For a rule of thumb, keep the summary to no more than about 10 percent of the presentation. Here are the key elements (Figure 6-7):

- *Reiterate main points.* This is the final leg of the "tell 'em" triad, often presented on a visual aid as the summary chart. Restate only what you've covered during the talk; no new material should surface here. Figure 6-8 shows an example of an actual summary (restatement) chart.

- *Give conclusions and recommendations,* as appropriate.

- *Ask for specific action.* Many presenters either are not well prepared for this or omit it. What do you want the audience to do? Even for an informational presentation, offer suggestions as to how they might use your information.

- *Close with punch.* This provides the final flourish that reinforces the impression of assurance and professionalism you want to convey. This also ties

Figure 6-7. The summary ties it all together. Select specific parts to fit the presentation best.

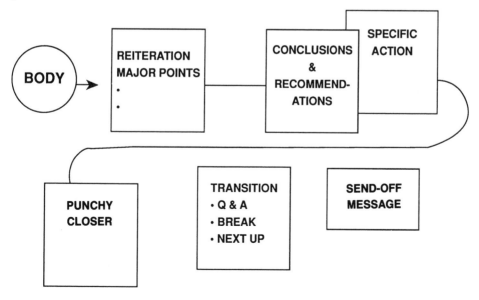

Figure 6-8. The most important chart is the summary, which reiterates the main theme and primary points.

BIOTEK -- PRIMED FOR GROWTH

- Market niche established

- Solid management team in place

- Key contracts secured

- Financing plan is sound

the presentation together, puts the final bow onto the package, and says "*Finis. Applaud now.*"

The wrap-up can be a simple sentence: "At this point, winning the proposal is entirely up to us—let's get at it." It may be an example, quotation, or statistic. A good way to show unity is to refer again to the illustration with which you began the talk. I commented earlier in the guidelines on the introduction how one speaker effectively held up a printed circuit board and called attention to the fact that the cost had been substantially cut by use of a new technique, which the presenter then went on to describe. As a wrap-up, he might again hold up the board and say, "Remember, we cut the cost of producing this $500 printed circuit board to $3. How many more $500 boards are just waiting to be discovered?"

It's hard to top the wrap-up used by Ross Smythe of Air Canada: "As I now glance at the hour, I am reminded of a poem:

> 'The coffee's cold, the sherbet wanes,
> The speech drones on and on . . .
> O Speaker, heed the ancient rule:
> Be brief. Be gay. Be gone!' "

And he was.[14]

What about a final thank you? Many speakers feel compelled to say "Thank you" upon concluding their presentations. Occasionally this is appropriate, for example, when the speaker has requested time to make an appeal for funds from the audience. Generally a thank you is superfluous and detracts from the final punch achieved by the wrap-up statement. Skip unless obviously called for.

- *Provide a transition to the next phase.* Now what? Don't leave the audience sitting there bewildered. Do you want to take questions? Introduce the next speaker? Pass out materials? Take a break? Let them know.

To transfer to questions, use wording that will ease your audience into a new mode. "Any questions?"—the most common expression—is too abrupt and frequently means, "*Don't* ask questions." Try this: "We've covered the main points about my proposal. I'm sure you have more questions, and I'll be pleased to answer them now."

- *Conclude with a final send-off message.* The Q&A period may have been rough, and you may want to restore the right flavor to your message, or you sense a key player is about to leave and you'd like to get her ear one more time. Be assertive and close out the session with the message you'd like to have her carry out of the room: "Once again, the key point I'd like to leave you with is that our proposed new system will greatly add to our productivity."

OTHER ORGANIZATION FORMULAS

The basic formula just presented is the one most commonly used in business presentations. Several other formulas have useful applications as well.

The Motivated Sequence

Alan Monroe and Douglas Ehninger are associated with this formula, which may be effective for certain persuasive presentations. It may be the wisest organization for neutral to negative audiences, where revealing the true purpose and message early may bring the presentation to an abrupt halt. This formula does not "tell 'em" in advance. The main message is not stated until late in the talk, after an important need has been established and developed. This is roughly the approach used by Marc Antony in Shakespeare's *Julius Caesar* to turn around an audience that initially was opposed to Antony's proposition—that Brutus was a murderer, not a hero.

Here's an example of how the formula might be applied in a presentation. (If this sounds familiar, it's because you've been hit with it a thousand times from your television screen. It's a common technique television advertisers use to get us to buy their beer or deodorant.)

ATTENTION:	Catch the attention of listeners: "Losing the Program X contract was a major blow."
NEED:	Focus on a concern or problem: "To remain competitive, we must fix our main problem, namely high costs."
SATISFACTION:	Put forth your solution to that problem: "The Model H50 computer will reduce our costs."
VISUALIZATION:	Describe your solution's benefits to listeners: "With the H50, we can win the upcoming Program Y contract."
ACTION:	Ask for a commitment to your solution: "I ask your O.K. to buy the Model H50."

AIDA

AIDA does not refer to the Verdi opera; it is a mnemonic frequently used by Toastmasters, similar to the motivated sequence.

(CATCH) ATTENTION: "With your present setup, two dumptrucks a day go to the scrapyards."

(AROUSE) INTEREST: "Suppose you could cut that down to one per week."

(STIMULATE) DESIRE: "Our Framzis Fixit can do that. The proof is in the dozen units we've sold your competitors, which have averaged 90 percent scrap reduction."

(MOVE TO) ACTION: "Sign on the dotted line, and we'll deliver tomorrow."[16]

Borden's "Ho-Hum" Formula

These are the four stages of audience reaction to a speaker:

HO HUM. "Twenty-five billion dollars of prime real estate was sold last year to a new group of buyers—oil millionaires."

WHY BRING THAT UP? "You don't care about real estate? What about inflation? A major contributor is our outlay for foreign oil."

FOR INSTANCE. "Let's look at how our excessive oil imports contribute to inflation: Our dollar is devalued, housing prices are driven up . . ."

SO WHAT? "We can keep pouring our dollars out for foreign oil or cut down imports. Let's choose the latter."[17]

Example–Point–Reason

Dale Carnegie called this the "Magic Formula" for short talks to get action.[18] An example:

EXAMPLE: "I recently spent time with an enthusiastic bunch of businesspeople. They're making a flotzinjammer and selling them like hotcakes. These are teenagers, getting business experience through Junior Achievement."

POINT: "To get these kids started in business takes money. I'm here to ask you to donate $100 to get another group started."

REASON: "What will you get out of it? The satisfaction of helping kids understand our economic system."

PREP

Communications consultant June Guncheon discussed this formula in an article in *Nation's Business* and noted it was particularly useful for impromptu or short-notice situations.[19] Many of my students have commented favorably on the value of this formula. It can help quickly organize your thoughts prior to speaking or going into a meeting, or even before making a telephone call. It can help prevent that sinking feeling that often hits one minute after you've finished speaking: "Oh, why didn't I say that?" or "I forgot the main point!" Here's an example of PREP:

POINT: "Boss, I deserve a raise."
"Oh really, what makes you think so?"
REASON: "Because I've been doing good work this year."
"Oh? Such as?"
EXAMPLE: "The study you put me in charge of. We finished that under budget; the customer said it was great and gave us an add-on."
"Hmmm."
POINT: "I think that shows that I deserve a raise."
"Hmmm."

Straw Man, or Point/Counterpoint

This is my own formula, which quickly lays out an easily understood framework for argument. Setting a straw man (the opposing position) against your own view provides a dramatic confrontation, shows you have given some attention to opposing views, and allows flexibility of attack.

POINT: State a position: "Many people feel that nuclear energy is not safe because of the waste disposal problem."
COUNTERPOINT: State an opposing position: "Others feel the disposal methods are adequate and that we should proceed."
ARGUMENT: Present your case: "A study conducted by the Department of Energy shows . . ."
CONCLUSION: Sum up your now-proven position and ask for action as appropriate: "I believe these analyses have shown . . . and that we should . . ."

ORGANIZATION TOOLS

Sifting through ideas and material and arranging them in a logical and effective order is by no means simple. The process can be greatly aided with the help of several widely used (and still underused) tools.

Jim Dollard, president of Management Analysis Company, is a firm believer in taking time to organize: "After thirty years, I never cease to be amazed at how disorganized people are in preparing presentations. If people are too quick to get into chartmaking before they've focused their messages, it takes twice as long to turn them around. One of the most useful steps is to walk through your presentation, while it's still flexible, with these simple organizational tools."[20]

Brainstorming and Sorting

Once the main theme is set, a useful step early in the organizing phase is to list all the topics that the presentation might cover. Brainstorming, which can be done alone or by a group, lists all ideas as they come, with no attempt to evaluate or categorize. The fullest range of potential topics is the goal.

After the flow of ideas slackens, sorting and evaluation begins. The objective is to identify and establish priorities for the half-dozen or fewer major topics to be covered and to eliminate those of lesser value.

Visual Outlining

Many people are more spatially oriented than word oriented. For designers, computer programmers, and schedulers, diagrams are an integral part of the thinking process. PERT charts, decision trees, flowcharts, and exploded drawings are examples of spatial thinking.

The same concepts can be used to map out the design for a presentation, which is why one variation is called *mind mapping*. This process can provide insight and structure as it helps generate ideas and reveal relationships. Diagrams (Figure 6-9) often develop these better than verbal outlines.

Professional speaker Jane Handly is a long-time practitioner of visual outlining. For her talks, she draws a circle and places the main theme inside (e.g., "customer relations"). Around that she draws another circle, divides it into sections, and places key topics around like a clock (e.g., "motivation," "company experiences," "specific steps"). Then she chooses stories and examples for each topic. When speaking she often puts her "clock" on a note card.[21]

Cards and Stick-ons

Many people have found 3- by 5-inch cards valuable in the organizing process. Write key ideas, examples, stories, and so on one per card; arrange the cards into common groups on a table top.

A variation is to use small stick-on slips and a manila folder to brainstorm and develop a quick layout of key points (Figure 6-10). I've used this method for years to organize speeches, lesson plans, articles, and meetings quickly. I've introduced it to many people, who have provided ample feedback about its simplicity and value. Try it and see.

Outlining: Beneficial and Underemployed

"I had spent two weeks wrestling with this presentation," said one seasoned presenter. "I've been going round and round trying to tie all these visuals together and to get this thing to flow. Then I decided to go back to square one and write an outline. I spent one day working on it, and was absolutely amazed at what it did for my presentation. For the first time I could see what I was really trying to say. The outline sorted out a whole jumble of ideas that had been racing around in my head. The obvious question is, why didn't I do the outline first and save all that time and energy? Next time I'll know better."

Figure 6-9. A visual outline often helps stimulate and clarify ideas.

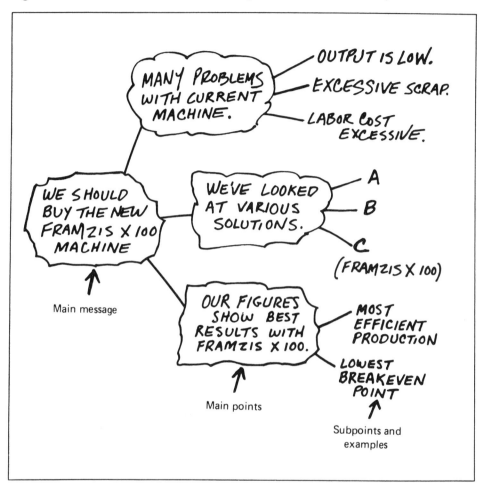

The outline is a planning tool. It is a way of forcing or disciplining the selection and ordering of ideas. Presenters sometimes say that they don't outline because it will constrain their thought process and take away their natural flow. Yet a presentation must be constrained. It must be tightly packaged, with all the extraneous ideas and material excluded. An audience deserves and will insist upon a concisely organized message that achieves its goals in the least possible time.

Writing an outline is a much better use of time than writing out a presentation. If there is one thing that constrains speakers, it is a written speech. The basic ideas are often poorly organized and are hard to assess and improve because they are often buried and rambling. Writing style is different from speaking style, and written speeches often sound dreary and lifeless. If you must write out a talk, first write an outline and then follow the principles noted in Chapter 15.

Figure 6-10.   A quick way to get thoughts organized is to place stick-on slips onto the wall or a manila folder.

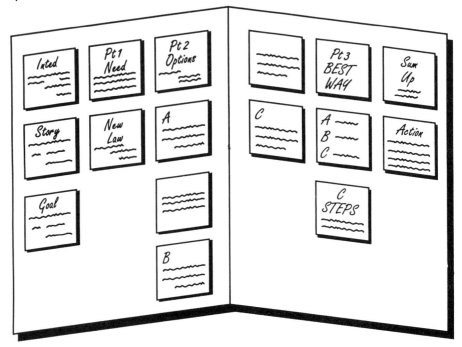

Outlines come in different forms. A complete-sentence outline, where main points and subpoints are written out in complete sentences (Figure 6-11), removes the vagueness associated with briefer outlines and permits the tests noted before to be readily applied. Particularly for people who have not done outlines before, I recommend the full-sentence outline. As a thought-disciplining tool, it is hard to beat. A less detailed outline, such as key words, can also be helpful.

The Storyboard—Combining Visual and Verbal Messages

This is a simple method for making the transition from an outline to visual aids. Don't be fooled by its simplicity. It is a most important and useful tool in the planning of visual aid presentations.

Because storyboards are part of the design process, they can be created, reviewed, and redone quickly and cheaply. Their visual nature is easier to follow than outlines or narratives, and the rough visual ideas give reviewers an actual picture of what the audience will be seeing during the presentation. Presentation length can also be quickly estimated from the storyboards. Business presentations typically take thirty seconds to two minutes per visual.

A storyboard (also called a thumbnail sketch) is a visual aid outline. It is a layout or flowchart of the presentation in a series of sketches (Figure 6-12), with each sketch representing one visual. Each should make one point only, and that

Figure 6-11. Some tips on outlining.

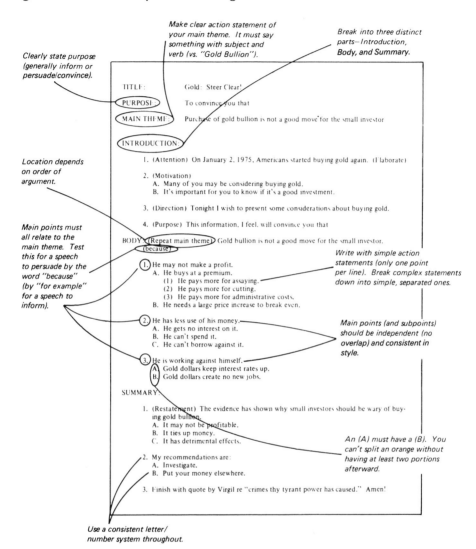

Make clear action statement of your main theme. It must say something with subject and verb (vs. "Gold Bullion").

Break into three distinct parts—Introduction, **Body, and Summary.**

Clearly state purpose (generally inform or persuade/convince).

TITLE: Gold: Steer Clear!

(PURPOSE) To convince you that

(MAIN THEME) Purchase of gold bullion is not a good move for the small investor

(INTRODUCTION)

Location depends on order of argument.

1. (Attention) On January 2, 1975, Americans started buying gold again. (Elaborate)

2. (Motivation)
   A. Many of you may be considering buying gold.
   B. It's important for you to know if it's a good investment.

3. (Direction) Tonight I wish to present some considerations about buying gold.

4. (Purpose) This information, I feel, will convince you that

Main points must all relate to the main theme. Test this for a speech to persuade by the word "because" (by "for example" for a speech to inform).

BODY (Repeat main theme) Gold bullion is not a good move for the small investor.
(because)

Write with simple action statements (only one point per line). Break complex statements down into simple, separated ones.

1. He may not make a profit.
   A. He buys at a premium.
      (1) He pays more for assaying.
      (2) He pays more for cutting.
      (3) He pays more for administrative costs.
   B. He needs a large price increase to break even.

2. He has less use of his money.
   A. He gets no interest on it.
   B. He can't spend it.
   C. He can't borrow against it.

Main points (and subpoints) should be independent (no overlap) and consistent in style.

3. He is working against himself.
   A. Gold dollars keep interest rates up.
   B. Gold dollars create no new jobs.

SUMMARY

1. (Restatement) The evidence has shown why small investors should be wary of buying gold bullion.
   A. It may not be profitable.
   B. It ties up money.
   C. It has detrimental effects.

An (A) must have a (B). You can't split an orange without having at least two portions afterward.

2. My recommendations are:
   A. Investigate.
   B. Put your money elsewhere.

3. Finish with quote by Virgil re "crimes thy tyrant power has caused." Amen!

Use a consistent letter/number system throughout.

Figure 6-12.   The storyboard is invaluable for planning the presentation and combining verbal or outline points with visual concerns.

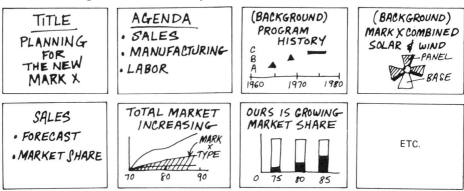

statement should be written out. These intended messages suggest the visual, not the other way around. A storyboard developed further will add the spoken points that would go with the visual. Storyboards come in various forms:

- *Small sheets or cards* (3 by 5 or 4 by 6 inches). Each card represents a visual concept. Some people prefer the smaller cards so presenters put less on them; with larger cards, visual and key notes can go on one card. The cards can be placed on a table for review or taped to a wall or chalkboard. Kodak offers a design for a wall-mounted cardholder.

- *A series of linked sketches* with spaces below or beside the sketches for comments. Four sketches per page (vertical or horizontal) works well.

- *Full-size sheets* (8½ by 11 inches), one sketch per sheet mounted to the wall for review. Some organizations have cork or magnetic walls in their presentation development rooms for this purpose.

Computers as Organizing Tools

Computers can greatly expedite the organizing process. Presenters can use software programs to develop outlines, shift each key point into a storyboard of visual aid concepts, and develop each concept into a finished visual. Some programs have back-and-forth linkages, so changing the outline can automatically change the visual content, and vice-versa (Figure 6-13).

A word of caution: Computers can streamline the process, but they don't ensure a sound presentation. That immediate bridge from outline to visual, for example, quickly provides high-quality visuals, but, without further development, they may be mostly words or imported tables. Presenters may be inclined to stop at this point, yet further development may lead to significantly better visuals.

Delivery Scripts and Speaker Notes

This is the bridge between organization and delivery. Again computers can help. Once the storyboard flowchart and each visual are finished, add the spoken

Figure 6-13. Computers are powerful tools to aid organizing.

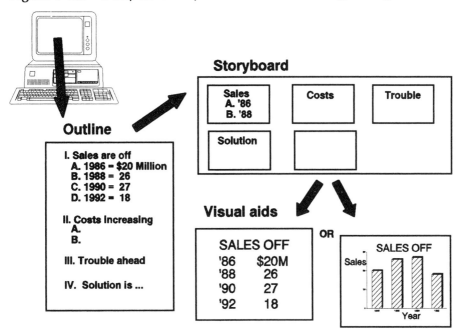

words that match each visual to form the delivery script (Figure 6-14). This helps tighten the spoken message, prevent rambling, and keep presenters within time limits. The same process can provide distribution materials of visuals and supplementary detailed information.

Speakers may use notes to help them stay on course or provide needed information. Well-used notes are barely noticed by the audience. Poorly used, they interfere with eye contact, lead to monotone delivery, and damage credibility. For these reasons, I advise caution about the use of notes. With visual aids, most speaker cues can be pulled right from the visuals.

Notes of large, key words only or sketches on 3- by 5-inch cards can be used unobtrusively, with a quick glance triggering the thoughts. Larger cards (4 by 6 or 5 by 7 inches) are better for lectern use than hand held.

TITLES—A FULL HOUSE MAY DEPEND ON THEM

For most everyday business presentations, titles are not particularly significant. In-house management and customers generally know what the subject will cover, and the titles' main function is for reference and to go on the front page of the visual aid brochure. In this category I would put "Proposal for NASA Electric Propulsion System" and "Production Readiness Review."

Titles take on much greater significance when the presentation is given to outside groups, particularly those whose members can be selective about whether they even show up. At a professional society's annual convention,

Figure 6-14. Delivery or talking scripts help to tighten spoken messages and meet time targets.

Visual

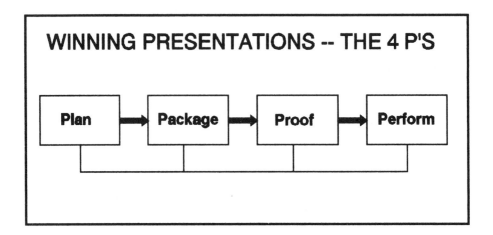

Key points to address orally:

● **Describe elements.**

● **Note value for developing presentations.**

● **Show use for critiquing presentations.**

attendees may be able to choose from a half-dozen presentations, all occurring simultaneously. The title may be the determining factor in the choice of which talk to attend.

If the title is to be used in advance publicity or the talk is to be printed in seminar proceedings or some other publication, a punchy title can help promote attendance and ensure that the talk will be read. A political club's newsletter announced that the speaker at the next club meeting would talk about penal reform and rehabilitation. The talk was titled, "Penal Reform and Rehabilitation." A real crowd puller. I suggest that an equally informative and much punchier title might have been "Ex-Cons—Recyclable or Lost Causes?"

A catchy and effective title has several key characteristics:

- It is appropriate to the occasion.
- It provides enough information about the subject so that potential attendees can tell if this is likely to be of interest to them.
- It is succinct and to the point.
- It piques the interest of the reader.

Here is a list of idea categories commonly used, with examples from actual speeches:

- *Play on words.* "The Yen to Make a Mark with the Dollar: A Franc Look at Our International Economic Policy" (from former Senator Frank Church); "Let's Put Some Esprit in de Corporation" (*Harvard Business Review* article).

- *Satire.* "Can't Nobody Here Use This Language?" (to professional communicators).

- *Variation of a common axiom.* "Guilty Until Proven Innocent—Advertising and the Consumer" (to an advertising club).

- *Tie to current topics* (movies, slogans, songs, books, etc.). "Organizational Encounters of the Third Kind: With the Ombudsman" (your author)

- *Figures of speech.* "Tomahawk Today"; "Resources, Results and the Seven Deadly Sins."

- *Use of slang, jargon, or "street" expressions.* Two papers on a similar subject given at a national speech conference illustrate this concept.[22] Which is likely to draw the bigger crowds? "Structural Coherence Production in the Conversations of Preschool Children" or " 'I'll Give You a Knuckle Sandwich!': Preschoolers' Resolution of Conflict"?

- *The "gather 'em all in" formula.* A writer set out to appeal to the largest number of people in the shortest possible time, so he decided to pull out the stops and combine all the magnetic techniques in the title for a new book. He sent his publisher this title: "I Had Intercourse with a Bear." The publisher said it wasn't bad but not universal enough. So the writer tried again: "I Had Intercourse with a Bear—for the FBI." The editor said it was better but still lacked a certain something. After much tinkering, the writer came out with his best and final effort: "I Had Intercourse with a Bear for the FBI—and Found God."[23]

IN SUMMARY: TAKE TIME TO ORGANIZE

In a world where people were willing to sit and listen to speakers go on at length about their specialties, organization wouldn't be much of a problem. In the real world of time pressures and priorities, having a clear, concise, and convincing organization is essential to success. By following sound principles for structuring ideas and applying tools to expedite the process, presenters can clarify their own thinking and help their audiences get the message.

Dottie Walters, head of Walters International Speakers Bureau, has spoken all around the world and worked with hundreds of speakers. She advises speakers to "start with humor and end with heart. Either a story from your own life or about someone else. People love it when someone gets knocked down and gets back up."[24]

Political writer Richard Bergholz described how effectively President Ronald Reagan applied this closing concept in a major address at a tenuous moment in international relations. He finished his speech and then reached into his inner coat pocket and pulled out a letter he'd received a few days before from a woman who'd just sent her son off the join the armed services. He read the moving words she'd written about the emotions that were flooding over her, with the close: "So tonight, here in the shadows, here in the quiet, a dumb orange stuffed tiger and I sit together absorbing the intensity of this special day.

"Thank you for taking the time while running a nation to listen to the passions of a mother's heart. I feel better now having shared my feelings tonight.

"And please, will you be especially careful with the country just now?"

Reagan paused, glanced quickly at his wife and then at the audience and said in a husky voice: "I will be very careful with the country just now."

Was it good? Wrote Bergholz: "Women sobbed. Nancy Reagan dabbed at her eyes and the huge convention hall was hushed."[25]

* * * 7 * * *

Support, Part I: Reinforcement

KEY POINTS OF THIS CHAPTER

* Ideas don't stand alone. They must be illustrated and supported to be listened to, understood, and accepted.
* Explanation—description, definitions, and ground rules—helps everybody get on the same wavelength.
* Winning presentations generally include a substantial amount of well-chosen forms of support: examples, analogies, statistical data, and references.
* The most effective supporting material is relevant, accurate, appropriate, and put in terms the audience will understand, respect, and respond to.

During the 1988 presidential campaign, Congressman Richard Gephardt (Missouri) was one of several candidates vying for the Democratic nomination. In spite of mighty efforts over many months, his campaign wasn't creating much of a stir. One of his central themes was the need to get a fairer trade system to keep American jobs from being lost to overseas manufacturers. That seemed to be a timely issue, but he wasn't stirring the electorate with it.

Following an adviser's suggestion, Gephardt started talking about the different rules U.S. and foreign manufacturers operate under. He noted that Hyundai autos were selling well in the United States at a price around $10,000. If Chrysler sold its comparable auto in Korea, import duties would result in a price of $48,000. "How many Hyundais would sell in the United States," he asked, "if they cost $48,000?" By using this analogy, Gephardt was able to get people to see the injustice of the system and get more excited about his candidacy. This becomes a staple of his speeches and ads, which became known as the $48,000 Hyundai ad.[1]

In late 1991, a $1 billion contract for small computers was awarded to Compuadd Corporation by the Defense Department. Among the losing bidders were giants Apple and Zenith. Compuadd was not the low bidder, so what rabbit did it pull out of the hat to achieve this success? Noted in press reports was its outstanding performance on a contract during the 1990–1991 Persian Gulf crisis. Compuadd came through admirably on a $21 million computer order, when its employees worked around the clock and started shipments two weeks before the deadline, and the computers worked as expected. So ten months later, Compuadd could cite that example of proof of its capability to a buyer with a sharp memory and appreciation.[2]

From the Organize phase came the presentation skeleton: the layout of themes, topics, and ideas. Now comes the time to flesh it out, adding the supporting material to illustrate and back up the main points. "Where's the beef?" is the cry from the audience, a slogan that Wendy's hamburgers coined to suggest that other products lacked substance. Presidential candidate Walter Mondale borrowed it to suggest the same about his opponent's ideas during the 1984 campaign.

Support has various roles. *Explanations* help people establish a common base of understanding. *Reinforcement* provides clarity, substantiation, and sometimes inspiration. *Visual aids* are a primary vehicle for presentations support.

Good supporting material is vital for success in presentations. Contracts and budgets are rarely won by passion alone, but by also making a solid case. Good support adds spark to presentations, much as the color analyst does in a sports broadcast. It offers one of the best ways to get an audience actively involved, and it helps a presenter add personality and experience to message and style.

Statesmen, religious leaders, and professional speakers, such as Paul Harvey, Tom Peters, and Billy Graham, are among the most proficient users of supporting material to inform and inspire. Humorists such as Bill Cosby and Garrison Keillor are masters at using support material to entrance audiences.

Using support well takes care. "Start with a joke" is common advice, and yet many people can't tell jokes well. "Dazzle 'em with statistics" is another old saw, which often quickly leads instead to the MEGO ("My Eyes Glaze Over") syndrome.

In this chapter we'll look at how to provide the "beef," using mostly spoken forms. Visual aids will be covered in the next chapter.

EXPLANATIONS: DESCRIPTIONS, DEFINITIONS, AND GROUND RULES

When people first hear about an idea, they may reject it immediately for a variety of reasons: They think it is far more complex than it really is, they think it is something different from what it is, or they just don't know enough about it. Three common forms of explanation are often used to combat this problem.

Descriptions

One way of overcoming hesitancy or fear is to describe what something looks like, how it works, what effects it will have, and what benefits it may bring. This is a particularly common form of support in presentations and often a firm requirement. "Show and tell" is not restricted to grade school classes.

People who must make decisions about whether to buy a product, authorize go-ahead on production or a new facility, start a sales campaign, or launch a rocket want to get into the nuts and bolts to various degrees. Detailed descriptions, including visual displays of hardware, flowcharts, inputs/outputs, and operations, are standard practice (Figure 7-1).

Definitions

Because of audiences' varying backgrounds and familiarity with the subject, terms must often be defined if everyone is to understand what is being addressed. In addition, words have different meanings for different people. Failing to define such terms as Theory X, M1, and supply-side economics can result in people on two or more wavelengths.

In a presentation about subcontracting on an aircraft program, a presenter several times referred to "indicators." It was at least five minutes into the talk before the members of the audience, all well versed in the aircraft program, realized the speaker was referring to indicators used in the cockpit for measurements of key pressures and not economic indicators. How much simpler it would have been to have explained at the start what indicators he was referring to or to have shown a photo or an actual indicator.

Ground Rules

Also important in clarifying terms and providing a common starting place for discussing topics are the ground rules or assumptions. These may also provide an immediate cause of disagreement if the listeners don't like the ground rules you've used. Such open disagreement seems better than listeners' thinking they are in agreement with your analyses while in fact they have erroneous judgments about your ground rules.

Key Points in Using Explanations

■ *Remember your audience.* A common mistake by presenters is misjudging the audience and spending far too much time in detailed explanations of how something works when the audience is interested only in applications or results.

■ *Watch your language*—terminology, references, jargon, and acronyms. Far too often the speaker's lengthy explanation loses the listeners in the first few sentences by speaking a language they don't know.

■ *Consider the use of visual aids or demonstrations.* A picture is worth a thousand words—that is, if it is a good picture.

■ *Give the big picture before going into the details.* This provides a reference point so listeners can more readily accept detailed data.

■ *Explain by example or analogy.* Disraeli was once asked to define the difference between a misfortune and a calamity. "Well," he said, "if Gladstone [his political opponent] were to fall into the river, it would be a misfortune. But if anybody dragged him out, it would be a calamity."

A presenter used this concept in explaining trade studies to a general

Figure 7-1. Descriptions—drawings, photos, and flow diagrams—are common forms of explanatory material.

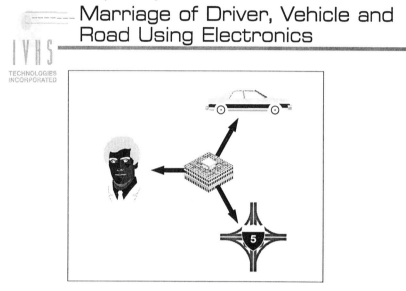

Marriage of Driver, Vehicle and Road Using Electronics

IVHS
TECHNOLOGIES
INCORPORATED

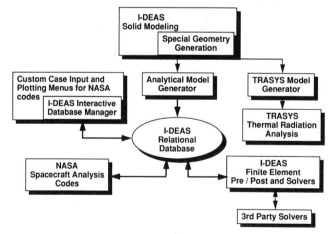

INTEGRATION HELPS AUTOMATE DESIGN AND ANALYSIS

Source: Courtesy IVHS Technologies Incorporated and Structural Dynamics Research Corporation.

audience: "You're familiar with the magazine *Consumer Reports.* In every issue they compare how different models of refrigerators or lawn mowers stack up against various set criteria. Those are trade studies." The formal definition would have taken longer and still left misconceptions.

An example can also drive the point home better and faster than a straight definition. *Assertiveness* is a term often used and often confused. Would it be more easily grasped by demonstration? Alberti and Emmons defined the terms by noting behaviors in a restaurant when Mr. A. has ordered a rare steak and gets one that was well done:

Nonassertive	Mr. A. grumbles to his wife but says nothing directly to the waiter. He leaves a tiny tip and later says he won't eat there again.
Aggressive	Angrily summons the waiter, berates him loudly, and demands another steak. Mrs. A. is embarrassed, but Mr. A doesn't care.
Assertive	Motions the waiter to the table. Notes he had ordered a rare steak but got a well-done piece of meat. Asks politely but firmly that it be replaced.[3]

These definitions could be made vivid and memorable by role-playing the various behaviors, creating punchy visuals, and drawing similar experiences from the audience. Other examples could be pulled from "Dear Abby" or the comic pages, using realism and humor to take it from abstract to something audiences can relate to better.

■ *Come at it from different directions.* An unfamiliar item or idea may be more easily understood by explaining what it is not rather than what it is or by comparing it to variations or contrasting concepts. "I'm an optimist in our battle against inflation," said the speaker. "An *optimist* will loan his or her new car to the teenager of the family who just got a driver's license. A *pessimist* won't. And the *cynic* already has."

■ *Avoid lengthy formal definitions*, especially if shown as a lengthy paragraph on a visual aid. This is one of the easiest ways to add lead to your presentation, as pure dictionary descriptions are deadly dull. Generally better are brief paraphrased definitions with specific examples used to create clearer understanding faster. "There's a difference between involvement and commitment," said one speaker. "Take a plate of ham and eggs. The chicken was involved, but the pig was committed."

■ *Use discretion in presenting ground rules.* I have seen many presentations quickly bog down because the speaker was so meticulous in presenting every assumption. Immediately some listeners started to argue about the appropriateness of certain minor assumptions. They took on an importance far beyond what they actually had and would have been much better left for the question period or as an exercise for the reader as he reviewed a written report giving all the details.

These and other key points are summarized in Figure 7-2.

THE REINFORCEMENT ROLE

Consider the following presentation by a representative from an electronics company to a potential customer:

Figure 7-2. Apply these tips to liven up explanations.

- Provide adequate explanatory material for background, but keep it brief.
- With any explanatory material, gauge your listeners and put it in terms they can understand.
- Describing what something looks like or how it works can be helpful to listeners if not overdone. Give a big picture before details.
- Define your terms initially so people are clear about your subject and references.
- Description and definition are often better expressed and understood by example, analogy, and contrast than by formal (dull) statements.
- Visual aids are particularly helpful in giving explanations.
- Provide enough ground rules to give listeners the necessary starting point, not so many as to bog down the talk in nitpicking.

Our innovative new Frim Mod II is the perfect solution to your problem. It has worked fine for many other companies. Maintenance costs are almost nothing. It is a significant technological advance over the brand X unit, but it's a bit complicated to explain and much of it is proprietary, so I can't say much about it. Suffice it to say it will do the job you need. Now, how many do you want?

It is possible for a presenter to make such a series of statements to a potential customer. It is also possible the customer will throw the presenter out on his ear. The presenter has made a series of claims, all of which the customer is supposed to accept on faith. The customer has been given no insight into how this "technological advance" is supposed to work, nothing to give him or her a warm feeling about the gadget.

That same presenter could have also given this presentation:

We believe our innovative new Frim Mod II is the perfect solution to your problem. The people at Magnacom had a problem similar to yours and the Mod II worked beautifully for them. ①

You asked about maintenance costs. Here's what Frank Gonzales, Magnacom chief of maintenance, said about the Frim Mod II: ② "Our experience with the Mod II has been phenomenal. It has been out of service only 1.3 days per month, a big improvement over the 5.7 of the unit it replaced." ③

What makes the Mod II so much more effective than the competition? You're familiar with the difference between a car alternator and a generator. The alternator is always charging, the generator often isn't. Our Mod II is a form of alternator—it never drains off energy from the system it works with. The competition units all operate like generators—they have periods of power drain . . . ④

Now, how many do you want?

Both presentations contain the same ideas and make the same claims. In the first version, however, none of the claims is substantiated; in the second, all of them are. The reinforcement not only adds support to the claims; it helps the listener understand the concepts presented. If the support material is effective, the listener may become convinced that the Mod II is indeed just what his or her company needs. If it is weak, no sale.

The principle here is, "Assertion needs reinforcement to be successful" (Figure 7-3). Winning over the audience to the proposition depends largely on how well the presenter uses supporting material to clarify, substantiate, and inspire. The reinforcement repertoire is sparked by the words "for example," as seen in the second Mod II presentation:

Examples: specific cases ①, illustrations, stories, and anecdotes.
References: testimonials ② and quotations.
Statistical data ③.
Analogies ④.

Several basic ideas relate to the use of any of the forms of supporting material (summarized in Figure 7-4). The material must:

■ *Fit the needs and style of the receivers.* Fundamental in planning support material is knowing how the principal listeners want material presented to them. Are they big on numbers? Are they no-nonsense, get-to-it-now types, or are they likely to allow a more leisurely pace? Do they enjoy a good story? This is where many presenters fall flat. In my organization, the engineering vice-president was a stickler for details, so people learned to be ready with lots of those. His successor was vastly different; his eyes would glaze over, and his interest would visibly shift after the second data chart. Would you present the same way to President Reagan as President Carter? Not at all. "Know thy audience" is a cardinal rule for getting through (Figure 7-5).

■ *Be relevant to the subject being discussed.* One of the problems with stories selected from published collections is that the speaker may not tie them well into

Figure 7-3. Assertion needs reinforcement. To clarify, substantiate, and stir, presenter's key words are "for example."

Figure 7-4. Apply these tips to use support material well.

- Make sure the material is relevant to the topic and in appropriate taste.
- Use several types of support to account for differing audience backgrounds.
- Provide enough support to illustrate and prove your case, but don't overkill or bore people.
- Be sure of your facts, and use them ethically.
- Use examples from your own experience where possible.
- In citing specific cases, three is the magic number. Fewer is often not enough; more is overkill.
- Capitalize on the power of analogies, but don't overdo their use. Make sure the comparisons are valid, and use interesting and powerful starting points.
- Be sparing in your use of statistics, round them off, and convey them in terms the audience can understand.
- Use sources the audience will respect and in the context the author intended. Identify sources where they will add to credibility.
- Keep your material nitpick-free by pronouncing names correctly, making sure numbers and totals match, and being ready for challenges.
- Practice so you can deliver material in a smooth and dynamic manner and so you don't forget the punch line.
- Don't rush your delivery. Make sure key points are clearly spoken and even repeated. Allow sink-in time.

the ideas he or she is presenting. In business presentations listeners are there to hear ideas put forth, not a series of jokes and one-liners. Unless your purpose is to entertain, make sure the balance is proper. Have something to say first; then have the examples to back that up.

■ *Be appropriate and nonoffensive.* Prior to a U.S.-Soviet summit conference, White House chief of staff Donald Regan said women would find the activities of the two president's wives more interesting "as they'd have trouble understanding the weightier issues."[4] You can imagine the outcry from an offended populace. It's surprisingly easy to shoot yourself in the foot by off-color humor, ethnic jokes, and sexist references.

■ *Be interesting and influential to the audience.* A speaker from the eastern United States might find a western audience puzzled by references to Kroger's or Mogen David wine. A speaker to a youth group might be better off speaking about Bo Jackson than Jesse Owens.

■ *Be accurate and fairly presented.* This avoids the biggest and most legitimate criticism; support material often is biased, phony, taken out of the original context, inaccurate, or selectively presented to show only the good and not the bad. Ethical speakers pride themselves on using material legitimately. Pragmatic ones know that phony material can come back to bite them. Senator Joe Biden's 1988 presidential campaign ground to a quick halt when it was discovered he'd borrowed much speech material from a British politician, without crediting the source.

■ *Be workable.* Will the presentation fit within the time allowed? Can it be completed as intended? During the 1984 presidential debates, each candidate

Figure 7-5. Receiver style—how they want information—is a key factor in deciding which support material is best.

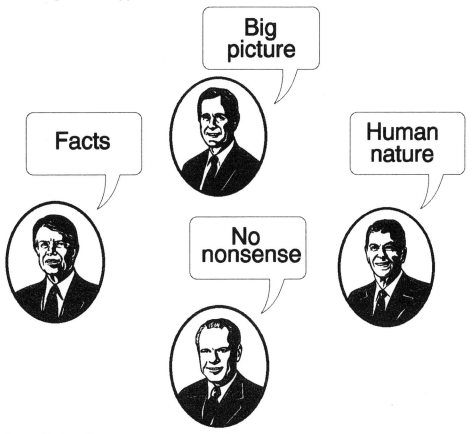

Source: Genigraphics.

was given three minutes for a final summary. Ronald Reagan launched into a story that wandered circuitously until the moderator interrupted him (a rare occasion when a U.S. president could be cut off). He never tied the story into anything or truly closed out this important speech. (This point also makes a good case for practicing, even though he won the election.)

■ *Prudently balance quantity and variety.* Because listeners bring different backgrounds and interests to a presentation, several types of material are generally desirable. What registers with one may not with another. It is also possible to saturate listeners with so much material that they lose interest. The "rule of three" has proven sound; citing more than three examples or statistics is overkill and sleep inducing.

■ *Be smoothly presented.* A great story falls flat if the speaker forgets the punch line. If she or stumbles when reading a testimonial or gets the numbers confused, credibility and impact suffer. Prepare material well, and practice so it goes smoothly. When delivering, read as little as possible, and pause long enough to let the punch line sink in.

Examples as a Form of Support

Business presentations make ample use of support in this category.

Specific cases are a common and effective form of example. These are references to specific instances, not detailed stories, that provide examples of the point being made. Here are some examples:

- "Drugs are bad news. You don't believe it? Neither did basketball superstar Lenny Bias, dead before he got to play with the Boston Celtics. Nor John Belushi, half of the Blues Brothers and a superb comic talent. Nor rock singer Janis Joplin. All done in by drugs."

- "You've raised an important question—what makes us think this new scheduling system will work here? The answer is that we know it will work here. This system is identical to one that has been working at Standard Oil for six months. IBM installed one a month ago, and they're ecstatic about it. The problem they solved is the same one that you have here."

- "In my own company, for every dollar spent in our Chemical Division for the development of new agricultural products—such as those chemicals that increase crop yields around the world—we spend an equal amount to prepare regulatory paperwork. A one-to-one ratio of productive to nonproductive. . . . I've read that a leading drug company spends more man-hours filling out government forms than it devotes to cancer and heart research combined."[5]

Stories and illustrations are among the most powerful forms of material a presenter can use. More than likely you have been part of a group in conversation and found yourself shifting your attention to an adjoining conversation. Why? Probably because someone started to tell a story. Or you may have been listening to a sermon or presentation and your interest had drifted when the speaker said something that brought you right back to full attention. Again, the most likely draw was a story.

The interest capability of a well-told story has been demonstrated throughout history. If the Greeks, Romans, Vikings, and American Indians have had one thing in common, it is that their cultures have been heavily flowered with myths and stories. The great religious leaders have made parables and stories a major force for getting their ideas across. Abe Lincoln and Mark Twain were noted as much for their storytelling ability as for their political or writing accomplishments.

How does a program manager convince her own management or a source selection board that she is the best one for the new project? Listing college degrees and job titles is only marginally effective and does little to distinguish this person from other candidates. One of the most effective ways is by telling about her experience on one or two similar assignments, with enough specifics to demonstrate she's been there, met tough challenges, and played a significant role in getting the job done. This is the place for one or two war stories, with enough detail to establish credibility and instill confidence.

Over and over again I've seen that the real stories—of successes and goofs—make people sit up and listen more intently, effectively impress upon them the importance of the issue under discussion, and be a major factor in winning their support. Wes Magnuson frequently spoke to suppliers of hardware and software for major defense programs. To make people more conscious of quality in their work, he used real examples of costly mistakes caused by lack of attention:

> I'd like now to review a few recent incidents. Some of you will recognize this as a rocket boost pump. In the photograph it's shown here on the table. We took some protective measures to prevent it from falling onto the floor. We put a screwdriver under this side, and a roll of masking tape under the other side. Unfortunately, one or both of them didn't do their jobs, because the pump fell on the floor. What makes this significant is that this pump cost $176,000.[6]

Stories don't have to be real to be interesting and powerful. As real examples can lend credence to a proposition, *hypothetical examples* can be effective in demonstrating a proposition.

> Ladies and gentlemen of the council, let's follow first-grader Johnny as he leaves his home on Randolph Street. A block away he meets his classmate, Maria. They walk to Second Avenue. Here they have to cross over because that's where the school is located. They've been well taught by their folks, so they stop and look both ways. It looks safe, so they head cross. As they get almost to the center, they're startled to hear a squealing of tires. It's two high-school kids drag-racing. The children run, but the drivers don't see them until it's too late. Johnny and Maria don't make it across the street, and they'll never make it to school. This story hasn't happened . . . yet. But it is inevitable, and the names won't be Johnny and Maria, but the names of some of our kids, unless you approve the new stoplight we've requested for that corner.

One final advantage of stories is their value in helping overcome nervousness. Stories are particularly helpful for this purpose at the start of a presentation. Speakers are at their most animated and natural when they are telling a story, especially one from their own experience.

Using Examples

■ Look for examples from your own experience. You don't have to go poring through books of 1,000 jokes to get material. You won't have to scratch very hard to come up with your own good examples, and they'll probably be more germane than borrowed material. You'll be more comfortable relating them, and they'll probably come across with more vitality to the audience. In particular, humor told on yourself almost always goes over well.

■ Make sure you know the specifics. An example that is vague and lacks key information is often better not told. The presenter who doesn't know the details is open to attack and embarrassment.

■ Don't try to con the audience. A classic story is about the traveling preacher who was a frequent speaker in many towns. In one town he stood confidently at the pulpit and said, "I'm really pleased to be here in [glancing at his notes] . . . Kendallville. What a marvelous congregation you have here in this magnificent [glancing at notes] . . . Methodist church. It's truly wonderful to see so many of you here tonight to worship our Lord [glancing at notes] . . . Jesus Christ."

■ Start with the story itself, not with "That reminds me of a story."

■ Match your nonverbal message to your verbal. If it's funny, enjoy it. An amusing story may be hampered if the teller's jaws are clenched. A story about John Kennedy's assassination will probably not be well received if the presenter is grinning from ear to ear.

Analogies as a Form of Support

The power of analogies was noted earlier as used by Representative Richard Gephart in his speeches during the 1988 Democratic primary. His $48,000 Hyundai analogy grabbed people when more traditional arguments didn't. Another powerful demonstration was provided by a business executive who gave a talk about the U.S. economic system to an elementary school class, not a group especially tuned into stocks and corporate takeovers. He introduced his topic by suggesting they form a company to make a product this group knew well: skateboards. He led them through the process of selecting the type of board, getting a facility to build them, buying the raw materials, and getting them built and sold. Where would the money come from to do this? With a few more of the right questions, the children got the sense of how the system works. How well can be seen from the newspaper headline about the story: WHEN THIS EXECUTIVE SPEAKS, 6TH-GRADERS LISTEN.

Analogies are special forms of illustrations and powerful generators of "ah so's" (what listeners often say when a point finally registers). They are most effectively used to provide insight, to help listeners understand and more fully appreciate the significance of complex concepts. They make comparisons between things that are familiar to the audience and those that are not.

Figurative analogies compare things that differ considerably in their appearance or function. They are a close cousin to the metaphor: "Your eyes are like diamonds." Figurative analogies are frequently used by experts in a field talking to lay persons not well versed in that field or to people from other disciplines. Here's an example. The Saturn V rocket was used to launch the *Apollo* astronauts to the moon. The engines of the first stage of Saturn V generated 160 million horsepower. Is that anything you can relate to, other than that it's probably a lot of power? Here's the way Rockwell International, builder of the first stage, explained it so all we space ignoramuses could comprehend it: "If you ran all the rivers and streams of America through steam turbines at the same time—you'd get only half the 160 million horsepower that all five of the Saturn's F-1 engines generate."[7] Well, if you put it that way, wow!

Literal analogies compare items with similar characteristics. They are comparisons of green apples to red apples, to use a figurative analogy, as distinct from comparisons of green apples to elephants.

Arthur Doerr of the University of West Florida used this literal analogy to demonstrate the imbalance in the use of natural resources:

> Suppose world population was compressed into a single city of 1,000 people. In this imaginary city 55 of the 1,000 people would be American citizens and 945 would represent all other nations. . . . These 55 people, representing 5½ percent of the population, would consume almost 15 percent of the town's food supply; use, on a per capita basis, 10 times as much oil, 40 times as much steel, and 40 times as much general equipment [as the rest of the population].[8]

During the Watergate hearings, Congressman William Hungate of Missouri presented this perspective on the question of the president's responsibility, as quoted by columnist Ernest Fergurson:

> "Suppose," he said as the House Judiciary Committee began that fateful week of impeachment proceedings, "suppose your mayor approved a plan by which the chief of your city's police department could illegally tap your phone, open your mail, and burglarize your apartment. Suppose your mayor withheld knowledge of a burglary from a local judge trying a case in which that knowledge was crucially important. . . ." He supposed a couple more times, and his point was strong and clear: The President of the United States should be held to moral and legal standards at least as high as those binding a small-town politician.[9]

Using Analogies

■ Make sure the analogy has a direct correlation to the idea it is intended to reinforce. "Olympian Charley Smith eats Smackos every morning for breakfast. Eat Smackos and you too can become an Olympic champion." As listeners, we are highly susceptible to analogies and far too frequently accept them as valid without questioning their logic. Common examples are found in political advertising, where a candidate is shown jogging to indicate he is vigorous and thus will make a good president. Or her success as a business executive shows she will be successful at running the government. Business audiences, particularly those neutral or negative toward the speaker, generally are extremely critical of shaky comparisons. A speaker who has not thought logic through carefully enough may swiftly come under a show-no-quarter attack.

During Senate confirmation hearings, the nominee for secretary of defense,

John Tower, was under heavy attack. In an appearance before the National Press Club, he defiantly vowed to fight on. "I shall never surrender or retreat," he said, quoting from the last letter written by Lt. Col. Travis, leader of the Alamo defenders in 1836. Applause ringing in his ears, he stepped away from the lectern. Moments later, he retook the lectern to say: "I'm a little sorry I brought up the Alamo analogy because it just occurred to me what happened at the Alamo." Tower's nomination had the same fate.[10]

■ Make sure the conditions of both parts of the analogy are close enough to render the comparison legitimate—especially important for literal analogies. "We turned the tide in the Korean War with a surprise amphibious landing at Inchon. We can do it again in the _____War by making a similar surprise attack on _____." While the first statement may be correct, the situations may be so different that the speaker's argument will be shot down immediately.

■ Be sure of your facts on the example chosen for comparison. If the speaker in the previous example had been wrong—if the surprise landing at Inchon had not been instrumental in winning the war or if he or she had been mistaken about the location and said *Pusan* instead of *Inchon*—the analogy would have been immediately flawed. (And, of course, if the audience never heard of any of them, try another war.)

■ Use analogies sparingly. Analogies are powerful because they present an interesting and possibly unusual way of looking at something. If used to excess, they lose their novelty.

■ Don't put too much faith in them. Analogies are good as attention getters and clarifiers but rarely have enough clout to stand alone. Combine them with the other forms that are more valid as support to back up your ideas.

Statistical Data

"Somewhere on this globe, every ten seconds, there is a woman giving birth to a child," observed Sam Levenson. "She must be found and stopped!"

While any of the forms of supporting material can be used in a confusing and questionable manner, statistics are perhaps subject to more chicanery and selective use than any of the others. It was Disraeli who observed, "There are three kinds of lies—lies, damned lies, and statistics." Yet statistics that are demonstrably valid can add powerful support to an idea. For many presentations they are essential.

Edward Ball, former chairman of Florida East Coast Railroad, was arguing that privately owned railroads are more efficient than nationalized railroads. He pointed out that U.S. rail lines, even with their archaic work rules (his words), have an average of 2.7 employees per mile of track. He compared this with the equivalent figures for countries with nationalized rail systems: Germany, 22.1; England, 20.9; and France, 12.9. The statistics would seem to add real clout to his thesis.[11]

Joseph Flannery, former president of Uniroyal, put an interesting perspective on the subject of government regulation this way: "Federal regulations cost each American family some $1,000 a year. In 1976 it cost $1.7 billion just to store the forms Americans are asked to comply with and fill out. Government regulations last year cost General Motors more than $1.3 billion. That, in one year alone, is slightly more than it cost to operate the *entire* Federal government during its first 100 years."[12]

Using Statistical Data

▪ Be prudent in your use of statistics. It's easy to overwhelm listeners with too many numbers.

▪ State the truly significant point about the statistics. Is the value for 1993 significant, or is it that the 1993 value is up 30 percent over 1992? Often the trend is more useful than absolute values. If you present a visual array of numbers, listeners are likely to have a hard time ferreting out the hot stuff unless you do it for them. You may be better off showing the data in graphic rather than tabular form.

▪ Round the data off; $505 million is probably close enough, $500 million is often just as good, $532,505,279 is probably deadly—especially if it follows $276,597,873.52. See, you can hardly read it without having your eyes glaze over.

▪ Pronounce the key figures so they can be clearly heard. "Five [*mumble, mumble*] . . . What do you think about that?" Huh?

▪ Be prepared to provide the assumptions behind the numbers and the procedures followed to develop them. I can offer personal testimonials to many of the difficulties with use of support data. Once I was presenting data generated by someone else and was not clear about all the ground rules used. Sure enough, the key member of the audience queried me on those, and when I was not able to answer adequately, there went the presentation.

▪ Make sure the numbers add up. Don't give your listeners golden opportunities for nitpicking by having columns that don't add up or figures that aren't consistent. The *Chicago Sun-Times* gleefully pointed out an error in an ad run in *Forbes* and *Fortune*. A sample tax return shown in the ad contained a subtraction error of $1 million. Adding to the embarrassment of the advertiser was the fact that it was a major accounting firm, and the ad was touting the value of its services in preparing tax forms.[13]

▪ Increase the impact by putting them in terms the audience can relate to and by using appropriate drama. Peter Kurzhals of the National Aeronautics and Space Administration noted that the data-handling implications associated with space operations were immense. As an example, he said that NASA already was handling 10^{15} bits of information per year. To put that in terms lay people could grasp, he said that was the equivalent of 100 million Sears Roebuck catalogs.[14]

References—Testimonials and Quotations

Early in this chapter, I cited the example of the $1 billion contract Compuadd Corporation had won to build computers for the Department of Defense.

Perhaps another contribution to that win over two, much larger, competitors was a testimonial letter from an Army commander. In it he described how during the Gulf War a Compuadd 486 computer was blown through a wall after a nearly direct hit from an Iraqi missile. The computer's case was undamaged, and after a damaged circuit breaker was replaced, it was back in service.[15]

Statements by other people are the final form of supporting material. As in a courtroom, the testimony of recognized authorities can provide important support to a presentation. People may not be swayed by statistical analyses or specific cases, no matter how powerful they seem, but they may listen to and believe the comments of someone else they respect. This is widely recognized in running for office, selling new cars, or plugging a new movie.

A department director may have difficulty convincing her subordinate supervisors that affirmative action is important by showing the ethnic and racial makeup of the work force relative to the local community, but she may be successful by quoting the company president's statement in favor of the program: "Affirmative action is a fundamental part of our operation. I expect all supervisors to comply fully with both the spirit and the intent of our program. Each supervisor will be evaluated on how well he or she contributes toward achieving our goals."

A salesperson may find it invaluable to have on hand a few unsolicited testimonials from previous buyers on the virtues of the salesperson's gadget.

Other uses of references are to add flavoring, entertainment, or a dramatic touch to the message. Quotations from the Bible or from Shakespeare, old saws from the *Farmer's Almanac*, and selections from *Bartlett's Quotations* are used for these purposes rather than as true evidence. These are often used to open talks, at pertinent spots throughout the talk, and as a punchy ending.

Here is how Robert Griffin, former U.S. senator from Michigan, used a quotation:

> Perhaps because of my own particular experience, I happen to believe that—of the five aspects of leadership that you are studying at this conference—none is more important than the institution.
>
> As Watergate demonstrated, if the institution or system is sound, it will survive and be effective long after a leader is replaced; if it is not, no strength of leadership can, or should, save it.
>
> Perhaps that's what Will Rogers tried to recognize when he said: "A good man can't do nothing in office, because the system is against him—and a bad one can't do anything for the same reason. So bad as we are, we are better off than any other nation."
>
> It's astonishing, isn't it, how Will Rogers' observations seem to be timeless?[16]

Of course, your sources may have superb credentials and lousy insights. In 1945, Admiral William Leahy, President Truman's chief-of-staff, pronounced: "This is the biggest fool thing we have ever done. The atomic bomb will never go off. And I speak as an expert in explosives."[17]

Using References

■ Use legitimate authorities with valid and current credentials. President Jimmy Carter lost points by citing his daughter, Amy, as a source on the subject of nuclear proliferation during the 1980 campaign debate.

■ Select sources the audience will respect and that are applicable to the specific subject discussed. A speaker advocating expanded use of solar energy quoted the head of the solar manufacturing lobby. If his audience had been totally positive, this would have been no problem. Since he was trying to convince neutral-to-negative listeners, they rejected his source as biased in favor of the speaker's position. His testimony may have been legitimate, but it was not even considered by the listeners.

■ Use references sparingly, especially quotations. Some speakers take half their talks from other places. What the audience is most interested in is not what others have said but what the speaker thinks about the subject.

■ Give sources where appropriate. It may be helpful to identify the authority or document from which the information came. If a business audience knows your information came from the *Wall Street Journal* of August 5, 1992, this might give it more credibility.

■ Above all, get it right. Here are three who didn't:

—Vice-President Dan Quayle developed some unwelcome fame due to his frequent gaffes in speaking. An oft-cited one is his speech to the United Negro College Fund. His attempt to quote the fund's motto, "A mind is a terrible thing to waste," came out instead as, "What a waste it is to lose one's mind or not to have a mind. How true that is."[18]

—Xerox Corporation speechwriter Tony Francis prepared a talk for a company executive, smooth at manufacturing but rough at speaking. He wove in a quotation, which the executive delivered thusly: "To quote the famous British author, W. Somerset Muggam . . ."[19]

—Even the great communicators can blow it occasionally, usually to the amusement of the audiences. President Ronald Reagan closed out a speech to the United Nations with a reflection from "Mahatga Magandi"; he meant Mahatma Ghandi.[20]

WHAT ABOUT HUMOR?

"Now that reminds me of a story." This statement can bring on a pleasant interlude or cause the audience to groan, "Oh, not again!" Do jokes or humorous stories have a place in business presentations? Maybe. Almost any audience appreciates a bit of levity, and I have seen many business presenters incorporate humor into their talks with good effect. The "maybe" is to put up a caution that humor can fall flat if it is out of place, is not pertinent to the subject, or is atrociously told. We're not all great joke tellers, and obvious attempts to add levity at any cost generally backfire.

Why use humor at all? Dr. Jerry Tarver of the University of Richmond asked that question and answered it this way:

> Mainly because it can help hold attention and interest. Also, humor helps establish a friendly atmosphere. It can relieve tension and allow an audience to appreciate the human qualities of a speaker. I recall watching John F. Kennedy on television as he won over an audience by explaining his reaction to a political setback. "I feel like the old pioneer lying on the ground after being shot full of arrows," he said. "It only hurts when I laugh."[21]

Ross Smythe, retired communication projects manager of Air Canada suggests that *any* person who has to give a speech insert a little humor into it.

> Let's look at it this way. If you give a factual statistic-laden 30-minute speech about your profession or business, it is likely to be boringly dull—and may even put the audience to sleep—*unless* you have developed the ability to insert a little anecdote or a little story every few minutes that will advance or support the theme of your talk. This will provide a refreshing change of pace, keeping your audience alert and interested in your subject. Isn't this your goal? To be successful, you don't have to make them roll in the aisles with laughter. A simple, smile-producing anecdote will provide that change of pace to facilitate better audience comprehension of the more serious parts of your presentation.[22]

Fluor Corporation chairman Les McCraw, Jr., uses humor often in presentations, "in a tempered way." He finds humor useful for helping to establish rapport with an audience. "You can say something about yourself, tell a story. It shows them you are a regular guy and that they can relate to you as someone who is not too egotistical, who can make a mistake and keep the right perspective."[23]

Keep in mind that humor will not guarantee success. A 1972 study tested results from speeches delivered with and without humor. Results showed that no significant difference in content retention for a speech on totalitarianism, and for a speech about a more technical topic (the Whorf hypothesis), significantly less learning occurred with the humorous approach.[24]

From speechwriter Jean Pope comes this advice: "The rule of thumb concerning a joke is threefold: the speaker can deliver it effectively; it flows out of the experience of the speaker; it is appropriate to the subject."[25]

A company president speaking to a large business audience opened his presentation with a joke. But as he went through the story, his brain quit, and he forgot the punch line entirely.

"The single most common mistake in the delivery of humor is announcing you're going to tell a joke," said humor consultant Michael Kushner. Rather than, "That reminds me of a joke," he suggests substituting, "It's like . . ." and then the humor arrives as a surprise.[26]

"But I can't tell jokes!" you may protest. So don't. Professional speaker Gary Beals says humor isn't just telling jokes: "Everybody has a sense of humor. To sharpen it, find out whose humor you like by watching other speakers or comedians on T.V. Write down what you like and you'll start to find your own humor. This is better than reading a book of jokes."[27]

Look for opportunities to bring in a light touch. In many years of working with companies, I've found those most likely to use humor are the presidents; most cautious are those lower in the ranks. Here are some ways to use humor to help get your message across. Be sure to test your material in advance; humor can backfire if it is inappropriate.

- Weave in current items from newspaper, magazines, radio, T.V., movies, cartoons, columns, real-life stories. This book contains several, many of which I use in speeches. Ample other sources abound: poetry, the classics, religion, and your own experiences at work, play, home, or daily encounters (these may be the richest and funniest sources available).

- Have fun with your audience. Here is an opening from a talk by Walter Beran, a partner in Ernst & Ernst:

> It certainly was an act of reckless courage on someone's part to have selected an auditor as your speaker today. For some of you will recall Elbert Hubbard's damning description of the typical auditor as "a man past middle age, spare, wrinkled, intelligent, cold, passive, non-committal, with eyes like codfish, polite in contact, but at the same time unresponsive, calm, and damnably composed as a concrete post or a plaster of paris cast. A human petrification with heart of feldspar and without the charm of the friendly germ, minus bowels, passion, or sense of humor." "Happily," he said, "they never reproduce, and all of them finally go to hell."[28]

- Stretch your creativity as you develop material. Consider visuals, props, demonstrations, activities, and concepts adapted from late-night shows. One manager livened up the dreary annual lecture on time cards by using a cartoon character on each chart. "First time I ever paid any attention," said one grizzled supervisor.

- Try humor to help grab or revive audience attention. In a manufacturing organization, funding for a new idea had to be approved by a review board, notorious for its negative attitude. A designer opened his presentation to the board with a viewgraph cartoon. In it a medieval general was surrounded by enemies, armed to the teeth with bows and arrows. A salesman attempts to sell him a new product, but the general rebuffs him: "Don't bother me. I have a battle to fight." The salesman's product? A gatling gun. The board members recognized his point in good humor and heard him out, something they'd never done before.

- Add punch to your purpose. In a competition I worked on for a contract to be performed in Washington, the source selection board required presentations from eight proposed project team members who would all move to the Washington area should we win the contract. To close the four-hour presentation, our team leader reaffirmed our commitment to the project: "And finally all of our team members have made their personal commitments to working with you all in Washington, by publicly declaring loyalty to *their* new team." At that point all eight team members stood up and placed new Washington Redskins hats on their heads. The audience roared with laughter. Was it effective? The team leader noted we did win the contract and that several board members often chuckled about our ploy in later project meetings.

■ Look for opportunities to do something unique—perhaps even outrageous—to make your message more memorable. Mike Hale, MagneTek corporate director of industrial relations, told of an executive who started a meeting in a gorilla outfit. "We laughed and relaxed. Then we listened and remembered. Fourteen months later, I can still tell you several points he made."[29]

■ Even puns have a place. David Goodstein, chairman of the faculty at California Institute of Technology, likes to end his lectures with puns because, he said, they bring forth a loud and exquisitely predictable groan, waking up everyone for lunch—for example: "Heroes in the history of science may come and go, but Ampere's name will always be current."[30] You may now groan.

USING SUPPORT MATERIAL FOR INCREASED AUDIENCE PARTICIPATION

As Aggertt, Bowen, and Rickert note:

> The attention span of even an interested cooperative listener is startlingly short. . . . Experimentation indicated that listening spans are a matter of only seconds or fractions of a second. . . . The speaker is faced not with holding attention but with constantly regaining it, performing in such a way as to bring the listeners back alive as often as possible."[31]

A proven way of increasing audience interest and degree of learning is to get members of the audience to participate, physically and mentally, in the presentation.[32] (See Figure 7-6.)

Professional speaker and master humorist Joe Griffith advises:

> By sprinkling illustrations [like these] throughout your presentation, you will grab the imagination of listeners in a way that films or television are hard pressed to duplicate. Never forget that as a communicator you are appealing to the most powerful image-producing mechanism on earth . . . the human mind. It thrives on images. Good stories are a trigger that release an explosive, powerful, positive form of communication energy.[33]

Figure 7-6. Involve your audience to keep them tuned in.

I HEAR and I forget

I SEE and I retain

I DO and I
understand

Support material is a powerful means of getting audiences involved in your presentation. Here are some specific ways to do that:

■ *Make their activity an essential part of the communication process.* Role playing, exercises, and application activities are methods commonly used in presentations.

A nutrition expert spoke to an elementary school class about the importance of eating better foods. To spice up the talk, she had the students work through a puzzle similar to a children's game. She was a hit on a subject the children normally paid little attention to.

A lecturer on intercultural communication divided the audience into two artificially created nations. Each group quickly learned the rules of its new culture and then interacted with the other culture. By making the audience experience the intercultural difficulties, the key concepts were driven home far more effectively than would have been possible with a straight lecture.

■ *Let them handle the gadgetry.* Let the designer try out the new interaction graphic computer terminal—take the customer's production experts out to the factory floor and let them operate the proposed assembly tool. If you don't have real objects, have models, hardware samples, cutaways—anything people can touch, handle, or operate. In a presentation about the effects of employees' drinking on job safety and quality, bring in a current *Wall Street Journal* article about the subject, a box of liquor bottles confiscated from employees in the plant, and a damaged part produced by an intoxicated employee.

■ *Have them assist with demonstrations.* A thoroughly engrossing presentation was given by a student demonstrating how to make margaritas from scratch.

The choice of subject and promise at the end was a good starter for keeping our interest. In addition, he brought several listeners into the demonstration by having them squeeze the lemons, measure out some of the ingredients, operate the blender and ice crusher, and, most important, do the sampling of the finished product.

■ *Ask them to supply material for illustrations.* The most effective professor I ever had was a master at keeping his students active. One of his methods was to ask them to provide material he needed to illustrate propositions. In a discussion of statistical probabilities, he needed three choices of different degrees of value. He could have said A, B, and C or provided his own examples of real choices. What he did was have *us* generate them—specifically, three restaurants, in deluxe, not bad, and everyday categories. I can still tell you the names of the three restaurants we chose and, more important, something about the concept he was discussing. He not only kept us awake and involved, he came up with choices that were more significant to us because they were ours.

■ *Integrate audience responses into your speech or visuals.* Take a tip from the politicians, who love repeated themes (e.g., "I have a dream . . ."). Once the pattern is seen, the audience gets on board and joins in each time the theme is repeated. In a training session, leave some blanks on the slide or lecture notes for participants to fill in with responses. Ask questions. Get the left side of the room into competition with the right side ("Tastes better!" "Less filling!").

DEVELOPING SUPPORT MATERIAL

Support material doesn't materialize out of thin air. Business presenters and public speakers develop such material from three basic sources.

Studies and Analyses

Statistical data in particular are developed during efforts undertaken prior to the presentation, and those studies, analyses, and investigations may be key parts of the presentation.

Specific Research

A presenter may need to conduct a literature research to locate material to support a topic. A wealth of written and oral communication about any subject can be readily accessed using computer search methods or manually through the many reference systems found in public, educational, and corporate libraries. Identifying journals or digests pertinent to the presenter's general area of interest can be of value when the need arises to conduct a literature search.

Ongoing Accumulation

Here are some suggestions for accumulating and organizing material so that it will be of best use to you when needed.

■ Identify topics of relevance. If you start accumulating material on all topics, you'll soon be driven out of the house by paper.

■ Transcribe key material into a database or onto cards. Even if noting only a single anecdote, quotation, statistic, idea, or personal reaction, this will record and make retrievable at least a part of many articles, which typically will soon find their way into a stack of unread or hard-to-find articles. By noting the source, you can easily go back to the full document if needed.

■ Carry 3- by 5-inch cards with you. You will find a rich source of material in the experiences, observations, and thoughts that are part of your everyday business or personal life. You will be amazed at how often you will see or hear something useful to you and how quickly you will develop a rich resource, and one that is all the more valuable because it is from your own experience.

■ Document the source information completely. You may not be able to use it if the source is not specified adequately, or you may find yourself spending valuable time searching for the missing information. (This is a personal testimonial. Wait until *you* write a book and see.) Write down full names of authors or persons quoted; the exact title of the article, periodical, or book; publisher name and city; date and volume number; specific page.

IN SUMMARY: GOOD SUPPORTING MATERIAL IS POWERFUL

A presentation without supporting material is hard to conceive of. Examples, references, statistical data, and analogies add color to a presentation, in addition to providing their main service: clarifying points and backing up claims.

Support material needs to be chosen and used with care. Excessive statistics, irrelevant and badly told stories, questionable sources, and overdone analogies damage rather than help. Material that is relevant, accurate, and significant to the audience makes a necessary and valuable contribution.

* * * 8 * * *

Support, Part II: Visual Aids

KEY POINTS OF THIS CHAPTER

* Visual aids are essential media through which much of support is presented; they are integral parts of most business presentations.
* Good visuals can help a presentation's success. Poor ones can destroy it.
* The key to good visuals is getting a clear message visually conceived and then applying graphics sense to make sure it works.
* Computer technology has made high-quality visuals much easier to prepare, but having the tools doesn't guarantee wise use of them.

"A picture is worth a thousand words" is an axiom widely cited touting the value of visual aids. Add, "unless it *is* a thousand words."

Visual aids are staples of presentations. For many people the word *presentation* automatically implies "visuals" (Figure 8-1).

VISUALS: AIDS OR HINDRANCES?

Why Visuals?

Visuals can add greatly to a presentation—or do serious damage to it (Figure 8-2). The often-quoted statistic of 40 percent to 50 percent increases in communication effectiveness shows the possible gains from adding visuals to the spoken word. Another statistic should also be kept in mind: the 40 to 50 percent may in fact go the *other* way if the visuals are poor. "The battle for supremacy between seeing and hearing has been waged presumably ever since man was endowed with eyes and ears. . . . Because of between-channel interference, it is not by any means a rule that the audiovisual is always better than the audio or visual only."[1]

With that warning in mind and the proviso that the visuals are indeed well chosen and well prepared, here are the main reasons that visuals should be considered for presentations where they would be suitable:

Increased Audience Interest. People are attracted to what catches the eye as well as the ear. Adding punchy visuals to a talk can pique and revive interest.

Figure 8-1. Some people in business and government have trouble communicating *without* visuals.

Figure 8-2. Visuals can help or hinder.

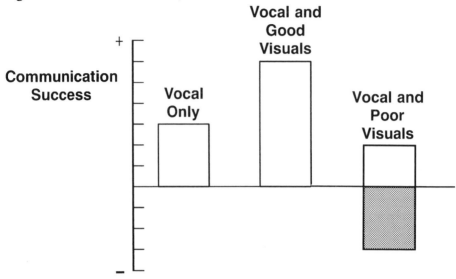

Source: Genigraphics.

Increased Understanding and Retention. The complex nature of business and technology demands that information be presented visually as well as verbally if it is to be communicated. Trying to understand the propulsion system of the space shuttle or a business plan is well-nigh impossible without visuals. Even simpler information, such as three main points, can be grasped and understood better if seen as well as heard. Often a visual treatment is necessary for clarity and insight. Many times in meetings, a disputed point is resolved by someone's going to the board and showing what she means or showing a chart. (Research in the field of neurolinguistics shows that people process information gained from one sensory channel better than from others. An auditory person picks up material readily by hearing it; a visual person needs to see it. For the latter, visuals are particularly important.)

Better Results—Maybe. In one well-known study at the Wharton School of Business, audiences significantly favored the presenter's proposition more when she used visuals (65 percent) than without (35 percent). This conclusion shouldn't be applied across the board because it depends on many factors, among them the quality of the visuals.[2]

A More Professional Image. The medium is the message, said Marshall McLuhan. A presenter who comes to a meeting with well-prepared visuals and uses them well conveys an image of competence, with the visuals adding a large part of the image. If the group is not used to visual presentations, it is often impressed by seeing them. In an organization where visuals are common, a presenter who shows up with no visuals or poor ones will be starting out with one strike against herself.

Increased Efficiency. Empirical data strongly indicate that the same message can be communicated faster, and as well, by using visuals instead of a strictly spoken method. A U.S. Department of Education study found that instructors could cut fifteen minutes off one-hour lectures by using the overhead projector. At the University of Wisconsin a fifty-minute lecture was boiled down to twenty minutes with audiovisuals. The Wharton study previously noted found that meeting time was reduced by 28 percent with visuals versus without them.

Thus, to be truly proficient in business presentations, one needs to know how to create good visuals and how to use them well. The term *oral communications*, used to describe almost every book on public speaking, is inadequate to describe business presentations. Because visuals are so integrally woven into presentations, the term *oral and visual communications* would seem to be more appropriate.

Too Many Bad Visuals

- At an annual convention, a highly paid and internationally known speaker showed visuals on a screen placed in a far corner of the room so that half the audience couldn't see them. The lettering was so small that the half who could see could barely read the visuals.
- At a major conference on energy sponsored by a prestigious university, roughly half the presenters showed visuals that were completely unreadable beyond the first few rows and were so cluttered as to make them impossible to follow.
- At a lecture by one of the country's leading thinkers on architecture, most of the visuals were copied from the detailed tables and drawings contained in the lecturer's book.

Each of these examples is a case of poor visuals' seriously damaging the presentation and the speaker's credibility, plus wasting the time of many people. In case you think that these are isolated cases or that I'm too critical a listener, hear the words of two people who have been on the short end of too many presentations with poor visuals:

"It's astounding how many people still use overhead transparencies with tons of information on them," said governmental executive Michael Bayer. "I can't believe how overly complex most of these presentations are."[4]

Jim Elms, consultant to business and former center director in both NASA and the Department of Transportation: "I still see it all over the place. *The most universal complaint people have in presentations is that they can't read the damn charts. It's so fundamental, yet we keep violating it all over the place.*"[5]

Why Not Better Visuals?

Almost anyone can make visuals. We started doing that as tots the first time we got crayons and walls together. Then we spent our early years drawing houses and trees and mommies. We soon stopped doing that, because crayons were for kids. Over the next decade or two we learned stuff. Our heads got filled with information, and we solved problems, wrote a lot of essays, and answered lots of multiple-choice questions. We did a lot of communicating—written and oral. Only rarely were we asked to do anything "visual," except to go to the blackboard occasionally and work through some formulas.

Then we went to work and got steeped in detail and specialization. We learned to turn out seventy-five-page reports and make illustrations sharing minute details of design and scheduling and cost analysis. And then the boss said, "Jones, I want a half-hour presentation on what you're doing." And since we already had a lot of that information, we went to the almighty reproduction machine and copied our illustrations and got instant transparencies showing all those minute details. Since we now have computer graphics, we added ten more charts. True, they're all words and a little busy, but they look clean. (Truth is, we never have mastered any of the fancier features of the software.)

So we gave the boss the presentation and she said, "Yeechhh!" And we were stunned because we thought she wanted a thorough report, and we had all these visual aids to help her get that. She said the visuals stunk.

Why, in this television and computer world, are many visuals still mediocre? One explanation—that society is afflicted with massive *visual atrophy*—is suggested by Robert McKim in *Experiences in Visual Thinking.* It is the result of an almost exclusive stress in school on the three Rs: reading, (w)riting, and (a)rithmetic. "Opportunity for visual expression usually ceases early in the primary grades," he said, adding that "any mental ability that is not exercised decays, and visual ability is no exception."[6]

Research into learning suggests that the two sides of the brain handle different types of information and activities:

Left	*Right*
Logic	Creativity
Order	Spatial
Analysis	Humor
Verbal	Images
Math	Music

For the typical business and technical person, the left side is continually exercised and well developed while the right side often gets little workout and thus may be only slightly developed. The result is stifled visualization and imaginative ability. Deliberate stretching of imagination exercises the right side and helps the visual ideas flow.

McKim said that most people have a large unrealized potential for visual thinking. To expand this ability, three stifling beliefs need to be overcome:

1. That seeing is believing. McKim noted that we don't all "see" equally well but that what we see is enormously affected by personal factors such as emotion, knowledge, and viewpoint. "Seeing is an active art, not a passive experience to be taken for granted."
2. That "I don't have any imagination." McKim said that anyone who

dreams has imagination and that everyone dreams. Imagination also can be developed, he says, by learning to contact the imagination consciously and direct it productively.

3. That drawing requires rare artistic talent. McKim pointed out that the impulse to draw is universal in young children. "No more habitual disclaimers about lack of artistic talent: almost everyone learns to read and write in our society; almost everyone can also learn to drive."

If these three factors—active seeing, imagination, and drawing—can be obstacles to visual thinking, they are also the avenues. And they are mutually beneficial, according to McKim. "A primary by-product of experiences on seeing should be an enhancement of visual imagination. . . . The person who can flexibly use his imagination to recenter his viewpoint sees creatively. . . . The value of drawing is that it stimulates seeing; it is an inducement to stop labeling and to look. It clarifies and records inner imagery." McKim's book offers many practical exercises to expand each of these three avenues to better visual thinking.

Computers Mean Better Visuals, Don't They?

The rules have dramatically changed for preparing presentation visual aids. Getting good-quality visuals in the past meant using the services of in-house or outside professional graphics designers. Those services were generally available only for major presentations and were costly. Visuals for most everyday presentations were made by the presenter: typed, cut-and-paste of whatever art existed, shrinking illustrations on the copy machine to fit viewgraphs, and even hand-printed.

Computers and laser printers provide an entire graphics department right in the office. Low-priced computer graphics software enables presenters to create bold titles, lay out flowcharts, instantly transform tables into six forms of graphs, and incorporate clip art. Most software comes with professionally designed templates to steer amateurs along the right paths.

With better graphics come a variety of output and display options that formerly were only in the domain of expensive presentations. All of this attention to desktop presentations has stimulated increased awareness and skill enhancement among the end users—those with the knowledge who actually prepare and deliver presentations. The quality of presentations has significantly increased for everyday presentations as well as for the major ones.

Nevertheless, poor visuals are still being used in presentations. Many can't be read, or they obscure more than illuminate. Some presenters can't resist trying out the many options, leading to presentations that are more exercises in technology than communication.

Having nifty tools is one thing; knowing how to use them is another. Graphic design is a specialty in its own right; having managerial or technical talent doesn't ensure graphics capability. Computer specialists have long used the term GIGO—"Garbage In, Garbage Out." If visual knowledge and presentation wisdom are weak, the computer will give only prettier garbage. If you do use the graphics pros, they must rely on you for strategy, organization, and content. By adding basic knowledge of visual aids, you can come up with more creative ways to get that knowledge across, whether making visuals yourself or working with experts.

The desktop presentations era has *not* reduced the need for visual aid wisdom by presenters. Computers must be combined with good presentations sense; the combination is powerful.

SELECTING THE RIGHT AUDIOVISUAL FORM

Projected and Electronic Media

Conference room visuals range from low-tech to high-tech. The lowly overhead projector and black-and-white *viewgraphs* (also called *transparencies* or *foils*) are still the staples for most conference room presentations. They can be quickly prepared and changed, allow high flexibility and interchange during meetings, and paper copies can be quickly made. The graphics today come mainly from computer graphics programs, but their operational use is much the same as in the 1970s. Color viewgraphs are common, obtained quickly and cheaply from paint-jet printers or in better quality from color printers.

Full-color *slide* presentations remain common, now boosted by the combination of computer graphics and fast, low-cost slide production. With a computer graphics program linked by modem to a slide service, presenters can get top-quality slides for $10 that would have cost $150 from a professional graphics department a few years back. Slides are a high-quality medium, with versatile capability through multiple projectors and special effects.

Opaque projectors display objects or printed materials on a screen without using photographic material or reproductions. One application is enabling large audiences to view objects without passing them around; another is to project examples of color advertisements without having to make slides.

Presenters have a wealth of new options linking desktop or laptop *computers with visual display devices* (Figure 8-3), often referred to as *electronic presentations*. These eliminate physical slides or viewgraphs. For small groups, the computer monitor may be adequate. In a marriage of high and low tech, LCD (liquid crystal display) panels are placed atop overhead projectors, perhaps the most common method in use today. Computer screen images are projected through the LCD panel onto a larger screen. Better-quality images, with more expensive gear, come from linking the computer with video projectors. Newer LCD projectors are more compact and mobile than older designs. Computers offer a high degree of flexibility. Changes can be made right up to the meeting or even while it is going on. In response to a question, the speaker can immediately call up the program and display the changed data with a new graph. A trainee can engage in an interactive dialogue to acquire knowledge or skills.

Expanding presenters' options is the emerging form known as *multimedia*. Once applied to combined use of two or more audiovisual forms, such as slides and video, "multimedia" now refers to computer-generated visual support that incorporates images, animation, video, sound, and who knows what next. This

Figure 8-3. Computers have expanded presenters' audiovisual options.

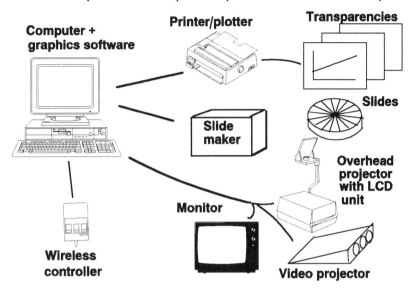

brings dynamic effects to presentations, much as video goes beyond slides, and can add power and interest to presentations.

Video is a powerful medium for presentation support, bringing realism or events, processes and people, into the conference room and generally enlivening the program. One application is for proposal oral presentations; a half-hour video summarizes the proposal and provides personal comments from key team members. Low-cost camcorders allow quick recording and playback of relevant happenings or interviews. They are often used during meetings or seminars for recording key activities or role plays and analyses. A portable "visual presenter" uses a tiny video camera to display objects or printed copy on a video monitor or projected onto a screen, somewhat as an opaque projector does. It is useful for videoconferencing, large audiences, or to focus on details. Copies of presentations can be made for about five dollars a copy and sent out to field operations or sales representatives. The convenience of video and the availability of video projectors have reduced the use of films for presentations.

Teleconferences incorporate many of the other forms for presentations linking different locations. This mode allows convenient and timely communication to occur while cutting out travel time, aggravation, and expenses. Simultaneous teleconferences with multiple locations was demonstrated to good effect by Apple Computer when it introduced a new computer line to thousands of potential consumers around the world all at one time.

Nonprojected Audiovisual Support

In a high-tech world, the nonprojected formats still have many applications and often are necessary because the setting precludes electric outlets, screens, or darkened rooms. After all, didn't one famous speaker use the lilies of the field to make a point?

Chalkboards, flipcharts, and posters are widely used. In his much-discussed Gulf War briefing, General Norman Schwartzkopf chose poster boards as his visual support. Architects rely heavily on paper drawings and pictures on poster boards. Sales people use small flipcharts for one-to-one desktop presentations. Quality or safety talks on the shop floor are often done from flipcharts. These can be hand written by the presenters in advance or during presentations and discussions. Large charts can be prepared with good quality by special printers or photo processes. Electronic chalkboards offer a useful capability by tying in a printer for making paper copies of chalkboard material. They are especially valuable for problem-solving sessions.

Hardware, models, and demonstrations are among the highest interest media when used well. They can add a change of pace from sitting through an hour of viewgraphs, bring in a dramatic or humorous touch, and add credibility. As an Air Force colonel said, "A picture is worth 1,000 words and a piece of hardware is worth 1,000 pictures." (What comes to mind when you think of TV ads for Timex or U.S. Sprint?)

People love to handle gadgetry, see real stuff, and watch things work, a bit like kicking the tires and test-driving an automobile before buying it. Care needs to be given to using these forms of support; interest fades fast if people can't see items or if some are actively engaged while others are waiting. Some highly effective examples:

- A Miami priest whipped out a handgun during his Palm Sunday sermon and then asked his flock to turn theirs in and stop shooting each other. Said one parishioner, "It was the most dramatic thing I've ever seen in a church in my life." (Only one gun got turned in; nevertheless, the presentation was dramatic.)[7]
- A speaker used puppets, such as Sergeant Sammy Sperm and his regiment, in sex education lectures to junior and senior classes. A reviewer described this as "the most comfortable, clearly-presented class I have ever attended on the subject."[8]
- Three entrepreneurs seeking backing for MovieFone, a computerized system providing free movie information, got nowhere until they came up with a working model. One of the founders said a prototype was imperative because without it, no one else can envision it and want to back it.[9]

Supplementary documents or displays can give audience members something to see and examine that demonstrates what you've done. In one presentation to several high-level executives, an electronics firm displayed a dozen detailed reports they had developed on previous, related contracts to add credibility to their claims of expertise and performance.

Factors in Selecting the Right Medium

For many presentations, this is an easy decision. Perhaps the organization always uses black-and-white viewgraphs. Or for major presentations, it might use color slides. But the easy decision may not be the best one. The "we've always done it this way" syndrome may stifle alternatives that achieve a better result, or it may not adequately consider related factors, which can lead to serious aggravation and rework later.

Before making that quick choice, consider four important questions:

1. *Do preset specifications apply?* In a request for proposal or for an ongoing contract, a customer may ask for viewgraphs, paper copies, and a thirty-minute video summary. (They may also say, "Don't spend much money on fancy presentations," thus driving marketing directors crazy trying to figure out how to do that and not get aced out by competitors.)

2. *How else might these visuals be presented?* It is increasingly common that visuals get used in several modes, each of which has different requirements. Viewgraphs designed for conference room use may not work well for a videoconference. When the boss says, "Great slides. Let's put them into a video program and send them to our field salespeople," you may quickly find out you're in trouble.

3. *Will they need to be printed as well as shown?* If you select color, how will that affect making paper copies?

4. *What capabilities do we have for producing visuals?* Do we have computer graphics programs that can do what we need? Do we know how to use them? How easy is it to bring in existing data or other visuals? What about getting finished products? What are turnaround times and costs? What lead times do we need?

These and other factors are summarized in Figure 8-4 for typical audiovisual forms.

GETTING THE MESSAGE CLEAR: CREATING VISUAL AID CONCEPTS

Here are some guidelines on creating visual aids that achieve their purpose. Figure 8-5 highlights the key points.

■ *Remember, they are aids.* The most important element in the presentation is you, the presenter. The aids may be your most important tool, but your words and the way you conduct yourself are primary. If the entire message is on the visuals, why do we need you? Just send a clerk, who costs a third as much, to flip the charts. If the aid does not help you convey your message, it's a poor visual.

■ *Plan for both primary and backup charts.* Presenters often end up with too many charts that are too complex, forgetting it may be wiser to show less and be ready for more. Brook Byers, principal partner in a major financial firm, advises, "It's very important to have backup overheads. When a question comes and you reach into the briefcase and have the perfect overhead, it shows you have anticipated questions. It can be more impressive than forty primary slides."[10]

Figure 8-4. The choice of audiovisual medium involves many factors.

TYPICAL PRESENTATION AUDIOVISUAL FORMS

Factor	Flipchart/Chalkboard (Manual or Electronic)	Viewgraph	35mm Slides	Film/Video	Computer-Linked or Electronic Output
Application	Small group, informal, high interaction, desktop	Small-medium group, interaction, complex information	Medium-large groups, formal, first-class, classy effects	Action, operations, people, scenic	Any of the previous
Quality	Often poor when hand-written; good quality, feasible	Can be good, but easy to get poor	Usually excellent	Varies; generally high if professionally prepared	Wide range, depending on projection mode and lighting
Production (art/content)	Often manual; can be created with photo methods, processes	Computer graphics, typed, manual	Computer graphics, cameras	Simple camcorders to complex studio	Computer graphics; office computers up to multimedia programs
End product method (cost)	Manual (low), photo repro (varies), electronic chalkboards ($3,000–5,000)	Laser printer and copy machine (low—$1 each); color with inkjets or printers ($1,000–8,000)	Typically uses in-house cameras or agencies ($5–20 if direct from computer; up to $100 for graphics art)	If editing or studio work, cost can be high	Computers plus: monitor (low); LCD panels ($1,000–3,000) and overhead projectors; video projectors ($5,000–20,000)
Ease of change	Can be on the spot	Swift if using low-cost modes; harder for color	May take overnight, with extra charges	Instant if unedited, camcorder; costly if studio quality	Can be instantaneous with right gear
Operations	Simple, high flexibility, and speaker control	High projector availability; lighted room, easy control (often awkward), manually supplemented	Darker room; smooth control but low interaction; punchy with multiprojectors	Usually run without interruption; gear needs attention to detail	High flexibility possible, but gear can be cumbersome and may need dark room
Distribution	Hard copies difficult in manual modes, easy from printers or electronic chalkboards	Hard copies are standard and easy	Hard copies easy if in computer, but likely need conversion from color	Video copies now fast and low cost from special shops	Diskettes and hard copies easy, unless motion and special effects are used

Figure 8-5. Apply these guidelines for creating punchy visual aids.

- Choose the best audiovisual medium or media to suit audience, purpose, situation, environment, and budget.
- Make sure each visual can be read without strain from all parts of the room.
- Ensure that each visual conveys only one main idea.
- Help the audience understand by simplifying, highlighting, comparing, and visualizing.
- KISS—Keep It Simple, Stupid.
- Use the title as a headline to state the essence of the chart.
- Remember, a picture may indeed be worth a thousand words, a live model or demonstration may be worth a thousand pictures, and a graph may be worth a thousand numbers. All may mean less time required to get the ideas across better.
- Present material in bite-size pieces to keep the audience's attention focused. Present complex material sequentially.
- Show only material you plan to discuss. Thin out unneeded detail, words, numbers.
- Present no more than seven items—lines, labels, blocks.
- Print all lettering horizontally.
- Proof visuals to make sure that all words are spelled correctly and that nothing detracts from the purpose.

■ *First ask, "What's the point?"* A visual serves one main purpose: to help make a point. This concept often gets forgotten, and charts are tossed into the presentation because they're there. It's better to figure out the message and then determine the best way to show that. Many visuals have been wisely eliminated or extensively modified by the question, "What point is this visual intended to make?" (Figure 8-6).

■ *Make sure each visual makes only one point.* More than one confuses the audience and often shows that the presenter hasn't thoroughly sorted out the ideas. Two messages on one chart also divide the attention of the audience. While you are explaining point 1 (say, the graphical data), the audience is thinking about point 2 (the conclusions about it) that you put on the same chart.

■ *Present more messages and less information.* Information overload is universally hated and, unfortunately, extremely common. It's the main contributor to the MEGO Syndrome: "My Eyes Glaze Over." The value of a presentation is to help listeners understand the essence of the subject, to be alerted to vital conditions.

■ *Interpret; don't just report.* As the presenter, you are the expert on the subject being discussed. "The data speak for themselves" is a common expression. The trouble is, they may say different things to different people. Your job is to apply your expertise and insights to help those not as expert as you understand the information.

■ *Focus on and highlight key information.* Out of three factors, which is the most crucial at this moment? When explaining a ten-step process, is one step

Figure 8-6.   Each visual must answer one primary question.

potentially the most likely to go wrong? If you've had five related assignments, did one in particular provide the best lessons learned for your proposed position? Design the visual so that these key items will be obvious and so they almost jump out at the audience. (Figure 8-7 illustrates this and the previous two concepts.)

■ *Ensure logical flow from chart to chart.* Consider how easy it is to follow a cartoon strip. Each visual logically leads to the next until the story is complete. It is much easier for the audience to follow your presentation if each visual ties in with the one before it. The storyboard helps this occur. If the visuals are disconnected, the audience has to reorient itself for each visual.

■ *KISS—Keep It Simple, Stupid!* Following a presentation is much like driving down a freeway. The passengers (listeners) have only a few moments to pick up the messages from the billboards, but they do, because the billboards are so simple. How many messages would they pick up if billboards looked like newspaper ads or articles with much more material? Not many. In the presentation, we want the audience to grasp our visual message quickly and listen to our words without moving on to other agendas in their heads or giving up because of information overload. Complex charts make that hard to achieve. "This may be the most common failing of [speakers]," says the Electro/Wescon

Figure 8-7. Select, focus, interpret.

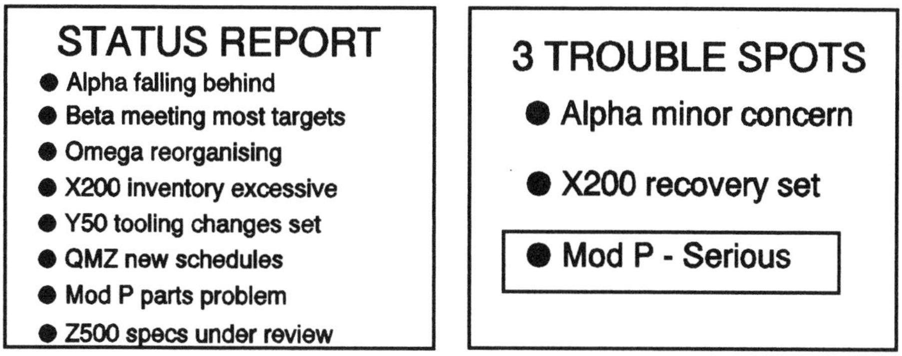

STATUS REPORT	3 TROUBLE SPOTS
● Alpha falling behind	● Alpha minor concern
● Beta meeting most targets	
● Omega reorganising	● X200 recovery set
● X200 inventory excessive	
● Y50 tooling changes set	● Mod P - Serious
● QMZ new schedules	
● Mod P parts problem	
● Z500 specs under review	

Midcom Speaker's Handbook, "trying to reproduce a 'novel' on the 35mm slide."[11]

■ *Present material so that it can be easily grasped by the audience.* Consider what you expect an audience to get from visuals. Generally these are trends, relationships, changes, impacts, and insights rather than raw data. Thus, it becomes important to present the data so that the desired concepts can be readily understood. This is an area of particularly rich potential for a presenter, where communication can be vastly enhanced by creative visual thinking. (See Figure 8-8.)

■ *Use visual power.* In this highly left-brain world, we often overlook the obvious. If a picture is worth a thousand words, why do we see so many words-only charts, especially ones describing things that can be pictured? A useful ground rule is this: if it's real, show it; if it flows, flow it.

■ *Think real and relationships.* Objects, processes, operations, sequences, time lines, and A versus B data lend themselves to visual displays (right brain) rather than wordy descriptions (left brain). If you have hardware, bring it in and hold it up. To help the audience more easily grasp an operation or sequence, show what it looks like with a series of sketches or a flowchart.

Seize every opportunity to visualize concepts, where it is appropriate. Pictures, sketches, abstractions, and cartoons are high-interest items, and they enable people to grasp ideas quickly—to "see the picture"—better than with words alone, spoken or written. Pictures or animation often can effectively complement the necessary words or phrases. Some examples are shown in Figure 8-9.

Low-key or highly apprehensive presenters can benefit greatly by using high-interest visuals—those with lots of pictures and few words. Perky visuals promote a more zestful delivery; dull visuals compound the dullness problem the speaker already has.

■ *Start with the general; move to the specific.* Frequently a presenter shows a complicated visual and proceeds to describe the detailed design or operation of some gadget or process. After five minutes of description of all the intimate workings, often comes a hesitant query from a bewildered audience member,

Figure 8-8. Show information in a format in which it can be readily grasped.

AUDIENCE HAS TO WORK HARD.   MORE QUICKLY PICKED UP.

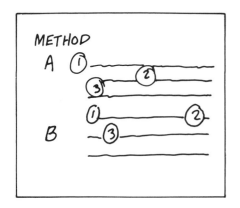

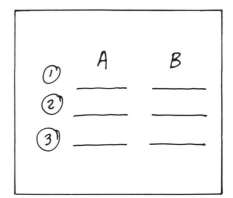

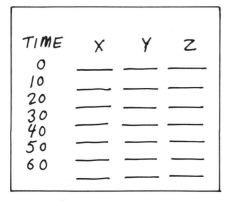

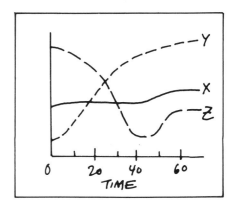

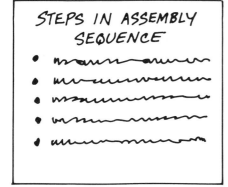

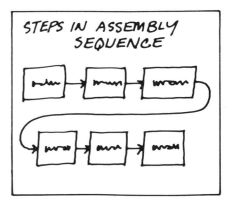

"Uh, what does this thing look like?" or "Just where does this gadget fit on the vehicle?" Then the presenter comes, belatedly, to the realization that these people haven't the foggiest idea of what he or she has been talking about for the past five minutes.

It's almost always worth an extra minute to give people the big picture before getting into the details. If it's an engine valve under discussion, shoot a photo of the entire engine. If you're explaining a computer software module to users, first show how that fits into the overall system and what it looks like (Figure 8-10).

■ *Show a reference (comparison, example, or analogy) for heightened insight and impact.* The significance of the accuracy achieved during a series of missile firings was barely grasped by an audience shown a visual aid giving the test results in the form of miss distances. An astute presenter changed the visual aid to a dartboard showing the actual miss distances all clustered tightly around the bull's-eye. Instant recognition of a sensational performance was achieved (Figure 8-11).

Often audiences have trouble catching key information (reflected by comments such as "That's interesting, but was it good or bad?") because the presenter has failed to give them a frame of reference.

Complex concepts are more quickly grasped if a familiar analogy is made. An instructor was able to get across the idea more quickly of how to steer a sailboat by relating it to the steering of a car. Another presenter drove home his point that a relatively simple structure was costing the government too much money by showing it next to four brand-new Cadillacs. Other examples are a pencil next to a circuit board, a woman holding a new cruise missile engine in her hands to show its compact size, and a changed procedure next to the old one.

■ *For data presentation, select the visual format that best portrays your message.* A major function of visual aids is to display statistical data—the figures. Of the many visual forms that exist to do this, the most frequently used are tables, line graphs, bar charts, and pie charts. Depending on the purpose of the visual, some formats may be better communication vehicles than others (Figure 8-12).

If you've followed an early suggestion in this section, you've identified the specific point you want the visual to help get across, rather than generated a bunch of data that probably ought to be shown. Knowing the purpose of the visual is a good starting point for choosing the best display method. For example:

Message: "We're losing market share." One way to show this would be with three side-by-side pie charts for three years.

Message: "The recession has barely affected sales, but it has hurt profits." You could use a column chart with two segments—sales and profits—for the past five years, or a line graph showing these changes over time.

Message: "The best alloy for required conditions is number 310." A good choice probably would be a line graph showing the strength of three candidate alloys over the temperature range.

Figure 8-9. A picture can be worth a thousand words, especially when used to explain real things and relationships.

QUALITY CIRCLES NEED TIMELY RESPONSE TO SUGGESTIONS.

GENERAL DYNAMICS
Space Systems Division

CONTRA-ROTATING CENTRIFUGAL DEPOT

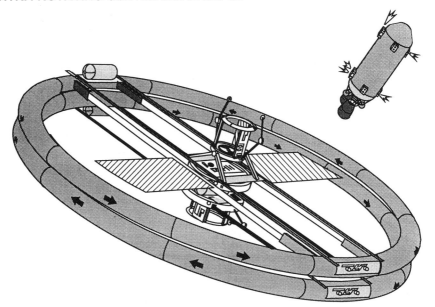

DAVID CAUDLE

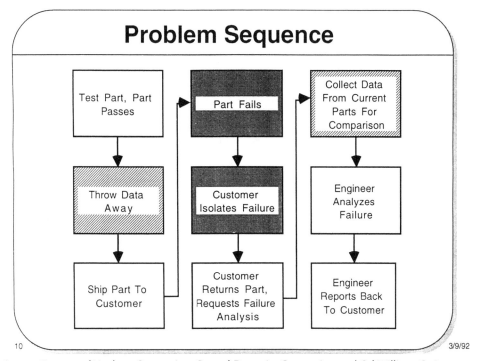

Problem Sequence

Test Part, Part Passes	Part Fails	Collect Data From Current Parts For Comparison
Throw Data Away	Customer Isolates Failure	Engineer Analyzes Failure
Ship Part To Customer	Customer Returns Part, Requests Failure Analysis	Engineer Reports Back To Customer

10   3/9/92

Source: Courtesy of Northrup Corporation, General Dynamics Corporation, and Cal Williams/Craig Bousquet.

■ *Design the graph so that the message will stand out.* For the three examples, **highlight the most pertinent pie segment, column, or line by shading, boldness, or color to focus the audience's attention.** If you are using tables, use a block, arrow, larger type, or color to focus attention on the vital entries.

In general, if your purpose requires that specific numbers be seen by a knowledgeable audience, the best method is probably a table. If you wish to show general trends, relationships, or changes, especially to a general audience, one of the more pictorial forms is probably better. Recall this headline from a Tektronix Company ad: "The difference between a page of numbers and a graph is ten minutes of explanation."

What works well for one audience may work poorly for another. A detailed financial table appropriate for internal top management review may baffle newly hired employees at an orientation program. A graph, bar chart, or pie chart may be a better choice.

■ *Apply your expertise so nonexperts get it.* Help decision makers assess options and make wise choices by giving different perspectives (Figure 8-13).

■ *Use progressive disclosure or overlays to build to complexity and for dramatic effect.* Since the eye is quicker than the mouth, showing lots of information is a sure way to lose your audience. Yet often considerable material has to be displayed. A way to do that and still hold the audience is to use progressive disclosure, also called "revelation." (See Figure 8-14.) The presenter shows only part of the

Figure 8-10. Provide a brief orientation before diving into details.

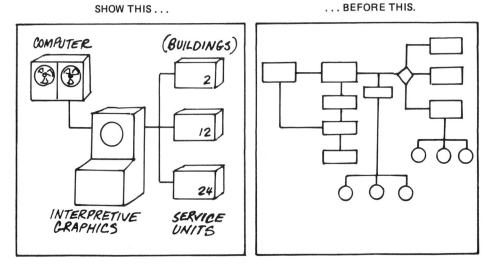

material and discusses that. Then he shows another part, discusses it, shows another, and so on, until all the material is displayed.

Another purpose is the dramatic effect of showing material juxtaposed on one visual. A presenter used this technique effectively as she explained why a new airport was needed in a major city. First she showed a graph of projected airline operations through 2000. Then on the same graph she displayed with an overlay the capacity of the existing airfield, which would be insufficient by 1995. Her final overlay showed the capacity of her proposed alternative, which was well above the 2000 forecast.

■ *Use headline titles.* The most powerful message in a newspaper article is the headline. Most people never read beyond it. In a visual aid, the most powerful position is the title. Yet few presenters take advantage of the potential power in the title. How many charts have you seen whose titles read "Cost versus Years" or "System Improvements"? As one observer said, that's like showing a picture of a horse and titling it "Horse." Of course it's a horse. These titles add little to the chart.

A headline title states in catchy terms the main message of the chart or interprets the chart. Even if readers don't get to or follow the body or detail of the chart, they will understand what the chart is intended to show. Like newspaper readers, they get the message from the headline and can then digest the rest of the material they choose to. For general audiences or those with mixed levels or disciplines, action or interpretive titles are particularly useful aids to understanding.

Since my experience shows many presenters have difficulty grasping the value of headline titles compared to topic or "horse" titles, consider these research findings. As cited in *Communication and Persuasion*, following a persuasive presentation, significantly more people (over 50 percent) changed toward

Figure 8-11. Giving a frame of reference increases comprehension.

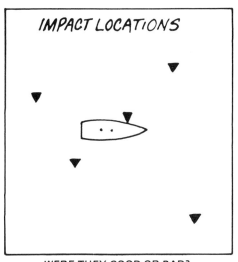

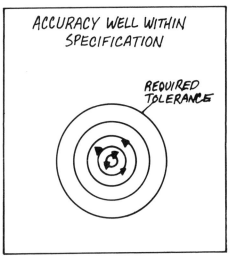

the speaker's proposition when the speaker explicitly stated conclusions than when he didn't (30 percent).[12] That's what a headline title does—state the point (or conclusion) of the chart.

Here are some examples of headline titles, with the proviso that the body of the chart must back up what the title says (see also Figure 8-15):

Subject Title	*Headline Title*
"Horse"	"Polka-dot horses run faster."
"Cost vs. Years"	"Initial cost outlay quickly recovered."
"System Improvements"	"System changes expand performance."

A headline title may not be appropriate for every chart, and the flavor of the message should match the situation and audience. A heavy sales flavor may turn off some listeners, particularly for a purely informational talk. A key top manager may prefer to draw his own conclusions. Generally, however, interpretive titles add to understanding.

Writing full titles can prove extremely beneficial for the presenter, as well as for the listener. This process can help focus and clarify the message the presenter wishes to convey, which often is clouded in a mass of data.

The location of the interpretive title varies. Many companies place it at the top of the chart. Others use a simple title or no title at the top and place the interpretive statement at the bottom, often adding the title after the chart is explained. My preference in most cases is for the top—it keeps the screen less busy, and I often use the action statement as a transition to the chart rather than as a summary after it is explained.

Figure 8-12.   Select graph to fit data type and message—four common graph styles.

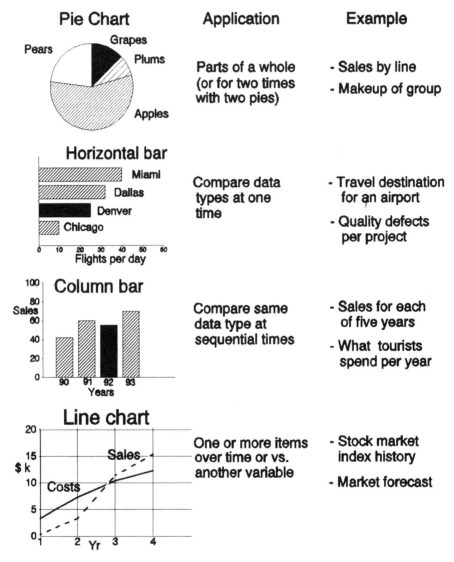

Pie Chart	Application	Example
	Parts of a whole (or for two times with two pies)	- Sales by line - Makeup of group
Horizontal bar	Compare data types at one time	- Travel destination for an airport - Quality defects per project
Column bar	Compare same data type at sequential times	- Sales for each of five years - What tourists spend per year
Line chart	One or more items over time or vs. another variable	- Stock market index history - Market forecast

MAKING VISUALS WORK: APPLYING GRAPHICS SENSE

Tightening Up the Message

The initial concept of a visual often needs refinement to make it a good one. Trimming the clutter, honing the message, and cleaning up the phrasing all help to make a better-focused and punchier visual. Here are several ways to do that.

Figure 8-13. Showing data in several ways may give a truer picture and help make your case better (another example of progressive disclosure).

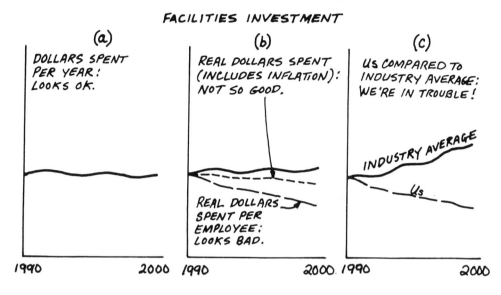

- *Present only information you plan to discuss.* This cleans up a lot of excess and potentially troublesome baggage off the visuals. Whatever you leave on is fair game for viewers to raise questions about. Exercise that red pencil, correction fluid, or delete command liberally.

- *Keep the visuals moving.* Audience members will be able to read your visual material much faster than you can talk it. They won't be listening to you if you give them too much material to look at. Simplify the visuals to aim for no more than one to two minutes per visual for talks of some substance with an in-person presenter. If a chart needs a longer time on screen, find a way to show it as a buildup of several charts.

- *Limit items to seven.* Show them more than seven, and you will lose control of their attention, and their comprehension will probably be less than you expect.[13] If more than seven items are needed, disclose them progressively.

- *Trim and punch up words.* Work toward the fewest and shortest words possible. Cut qualifiers, connectives, and articles. Active tense has more zip than passive. Compare the wordier version on the left to the trimmed on the right:

"The selected component is acquired."	"Buy part."
"Rigorous testing procedures will be employed."	"Test it."
"The production decision is ascertained, pending application of the various assessment factors."	"Evaluate and decide."

Figure 8-14. Present information in steps (progressive disclosure) for better understanding and focusing.

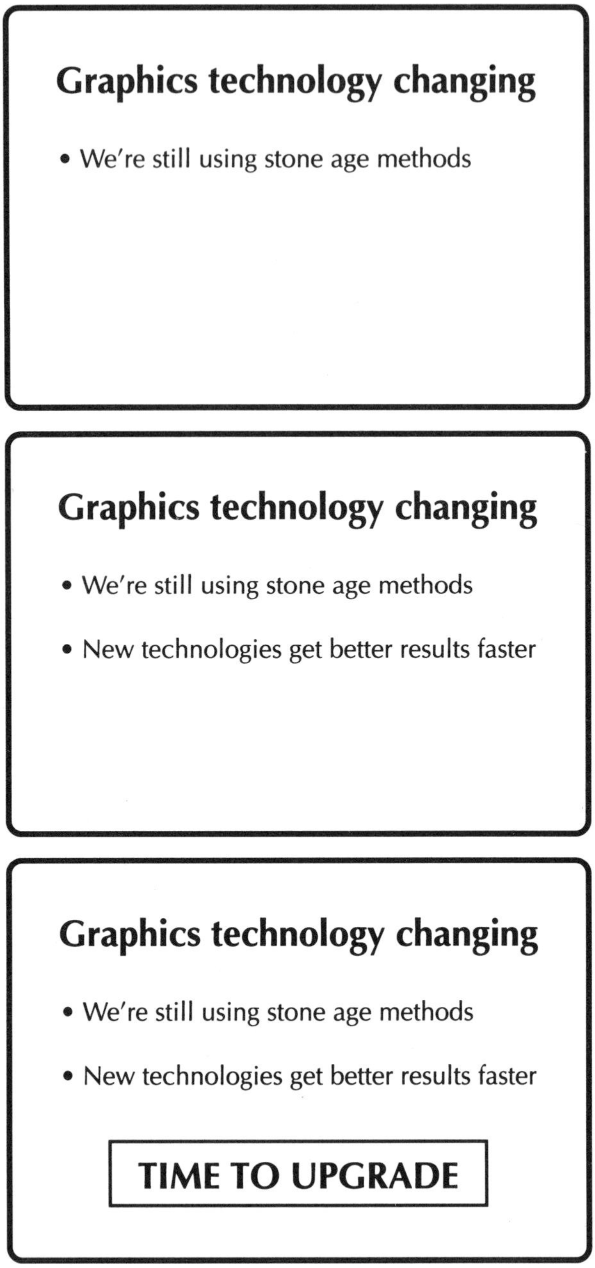

Graphics technology changing

• We're still using stone age methods

Graphics technology changing

• We're still using stone age methods

• New technologies get better results faster

Graphics technology changing

• We're still using stone age methods

• New technologies get better results faster

TIME TO UPGRADE

Figure 8-15. A headline or message title makes the point clear.

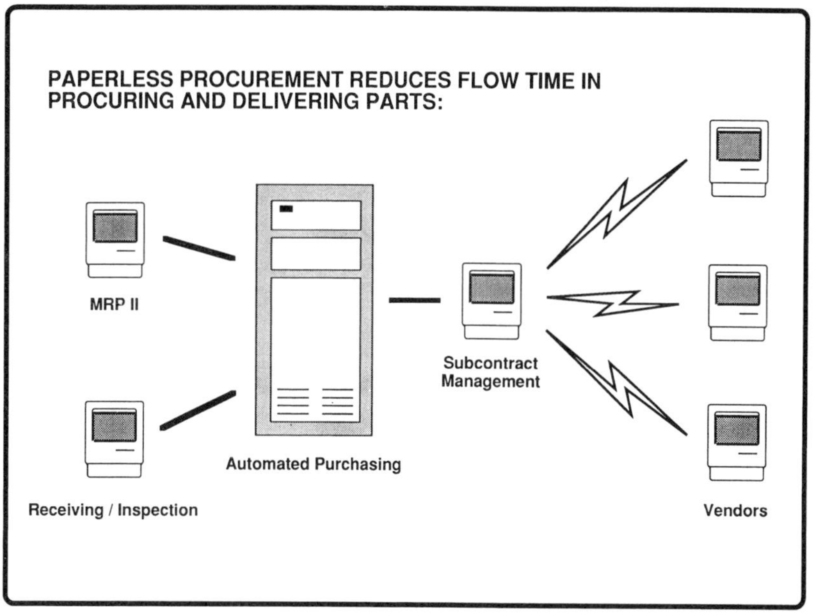

PAPERLESS PROCUREMENT REDUCES FLOW TIME IN
PROCURING AND DELIVERING PARTS:

MRP II

Subcontract
Management

Automated Purchasing

Receiving / Inspection

Vendors

Advance Warning =

IVHS
TECHNOLOGIES
INCORPORATED

Accident Reduction

	With: 1/2 second advance warning...	1 second advance warning...
Rear End Collisions	↓60%	↓90%
Intersection Collisions	↓50%	↓90%
Head-on Collisions	↓30%	↓60%

Source: Visuals courtesy of General Dynamics Space Systems and IVHS Technologies Inc.

■ *Delete superfluous detail.* Will anyone remember the last six digits in "The program cost will be $946,275,172"? Does anyone care? Try "$946 million."

■ *Use consistent style.* If you underline titles, underline all titles, so people don't start guessing about something that isn't there. If you establish a format, stick to it. Use consistent terminology—not:

■ Achieves goals.
■ Lowers costs.
■ Schedule is met.

Figure 8-16. People love to nitpick. Check your visuals carefully before you show them so that you are not guilty of making avoidable errors.

Change the last item to "Meets schedule."

■ *Spell words correctly.* Gremlins often creep into visuals, detracting from the message and the speaker's credibility (Figure 8-16). Pay attention to these little details, for their impact is way out of proportion to their actual importance. Use a computer spell-checker, have someone else review your visuals, and have a dry run with an audience.

■ *Present material that will advance your idea, not sabotage it.* Often presenters overlook words or pictures in their visuals that cause trouble as soon as the audience sees them. Special-interest groups or minorities can easily become offended when the wrong visual symbol is flashed before their eyes—for example: a new design being proposed to the U.S. Navy and shown with an Army logo, a presentation to Saudi Arabia that features a map identifying the Persian, not Arabian, Gulf, or visuals that show women only as secretaries.

GETTING BETTER VISUALS—THE MECHANICS

If you are using the services of graphics professionals, heed their advice about how to lay out visuals property. Get them on board early and have a schedule that allows time to consult with them. In other words, avoid showing up on Friday with thirty rough visual ideas and expecting them back in finished form for a Monday morning presentation.

If you're preparing visuals as many people today do, with computer graphics programs and their various output devices, you need to know certain mechanics about getting workable visuals prepared.

The first question is, *What uses will be required?* Multiple uses are not unusual today. It's important to know whether the visuals will be used as viewgraphs for a live audience, with a laptop computer and LCD projection on the road, or as paper copies for a teleconference, because the layout and type size requirements differ. Most computer graphics programs can adjust sizing automatically for different output forms. If you are using slides and video, for example, check requirements for both forms.

The second question is, *Is the intended screen properly sized for the room?* Many room designers ignore the standard for proper screen sizing (screen width equals one-sixth distance to the last viewer). An undersized screen can make good viewgraphs unreadable. We ran into this problem on a major customer presentation. By testing the layout, we saw the need to eliminate marginal lettering (which had crept in due to busy charts).

Now, Make Charts READABLE

Once more, let's hear from consultant Jim Elms: "With anybody I've ever talked to in the government, the first thing they'll bitch about is the viewgraph they can't read. This is so fundamental yet so commonly violated."

Keep in mind that many upper-level management audiences include older people. On numerous occasions, I've heard those executives remind presenters in this fashion: "This may surprise you, but my vision is not nearly as sharp as it was twenty years before. In other words, don't make these old eyes work so hard. Print larger."

To determine if a viewgraph will be readable when projected, place it on the floor (with paper behind it or use a paper copy). If you can read it *without strain* while standing, it's probably fine. If you aren't able to read it, neither will the audience. For slides, hold each up to a light. If you can read it, it's all right.

A better way is to prepare visuals correctly from the start. Figure 8-17 illustrates basic concepts to ensure adequate visual aid readability:

■ *Select readable type sizes.* With computer graphics so common, it pays to learn about type points, the standard measure of type size; 72 points is 1 inch high, with lower numbers meaning smaller type. What is readable depends on the application. For conference room viewgraphs, 14 point will generally be readable; slides or video-projected visuals and large groups may require larger type. Nevertheless, nonreadable charts, with 4- to 8-point type, are not uncommon.

■ *Don't overwhelm them.* Sixty-point lettering may backfire; it's too big.

■ *Use easily readable typefaces and fonts.* Use sans serif styles, such as Helvetica, rather than serif, such as this typing or Roman. Other sans serif styles are Futura, Optima, and Univers.

Figure 8-17. Choose type layouts wisely.

Poor design	Better design

Poor design:

TOO BIG

Serif type not most readable

SAN SERIF FONT, BUT
ALL CAPS LESS READABLE
Little spacing between items
Centering vs. left align

Fancy but hard to read

10 point type too small to be read, though
not rare on visuals (aids?)

Better design:

Title 24 - 36 point

● **San serif font, 18 pt for**
  subpoints, min. 14 pt bold

● **Lower case more readable**

● **Space between statements**
  1.5 (min.) times line height

For viewgraphs, -- slides may need larger.

■ *Adjust lettering to discriminate or emphasize.* Make titles a larger type size than body elements. Emphasize important statements or words with **bolder type,** *italics,* larger size, or a totally different typeface.

■ *But keep it simple.* Some people have to try out all the computer options, so the first bullet item is Old English Script, the second Broadway Bound Italics, and so forth, which makes for mass confusion. Stick with one family to be on the safe side. Using another font can add punch, but more may be distracting. Within one family, use no more than three variations per chart.[14]

■ *Choose lettering case with care.* To have phrases read most easily, use lower or mixed case, with only the first letter of the first word capitalized. (Some people capitalize each word, which I find confusing.) Receivers pick this up better than all capitals for two main reasons: we're used to seeing this form in print, and changes in lettering elevation with mixed case are easier to pick up than all-capitals with all the same height.[15] Still, if you want a specific phrase or line to stand out strongly, all-capital lettering can often focus attention (which is why many people prefer it for chart titles).

■ *Make it strong enough for good legibility.* Some computer fonts are thin; printers may make weak copies or transparencies. Test to establish if your chosen lettering needs to be made bold or standard. Especially check small type sizes (14 to 16 point), which often are marginally legible unless done in bold type. Also, use filled-in letters rather than open ones (they're much easier to read), and be careful using shadows because they may hamper legibility.

■ *Provide adequate spacing.* A simple rule is to keep a two-line statement tight and separate it distinctly from other parallel statements. Then make the space between statements a minimum of one and a half times the line height.[16] Increase this space as needed to fit the vertical page space well. If you're using bullets, add extra space between the bullet and first letter. Another key to tighter, more easily read lettering is kerning, which fills in spaces between letters. Most graphics programs do this automatically, but older, manual mechanical systems need special attention.

- *Keep all lettering horizontal,* even for *y* graph axes, unless your audiences have ostrich necks.

- *Be especially careful when choosing colors.* Using the wrong colors together can make good type barely readable.

Tune Up Chart Design

Besides readability, the way visual content is laid out also affects how well the information gets across. Consider these suggestions for increasing visual aid value.

- *Use bullets, not numbers.* Bullets (or dingbats) are symbols used before items in a list. Using bullets implies no significance to the order. When you do want to show rank or sequence, use numbers.

- *Prepare charts in horizontal format.* Vertical format has several drawbacks: (1) it requires readers to look lower on the screen, possibly through heads in front or projectors; (2) a mix of horizontal and vertical projected visuals dictates that less than full screen be used, because both horizontal and vertical needs must be met; (3) titles and body phrases of more than a few words, and many visual types such as processes and graphs, fit poorly to this format; (4) a mix of horizontal and vertical viewgraphs or flip charts is awkward to handle; and (5) vertical format visuals aren't usable in that form for other uses, such as video and videoconferencing.

- *Clean up data display confusion.* Often tables, graphs, and charts can be changed to help clarify information, make key points more readily grasped, and head off undesired trouble.

The first beneficial change is to figure out exactly what data you need and what you can do without. If you plan to talk only about total sales, don't show sales by product line. Prepare backup charts if needed to cover questions that might come up about secondary data.

Now cut out all the details—the assumptions, sources, document numbers, and so on—that only give the audience something else to think about and raise nettling questions about instead of making them listen to you. Put this kind of information on copies of visuals for later distribution.

Replace any vertical printing with horizontal printing. It's much easier to read. Viewers should not have to cock their heads sideways to read vertically aligned graph labels, column headings, or labels on bar or pie charts.

For the most common forms, here are further suggestions, taken in large part from Michael MacDonald-Ross's "How Numbers Are Shown."[17]

Tables

- Show information in the form in which you plan to discuss it. If you intend to talk only about unemployment, don't show data for employment. Don't make the audience do too many mental gymnastics.
- Make sure that all headings and numbers are readable. Try to round off all information to two significant digits. For most applications, that's plenty.
- If data are to be compared, put them in adjoining columns, not rows. If column data are to be added, make sure they're lined up properly and do add up to the totals. (See Figure 8-18.)
- Give other data, such as percentage changes, to help viewers understand the significance of numbers.

Graphs

- Position the graph on the page so that there is enough room to print the ordinate (vertical axis) label horizontally. Print words in full. Make sure that symbols will be understood.
- Broadly spaced grids rather than finely spaced ones improve chart visibility and reduce nitpicking. A few grid lines help viewers grasp numbers better than no grid lines. (The more general the audience, the fewer the grid lines.)
- Space grid markers at regular, fairly large, and easily handled magnitudes—for example, not 5, 10, 15 . . . or 35, 70, 105 . . . but 0, 25, 50, 100.
- Start the vertical axis at zero. If using a section (such as 700–800) to show detail, insert a break or separate chart with zero value.
- With a series of graphs of the same type of data (like sales histories for products X, Y, and Z), keep the same axes scales.
- Buildup graphs, where each line adds to the line below it, are often hard

Figure 8-18.   Tabular data can be hard or easy to read.

This way, it's hard to read and
to compare sales and earnings.   This way is easier to read and compare.

Sales	
Widget	75,325
Framzis	236,950
Gizmo	9,000
Total	321,275
Earnings	
Widget	8,295
Gizmo	952
Framzis	38,162
Total	47,409

	Sales (000)	Earnings (000)	% E/S
Framzis	$237	$38	16
Widget	75	8	11
Gizmo	9	1	11
Totals	$321	$47	15

to figure out. Make it clear that it is a buildup graph and that the lines are not independent. If changes in each segment are to be understood to any degree, separate charts for each segment or bar charts may be better.

- More than three lines on a graph gets confusing. If more lines are needed, use progressive disclosure or color coding to help keep lines straight.
- Tie identifiers directly to the lines instead of showing them as a separate legend. If color coding is used and black-and-white copies are to be made, distinguish the lines by other means, such as dashed and solid lines. (Figure 8-19 illustrates many of the concepts for graphs.)

Bar Charts

- Use three-dimensional effects with care. They can make values, such as vertical bar quantities, hard to read. For comparisons, it's clearer to change one dimension only (e.g., bar heights) rather than two (e.g., bar areas).
- Try using symbols instead of bars to establish a stronger relationship between numbers and the information. Look at *USA Today* for some creative ideas, such as stacking trucks, trains, planes, and ships to show different shipping quantities; using figures of a man, woman, and child to report incidence of diabetes. But don't let symbols or graphics interfere with clarity, as is often the case.
- Use shading, spacing, colors, and arrows to increase clarity and punch. Distinguish key information by the richest shading, an arrow, or notation of activating events.
- Reduce the clutter by thinning out axes markers, making all labels

Figure 8-19. Make graphs easily readable.

MAKE CHARTS QUICKLY READABLE

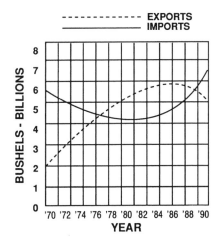
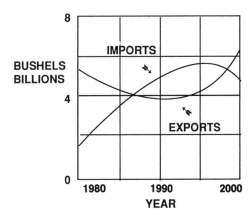

horizontal, and designing layouts to cut redundant information. Place labels close to the bars rather than using a reference legend.

- Subsets of data within bars can be effective, but categories except the first one from zero may be hard to compare. One category (e.g., profits as a subset of sales) can be easily grasped, but dividing sales into four product categories can be difficult.

Pie Charts

- Start a pie at twelve o'clock, and place the most important element clockwise from there. Make it obvious by strong shading or color or split out a key segment to focus extra attention.
- Too many pieces ruin the pie. Stick with no more than six, and put any other little segments into an "all other" category.
- Make all labels horizontal for easy readability. Color coding to match pie segments is also helpful.
- Pie charts work well with other graphical forms or for coding. The pie can be placed in a corner, with the key element highlighted, and presented more fully by a table, bar chart, or word chart.

Use Color Power—Wisely

With advances in computer graphics and output capabilities, color visuals are much more commonly used. Yet using color correctly is not automatic, in spite of the best efforts of the technologists.

According to *Audio-Visual Instruction: Technology, Media and Methods,* color can add to visual effect in three ways:[18]

1. To attract attention (e.g., using the Red Cross logo to stress safety).
2. To emphasize or contrast (e.g., highlighting the super sales trend of one product line relative to several others).
3. To create moods (e.g., a sunny logo for a solar energy company or lots of blue for a Caribbean cruise company advertisement).

The value of color has been demonstrated in numerous studies. For example, a Xerox Corporation study showed significant benefits in learning and retention from use of color materials over black and white.[19] Color can enhance visual clarity and strength by:

- Emphasizing specific words or lines, flagging key information as a highlighting marker does for the printed page.
- Distinguishing different or common parts of illustrations, schematics, or procedural charts (e.g., showing different liquids in a propulsion system or grouping safety features of a product).
- Showing changes such as the old and the new or different states of the liquid in the system.
- Highlighting a specific part of an object or illustration, such as the drive train of an automobile.

- Focusing attention on critical changes or problem areas, such as the part that failed during a test.
- Identifying or coding parts of a graph to their sources.
- Providing organizational clarity by introducing new material onto a visual or maintaining a color reference across several visuals.

Poor use of color can damage visuals seriously. Three primary ways in my experience are:

1. *Poor visibility.* Put green lettering against a gray background, and it is extremely hard to see with green lettering against a red background, the color-blind executive sees a blank screen.
2. *Misuse of color associations.* In a presentation to demonstrate how much better team A was than brand X, a bar chart compared financial performance. The team A bar was in red; brand X's was in black. Who had the red ink, a standard measure of financial loss?
3. *Culture traps.* What plays well in Peoria may backfire in Hong Kong.

The best way to make sure your color choices won't backfire is to follow the wisdom of the experts. If you're using an in-house graphics department or outside service, ask for advice and listen to it.

If you're using computer graphics, a generally sound approach is to stick with the choices the software designers used to create preset background/ lettering combination or templates. They've developed these following good color principles (you hope).

Watch out for the WYSIWYG trap. This means "*What You See* [on the computer monitor] *Is What You Get* [in the finished product]." Except you often don't get what you see. Many a good black-and-white graphics ace has made color choices because they looked fine on the monitor and then been dismayed to get back slides that could barely be read when projected on the screen.

If in doubt, run an early pilot test from computer to actual end use. If you're using a service bureau to produce slides, try out several color combinations. Try those slides in a projector with likely room lighting conditions.

For good legibility, the rule is to use light lettering on a dark background and dark lettering on a light background.

Background	Carrying Power in Decreasing Order
Dark	white, yellow, orange, green, red, blue, violet
Light	black, red, orange, green, blue, violet, yellow[20]

Use the color wheel (Figure 8-20) to help you make sound color choices.

- Warm-side colors are yellow, orange, and red and their combinations. They have associations of fire, sun, intensity, and movement. These are also called advancing colors, because they seem to move toward the audience. They

Figure 8-20. The color wheel is the key to wise use of color.

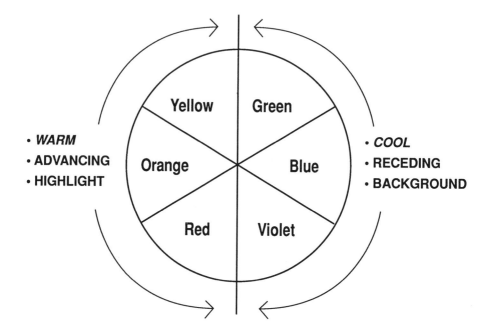

COLOR WHEEL KEY TO COLOR SENSE

are good choices for focusing areas or items and poor choices for large sections or backgrounds.

- Cool colors are violet, blue, and green. Associations are meadows, oceans, peace, and harmony. Because these seem to recede from the audience, they are better background colors than focusing colors.

- For best contrast or visibility, choose colors opposite from each other on the color wheel (called "complementary"). Thus, with a blue background, good visibility is likely with its opposite—orange—and generally with yellow and maybe with red.

- For subtle effects, choose colors adjacent to each other ("harmonious"). For example, with a blue background, a green or violet logo would show up subtly. Another choice is to use the same basic color in a lighter or darker shade (e.g., a dark blue background with a pale blue logo).

- Graphics experts advise caution about using gray for background. It is difficult to reproduce consistently and to make paper copies.

- Help color-blind people, roughly 10 percent of the population, get your visual message. Do *not* place red and green (the most common problem colors) next to each other—no red letters on green background and no red pie slices next to green ones, unless you place a line between them.

Some safe color combinations are shown in Figure 8-21. Remember these are guidelines; test your color production system from computer to screen.

Be moderate and consistent in color use. People often pull presentations together from previous ones or from other sources. Often the various sources have different color combinations; using them as is would lead to confusion and a slapdash look. Some graphics programs can apply the same design to all visuals, leading to a more uniform appearance.

Tips for Specific Audiovisual Forms

This section is only for those who want to get into the nitty gritty of preparing visual materials. Here are the nuts and bolts of the process:

Viewgraphs

■ *Layout.* Most viewgraphs are 11 inches wide by 8½ inches high. Keep viewgraph copy or artwork ¾ inch inside this; material placed out to the edge won't fit on the screen. To prevent this, set up computer graphics with ¾-inch margins or print on paper with nonreproducible border lines ¾ inch inside the edges.

■ *Black-and-white (B&W) viewgraphs.* The easiest way to create viewgraphs is to write with special markers directly on the plastic sheets. Most viewgraphs today are computer generated and produced by printer output directly onto transparencies or printed onto paper and then onto plastic with office copy machines or thermal processes. Laser or inkjet printers make high-quality viewgraphs quickly available at low cost, so last-minute changes are workable.

■ *Color backgrounds.* Office copiers or laser printers can produce black lettering or artwork on color transparencies. Avoid red and yellow—they're too harsh—and check other colors because visibility may suffer. You can also place one clear color transparency on the projector and lay B&W viewgraphs on it.

■ *Reverse image.* Thermal copiers can make color lettering on clear background or reverse image (dark background with light lettering).

■ *Full-color viewgraphs.* Manually write with color markers directly onto

Figure 8-21. Choose color combinations carefully. Here are some typical backgrounds and suitable emphasis colors.

Background color	Best legibility	Lower legibility
Blue or black (medium to dark)	Yellow, white, orange	Red, black, green, light blue
Green (medium to dark)	White, orange	Blue, yellow
Brown, rust	White, yellow, blue	Black, red
Red (spot areas)	White	Green (no), black

transparencies or add stick-on translucent color film to highlight areas. Paintjet or inkjet printers of modest cost take computer output and quickly produce color transparencies of quality sufficient for most presentations. Color printers or film recorders produce better-quality color but at a higher price (unless you own one).

■ *Overlays.* The easiest way to add to a visual is to make separate viewgraphs, with each overlay containing *only the new content* (e.g., new bullet items, flowchart sections, graph items). Use a portable Instaframe chart holder on the projector. Place the first visual into the framer, and then drop new ones on one at a time. Alternatively, overlays can be done by using a cardboard or plastic frame. Tape the first viewgraph to the frame, tape the others at one edge, and flip them onto the original.

Slides

■ *Size.* With computer graphics programs, verify that your working and output areas are set for the slide width:height ratio of 3:2. (This is different from viewgraphs, which is 4:3.) Most software has an adjustment for this. If the slides will be used for video or videoconferencing, check their constraints.

■ *Slide orientation.* Plan for all slides to project in horizontal format, and do not mix horizontal and vertical slides.

■ *Legibility.* The two primary culprits are tiny lettering and poor color combinations. Since slides are more often used than viewgraphs with larger audiences, I suggest you increase adequate viewgraph point sizes by one-third (e.g., 24-point viewgraph title equals 32-point slide title). Genigraphics recommends 36-point title and 24-point bullets.[21]

A quick test for readability from a slide on a computer monitor is to measure the width of on-screen copy, and then step back six times that dimension. If you can read it without strain, the copy is probably legible. Or print out a sample slide on paper and try that. For a finished slide, hold it up to a light; if you can read it, it's legible.

■ *Artboards.* Kodak suggests art layout size of 9 inches wide by 6 inches high, with minimum letter heights.[22]

- For a small conference room (32 feet to the last viewer, 6-foot wide screen): ⅛ inch minimum, ¼ inch recommended.
- For a large auditorium (80 feet to the last viewer, 15-foot-wide screen): 0.2 inch minimum, 0.4 inch recommended.

Computer-Based Presentation Visuals

This refers to mode of presentation, such as direct viewing on monitors or projected. The primary problem is ensuring adequate visibility.

■ *For viewing from monitors.* A common application displays information to ten people crowded around a computer monitor. The usual result is that half can't read the material. With several monitors in a classroom, the result is the same. If you can't get a larger monitor or use a projection system, increase the lettering sizes. Apply the "6W" test noted before: measure screen width, step back six times that, and try to read the screen.

- *For projected images.* For current projectors and with proper room lighting, the same standards suggested for viewgraphs (in a small room) or slides (a large room) should suffice. If you are using older LCD devices on overhead projectors, which may show dim images, stay away from marginal lettering.

Video and Videoconference Visuals

- *Image size.* The video screen aspect ratio (width:height) is 4:3. Visuals taken from a viewgraph layout are also about the same; the ratio for slides is 3:2, so some content may be cut off.

- *Safe areas.* With computer graphics, the different requirements can be accounted for by setting larger inside borders. For slides laid out on 9-inch by 6-inch artboards, Kodak recommends a visually safe area of 6 inches by 4.5 inches for any vital information.[23] For those made on computer, use the slide aspect ratio but adjust the content area as for an artboard. If using paper copies of viewgraphs, the aspect ratio is the same as video, but you need a larger border for the video safe area. For videoconference facilities, inquire about requirements before you make your visuals. One facility requires paper copies 8 inches wide by 6 inches high, smaller than the standard viewgraph layout of 9.5 inches by 7.5 inches.

Flipcharts and Posters

These present special problems in preparing, transporting, and displaying. Illustrations and layouts, such as those used by architects and planners, come in all sizes. They work well for small groups but are often disasters when used for large. Ensuring adequate visibility is one problem; displaying them another.

- *Choosing the size.* Flipcharts come in several common sizes: small (8½ by 11 inches) for use with three-ring binders or special holders when speaking to one or two people; intermediate (one is 19 by 24 inches) with table-top easels for three to five people; and large (one is 27 by 34 inches) for use with floor easels and suited for groups of five to twenty-five. Larger sizes are often used for such applications as architectural presentations or courtroom use. Poster boards are much like flipcharts, except they sit on easels (or other objects) rather than hang from them.

- *Ensuring legibility.* Lettering size needed depends on the distance to the last viewers.

For charts and posters to be seen from up to 32 feet away, minimum lettering size is 1 inch and drawn bold (according to Kodak). Use 1¼ inch minimum for titles or to be on the safe side. Farther than 32 feet means larger lettering (e.g., for 64 feet, 2 inches high).

For desktop charts, use the same guidelines suggested for viewgraphs. If you pass out copies, regular typing will be legible, but loading up the page may hamper your ability to direct attention.

▪ *Producing materials.* Many visuals in this category are hand drawn, either in advance or at the moment of presentation. If they are legible and reasonably neat, there's nothing wrong with doing it this way. Wide markers (e.g., ½-inch felt tips) give bolder lines and lettering. Machines that make large stick-on letters help make a better-quality chart. Large-size, high-quality visuals can be made from page-size artwork photographically with a Varitronic system.

▪ *Keeping it undercover.* Since the charts may be in place right from the start, put a cover on the front, using either a blank or a simple title. To keep the upcoming page from being seen prematurely, insert blank sheets and staple them for easy flipping.

▪ *Problem prevention.* Check how your charts will be attached. Top-mounting to an easel means the top three inches of chart are not usable.

MULTIVISUAL/MIXED MEDIA PRESENTATIONS

So far we've been dealing with one visual image up on the screen at a time and usually with one presenter using the visual to help make a point or get information across. Even in this high-tech world, this is by far still the way most presentations are done.

Yet other ways of using visuals in presentations are commonly seen, ranging from two overhead projectors to eighteen-projector slide spectaculars to computer-based presentations weaving in animation, sound, and video. We'll touch lightly in this area; it's easy territory to mess up without a professional.

Multiple Image Presentations

In many organizations, a presenter (or team) may use two overhead projectors to show either single or side-by-side images. The presenter may stand between two separated screens, sit at a console facing the audience with images displayed on one large screen behind him or her, or work with an associate who handles the viewgraphs. And sometimes the presenter uses three slide projectors located behind the screen (rear projection).

Seeing two or three images side by side can help get the message across—for example:

▪ Something can be shown from several angles or perspectives. This can be done with two images shown simultaneously or by showing an abstraction of an object plus a real picture.

▪ Multi-image is particularly desirable for showing comparisons, such as before and after photos used for weight reduction ads or desirable and undesirable ways of doing something. Results from two different actions can be compared.

▪ Relationships become clearer. A close-up and a more distant photo often are helpful—for example, seeing a picture of a house while also seeing its neighborhood setting. An automobile engine might be shown as a photo or system diagram; then one component, such as the distributor, might be shown separately in detail. A cause and effect can also be effectively shown, such as poor machining technique and a broken arm.

■ A process or operation can be shown in both static and dynamic form. Following the process of making wire while also seeing a flowchart may increase understanding.

■ Understanding is often increased by repetition and reinforcement. Multi-image gives opportunities to do this in different ways.

■ Orientation of the presentation can be aided by multi-images. The agenda may be shown and referred to periodically on one screen or on a flipchart; then the discussion of the first, second, third, and so on, section can be done on the other screen (see Figure 8-22). The classic example of this was the use of placards announcing each act during vaudeville.

■ A presentation can be conducted visually in two languages by showing the same visual on two screens, with annotations for the two images in different languages.

Mixed Media Presentations

These use several visual media forms and are extremely common. Some examples:

- At a training seminar, the speaker opens with an overview slide show, switches to viewgraphs for an interactive segment, and closes with an instructional movie.
- An architect presenting to a prospective client reviews her firm's background with color slides, presents the proposed design from illustrations on poster boards, and goes into detail using copies on paper.
- For a program review, the first speaker uses viewgraphs, the second a laptop computer linked to an LCD device on the overhead project, and the third closes with a video showing test results.

Figure 8-22. Multiple images are often used to enhance understanding.

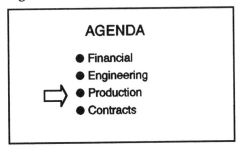
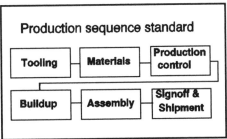

Using Multi-Images and Media

- Carefully design and coordinate multi-images so the audience's attention is logically directed and not scattered. The images should not compete.
- Facilities requirements are more complex. More space will be required for equipment. Power outlets and power-handling ability must be adequate. Rear screens will take a larger chunk of the room than front screens, and lights behind the screen must be restricted.
- Consider transportation, display, visibility, and use in your planning. Where will you hang or mount those large poster boards in a customer's conference room? A major presentation came to a swift halt when a dozen large drawings attached to a wall with masking tape came tumbling down simultaneously. A design firm was prevented from carrying its large rolled charts onto the plane and was dismayed to find they'd then gotten lost enroute—on a nonstop flight. A briefer discovered at show time that none of his carefully crafted visual aids—wall-mounted renderings, slides, and working models—could be seen adequately by the audience of 300 at a public hearing.
- Check readability effects early. Multi-image may mean two images on one screen or smaller screens, so visual lettering sizes may need to be increased. A last-minute panic ensued for one presentation when it was realized that the screen size would be half of that expected.
- Operations are likely to be more complicated than for single-image presentations. Check the layout, establish how visuals will be managed, and rehearse. Plan timing of visuals to hold audience attention and not compete with each other.

Multimedia Computer-Based Presentations

This is one of the hot technologies of the 1990s, which will see increasingly wider application as software and hardware capabilities improve. Still graphics can be shown on a single computer monitor or projected onto a large screen; full sound and motion sequences can be woven in from video or compact disc storage; processes can be illustrated vividly with animation and changed according to audience requests.

Multimedia presentations come in many forms and sophistication levels. Equipment needed can be slightly or considerably beyond that used for basic desktop computer presentations, depending on the application. Preparing and using them typically requires four elements:

- The basic computer platform, high speed and memory, with sound and video capability
- Development and operational multimedia software
- Input and storage, such as CD-ROM, laser disk video recorder or computer-compatible VCR, scanner, digitizers, graphics, and text programs
- End-use systems for receivers/users, e.g., computer monitor, video projector or monitor, overhead projector and LCD panel, interactive storage/access (CD-ROM, video), audio speakers, computer diskettes

Using this presentation mode means working closely with technology providers and service bureaus. Get them on-board early before buying systems or preparing such presentations.

IN SUMMARY: MAKE THEM AIDS, NOT AILMENTS

Visual aids are integral with presentations. Good visuals can add greatly to presentation success, and computer technology has brought high-quality graphics capability out of the realm of graphics designers only and onto office desktops. Yet poor-quality visuals are still commonly seen, even with computer graphics.

Success comes from understanding the role of visual aids, sharpening visual creativity, and applying sound graphics principles.

One of the pioneer high-tech presentations was given during the 1950s by a top marketing man for a major automobile manufacturer. Excerpts from John Brooks's *Business Adventures* describe his work in promoting the new Edsel car:

> [He] brightened up his lectures by showing such a bewildering array of animated graphs, cartoons, charts, and pictures, of parts of the [new car]—all flashed on a Cinemascope screen—that his listeners usually got halfway home before they realized that he hadn't shown them [the car]. He wandered restlessly around the auditorium as he spoke, shifting the kaleidoscopic images on the screen at will with the aid of an automatic slide changer—a trick made possible by a crew of electricians who laced the place in advance with a maze of wires linking the device to dozens of floor switches, which, scattered about the hall, responded when he kicked them.[24]

Brooks went on to describe how the speaker would deliver his lines while giving a kick at a switch here, then a switch there. The presentation built toward the grand finale, with the speaker kicking switches right and left and shouting, "We are proud of the Edsel!" It was a sensational presentation and a great success. Many dealers left thriving agencies to become Edsel dealers, never having seen the car. Apparently the rest of the Edsel presentations weren't so successful.

✻ ✻ ✻ 9 ✻ ✻ ✻

Stage

Key Points of This Chapter

✻ The medium may become the message; or, *how* you do the presentation may be as influential as what you say.

✻ Pay attention to the little things; they can do you in.

✻ Care with arrangements pays off in productivity, impression, and confidence.

✻ Today's computer graphics capabilities offer opportunities for better presentations—or more traps to mess them up.

✻ Using your visual aids properly can enhance their value and power.

✻ Test your product and yourself before delivery—common sense that is often ignored (see Figure 9-1).

The audience of 300 was gathered to hear about the latest in presentations computer technology. Following introductory comments, the speaker brought up the video projection system and showed several dazzling demonstrations of great presentations using his company's software/hardware technology. Many in the audience were ready to whip out their checkbooks and buy on the spot. Continuing the presentation, the speaker activated the computer program so we could all see the monitor projected onto the large screen. He swiftly moved through several instructions until it went "tilt" and froze up. Must have done something wrong, so restart the program. Oops, same point, same "tilt." Possibly a hardware problem, so now helpers were testing connections and kicking projectors, "Oh, no," came the plaintive wail of another wounded presenter as he examined the software program's diskette. "I grabbed the wrong one." By now, twenty minutes into the aborted presentation, most of the checkbooks had gone back into the pockets.

In today's presentation world, a host of potential problems lies in wait to sabotage unsuspecting or careless presenters. Yet never have presenters had more readily available technology to aid them as they're trying to get their messages across. Winning presenters are on top of the operational aspects; they know that wise planning and attention to detail are vital to success. This chapter thus examines the *how* of presentation, as distinct from the *what*.

Figure 9-1. Careful staging averts embarrassment.

"The feed and return manifolds
are connected by a solenoid valve
allowing fresh coolant to circulate
through a cooling coil.....
as would be shown on this slide
if I had brought a spare bulb."

Source: Copyright Aaron Bacall.

ARRANGEMENTS

A nationally known financial adviser booked a large room in a major convention facility. Newspaper ads pulled hundreds of people to the meeting, which was aimed at enticing them to sign up for the full seminar. The presentation was well prepared, with good visuals, smooth delivery, and skillful handling of mechanics. Unfortunately, in the adjoining room, separated only by a thin partition, an est (Erhard Seminars Training) inspirational meeting was in progress. The frequent cheers and shrieks of the excited est members kept drowning out the terribly frustrated financial adviser, who watched substantial investment go down the drain.

Proper attention to arrangements results in trouble-free operations, thus making a valuable contribution to presentations success and meeting productivity. Missed planes, lost visual aids, burned-out projector bulbs, and upside-down slides can sabotage a presentation beyond repair.

These irritants or disasters may be *amusing* to audience members, especially when it happens to the competition. They are *embarrassing* to the presenter, who is now trying to recover from sloppy preparation (and occasionally fate). And they quickly become *costly* as the meeting is delayed while problems get fixed (maybe) or principal listeners get fed up and move on to something else.

Finally, the long-term effects may be doubly costly if the mishap hangs on to the presenter for life. As Mark Antony said in his eulogy of Julius Caesar: "The evil men do lives after them; the good is oft interred with their bones." When presentations go smoothly, audience members scarcely notice anything about the mechanics; when something goes wrong, that may become the most dominant and lasting impression: *"I don't recall anything he said, but I'll never forget what he did."*

Here are six general axioms about arrangements that will serve you well if you rigorously apply them. They've been developed over years of hard lessons—learned from my own and others' painful experiences:

1. *The medium may be the message.* Marshall McLuhan's famous observation definitely applies to presentations. A smoothly run presentation not only aids in getting the message across but adds to the confidence listeners have in the speaker and the material. The image of professionalism is enhanced. Conversely, a speaker who doesn't have the necessary equipment on hand and ready, can't figure out how to operate the equipment, and mixes up the slides is doing serious damage to his or her cause. Observers may assume that such carelessness applies to the work being presented as well.

2. *Be prepared.* Give thorough attention to every detail necessary for putting on the presentation smoothly: the who, what, when, where, and why questions. Assurance comes from knowing all the incidentals have been taken care of and all the necessary equipment is in place and working. Few things can more quickly sap the confidence of an already apprehensive speaker than discovering at presentation time that some key incidental has been overlooked.

3. *Anticipate disasters.* The classic example is the projector bulb that burns out—generally at the most critical part of your talk. If you follow this axiom, you will *assume* the bulb is going to burn out and will have a spare with you. And you will know how to put it in.

4. *Test everything.* In spite of extreme exhortations to inexperienced presenters, it usually takes one or two trials under fire before the critical importance of this axiom truly registers in the "MANDATORY" section of the brain. *Show time is not the time for on-the-job training.*

5. *Trust no one implicitly.* The wise presenters—those who have tired of being burned by faulty arrangements—make sure that all the mechanics needed for the success of their shows have been handled properly. By sorry experience they've learned that delegation, promises, and intentions don't always get carried out as intended. Clear communication, feedback, and personal checking by the

presenter (to the degree practical) are mandatory. The presenter, not the support people, will be embarrassed and set back when a promised projector isn't there. Unless it comes from a trusted and experienced helper—a most valuable resource—be wary whenever you hear, "It'll work. Trust me." or "Joe said it's all set."

6. *Never underestimate the power of Murphy's Law.* Lest there be some among us who do not know what Murphy's Law is, let me explain now. Murphy's Law says that whatever can go wrong, will. Various corollaries and axioms have been put forth over the years, and I suspect many of those were derived during business presentations. My set is offered in Figure 9-2.

Leave It to the Pros?

Large organizations have specialists who know all about the areas we're about to examine. Outside experts are also often hired to take care of many arrangements. For most informal or routine presentations without much professional help, presenters must make their own arrangements, and even in organizations with technical experts, speakers themselves do most of their own arranging for informal or lower-priority presentations.

Whatever the degree of expert assistance available, it is important that presenters themselves have a good understanding of facility factors that affect

Figure 9-2. Murphy's devious law applies to presentations, too.

- Visual aids packed with luggage headed for Cleveland will end up in Detroit.
- An upside-down slide or viewgraph will not be projected correctly until all other erroneous positions are tried.
- In a major two-speaker presentation, the other speaker will get hit with the flu thirty minutes before show time.
- A person can partake of coffee hundreds of times without incident until he is the next presenter—and then he spills coffee all over himself.
- A loose coat button will pop the first time the speaker points to the screen—and the button will go into the admiral's coffee.
- The one time the presenter fails to check the projector bulb is the time just after the last person who used the projector burned out the bulb—and didn't replace it.
- If you bring the resident expert on a specific subject to the meeting, that subject will never come up.
- The pointer that is always there, won't be.
- When the graphics expert advises, "You don't need to check it—it will work fine," it won't.
- If a presenter must have a specific type of equipment, such as a cassette recorder, the wrong type will be delivered, such as a reel-to-reel recorder.
- Whenever a speaker says, "As you can all see . . . ," half the audience can't.
- When the speaker makes a final run to the restroom, a prominent zipper will catch, in either the closed (before) or open (after) position.
- While racing to a meeting across town, the harried presenter will suddenly remember she forgot to put gas in the car . . . just before it starts to cough.

the presentation. Familiarity with equipment capabilities and restrictions is essential for sound planning for use of such equipment. Many of the other incidental arrangements are definitely within the responsibility of the presenter.

My philosophy is that *all* arrangements are the responsibility of the presenter. Arrangement decisions significantly affect the cost, the style, and ultimately the success of the presentation. The presenter with adequate knowledge and experience is much better equipped to make decisions about arrangements than one who fails to acquire such knowledge.

Presenters often make the mistake of leaving decisions and arrangements about conference room facilities and visual aid equipment entirely in the hands of the technicians. The experts who sell, maintain, and operate presentation facilities are valuable resources, but their perspective is different from that of the presenter, the person actually standing in front of the audience and *using* that equipment. What seems adequate from a technician's standpoint may cause problems for a presenter.

Presenters seem to be rarely consulted when an organization's facilities planners design presentation rooms or buy audiovisual equipment. Presenters themselves seldom have raised their voices in advance about their needs, because they don't know such planning or buying is going on, and they have other priorities—until the time comes when they have to present there. Then the cries of despair bellow forth: "What idiot designed this room!!?"

Here's a plea to people in organizations who are responsible for planning and acquiring facilities and equipment that presenters will have to use: *Get input from the users of that facility and equipment and pay attention to it.* That might help prevent some of the problems that presenters are continually faced with, such as lecterns that won't hold notes, lights that shine directly onto the screen, projector tables with no room for visual aids, and sound systems that blast here and squeal there. Key items for consideration of arrangements are shown in Figure 9-3.

Figure 9-3. Key how-to's of arrangements.

- Assume responsibility for specifying facility, equipment, personnel, material, transportation, and other requirements.
- Make a detailed checklist well in advance. Have checkpoints to ensure that arrangements are being met as planned.
- Give deliberate consideration to how the presentation will be affected by timing, location, and attendees.
- Know the facility and equipment and have access to needed controls.
- Make sure all equipment is in place and tested well enough in advance that fixes can be made.
- Public address systems are notoriously poor quality and cantankerous. Check in advance or bring your own.
- When traveling, allow enough time to get there and inside. Do not entrust your visuals to the baggage department.

Meeting Rooms

The quality of the meeting room should match the level of the audience and the importance of the meeting. People typically behave in the manner the environment seems to call for. They shout and become unruly in the boxing arena and conduct themselves in a civilized manner in church. Unfortunately, the low quality of many presentation rooms and classrooms results in the same demeanor as at a boxing match.

A change in setting for a weekly production meeting had dramatic effects. The meeting had always been held in the factory area in a poorly maintained and crowded room. Speakers and other audience members were continually interrupted, foul language was prevalent, and shouting was the normal level of discourse. The meeting was shifted to a first-class conference room, with carpeting, a controlled environment, and comfortable seating. Said one regular attendee: "I couldn't believe the change. People stopped interrupting each other, cleaned up their language (a little bit), and started giving the presenters a chance. Things got done a whole lot faster."

An off-site location may be more desirable than a room within the company or agency facilities, with increased attentiveness, self-image, and productivity often offsetting the cost of the facility.

Check soundproofing carefully. Find out who will be using adjacent facilities and what effects this will have on your meeting.

The room walls should be plain—no photos, charts, or drawings. These are powerful attention getters, and they compete with the presenter.

Entrance and exit should be at the opposite end from the speaker. Latecomers and early departers create less disturbance than when the door is near the speaker. Also, message bearers or refreshment servers can do their tasks more discreetly.

The fewer barriers between speaker and audience, the better. Elevation, distance, podiums, microphones, and other obstacles between speaker and audience serve to impede communication. (This is the way most courtrooms and city council chambers are designed, which serves only to increase the anxiety the average citizen has about appearing before the judge or city hall. Perhaps one day a city chamber will be designed so that the elected officials have to look up to the taxpayer instead of the other way around.)

Room Lighting and Darkening. Different presentations require different room lighting conditions, so flexibility is important. During discussions without visuals, a lighted room is best. To see some projected images, a darker room may be necessary, *at least on the screen.*

To allow for flexibility, many rooms have rheostat controls to adjust lighting as desired (not feasible with fluorescent lighting), or they have banked lights and separate switches to control specific sections. Unfortunately, the on-off sections are often unrelated to the darkening need and don't kill the lights in the right place.

Many rooms are set up with a light that shines directly onto the screen. If the screen is portable, the problem can be overcome by moving it. To get workable conditions, some presenters have been known to remove the bulbs near the screen.

In their zeal to ensure superb conditions for the on-screen images, presenters (or arrangers) may end up with a totally dark room and a speaker who can't be seen—a poor solution for the speaker-audience relationship. This is occurring more often with increased use of computer-controlled presentations. Tip: Keep some light on in the room, and especially on the presenter.

Outside light can be another problem, and that may change throughout the day. I once overlooked this basic fact. I had checked the room conditions in the morning, but at 3 P.M. when I turned on the projector, nothing could be seen on the screen. The afternoon sun now beat powerfully through the thin curtains.

Lecterns. Since most people aren't clear about what people speak from, here's some help. People stand on the *podium* and speak behind or from a *lectern*. For most presentations, lecterns are not used. For more formal speeches, they typically are. Many people insist on a lectern, which serves as protection from the savages in the audience and provides a crutch to lean upon and hang onto fiercely.

For presentations, a lectern, placed not to interfere with audience ability to see the screen, may be helpful as a place to keep notes, copies of visual aids, or other props. I advise presenters to speak generally without a lectern, but, if one is used, to speak from the side. This allows ready access to materials as needed while still keeping good audience interaction and personal delivery. Short presenters can get lost behind a bulky lectern; they are better off speaking at the side or standing on a box.

Lectern designers seem not to have asked speakers what they'll use the lectern for. The ¼-inch back edges of lecterns are sure bets to have materials sliding to the floor at inappropriate times. Lights shine directly into the speaker's face, preventing him or her from seeing materials and creating a Dracula-like glow. A solution to the slipping notes problem is to use a note or manuscript holder, such as Script-Master.

Power and Environmental Capabilities. If you want that equipment to work, it probably needs electrical power—and the more gear there is, the more power you need. Say you put two slide projectors in the rear and an overhead projector in the front and throw in a video monitor on each side. Then you show up without making sure the power requirements can be met. Watch out.

Are the outlets in the room adequate and located where you need them? Do you need power extensions? Who provides them? How will you keep people from tripping over the wires and killing the power at a crucial moment? (*Tip:* Wide duct or cloth tape is most helpful for disaster prevention.)

And what kills meeting productivity faster than an overly warm room, after lunch, with slides and a totally dark room. Keep the room too cool rather than too hot. If you as the presenter do not have the capability to control the room temperature—often not the case—at least try to specify the desired temperature, with 68°F to 70°F a safe range. (Keeping it too cold will irritate audience members also.)

Another environmental factor that may be trouble if not considered properly (and tactfully) is smoking. In many facilities, smoking is banned in conference rooms. Since broad agreement now exists about the detrimental effects of tobacco smoke and it can severely interfere with meeting productivity, you may want to specify a smoke-free environment and provide smoking breaks. With smoking allowed, filters can alleviate some of the problem and irritation, or you can arrange the room with smokers on one side and nonsmokers on the other.

Seating and Tables. Adequate and comfortable seating for all attendees is essential. Each member of the audience should be able to see the key elements of the presentation—speaker, screen, displays—without strain.

The table and seating layout should consider the purpose of the presentation and the nature of interaction. Higher participation can be facilitated by arranging tables so that audience members can see one another as well as the speaker. In contrast, theater seating, common in most classrooms and auditoriums, defeats audience interaction. For small groups (ten to fifteen people), a large conference table with attendees seated on three sides works well. By opening up the center and making a U-shaped table arrangement, the speaker can operate with the group better. For larger audiences, groupings of five to six people at tables are still preferable to theater seating. (See Figure 9-4.)

Fitting seating to presentations means that flexibility of tables and chairs is needed. One large conference table gives no flexibility; it can't be changed. Smaller tables can be set up separately or joined together to make a single large conference table.

Theater seating is often required to accommodate large groups or is mandated. If the number of seats is considerably larger than the number of attendees and you want to have the audience up close, rope off rear sections so they are inaccessible. Be sure to check your visuals for visibility; what worked well in a small room may be barely visible in the larger and longer auditorium.

Projection Screens

A large audience was assembled to hear a high-level military briefing by an admiral and several senior officers. Each gave a twenty-minute presentation, profusely illustrated with excellent full-color slides. There was one problem: at least half the audience was unable to see the slides from where they were seated because the screen was too small for the room. Scratch another well-intended and expensive presentation.

Size. Make sure the screen is large enough. The standard guideline is to use a screen width at least one-sixth the distance from the screen to the last viewer (Figure 9-5).[1]

Location. Place the screen so all viewers can see it. Consider both side angle and elevation. Depending on the screen type, anyone seated more than 20 to 30 degrees to either side of the screen center won't be able to see the image. (For a beaded screen, the angle is about 20 degrees; for matte or lenticular, up to 30 degrees and perhaps more.[2]

Figure 9-4.   Seating and equipment arrangements ensure visibility and facilitate productive dialogue among participants.

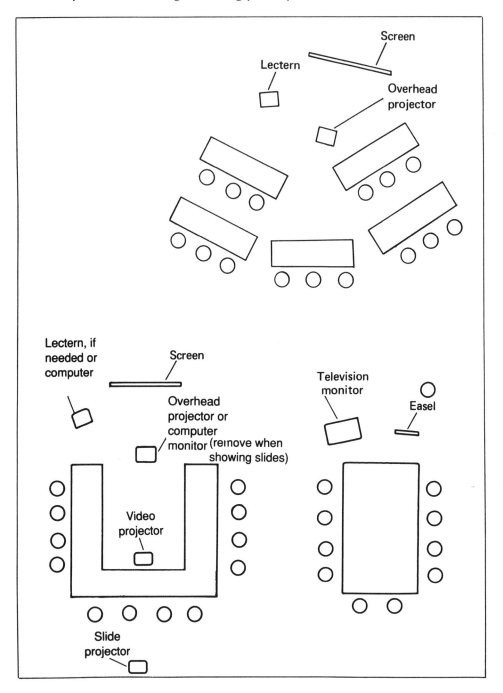

Figure 9-5. Make sure they can read what's on the screen. Audience-to-screen distance to the last viewer should not exceed six times the screen width.

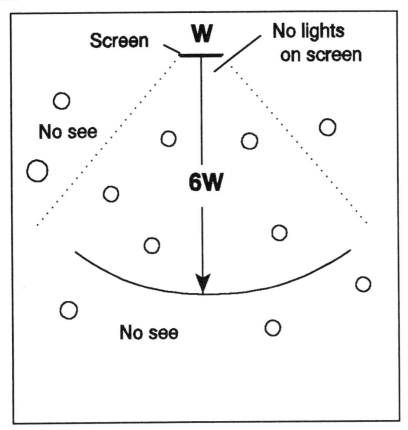

The screen image should be projected high enough that viewers won't be trying to look through the heads of those in front of them. The screen bottom should be at least 4 feet above the floor if everybody is seated at the same level. For many conference rooms, however, the room height may be only 8 or 10 feet; thus, the 4-foot minimum won't work for large screens. You may need to arrange seating to ensure clear lines of sight, or use a different room.

Columns, hanging fixtures, other lights, and inadequate darkening capability can all cause snags. Angled projection makes a distorted image. With overhead projectors, this "keystoning" is often severe. Slanting the screen forward from the top will help keep the top and bottom image widths constant.

Brightness. Type and age of screen, projector powers, lens type, room darkness, and extraneous lights affect brightness. The type of visual material is also a factor. Full-color slides require brighter projection or a darker room than black-and-white slides or viewgraphs. Highly reflective screens, such as beaded or lenticular, can be used in a dim light; a matte screen will require a darker room or brighter projection. In general, keep the room dim rather than completely dark. Make sure lights from the lectern, exit signs, or outside sources don't interfere with the image. Check that window coverings block the sun or nighttime lights outside.

Quality. Yellowed, damaged, or patched screens create problems for visuals by reducing image sharpness or adding distracting marks.

Sound Systems

Standing at the side of the conference room, the upcoming presenter listened as the current presenter spoke into the microphone to the large audience. Knowing he had several minutes before he was due up, he stepped out into the hallway and into the men's room for some final personal arrangements. He proceeded to comb his hair, straighten his tie, and, being a bit nervous, go to the bathroom. Unfortunately, he was wearing a wireless microphone, switched to "on." The current speaker's words on the public address system were joined by the unmistakable sounds of a gentleman relieving himself. The audience roared with delight, and as the new speaker took the podium, cheered mightily. In the movie *Naked Gun*, the same thing happened to the hapless but cool detective, Frank Drebin.

In fiction or reality, sound systems can be tricky. In large meetings, if anything is likely to go wrong, it is the sound system.

Presenters generally don't use a sound system, but on some occasions it is required—for example, delivering a program to a large conference, speaking to a civic group or at a management club dinner, conducting a walk-around tour through the factory, serving as a panelist or emcee. When that happens, it pays to be able to use sound systems properly.

For starters, work with the professional sound specialist, who is usually on the scene. If none is there, you're on your own. Here are some useful tips.

- If you're speaking away from your office, you will be taking your chances about the adequacy of the sound system. Either you or a trusted aide should visit the facility in advance and check out the system or take along your own equipment. Try out the system with a helper located where the audience will sit (all locations). Remember that the noise level will go up with a real audience as compared to an empty room.

- Have each presenter become comfortable with the microphone. A rule of thumb is to hold the mike at a 45-degree angle 6 to 10 inches from the mouth or vertically near the chin. Holding it too close can create a popping effect.

- Know where the system controls are, how they work, and that they will be operating or accessible when needed. Note the desired settings, so the system can be instantly activated without experimenting before a live audience.

- Fixed or hand-held mikes are common problems. Practice with presenters so they can tell when the mike is not adequately picking up their voices. Clip-on, lavaliere, or wireless mikes may work better; they allow the presenters to move their heads or bodies freely. Practice so each can put the mike on smoothly. A mike windscreen can help reduce wind noise if outside or popping from presenters who talk too closely into the mike.

- What about the painful squeal caused by sound system feedback? Often the cause is having the mike located in front of the speakers.

- Small, portable systems are good for multistop talks, such as plant tours. Make sure the quality is good and the batteries are fresh.

Incidentals

This category covers the whole raft of things that must often be taken care of to make the presentation go well. Because overlooked factors can have repercussions far greater than one would think possible, attention to detail is the byword. Some of the areas to consider are:

- Transportation of people, gadgetry, and written material.
- Human needs, such as refreshments and meals.
- Arrival/departure needs, such as directions, security clearances, greetings, and movement.
- Rank and ritual needs, such as protocol and special appearances.
- Operational details, such as who does what and when, name tags, ID badges, and message processing.

Incidentals need rigorous care. Putting it in writing is essential, as is a system that ensures that all details are adequately planned for and implemented.

PRESENTATION EQUIPMENT

Today's presenters have a vast array of tools at their disposal. Here we'll examine the audiovisual equipment options and their setup and use, proceeding from low to high tech.

Flipcharts and Posters

The first question to ask is: Will the easel hold the charts I intend to use? Some easels hold only a certain type of flipchart pad; if you have another type of pad or prepared charts, you're in trouble. More versatile is a clamp.

The second question is: Does the easel hang charts or prop them up? An experienced presenter, assured an easel would be provided, found himself in difficulty when the easel was fine for holding up cardboard posters but not for hanging his flimsy paper charts.

Overhead Projectors

In today's increasingly high-tech world, the lowly overhead projector is still by far the most commonly used presentation device. Nearly every conference room has one, and presenters can easily tote small portable ones with them.

They will continue to be around for a long time, especially as they are used in combination with computer-controlled liquid crystal display (LCD) units.

Being used *widely* does *not* ensure their being used *wisely*. Complaints abound because of poor visuals or improper use of the projection equipment. Here are some tips for effective use.

■ *Make sure the equipment is there, and know how to operate it.* I've seen dozens of presentations get off to poor starts because the projector wasn't there, it was the wrong projector, or the speaker didn't know how to operate it or even turn it on. That's a terrible first impression and a disservice to the audience, which may now have to wait several minutes while the presenter does what should have been done in advance. On-off switches and adjusters vary for different projectors, so be sure to check the actual one being used. Don't forget to check that the power cord is long enough to reach the outlet.

■ *Make sure the images are large enough.* Good visuals are hampered badly if they're hard to read. In advance, position the projector (and screen if you have that option) so the image fills the screen. Many projectors stationed in conference rooms don't match the rooms; finding that out at show time can be painful. If it's awkward to position the projector where it needs to be, change the projector. Get one with a wide-angle lens (e.g., 11- or 12½-inch focal length creates an image 51–20% wider than the 14-inch standard). Some projectors have a dual capability for either standard or wide angle by flipping a switch.

■ *Test it with the visual materials you intend to use.* Place the actual transparencies/viewgraphs, framers, or LCD device on the projector and check the image quality. If the image is fuzzy, the projector optics may require that transparencies lie flat on the glass surface, precluding use of framers or LCD devices.

■ *Choose a projector with a built-in spare bulb.* This is a high confidence builder, if you've remembered to check both main and backup bulbs and know how to change them. If the projector doesn't have a built-in bulb, keep the correct spare handy and know how to insert it.

■ *Place the projector on a waist-high table.* A chest-high table interferes with the audience members' ability to see the screen.

■ *Make sure the table has space for your viewgraphs*—two stacks for upcoming and past, with both on the same side. This is so obvious yet frequently overlooked.

■ *Arrange for a chart flipper if beneficial.* Some presenters operate their own visuals. In some instances, a better solution is to work with an associate who operates the projector and gets visuals on and off. Examples are for lengthy or particularly important presentations, such as proposal orals. The operator sits unobtrusively next to the projector, and the speaker stands on the opposite side of the projector, not behind the operator.

■ *Take extra care with multiple projectors.* It's not unusual for presentations to use two or three projectors. Used well, they can help. Used poorly, they provide twice as much opportunity to confuse the audience. Here are some tips for wise use, using two overhead projectors as an example:

—Make sure the projectors are compatible with the layout. If you mix a wide angle with a standard lens, you need different projector-screen distances, which may not be feasible.

—Consider screen sizes relative to image readability by the audience. If you're putting two images on one screen, does that cut image size in half?

—If images are close together, don't let them overlap.

—Where will you place transparencies, and who will operate them? Where will the speaker be positioned—seated or standing? How will pointing to screen items be done?

35mm Slide Projectors

With more widespread use of computer graphics, 35mm slides have become more common as a projection medium. Here are some considerations for effective use.

■ *When requesting equipment, be explicit about your needs.* You don't want to show up with a Kodak Carousel tray full of slides and be greeted with a noncompatible projector or condition. *This is especially a problem outside the United States.* Specify projector type, manufacturer, and model. The automatic focus option is handy and will help you focus on your message and audience rather than having to focus the image constantly.

■ *Ensure that you have the right lens.* Many people overlook this consideration and end up with mediocre results. The typical culprit is a fixed lens that is not suited to the room conditions and leads to tiny screen images or having to move the projector way to the rear of the room. For flexibility, use a zoom lens, which adjusts the image to fit the screen without moving the projector.

■ *Determine whether the bulb is strong enough.* If you can't see much on the screen, maybe the bulb is too weak for the room conditions or the images you're trying to project. First try to make the room darker, especially around the screen. Then consider a higher-powered lens, such as a xenon.

■ *Make sure that the tray or slide holder compatible with the projector and slides.* If you are using a Kodak Carousel type, use only the 80-capacity tray (the 140 size is more prone to jamming).

■ *Put the slides in properly.* Who hasn't seen an upside-down slide, or several of them? This is so common that it's almost expected—and it's always embarrassing to the presenter. For front-screen projection, hold the slide so you can read it. Turn it top to bottom, and place it in the tray. Once you know a position is correct, mark or number it in order in the upper right corner (as in the tray). For rear-screen projection, follow the same procedure but reverse front to back.

■ *Lock the slides into the tray.* Failing to do this is extending an invitation to disaster.

■ *Know how to control the projector, and from where.* Most projectors come with a control device and a wire that is never long enough. Two solutions are to use a wire extension cord for the controller or a wireless remote (an excellent investment). With either one, get focusing control plus forward/reverse. Another handy option is a projector on-off control.

■ *Get a workable projector table.* The projector has to sit on something, and mostly it's a jury-rig (a projector box, a TV set in the back of the room, a carton). State your needs clearly. Often the projector can sit on the conference table. Other situations dictate a high table at the rear of the room for projection over the heads of the audience. One more trap is that the built-in height adjusters never have enough range, so it's wise to carry along a 1-inch-high portable shim.

■ *Make sure the images appear properly on the screen.* Often a slide image is crooked or tiny or overlaps onto the wall behind. Check it out. If you're using a mix of horizontal and vertical slides (not advised), be sure to check both. If you fill the screen to optimum size with a horizontal, the vertical will overlap.

■ *Know in advance if you'll need a power extension cord.* As standard practice, I always carry an extension cord with my personal projector.

Movie Projectors

These come in all types and sizes, and with lots of problems.

If you have a film to show, specify precisely the type of projector needed. Is it 16mm, 8mm, or Super 8? Is it reel-to-reel or cartridge?

Since every projector manufacturer seems to have its own system, know all the mechanics in advance, including how to thread the film, how to turn the projector on and off, and where the volume control is. And what do you do when the film starts jumping?

Size and location of screen and location of projector must be carefully planned to ensure visibility. This is so fundamental that it is often forgotten. Some projectors carry their own built-in screens. They are extremely flexible, but don't try to show an audience of thirty people a 12- by 12-inch image.

What about darkening? Will people be able to see the image? At the time of day you plan to show the film?

Never assume the film will work. Wherever possible, test it out to ensure that it is not worn out and will indeed operate.

Don't forget the take-up reel.

Video Systems

Video is used for a variety of presentation purposes: playback only of prerecorded segments or tapes; interactive live video of remote events; teleconferences; record and play during sessions; computer-controlled presentations using video monitors or projectors for images. Video can be a powerful part of the presentation, but it offers plenty of traps for the unwary. Because video typically involves several pieces of equipment, special care in planning, specifications, setup, and operation is especially important.

Video Record and Play Gear. Specify equipment needs in detail. Video system X may differ from Video system Y (e.g., a ½-inch VHS cassette won't work with

Beta or ¾-inch systems). If the system has several components, it needs connecting cables. Are they all there?

Recording steps up possible complications. All-in-one camcorders have reduced much of the nettlesome complexity of older systems, but they need to be mastered nevertheless. Forgetting to mention to the equipment setup person that you'll be recording may result in a play-only system being delivered, without camera. Zoom lenses and low-light capability cut error possibilities, but it's wise to make an on-site inspection of room conditions, lighting, and distances. Special lighting may be required to get the desired quality. Don't forget about audio and a tripod for the camera. I'm often amazed at how many organizations rest $2,000 cameras on shaky, rusty tripods instead of investing $100 in a decent one.

For a serious video recording, bring in the experts. Preparing a video summary of a major proposal, for example, is too important for amateurs. Experts can ensure proper lighting, backgrounds, and clothing; eliminate distractions; and make good use of teleprompters.

Who is going to operate the equipment? That needs to be arranged, and the operator needs to be instructed and clued.

Above all, do a test run with the equipment in the actual conditions you'll be using, and *test the entire system*. Few things are more embarrassing and damaging to a meeting purpose than to find out the video you've been recording is no good or the audio is absent. (I know. In spite of constant reminders and checking, it has happened to me—several times.) Check it yourself, even if you've been assured the video is all set.

Video Monitors. The most common problem is having a monitor that is too small, yet many people persist in using one 19-inch video monitor for a large meeting of thirty to forty people. Even several monitors may not be enough. I watched a presentation die in a large auditorium with 500 people; the dozen video monitors placed around the room were not enough.

Here are some guidelines from General Telephone Company of California, one of the nation's largest in-house corporate video producers.[3]

Monitor Size	Number of people
19 inches	5–6
25 inches	12–18 (up to 30 if dark, quiet room)
4–6 feet	50–75 (check for side visibility)

Video Projectors. These come in a variety of types, from large floor-hogging three-gun systems to small table-top LCD devices projecting onto the screen, and from super-sharp color quality to dim, hard-to see images. Here are some specific cautions:

- Be specific about the type of gear you want.
- Verify that the unit is in correct working order. Older, lightly used projectors are cantankerous and may need adjustment for proper colors.

■ Check out lines of sight and lighting needed for visibility. Some models have a narrow visibility angle of coverage. You may need to block off seating where the image quality is poor.

Video Primer for Executives. As a member of the proposed team, you will be part of a video summary of the proposal, or you will appear live on a local video interview program. Here are some general aids to help you get ready for a video appearance:

■ *Early on, get help from the producer/video experts.* You need to know about schedules, setting, specific agenda and segment times, visuals, procedure, and wardrobe for starters.

■ *Develop content.* The time allocated is an overriding factor. Figure out your central message. Identify the core two or three main points that are essential and workable. Pick the best support material (examples, visuals, demonstrations). Because this is a dynamic, visual medium, think hard about how to include visuals, objects, pictures, demonstrations, and action.

■ *Meet early and often with helpers* to get the content ready: writer, graphics, director. If using visuals, make sure what you have will work. Set strong clues so helpers can match each visual to your spoken words.

■ *Check over the setting.* What are the rules? Where do you look? Where must you stand or sit?

■ *Rehearse.* Go over all facets, with actual wardrobe. Practice the delivery mode, especially if you will be required to speak directly to the camera. (It's not so easy.) If you will be using a script or teleprompter, mark it to help you get the right punch and natural flavor (often a major deficiency). Check how you come across. Modify the script as needed, and try it a few more times.

■ *Carefully consider wardrobe and appearance.* Your basic wardrobe color depends on the background color; don't wear brown if the set is brown, for example, or you'll get lost. Pastel colors are recommended over white, but white shirts are okay if worn under a dark jacket. Avoid blue button-down shirts—the white buttons become the main attraction. Go for simplicity over flash, and eschew gaudy patterns or polka-dot ties (they seem to wriggle on TV). Avoid dangling, noisy jewelry. (A well-known political expert participated in a lengthy discussion on national TV. Her dangling earrings kept clinking into the mike as well as flashing on the screen.)

■ *Get there early.* Be totally cooperative with the technical team. If they say to use makeup, do. Get a sound check. Recheck rules for talking, looking, and time signals. Put gadgetry in place, and have a glass of water ready for dry throat.

■ *Deliver.* Remember, close-up mode amplifies certain things:

—If the presentation will be a discussion, talk with the moderator, not the camera.
—If speaking directly into the camera, such as for a presentation segment,

practice beforehand. Typical problems are shifty eye contact, obviously looking at notes or teleprompter, and not looking at the camera/viewing audience.

—If someone else is talking, give the person your attention because the camera may be on you.

—If you are using visuals, make sure your clues are strong and clear. If a monitor is convenient and you're skilled, check it to ensure the right visual is displayed.

—Stay within the specified area.

—Watch your posture and mannerisms. Slouching, waving arms flamboyantly, gesturing toward camera, scratching your nose—all get amplified, not in your favor.

Videoconferencing. Videoconferencing links two or more locations by video and provides the capability of having live presentations and discussions between people who may be thousands of miles apart. This can greatly reduce travel time, expense, and aggravation. As companies and agencies increasingly use videoconferencing, more people have found themselves giving presentations under vastly different conditions from the usual face-to-face conference room situation.

If you are called upon to participate in a videoconference, don't assume it is business as usual. Lack of awareness and preparation have humbled many seasoned presenters. *The first rule is to seek out the experts and follow their advice.* Someone in your organization or a service contractor has the responsibility and experience with the specific facility and conditions you'll be adhering to.

Videoconferencing setups vary widely, but a typical corporate facility is shown in Figure 9-6. Participants are likely to be seated, facing a camera (either obvious or hidden), and a video screen showing the people on the other end. A separate camera probably will be focused on visual aids. A facilitator, program manager, or moderator is likely to be in charge.

Review the suggestions noted for appearing on television, and find out anything more specific to the setup and procedure. Be aware of these additional key elements:

■ Time is definitely money. Agreed-upon objectives, an agenda with timed targets for each segment, and speaker preparation are more important in videoconferences than in regular presentations. All participants need to cooperate by sticking with the agenda so that all topics get suitable attention and people interested in upcoming topics don't get fidgety or short-changed.

■ Visual aids, props, or hardware are especially valuable but need to be checked for suitability and possibly adapted to meet video's stringent requirements. Visuals passable in conference rooms may be inadequate for videoconferences. Some specific recommendations:

—Only horizontal format visuals.

—Easily readable type (review standards for visuals in previous section).

Figure 9-6. Videoconferencing is an increasingly common presentation mode.

Source: Courtesy of United Technologies Sikorsky Aircraft.

—Simple visual, graphic treatments rather than complex, wordy paragraphs and tables. (If the facility has a zoom lens, marginal material can be blown up, but this complicates the process.)
—Important content within the video safe area.
—No glossy finish photos.

■ Timing is definitely trickier than for standard presentations. Since visuals may not be under your control, you will have to give strong clues to the operator so that your words match the visual on the screen.

Computer-Based Presentations. With these presentations, the physical visual aid is gone. Instead, visuals are linked from the computer directly to a monitor or projectors, generally video or LCD devices atop overhead projectors. (Figure 9-7 illustrates one such concept.) Computers may be in the actual presentation room as permanent setups or brought in by speakers with laptop computers;

Figure 9-7. This setup enables projection of computer monitor images onto the large screen via overhead projector and LCD projection level.

located elsewhere in the building and wired into the presentation room; or located hundreds of miles away and linked in via telecommunication systems. Here are some tips for use:

- With LCD projection pads, *make sure you have the right overhead projector,* the transmissive, light-from-below type. With reflective mirror systems, commonly used in small portable projectors, the image will be blurry.

- Determine image readability. See the previous guidelines for video monitors and audience sizes. With video or LCD projectors, test for adequate image sharpness and visibility from likely audience locations.

- Make sure computers or other equipment are positioned for easy access while not blocking audience line of sight to screen.

- Audience contact often suffers badly when presenters are hidden behind computer equipment. A better choice is to use a remote device to operate the computer, call up programs, and advance graphic images. Hand-held devices include controllers built into a pointer (Figure 9-8), a small hand-held mouse clicker, or a portable hand-held keyboard.

Figure 9-8.   Using a wireless control unit, such as this Cyclops™ interactive point and click system, lets the presenter operate away from the computer.

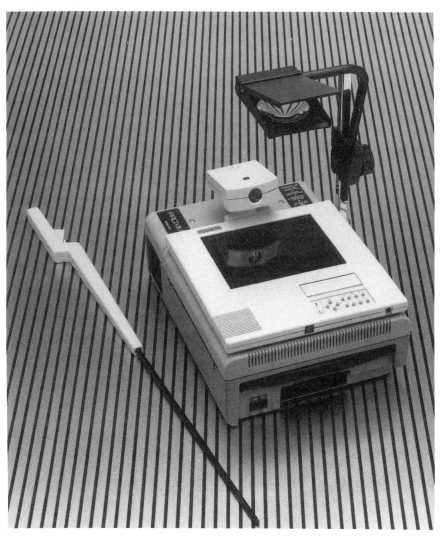

Source: Courtesy of Proxima Corporation.

- Since various pieces of equipment and software are involved, make a complete systems run-through.

- Exercise all systems involved in remotely located computers. Arrange for dedicated telecommunication hookups at necessary times.

Reducing the Unknowns—An Arrangements Checklist

The best way to ward off the insidious sneak attacks of Murphy's Law is by a rigorous checklist of all arrangements requirements, such as those shown in Figure 9-9. (For an even more comprehensive treatment, get the *Meetings and Conventions Magazine* All-Purpose Checklist.) If only a few areas are regularly of concern, use a simpler list. Whatever the form, a thorough, trust-no-one system is essential. Remember—Murphy is waiting.

USING AUDIOVISUAL EQUIPMENT AND VISUAL AIDS

How well visuals are used can have a major influence on how effective they truly are. Poor use of good aids can make a very bad presentation. The major points are summarized in Figure 9-10.

Use Aids to Complement, Not Compete with, the Message

Visuals are powerful attention getters; they can draw us to them as a light draws a moth. They also offer ample opportunities for viewers to go off on their own and look where they will rather than at what the presenter intends. The task for a presenter is to use equipment and display visuals in such a way as to keep the audience's attention. Here are some ways to help make that happen.

- *Make sure spoken words and visuals match.* Often the speaker's words don't readily relate to the visual displayed. The result is internal disorientation, quickly leading to a switch in channels in the brains of the listeners.

- *Introduce a chart before showing it. This is one of the most effective techniques in the use of visual aids.* It provides an opportunity to recapture attention with each visual, because listeners respond to words that suggest change is about to occur. This is the way a visual might be introduced: "The data just shown suggest that a significant benefit can result from a new marketing approach. We've looked at several of these, and now I'd like to show you the one we regard as most promising." At that time, and not before, show the visual. With many speakers, the time between charts is dead time, as the speaker changes charts, then looks up at the screen to verify that it really is there—surprise, it is—and then starts to address the chart, which audience members have thoroughly examined.

- *Scope a chart before diving into the details.* Too often the speaker is busily explaining the significance of point A on a graph while the listeners are still trying to discover what the x and y axes are. Astute presenters first provide perspective for the listeners by explaining such things as graph axes or column/

Figure 9-9.   Pay attention to detail with a staging checklist.

GENERAL INFORMATION

Presentation _____
Event _____ Date _____ Time _____
Location _____
Address _____
Directions _____
Travel plans/times _____
Parking _____
Entrance _____ Contact _____ Phone _____
Building _____ Floor _____ Room_____

PRESENTATION BASICS

Presenter(s) _____
Length _____ Q&A type/length _____
Audience size _____ Makeup _____

CONFERENCE ROOM (Provide diagram if needed)

Seating/table layout _____
Specific seating _____
Other audience amenities _____
Room lighting/darkening _____
Equipment placements _____
Environment _____
Dimensions: screen width _____ Distance to audience last seat _____

EQUIPMENT

Projector(s) _____
Computer _____ Monitor _____
Electronic projection _____
Controls wired _____ Wireless _____
Video _____ Recording? _____
16mm movie _____ Audio _____
Tapes/films pre-recorded _____ For on-site use _____
Flipchart/posters _____ Easels _____
Electronic chalkboard _____
Displays, models, demonstrations _____
Sound systems _____ Controls _____
Screens/monitors _____
Equipment stands _____
Power requirements _____ Extensions _____
Paper copies/brochures _____

PROVISIONS, INCIDENTALS

Breaks/lunch times _____
Refreshments _____
Need audience materials ready _____
Support personnel _____
Services needed _____
Escort/tours/security _____
Shipments _____
Anything else

Figure 9-10. Apply these tips for using audiovisual equipment and aids.

- Test all equipment and aids in advance.
- Have equipment in place and know how to operate it and who will do it.
- Once equipment is ready, keep your eye on it.
- If using viewgraphs, have them in frames for easier handling and correct placement.
- Turn equipment on only when you are ready to use it.
- Stand so you do not block the audience from seeing your visuals.
- Talk to the audience, not the screen.
- Use gadgetry in an efficient and nondistracting manner.
- Keep the visuals moving. Show only enough material at a time to keep audience attention where you want it.
- Introduce a chart before showing it. Then orient listeners before delving into details.
- Make sure the spoken message tracks the visual message.
- Keep attention focused by pointing at the specific items being discussed.
- Paraphrase word charts; don't read them verbatim, if you want to escape alive.
- Discuss everything on a chart unless time runs short.
- If you've finished with a visual, get it off or move away from it.
- Pass around real objects or models when the audience will not be unduly distracted from listening to you.

row headings for tables. Then, having brought all listeners up to the same level of awareness, they go on to the details.

■ *Use progressive disclosure to develop complex charts.* This technique, also called revelation, was discussed when we looked at the creation of visual aids. Rather than show a figure with twenty-five labels and lose the audience immediately, show the figure with only a half-dozen labels. Explain those. Then introduce the next set of labels, and continue bit by bit until the complete chart is presented.

With slides or computer-driven visuals, this is a simple process. With viewgraphs, overlays or buildups can be effective if done smoothly and without blocking line of sight.

Some speakers use a blocking sheet to cover a chart and then to uncover a line at a time. Be judicious in your use of this technique, as it often gets this response: "I feel as if I'm being given the idiot treatment."

■ *Give an overview of all main points on a chart; then go back and cover each in detail.* Suppose you show a visual with three lines:

—Initial cost is 20 percent less.
—Maintenance cost is competitive.
—Total life-cycle cost savings total 25 percent.

One approach is to discuss the first item, then the second, and then the third. The overview approach seems to condition the listeners better and could sound like this: "The three benefits our program offers are lower initial cost, competitive maintenance costs, and significant savings in life-cycle costs. Let's first look at the initial cost differences."

■ *Address all elements of a chart.* In the previous example, failing to address the third point would raise questions in the minds of the listeners. The rule is: If you show it, talk about it.

■ *Paraphrase rather than read lines verbatim.* Perhaps the most detested practice in the use of visuals is when the presenter reads aloud every word of a busy chart. This is palatable if the chart contains only a few key words but is regarded as insulting if the chart is composed of ten lengthy sentences. In the eyes of the viewer, the chart itself is a misdemeanor offense in the first place; reading it verbatim elevates the crime to the felony level.

■ *Use a pointer to keep listeners oriented to the specific item being discussed.* When faced with a complex visual, viewers can easily lose track of what is being discussed, especially if the spoken words don't match the written ones. While you are discussing one subject, the audience thinks you're discussing another, not a desirable situation. Use the pointer sparingly.

■ *Talk to the audience, not the screen or equipment.* This is one of the most important and commonly violated points. Once a slide comes onto the screen, that is the last audience members may see of the presenter's face. This is a big mistake. Certainly you will need to look at the screen as you point to specific items or lead the audience through a complex diagram or flowchart. But remember to face the audience while you are talking about the information (see Figure 9-11). Here's a useful formula:

- *Direct* the audience to a specific item on the screen
- *Connect* with your listeners by looking at them
- *Project* your spoken comments to them

Use Aids Professionally

Aids and equipment have made a marvelous contribution to communication. However, what can contribute can also clobber. Here are some ways to keep aids and equipment working *for* you.

■ *Make sure all gadgetry, aids, and other supporting material are ready.* This means in place, checked out, and focused. Test equipment placement from all parts of the room to ensure that all audience members will be able to see visuals easily. Learn from my own painful experience. For our general manager's quarterly report to supervisors, I was assigned to handle the viewgraphs. I had arrived early to get everything ready, checked the projector bulbs, and waited for the tardy general manager and his viewgraphs. The 400 supervisors were already in place when he walked in, handed me his visuals, and started his talk. When it came time for the first viewgraph, I placed it on the machine. It was both cockeyed and out of focus, and my best efforts helped little as it was an old machine. Already chortling was echoing through the hall as many knew I was such a firm believer of checking things out. Finally it got resolved, and I resolved

Figure 9-11. Talk to people, not the screen. Direct, connect, and project.

to check projectors and their visuals totally. (*Tip*: If you don't have a viewgraph in hand, place a pencil on the projector and focus on that.)

■ *Mark visuals for efficient and correct handling and placement.* Always lock slides into trays (eighty capacity). For discussion-type meetings, have a list of slides so they can be located as needed. Number viewgraphs in order on individual frames, on opaque stripes, which is why I prefer this transparency style, or in one corner if using a framer that will cover them up. (You can also write transitional notes there.) During setup for a crucial customer competitive presentation with a half-dozen speakers, the person in charge of the viewgraphs dropped them, and they scattered on the floor. Fortunately, he'd numbered each chart during final rehearsal and was able to get them back in order quickly.

■ *Make sure visuals are properly aligned.* A major irritant is the viewgraph that isn't on straight, or that moves around. An effective and simple solution is to use an InstaFrame, a movable, reusable framer that sits on top of an overhead projector. Viewgraphs are placed in the framer, which provides correct, stable alignment and a border around the copy. It also smooths transitions between viewgraphs and automatically lines up overlays (Figure 9-12).

■ *Display images and activate equipment only when ready to use them.* Often the first act of presenters, before they even say anything, is to turn on the projector. Then for the next five minutes, listeners look at a lighted screen, with no image

Figure 9-12.   With an overhead projector, visuals are easily aligned, framed, and overlaid with a portable Instaframe™.

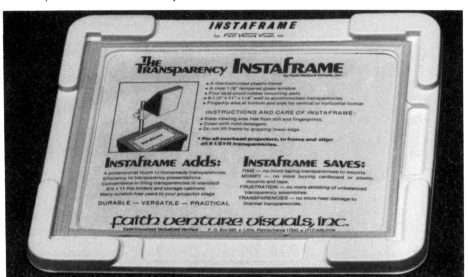

Source: Courtesy of Faith Venture Visuals, Inc., Lititz, Pa.

on it. Proper timing of events helps hold attention and adds flair to the proceedings.

—*Slide projectors.* Several options are available: (1) use the remote on-off capability; (2) coordinate on-offs with a helper; or (3) start with an opaque slide and turn the projector on before you start to speak, thus keeping a dark screen until you advance to the first visual (not needed with newer design projectors).

—*Overhead projector.* Place the first viewgraph on the projector, and focus it. Then turn off the projector until you are ready for the first visual.

—*Chalkboard.* Start with a clean board or a blank chart or simple title.

Coordinate projectors and room lighting/dimming. Make sure people never sit in a completely dark room. To start, projector on, lights off; to finish, lights on, then projector off.

■ *Don't make people try to see through you.* Whatever the medium, the audience should be able to see the images, charts, or models. I have already noted the importance of proper placement of equipment. Using the equipment, another potential vision impediment must be considered—the presenter.

By far the most common problem occurs with overhead projectors. Some manufacturers and salespeople advise speakers to stand next to the machine as they make their presentations. They point out the advantages of being able to write on the transparencies, standing close to and facing the audience, and handling the visuals. These are all true if the audience can see the screen while the presenter stands there. This is rarely the case. What is the solution, assuming the screen can't be moved?

—Place visuals, step away, and use a pointer. Thus, you can talk directly to the audience or turn slightly and point at items on the screen.

—Place a pointer directly onto the transparency to highlight specific items. Move to the side so as not to block the line of sight to the screen.

—Use a helper to operate the visuals while you stand away from the projector and point to items on the screen. To work smoothly, both people should practice so the chart flipper can pick up verbal cues from the presenter. Strong transition statements, such as "We've looked at the technical considerations of our proposal; let's now look at the marketing aspect" are preferable to "Next slide please" or raps to the side of the head.

■ *Don't create your own shadows.* A favorite parlor game for kids looking at home movies is to make shapes from hand shadows. The projected alligators and hound dogs are real eye-catchers. So are the shadows from the waving hands over a projector or from an entire body that has drifted in front of the projector. (Figure 9-13 shows two of the most common problems with projectors.)

■ *Handle viewgraphs or other aids smoothly and efficiently.* Getting viewgraphs on and off is not a simple task for many presenters. Smooth handling of mechanics means the presenter can use the time between visuals effectively to summarize the last visual and make the transition to the next one. Four tips:

1. Use a portable framer, which lines up viewgraphs and provides a neat border.
2. Insert viewgraphs in individual frames and number them.
3. Carefully tape or mark the position on the projector to place viewgraphs so they all line up. (Do not put tape on the optical glass.)
4. Eliminate papers between visuals; if they stick together, lightly wipe them with an antistatic cloth.

■ *Remove visuals when they have served their purpose.* There is something fascinating about a visual aid; as long as it is there, it compels us to keep coming back to it, even if the speaker has moved onto another subject. If you discuss material beyond the visual already on the screen, remove the distraction of that visual. Otherwise, you'll lose the competition for attention. Erase the board, turn to a blank flipchart, advance to a blank slide, or turn off the overhead projector or television monitor.

■ *Correct a problem immediately without calling further attention to it.* Ignoring an upside-down viewgraph, a badly focused projector, or improper lighting prolongs the poor conditions. Apologizing, joking, or insulting the equipment or operators adds to the negative impressions possibly already created. What *is* of interest to the audience is getting on with it and watching how the presenter performs under adversity.

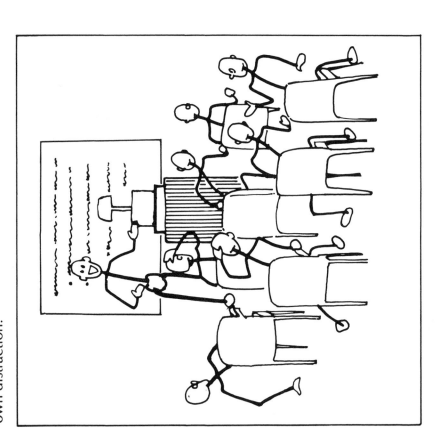

Figure 9-13. Don't block the audience's view of the screen or create your own distraction.

- *Use gadgetry only as intended, not to juggle, lead the band, or toy with.* It's among the most common sights to see—a presenter playing with gadgetry. It is absolutely riveting to watch a speaker juggle the chalk or wave the pointer in the air. How much of the message do you suppose is being heard while the sideshow is going on? (See Figure 9-14.)

- *Look at the screen only when you want the audience to do the same.* If you look at the screen, we will presume you want us to do that too. If you frequently look at the screen as a nervous mannerism, you create your own distraction.

- *Pass objects around the audience only after you have completed your presentation.* This common occurrence always creates a whole series of little distractions as objects are inspected, passed along, or dropped. Show it, discuss it, and invite them to examine it when you don't mind losing their attention.

TEST, EVALUATE, AND POLISH

The final phase of staging is to test the product, identify the weak spots, and fix them before taking the presentation to the actual audience. Many people

Figure 9-14. Use a pointer to direct attention to information on visuals, not to skewer audience members.

firmly agree with the wisdom of doing this, yet in practice this step often gets skipped. Making sure some form of testing happens can do much to head off trouble, polish delivery and operations, and greatly enhance comfort.

The test phase may be as simple as one speaker going to an empty conference room and talking the presentation through or, for major presentations, a team of speakers going through a series of dry runs before a team of reviewers and a video camera.

As in most other parts of presentation development, how the test phase is done makes a difference in how effective it is. Follow the procedures noted here for sharpening presentations and presenters.

Some experienced people state firmly they don't need to practice, get coaching, or attend training seminars, so it's worth noting that the top tennis players, opera singers, and professional speakers regularly get coaching, practice, and feedback. In preparing for a major presentation for a competitive contract, I was coaching the team of four. When I discussed the need for dry runs, the main presenter (the assigned program director for the contract) resisted: "I don't believe in rehearsals. You can get too programmed." We did the dry run, anyway, and it was obvious the one presenter most in need of coaching was that person. Vigorous feedback and seeing himself on video convinced him of that need. With a new attitude, he made the needed changes and did an excellent job for the actual presentation. Later he stated that forcing him to do the dry runs was valuable and would be standard practice henceforth.

Others have observed, "There's always a dry run." My question is, Do you want to have that occur before your real audience or in the privacy of your own conference room and in front of a couple of friendly colleagues? Put practice high on your list. Otherwise you may find yourself saying as I've heard many others say, "Why didn't I do a dry run?"

A key to improvement is having helpful colleagues play the roles of audience simulator, feedback provider, and presentations coach. An old adage says, "Practice makes perfect." When it comes to presentations, this is only partly true. If you're doing something wrong and don't realize it, you can practice all day and improve some parts of the presentation and have no effect on others. This is why having knowledgeable people give feedback is so important, if they do it in the proper way.

What a Dry Run Can Do for You

A dry run serves several important functions:

■ It prevents embarrassment, the kind that comes from finding out during the presentation that the print on the visual aid is so small it can't be read beyond the first row or that several misspelled words weren't caught earlier.

■ It checks scope, balance, and structure. Presenters are notorious for miscalculating the amount of material they think they can cover in the allotted time. The presenter who shows up for a fifteen-minute presentation with seventy-five viewgraphs, which would require two hours to present, is not unusual.

■ It surfaces fundamental miscalculations. Often the presenter is so close to the topic, he or she overlooks basic points—such as that the vice-president doesn't care about all the technical details the presenter plans to cover. The dry run can refocus a presenter back on the true purpose and the method for achieving it. Higher management has an intense dislike for hearing messages put forth to customers that are at variance with the company strategy and theme song. The dry run gives the presenter the latest information so it can be incorporated.

■ It uncovers holes in the material. A presenter may discover while speaking that what he or she thought was valid or complete isn't. A detached observer can often spot these holes more quickly than the presenter, who may be too close to the issue.

■ It prepares for the unknown. Since most presentations are interactive, with listeners commenting and asking questions, the presenter needs to be ready for more than what he or she is planning to cover. The unthought-of question can sabotage an otherwise sound presentation. A good dry run can go far toward surfacing questions that are likely to come up.

■ It makes a smoother, more professional-appearing presentation.

Planning the Test Phase

Planning for a simple dry run may take little effort. For major presentations, careful planning is key to a productive test phase. Here are some suggestions, summarized in Figure 9-15.

■ *Test early and often.* Much helpful reaction can be given at several key steps of development. The further along in the presentation, the more difficult and

Figure 9-15. Testing and evaluation can greatly improve presentations if done correctly.

- Plan to test at several steps during the development process, particularly after completion of storyboards, rough visuals, and final visuals.
- Definitely conduct one or more dry runs, simulating the setting and audience as closely as possible.
- Conduct dry runs far enough in advance that recommended changes can be implemented.
- Prepare carefully for dry runs so that time is efficiently used and productive results are obtained.
- Test the presenter, the spoken words, and supporting operations, not just the visual aids.
- Evaluate to improve the presentation, not to cut down the speaker.
- All participants have a role in maintaining a positive environment during dry runs.
- Use video recording for self-evaluation.
- Speakers should consider all comments and incorporate changes where feasible and desirable.

expensive changes become. Making changes at the storyboard or rough-visual-aid level is simple and cheap compared to waiting until all material has been gathered and finished visuals have been prepared, only to discover the presentation is off base and needs major work.

■ *Determine the specific purpose of each part of the test phase.* For a major presentation, several test formats may be in order. The intent of each may be different, which may mean different participants or procedures. If the purpose is to review visual aids for content, the best procedure may be to tape all the visuals on the wall or spread them on a table and have evaluators peruse them. To test the timing, the speaker's verbal and nonverbal performance, and the mechanical aspects, a full-blown dry run is in order. To surface potential questions, the evaluators will be active participants rather than passive listeners.

■ *Schedule it at the start.* Often the test phase is done as an afterthought or skipped entirely. Planning and scheduling the test program enables it to make a key contribution to presentation development.

■ *Conduct dry runs well enough in advance that needed revisions can be accomplished.* If the dry run is not held until the day before the presentation, it is difficult to incorporate the suggestions of the evaluators.

■ *Simulate the setting and the facilities.* Projector A is not the same as projector B. Conference room A is not the same as conference room B. Determine the necessary facts about the specific equipment and facilities that will be used. If possible, conduct the dry runs with the exact equipment in the actual facility. If that is not possible, simulate the conditions fully. One major presentation involved extensive last-minute rework because the preliminary dry run failed to simulate the exact screen size and audience location. When these were later simulated, it was obvious that most of the visuals had to be redone.

■ *Simulate the audience.* Often people in the presenter's organization have backgrounds like those of key people in the real audience. A marketing manager who is a former Air Force colonel may be a good person to have as an evaluator for a military presentation. Fellow professionals can listen much like the technical experts in the audience.

■ *Determine other participants.* Key people may include a moderator to conduct the evaluation phase; a recorder to note comments, suggestions, and agreed-upon changes; and support people such as graphics designers, video equipment operators, and presentation advisers.

■ *Provide background and schedule to all participants.* It helps reviewers if they have some advance knowledge of what the presentation is all about.

■ *Arrange for dry-run support gear.* This may include video or audio recording and playback equipment, copies of visual aids (with numbers on each page), scratch pads, pencils, a chalkboard or easel, evaluation forms, timing signs, and a stop watch.

Conducting a Productive Dry Run

Set the Stage. A few orientation tasks will aid the evaluators and the session.

- *Agree on the ground rules.* Let all participants know what procedure is to be followed, when comments are to be made, and whether to ask questions.
- *Provide background.* Briefly summarize the purpose of the presentation, the audience, the locale, and any other factors that may help the audience do a better job of evaluating.
- *Distribute copies of the visual aids if you want evaluators to mark comments on the visuals.*
- *Mark the start time if the dry run is to be timed.*

Make the Presentation. My preference is to have the presenter give the presentation exactly as it would be given, from start to finish, without interruption. Much time is typically wasted during dry runs with continual interruptions, many of which are about material that is yet to come. Often presenters show the visuals and merely state, "Here, I intend to say . . ." This process exercises only the visuals, not the speaker. If the purpose of the dry run is to surface potential questions and give the speaker an opportunity to perform under fire, then questions during the talk are essential.

During the presentation, the reviewers' task is to listen, observe, and react as they think the real audience would. If they have copies of the visuals, they can mark directly on those.

Conduct the Evaluation. The key to success is maintaining a positive environment, not always easy when one's best efforts are being dissected. Presenters and evaluators both must work to keep the environment productive. Use of a moderator to conduct this part of the dry run may be helpful.

- Give an overview evaluation as well as an evaluation of specific parts. In a detailed evaluation, the speaker may conclude that the whole presentation is a disaster and needs to be redone completely. An overview helps keep the proper perspective.
- Comment on strengths as well as deficiencies. The expression "throwing the baby out with the bathwater" is appropriate. If the emphasis is almost exclusively on the negative side, the presenter may overcorrect and discard useful material or practices.
- Offer specific observations, not vague generalities. This greatly facilitates communication between the parties. "The organization needs work" is not particularly useful to the presenter. "I was confused by your first two points. I think there is some duplication there," gives the presenter something specific to look at.
- Offer alternatives wherever possible. One of the strengths of evaluators is that they offer a different perspective from the speaker's. It is much more helpful to a speaker to see a quick sketch of an alternative to the concept presented than just to hear, "I thought chart four was too busy." This places a greater burden on evaluators, but it is a justifiable one.
- Focus on the major, but don't ignore the "minor." In the process of detailed analysis, it is easy to spend a disproportionate amount of time on

relatively minor flaws. The impact on the presentation of the apparent short-comings must be kept in mind. If all the attention is given to improving the speaker's eye contact and reducing the number of "uh's," the fact that the presentation completely missed the mark because it was at the wrong level might be overlooked.

Some Criteria for Evaluating and Coaching

Here are some questions evaluators can use as guidelines to help improve the presentation:

Big Picture

- How effective is the presentation? How well does it achieve objectives?
- Is the basic strategy sound? Does this presentation make a useful contribution to the overall program goals? Is this the right speaker to the right audience at the right time?
- Are the basic elements correct, or is a major revision in order?
- Will anything turn the audience off?
- What are major strengths or weaknesses?
- Were time allocations appropriate and met?

Planning

- Were objectives clear and appropriate?
- Did the theme come through clearly, and was it the right one?
- Are the strongest messages being put forth? Have any key ones been overlooked?
- Is the presentation properly targeting the audience?

Organization

- Did the introduction grab the audience and get them ready to listen? Was the format adequately covered and was the purpose clearly stated?
- Could the talk be easily followed? Was it clear and concise, with major points illuminated? Was topic coverage adequate? Were sections in the best order and depth? What should be cut or expanded? Were arguments presented in a logical and persuasive manner, and were transitions clear?
- Was the summary clear? Did it make a strong restatement of key points and main theme? Was the desired action clear? Did the summary close with punch and make a smooth transition to questions and answers or the next speaker or other event?

Support

- Were the points adequately explained, illustrated, and supported? How can the use of reinforcement material, such as statistics and stories, be improved?
- Did the visual aids truly help the presentation?
- Are the chosen support forms the best that can be used? Will other

activities, demonstrations, props, or something else increase audience interest and acceptance?

Staging

- Was the room setup adequate? Were audiovisual equipment and material in place?
- How smoothly did the speaker handle visuals, equipment, gadgetry, and distributions?
- Did the presentation begin promptly, stay on course, and finish on time?
- Was the teamwork between speaker and support team good?

Delivery

- Did the speaker come through as believable, forceful, and competent?
- Did the speaker hold audience interest? focus attention with vocal inflection and language?
- Was the speaker's body language natural and additive to messages? Were there any distractions to eliminate?
- Were the speaker's wardrobe and appearance appropriate?
- How well did the speaker handle audience questions and interruptions?

IN SUMMARY: PAY ATTENTION TO STAGING—IT CAN BE FRIEND OR FOE

Staging of presentations often gets cavalier treatment as speakers get swept up in developing and preparing presentations. If the arrangements and operations are well taken care of, these help the message get across. If not taken care of, they can prevent the message from being heard, and the medium may dominate the message. For final reinforcement, I offer the following poem, compendium of mostly true snafus that have occurred to many colleagues. They laugh about them now. They didn't at the time.

ODE TO MURPHY

It's away to Washington for a major pitch,
A Winning Presentation and they'll all be rich.
They've busted their fannies to lay out their story,
They're loaded for bear, Brand X better worry.

The team of four aces, came together at two,
Was sabotaged early by the Asiatic flu.
Joe arrived looking green and lurched back on the plane,
Anne's charts came up missing, with the luggage again.

But the show must go on, the general won't wait.
So the rest of the team ran for the interstate.
But Avis said "What car?" and Hertz said the same.
"Hey taxi, over here, get us out of this rain."

Finally at the Pentagon, half an hour late,
Mac's clearance has lapsed, he's stuck at the gate.
The team's last two members, polishing their boots,
Dashed to Conference Room A, in their power suits.

"Oh no, no one's there! How can that be?"
Simple, they're all waiting in Conference Room C.
To C they then headed, by now a bit whiffy,
"Turn on the projector, we're on in a jiffy."

What projector? There's none to be seen!
"Didn't you?" whispered Anne. "I thought you . . . ," said Dean.
A projector arrived. "Let's go!" came a shout.
But 'twas not yet to be, the bulb was burned out.

Patience was fading as a new bulb was found.
Now the show did commence—oops, chart upside down.
Dean moved through the data, waving pointer with zest,
One swoop pitched hot coffee on the general's vest.

Anne then took the floor for the final appeal,
One nifty demo the proposal would seal.
First sparks, then much smoke—yep, incorrect power.
The gen'ral was drenched by the sprinkler's shower.

Later Anne and Dean, joined once more by Mac,
Cried in their beer, "We'll all get the sack!"
The moral is clear, as in that old saw:
Remember the power of old Murphy's Law.

* * * 10 * * *

Deliver: Show Time!

KEY POINTS OF THIS CHAPTER

* Competence, sincerity, and enthusiasm will serve a speaker well, especially if backed up by careful preparation.
* Talking to one person at a time helps to control nervousness and achieve a natural, conversational manner.
* Nonverbal communication may be more important than the ideas or content of a presentation.
* The language with which ideas and material are presented can put people to sleep or jolt them to life and support.
* The voice is a powerful tool for communication and is often used at far below its true potential.

Robert E. Levinson said in an article in *Dun's Review,* "In a sense, every executive speechmaker is an actor, giving a performance for the edification, entertainment, and approval of a highly specialized audience. Since the delivery is as important as the content, an executive needs a bit of the ham."[1] A century earlier, Emily Dickinson described a fellow author: "She has the facts, but not the phosphorescence."[2] That could fit many of today's presenters: knowledgeable, thorough—and boring.

Or it could give a simple guide to winning presenters—those with *both the facts and the phosphorescence.* On lists identifying characteristics of outstanding speakers, certain terms keep appearing:

- "Forceful, dynamic," "Speaks with energy, enthusiasm, conviction."
- "A winning presence," "Commanding."
- "Sincere, warm, real, natural."
- "Personal—I felt she was speaking right to me," "Direct—looked us right in the eye."
- "Handled himself well."
- "Certainly knew what she was talking about."
- "Lively, kept us awake, made it fun to listen to."

These attributes reveal themselves in the way speakers deliver their messages. They determine if those messages are listened to, received correctly, believed, and acted upon. All our hard work in preparation may be for naught if we don't deliver well.

This chapter examines how to improve delivery skills in three key areas: nonverbal communication, including appearance; language/verbal communication; and voice. Another critical aspect of delivery is handling questions, the subject of the next chapter.

OVERVIEW: SOME BASIC POINTS

You've done your homework: carefully analyzed the audience, developed a sound organization, gathered solid supporting material, covered the arrangements, rehearsed, dressed right, checked out the room. The odds are you're going to do fine. On the other hand, if you've been a bit loose about the preparation and your material is a mite shaky, experience fully that queasy feeling and write yourself a mental note not to put yourself into this position again.

Review
Some of Those Core Elements

Before we get wrapped up in the specifics of a winning delivery, let's step back to basics:

■ *Character counts,* sized up by audience perceptions. If you're a jerk at heart or come across like one, expensive visual aids won't save you. Ralph Waldo Emerson agreed: "What you are stands over you the while, and thunders so that I cannot hear what you say to the contrary."[3]

■ *Have something worthwhile to say.* Fire and technique lacking substance (e.g., all phosphorescence, no facts) are "a tale told by an idiot, full of sound and fury, signifying nothing," as Shakespeare put it.

■ *Know your subject and the presentation.* Executives who have others prepare material for them sometimes walk into the conference room with limited familarity with their material, and it quickly shows.

■ *Want to communicate.* Recognize this for the opportunity it is.

■ *Let the real you show up.* Tight nerves, high stakes, rusty skills, thin preparation . . . all can result in a wooden imitation of yourself standing up before that audience.

■ *Speak from the heart.* From lawyer Louis Nizer comes this advice: "Persuasion does not come from affection or from charm or from wit. It is derived from sincerity. That is why illiterate witnesses or those from humble stations in life, who are awed by the courtroom, may nevertheless be the best witnesses."[4]

■ *Believe in yourself and your idea.* "Two very important factors," said Ron Stoneburner, General Dynamics vice-president. "One—project absolute sincerity, which comes from belief in your topic. Two—project confidence, which comes from your knowing what's in every bit of that sucker. I've watched well-packaged presentations taken on by people who had one or both factors missing, and they fell apart. And yet you know the data was super."[5]

■ *Live it; breathe it.* Ashleigh Groce, senior vice-president of Leo Burnett advertising, told of seeing back-to-back presentations about advertising successes: "Such a difference. One case was so eloquently related, the speaker bubbled up from pride in her work and spoke with a true passion. The others had just as good a case, but they read from a script, and didn't demonstrate they believed in the work. We came away feeling the first was a better story, when the opposite was the case."[6]

■ *Connect with your audience.* Talk with them, not at them.

■ *Enjoy.* Don't you love watching speakers in action who seem to be enjoying themselves? Take note. When you enjoy something, you're less tight and more yourself. Audiences respond positively, which adds to your own confidence.

■ *Ham rarely hurts.* Remember the opening quotation from Robert Levinson.

It's almost show time. Here is some preshow advice:

■ *Dress suitably for a positive impression.* You may not think it counts but listen to what Les McCraw, Jr., CEO of Fluor Corporation, one of the country's top contracting firms, says: "Appearance is absolutely one of the very important elements. A person who is well attired commands more respect than one who is sloppy. Being dressed neatly bespeaks a neat and hopefully uncluttered mind."[7]

■ *Get there early.* Do your part to make sure the meeting will begin on time. This also gives you plenty of time to set up, check room essentials, locate needed controls, and try out equipment. (Of course, if it's your own facility, you will have already checked all this.) Not being able to turn on the overhead projector is a terrible way to begin a presentation, yet I've seen it occur dozens of times.

■ *Loosen up,* just as if you were an athlete about to perform. Presenting is a physical activity, involving body, mouth, and mind. Stretch, do a few jumping jacks, shadow box, wave your arms in the air, hum, sing. These all will help you get rid of the stiffness that so often characterizes speakers.

■ *Step into the restroom for a final physical check.* This final check pays off. To get a demonstration video, I had arranged for a taping of one of my speeches. I was well prepared, and the audience and setting would be just right. I delivered the speech to good response and felt great until I reviewed the video and saw my badly mussed hair. Totally out of my normal, careful pattern, I had not made my usual final prespeech check.

■ *If the meeting is in progress, slip into the back and case the joint unobtrusively.* Observe the speaker, note the setup, and identify any problems. This will ease your entree onto the scene and allow you to change the setup as needed. At a national conference, I sat in on the presentation given before mine. The presenters kept the room entirely in the dark, so you couldn't see them, only their slides. I didn't like that setup and during the transition was able to change it so room lights could be kept partly on, a much better arrangement.

What About Stage Fright?

A classic story concerns the woman who had just been elected president of the local financial analysts society. Just prior to the meeting at which she would be giving her acceptance speech, she stepped into a room nearby to go over her speech one last time. As she was pacing back and forth, working on word emphasis and gestures, a man came in and, apparently a curious sort, asked her what she was doing. She said, "I'm going to give a speech in a few minutes and I'm practicing for it."

The man said, "Very interesting. Tell me, do you ever get nervous before you give a speech?"

"Of course not," the woman replied.

"Well," he said, "would you tell me what you're doing in the men's room?"

Tight nerves, speaking anxiety, and stage fright are not unusual, even among experienced speakers, but excessive stage fright can sap your confidence and prevent the real you from going on display. It's worth knowing how to keep the butterflies at a manageable level, or, as one speaker put it, "to get them to fly in formation." (You may find it helpful to review chapter 3, where this subject was covered fully.)

The best stage fright preventive is diligent preparation. Applying the principles previously discussed, including practice and helpful feedback, will bring you to show time well prepared. The other key is speaking often, getting up before groups, keeping your skills honed, and raising your self-assurance.

What you say to yourself and how you perceive this event can greatly affect your confidence. Look at it as a feeding frenzy about to occur, and down goes your zeal. Instead, consider it a golden opportunity, with the audience there to hear *you*, the most knowledgeable person in the room (which is true). Make "I can't wait to get in there" your credo.

Les McCraw, Jr., is a firm believer in the power of imagery: "It can be powerful to see how you want the audience to respond, how you're going to feel. I start a couple of days ahead and think through how I want to project, where I will sit, how the elements of the talk go over, what the audience will do. It works."[8]

Some further tips:

- Don't be a wallflower. Start talking to people informally before the meeting, if that is possible. This breaks the ice and lessens the barriers. It also gets you presenting, as a warmup to the real thing.
- Try isometric exercises. Force your muscles to work against each other; tense strongly, then relax. Take a few giant, drawn-out yawns (quietly, if the meeting is in process). Exhaling long and slowly helps you relax and gets your breathing under control.
- Talk to your audience as individuals, conversationally and one at a time. You're not giving a speech; you're communicating interactively.
- Look them directly in the eyes. If you're nervous, look for the friendly faces. Move your gaze to various people in all parts of the room.
- Keep talking to one person at a time. Your hands will start to take care of

themselves, the breath will stay under control, and natural expressiveness will come through.

- Have your opening down pat. This is when the nerves are tightest, and getting off to a good start is a great confidence builder.

What About Notes?

During the dry run for a proposal presentation, the program manager insisted on using a plethora of notes. He would be the key person on the contract, so a strong presentation was vital. But by constantly referring to notes, he created a poor impression. When he viewed himself on video—the first time he'd ever seen himself—he heartily concurred, and with some effort got rid of most of the notes and came through in good style.

"Nothing is so unnerving as the guy giving a presentation and reading a script," says Department of Energy executive Michael Bayer. "This is an instant, 'Hey, this guy doesn't know what he's talking about. Where's the guy who wrote the script, and why aren't we talking to him?' "[9]

For presentations, read as little as possible. Many people read poorly, and audiences dislike being read to. If you have to read, you're probably not the right speaker or haven't prepared well enough. (For formal scripted speeches, use the techniques noted in Chapter 15.)

If you're using visual aids, you'll be better off with minimal notes. They get in the way and interfere with effective use of visuals; it's like trying to serve two masters. Assuming you know your material and have prepared well, the visuals should provide all the thought triggers you will need.

You can provide simple notes with the visuals themselves for example, on viewgraph frames or flipcharts (lightly, at eyeball height, and on the side where you'll stand). If a lectern is mandatory, notes can be printed directly onto visual copies.

Notes are useful for formal speeches or parts of presentations with no visuals. They can help you stay on course and get the right things said. They're also handy when you can't remember what comes next.

Various card systems work, as long as they can provide the necessary thought triggers quickly and with little distraction. Index cards are usually more manageable than papers. Number each card, write large, and use only key information. Sketches or flow diagrams may be preferable to words only.

Place the notes on the lectern so they can be easily seen and handled. If you have no lectern or want to move around, either place the notes on a handy table before you or keep them in your hand (preferably small index cards only). A quick glance should be all you need to get the next move. To go to the next card, slide the old one to the side or behind the pack in a nondistracting manner. Practice with notes in advance to smooth it out.

Make a Last-Minute Reality Check

Before launching into your presentation, do a reality check of the current situation. Do the same conditions still hold as you planned for? Has the last discussion left the meeting in a shambles? Has the meeting gone way longer than expected, with now-worn-out audience members and the key players showing signs of imminent departure? Maybe it's time to enact plan B.

Recall retired executive Grant Hansen's advice about the importance of flexibility: "When you walk into the room, have under your right arm the thirty-minute presentation you were asked to give. Under your left arm, have the ten-minute presentation you now will be able to give"[10]

Show Time! You're On and in Charge

Here are several tasks often overlooked or poorly done:

■ Let the room come to order, look people in the eyes, and begin. Don't start speaking until you and audience are ready.

■ Do the steps in the introduction formula noted in Chapter 6. Have these well polished to get the presentation off in good fashion. These may include an opening hook, introduction of participants and other courtesies, the presentation road map or agenda, and clarification of meeting process and objectives.

■ Make sure the first visual is properly aligned (since it is usually the one that goes on crooked, upside down, or off the screen).

■ Move smoothly into the body of the presentation.

Feedback and Effective Response Are Essential

Keep reading the sensors—the verbal and nonverbal signals that come from each audience member, especially key people. Are they fidgeting, daydreaming, or inspecting fingernails? If so, these are strong signals to change—fast.

"When I speak," said Eric Herz, general manager of the Institute of Electrical and Electronics Engineers, "I look directly into people's eyes and determine if I'm coming across. Or, if I'm not sure, I may ask them, 'Is what I'm saying having any meaning for you?' If I get a bunch of deadpans, I stop."[12]

Adapt your material to what is happening. If it is clear that your listeners have grasped something faster than you thought they would, cut the rest of the material on that subject and go on to something they'd rather hear. Or you may have guessed wrong and assumed the audience knew more than it does, so you may need to dwell a bit longer on some material.

Respond to the comments and questions of the audience. How you conduct yourself under fire is a strong factor in acceptance or rejection of your ideas.

It's Your Show—Stay in Charge

This may sound idealistic when the audience is composed of the president and the board of directors. Or when you're a junior scheduler and the audience is twenty howling program and production managers. You put your first visual on, and thirty minutes later, there sits that same visual while the battle rages around you. But let's have a go anyway.

Consider the well-honed style of a successful party crasher. He strides into the room as though he owns the place, marches up to the bar and gets a drink, perhaps while exchanging a wave or two with imaginary friends across the room. No one challenges him because he is so much at home. In contrast, the amateur gate crasher tentatively slips into the room, looks furtively around for someplace to hide, and apologetically takes an hors d'oeuvre from a passing tray. He is swiftly shown the door.

The winning presenter is assertive without being arrogant, a contributing member of the team and in a leading role during this presentation. She came ready to do her part in making this a successful meeting. While likely outranked by others in the room, she assumes the responsibility that comes with the presenter's role—that is, as a professional. Here are some specific techniques to help you stay somewhat in charge:

1. Be prepared, and conduct yourself in a professional manner.

2. Give clear direction at the start and provide frequent summaries and direction signs as you go.

3. Use language and vocal emphasis to clue listeners to key information.

4. Provide lead-ins to visuals and verbal and physical direction to focus key information.

5. Be aware whether you are adhering to your time milestones and adjust as needed, recalling which of your material is in the *must* category and which in the *maybe*. Do not go over the allotted time unless the principal audience member gives you more time.

"The craziest thing you see," said consultant Jim Elms, "is the person who's running out of time. When the audience leader asks, "How many viewgraphs do you have? We're kind of running out of time," the worst thing that happens, and I've seen it lots of times, is for the person to say, "Oh, yes, well, let's have it a little faster. Here's so and so, and this is so and so, and I'll skip that and . . . here's the answer." Full speed ahead. Even dumber is the person who says, "Thank you very much," and goes on as though he never heard you. He made twenty viewgraphs, and by God, the fact that he's out of time doesn't mean he's going to throw any of them away. He forgot his effectivity. This makes me so mad, and you can't shut 'em up. The best answer is to say, "Oh, yes, we are [running out of time]. What I was going to say in the rest of the presentation is that because of _____, what we need to do is _____, and sit down."[11]

6. Do not shortchange the summary. If you find yourself running out of time, cut material and visuals, but save enough time to give the summary a good treatment. Make a clear transition to the next phase—questions, break, or next speaker.

7. Hold cleanup activities until later. Speakers often gather up viewgraphs or erase the board while trying to respond to audience questions.

8. Wrap it up. What about distributions? Are action items understood? Do audience members know how to reach you? Is another meeting planned?

9. Thank the audience for their time and attention only if appropriate, such as when you've asked to speak to a civic group to get their support. Even this may be unnecessary if you thanked them initially.

ACHIEVING POSITIVE NONVERBAL MESSAGES

The nonverbal messages may prevent the verbal and visual message from being heard or given proper attention. A presenter's appearance, posture, style, or mannerisms can be so strongly sensed and interpreted as poor by audience members that the true intended message—the ideas, arguments, substantiating material, visual aids—will be seen through clouded eyes or their eyes may even be closed. The contrary is true as well; audience members may become better inclined to listen to what a speaker has to say because his or her nonverbal messages are pleasing to them.

Psychologist Albert Mehrabian, in *Silent Messages,* underscores the importance of nonverbal communication (Figure 10-1). His studies show that when two people communicate, less than 10 percent of a key measure of communication success—total liking—comes from the words that are spoken. More than half the message comes from facial expressions and nearly 40 percent by vocal tone or expression, called paralanguage (how something is said).[13] The numbers may differ somewhat for formal presentations, but nonverbal communication is clearly a strong factor in what message is received.

Now consider what happens to many presenters. They grip the lectern tightly with both hands or keep their hands stuck together in front of or behind them. They adopt a rigid position and stare straight ahead, thus stifling their natural facial and body expression. Then they speak in a monotone, particularly if they are reading material. There goes the bulk of their normal nonverbal capability. Not exactly, however. Nonverbal communication definitely continues

Figure 10-1.   Nonverbal messages carry more weight than spoken ones.

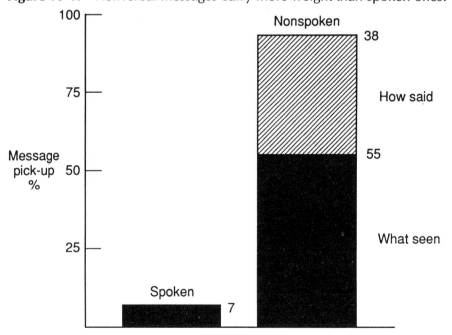

and is still a major part of the communication. The receivers see apprehension, unpreparedness, and possibly deception—not exactly what the presenter would hope to be sending.

Nonverbal Messages—Basis for Many Listener Judgments

Nonverbal messages can be door openers or door closers. We often immediately accept someone whose appearance we are comfortable with and reject another because we don't like his or her looks. We turn *on* to speakers for reasons that have less to do with their words than with their style. We turn *off* to speakers for reasons we ourselves are not entirely clear about: "There's something about that person I don't like. Can't exactly put my finger on it, but he's just not my cup of tea."

Often we *can* "put our finger on it" and are clear about it: "I won't do business with a guy who wears a beard." "I don't trust a person who won't look me in the eye." "I don't like that woman—she's always smiling."

Other times we know what it is but are reluctant to put it into words, because it makes us uncomfortable or reveals our own prejudices: "Why does he keep telling those vulgar jokes?" "They expect us to listen to a woman?" "Why doesn't somebody tell that guy to use a deodorant?"

Nonverbal messages are also tricky. We often misread messages. The person in the sloppy jeans and sweatshirt turns out to be the vice-president. We say, "Aha, you're being defensive," to a person with her arms folded, and it turns out she has a bad back and feels more comfortable with her arms folded.

Is It Natural? Congruent?

"Suit the words to the action, the action to the words," Shakespeare wrote. When words and nonverbal messages don't match, we tend to believe the nonverbal. Thus, when the speaker says, "We have tested this design under extreme conditions, and it passed them all," while fidgeting, shifting his gaze, and speaking hesitantly, the listener's tendency is to say "Baloney!" Conversely, when a speaker lacks fluency but has an earnest manner, we may accept the proposition in spite of the weak delivery.

This also means it is hard to deceive an astute audience. The words may be good, but if they are false, the nonverbal language that goes with them will give us away. It is easy to lie verbally, but hard nonverbally.

Much has been said and written about the importance of dress in business. Dress is, however, only one of many factors to which audiences may have knee-jerk reactions. Consider, for example, the well-groomed presenter in his perfectly tailored conservative three-piece suit who opens his mouth and says, "Gemmen, y'know it's a y'know real pleasure ta be witcha tidday." Or whose arrogant or abusive style turns off the audience members or arouses them to an equally abusing counterattack.

Consideration of all these factors is much more important during a presentation than during regular business activities. When presenting, you are in a spotlight, on display, and performing in an arena in which listeners have much more critical eyes and ears than in daily conversation or business matters. In addition, you are often speaking to higher management and customers, who may not know what a warm and competent human being you are. Because of the significance— positive and negative—of the nonverbal impressions, astute presenters get these working for them and correct those working against them (Figure 10-2).

A consideration often overlooked by speakers whose motto is "I'll do it my way" is that *as a presenter you are representing your organization, not just yourself.* The impression you create will carry into other business activities with your organization.

Yet nonverbal "flaws" may count little—if you're Albert Einstein. The best nonverbal impressions are those that come with a message of value, a true desire to communicate that message, and preparation. At a conference on future lifestyles, the speaker shuffled forward. He wore a frayed suit coat with rumpled and badly matched pants. His hair was long overdue for trimming. He looked a bit hung over, and he slouched. All the things speakers are cautioned to avoid in the power/success books, he displayed.

Several people near me snickered when they saw him. My first thought was, "Where did they dig up this character?" The snickers quickly stopped, however, as he began to speak. It was immediately evident that this was a person to listen to, and everyone did, intently. His talk was the hit of the conference and the subject of much discussion afterward. No one cared anymore that he needed a haircut and a shoe shine.

Given a choice, I would much rather be a speaker in a rumpled suit to whom people listened intently because of the power of my words than one perfectly tailored without substance!

Sending Positive Body-Related Messages

In this part, we'll examine matters related to what the *body* does as it creates positive or negative impressions for presenters.

Figure 10-2.   Here are some ways to positive nonverbal communication.

- Eye contact is important—look at your audience. Be especially careful not to look too much at the screen.
- Talk to all people in the room, not just the leaders or one side.
- Stand straight and comfortably, with weight evenly balanced. Avoid slouching or the fig-leaf/reverse fig-leaf arm positions.
- Strive for natural movement—gestures, facial animation, body expression. Talking to one person at a time will promote this.
- Avoid creating your own nonverbal distractors—coin jangling, chalk tossing, pointer waving, dangling jewelry, low necklines, "cause" symbols.
- Do not smoke or chew gum, especially at the same time.
- In choosing a wardrobe, be comfortable, appropriate, and yourself. When in doubt, dress toward the conservative direction.
- Ill-fitting clothes, poorly chosen accessories, and sloppy appearance detract from the positive image.
- Your style of relating to others—professionalism, courtesy, sensitivity, humor, and behavior under fire—carries a strong message.

The Total Body as a Communication Vehicle. Audience members make an instant judgment of a speaker's competence, character, confidence, and openness by their first views of the speaker as a complete physical being.

The beginning of the presentation offers an opportunity to start sending positive nonverbal messages:

■ Watch your nonverbal behavior while you're in the wings. Often a presentation is part of other activities, such as other presentations, group discussions, or preliminaries. Audience members start forming their impressions of you as soon as they see you (and often before that).

■ You're on. Stride with assurance and eagerness to the podium or proper place in the room and take command.

■ Adopt a comfortable stance, with weight evenly balanced on both feet. Directly face the audience, and stand as close to it as makes sense (if not speaking from a lectern). Your posture should be natural. An erect posture, with all parts in alignment, projects an image of assurance and is better for voice production than one that is slouching, ramrod-straight, or cockeyed. Here are three easy checks on posture: (1) Stand against a wall, with fanny, back, and head against the wall. Now walk away holding this position. If your normal position isn't close to this, you're probably slouching. (2) To reduce the shoulder-slumping tendency, force your elbows backward several times to loosen your chest and shoulder area. Then, with elbows extended to the rear, drop your arms. (3) As a check of posture, look where your hands rest along your legs. If they are either in front of or to the rear of your pants or skirt seams, you are probably slouching or excessively erect. Moving them to the seams will probably be an improvement.

■ Disciplined movement adds to an assured impression. You need not be cemented to one place. You can speak from different locations, such as in front of the projector table, at the screen, or close to specific audience members. Move deliberately, stop, and talk. Do not pace back and forth, bounce, or fidget as these are distracting.

Hands and Arms. "What do I do with my hands?" is probably the most common question I hear. My answer is, "What do you normally do with them when you are talking about a subject you're strongly interested in?"

Hands, arms, and body are an important part of how we communicate. Yet when presenting, many people cut their hands out of the action by adopting one of several common wooden-speaker positions (Figure 10-3):

Fig leaf: Both hands gripped together and covering the groin.
Reverse fig leaf: Hands gripped behind the back. (Its cousin is the military at-ease position.)
Mortician or concert singer: Hands gripped together at the navel.
Gunfighter or gorilla: Both arms hanging stiffly away from both sides.
Casual: Hands in pockets.
Challenger: Hands on both hips.

Figure 10-3. What do I do with my hands? "Wooden speaker" positions are not uncommon.

Death Grip

Fig Leaf   Tight-Rope Walker

Death grip: Hands firmly holding onto a lectern, chair, pointer, or papers.
Tightrope walker: Both hands on the pointer across the waist.

Follow this advice to let the hands operate naturally and forcefully:

■ Review the above list, and identify your standard position. Then be conscious of how you use your hands in normal conversation. Check your body language while formally presenting and while responding to audience questions. Videotape can vividly show you these patterns.

■ Don't let both hands grip things or each other. If you start to go to one of these wooden positions, break from it.

■ Once the hands get ungripped, let them do what they would do as you normally talk to someone at the coffee machine or at a party. Most people have a reasonable amount of hand movement. Some people can hardly talk without it.

■ Now work for refinements. Tone down excessive arm waving or hand waving. Broaden gestures, away from limited hand-only gestures or short movements of the forearm, toward broader, more sweeping movements involving one or both arms. Develop more forceful gestures, with increased vigor and fire going into them.

■ Eliminate irritating nonverbal mannerisms. Coin and key jingling head the list. One division general manager was advised by the corporation chief executive officer that he was paying one of his top executives too much money. This was just after the executive had given the CEO and others a presentation. The general manager asked why. "Because," came the answer, "he doesn't know enough not to jangle the change in his pockets when he is giving a presentation."

Facial and Eye-to-Eye Communication. What the face and eyes say is tremendously important for communication, and perhaps the most important factor, according to psychologist Mehrabian. Let's look at how we can use this avenue *for* us, not *against* us, starting with that all-important eye contact:

■ As you present, connect with your audience, one person at a time. Establish eye contact and truly engage that person with you for a brief moment. Eye contact helps gain their attention, adds to an assured impression, and gives you valuable feedback.
■ Be sensitive to proper duration of eye contact (from three to five seconds). Gaze intently at a person too long, and he or she becomes uncomfortable; too short and you appear fidgety.
■ Look at and face people directly. Side glances do not instill confidence.
■ Speak to everyone. Many presenters direct their attention solely to the highest-ranking person, irritating the lesser folks. Definitely talk to that person but also to the others. Even when answering a question, keep the whole group in the dialogue.
■ Don't shift your gaze from left to right and back as though watching a Ping-Pong game.
■ Even when using notes or visuals, remember to talk to your audience, not the screen, projector, ceiling, or lectern.

Other parts of the face play a role as well. The smile is a great resource and often never allowed to serve. Tightness and excessive concentration on the material may prevent a natural smile from shining through. "Put your best face forward" is not an empty slogan. Everybody wins with a natural and appropriate smile. The audience warms up and often smiles back, adding to the speaker's confidence. A smile is linked to a more pleasant voice too.

Overall facial expression has an impact as well. Often speakers are not aware how their faces look to others. A constant sneer, glare, or frown may lead receivers to assume the speaker is belittling or challenging them. It is hard to be enthusiastic about propositions coming from a person who looks sour or downcast. Confidence will be low in a person with a frightened-rabbit or bewildered look. A person who speaks out of the side of his mouth may come across as secretive.

Style and Manner Speak Volumes

A variety of nonverbal behaviors in the area of presenter style and manner interplay to communicate strong messages. Competence, trust, maturity, sensitivity, sophistication, and strength of character are all measured to a great extent by nonverbal factors. So are arrogance, boorishness, evasiveness, nonprofessionalism, and weakness. Much of this is sensed from tone of voice; sensitivity to space, time, protocol, and touch; and operation under fire.

■ *Understand rank and protocol.* Grant Hansen, a retired executive, says protocol is with us every day of our lives. "If you don't believe it, picture a desk and two chairs. Two guys walk in and the visitor sits in the resident's chair. The resident is too polite to say anything, but he won't hear a word. He'll be wondering why the guy is sitting in his chair."[14]

With any audience, powerful unspoken rules function: showing up late or wasting time, excessive familiarity, failure to know or use military ranks, or violation of space "bubbles."

■ *Respect your audience.* A senior program director said, "A presenter should approach an audience with respect. If you project a note of arrogance, you get them mad at you right away. Particularly if they are customers, they have something you're after, and thus they are in charge. It's good for the presenter to have a humble attitude, not to be a patsy, but one that says you recognize their position. This defuses the possibility of them having to show how smart they are. Your manner can get them on your side or against you right at the start."

Respect is demonstrated in many forms and is barely noticed. Disrespect is immediately noticed. Wasting the time of others by poor preparation, insulting the local facilities, badmouthing the competition, using profane language, or telling ethnic or sexist jokes can cause the audience to walk out, literally and figuratively.

■ *Be and stay positive.* With their opening words, many presenters doom their purpose. "I really didn't have much time to prepare these visuals, so I hope you'll bear with me." Apologizing for an about-to-be watched performance loses points immediately. This applies to problems during the talk too. When Murphy's Law prevails, speakers often go to pieces or apologize profusely, focusing attention on something the audience had perhaps barely noticed. When a mishap occurs, fix it and get on with the business.

As a speaker you naturally feel that you deserve attention. You have worked hard and are presenting material of validity and importance. When you are subjected to questions or opposing viewpoints, several undesirable tendencies may surface: to ignore the questioner, to attack back, to become defensive, or to cave in. Resist them all. You will lose if you give in to any of these options. Stay positive; keep your cool and your perspective.

■ *Let your human side show.* A characteristic shared by several outstanding speakers I know is that they are comfortable with their audiences. They come across as real human beings, with humor, vitality, and feelings.

■ *Be considerate of others besides the audience.* A dozen years ago I attended a sports lecture in which the speaker was to narrate the film. When the projector failed, the speaker became sarcastic and insulting to the equipment operator. Making snide comments to the operator may have helped relieve the speaker's frustration, but it turned many listeners off and led them to support the beleaguered operator.

The program director of a group of presenters became irritated at one of his speakers, and proceeded to berate him for his deficiencies in front of the audience. "Isn't he a big man," a key listener next to me said.

You don't win by being domineering to others, especially those not in a position to fight back.

- *Polish your business etiquette.* One after-dinner speaker had already lost many of his audience by loudly slurping his soup and belching during the dinner. A speaker failed to shake the hand that was extended to him by a listener as they were introduced before the talk. While waiting his turn to talk, the same speaker put his feet on the walnut conference table.

Perhaps the trickiest set of potential turnoffs is that associated with what people use to measure "class." The criteria vary widely across cultures, professions, and age, sex, and economic groups. Acceptance or rejection is often subtle and unspoken and the causes hard to identify. Much of what is called "sophistication" comes with experience, but the critical ingredients are the old standbys: strength of character and respect for other people. These will serve you well even if the sophistication is lean.

- *Be professional.* This final aspect of the speaker's style encompasses all the previous ones. The way you prepare for and conduct yourself during a business presentation says much about the type of manager, scientist, or person you are.

Dress and Grooming Do Matter

Like it or not—and some people don't—dress is important in business. Listeners are sizing you up long before you open your mouth, and probably the first "sizing" factor is your outward appearance—wardrobe, neatness, haircut, shoe shine.

Fluor CEO McCraw's words of wisdom about appearance were quoted earlier. Bruce Blechman, president of the Capital Institute, helps people get financing for their businesses. "Most people don't dress properly for presentations—for example the guy who showed up in my office in shorts, sneakers and a T-shirt. Audiences judge people quickly, and you go down the drain if you don't dress properly. It's a quick way to lose credibility."[15]

Dress is more important in some settings than in others. An audience of engineers at a technical seminar is less likely to be concerned about dress than a banker's loan approval committee hearing a pitch for a $10 million loan or a top-level military audience hearing the proposal for a major new contract.

Presenters talking outside the organization need to be particularly aware of their appearance. Sometimes they will wear casual or flashy clothing. That may be acceptable when speaking to some internal groups, but all speakers should keep in mind that they are *representing the organization as well as themselves.* A talk may be part of a broad marketing campaign or a team presentation, and the presenter's image can help or hamper achieving the main objective.

Yet it is a mistake to assume that dress is not also important for internal presentations. The sloppy presenter may never get the chance to speak externally and miss out on opportunities.

A suitable wardrobe is thus an important investment. People often stick with a marginal wardrobe because of cost concerns, but a decent wardrobe need not be expensive. Before reworking your wardrobe, take some time to plan. Read books on selecting a wardrobe or hire an image consultant. Investing a few hours before buying can save plenty in the long run because your choices will be sound ones.

The final point about appearance has to do with the effect of wardrobe and grooming on yourself as the speaker, independent of how that affects the audience. If you look good, your clothes fit well, and you know you are perfectly in tune with the situation, you will perform better. Your confidence will zoom, you will stand straighter, and you will move and speak with more assurance.

Wardrobe. As general guidelines for a presentation wardrobe, I recommend these three: be comfortable, be appropriate, and be yourself.

1. *Be comfortable.* Presentations can be stressful situations. Your clothing should do nothing to add to that stress. If your tie is too tight, your underwear grabs, or you feel squeezed in the arms and shoulders, you'll be aware of this discomfort during the presentation. So when you choose your clothing for a presentation, make sure all the pieces feel good.

It's hard to pick clothes that feel comfortable if they are poorly fitted in the first place. Consider having your clothes custom-tailored, particularly if your figure is hard to fit.

When speaking, many presenters perspire more than normally. Choose your wardrobe so you will stay cool. Undershirts, vests, and all-polyester shirts and suits can cause you to feel extra warm.

2. *Be appropriate.* As has so often been stated in this book, know your audience and situation. If you're speaking at the Little League winners' picnic, don't show up in your Brooks Brothers dark-blue suit, unless you're the umpire. If your presentation is to a joint services proposal review team, don't wear your casual outfits even if some of the review team members are wearing theirs. Dress to fit the occasion.

Different professions, industries, and locations have different standards for what is appropriate. The corporate office in New York, the division in Cincinnati, and the field operations group in Roswell, New Mexico, may differ significantly as to what is appropriate dress. "When in Rome" is not a bad rule. If you are the manager in Roswell and are going to New York to present to the board of directors, perhaps wisdom would say dress as the corporate office people do. A group of creative directors from the advertising industry usually looks different from a group of bank controllers and a gathering of college deans. While the wardrobe *within* a profession or industry group may be distinct from the wardrobes of other groups, the wardrobes of all those business groups may be reasonably similar for business or presentations *outside* the group. Thus, when any of them come to testify before a congressional subcommittee, the differences may be small. Again, the key for any situation is *to know your audience and select your wardrobe so that it will not harm your presentation and may enhance it.* If in doubt, dress toward the conservative side. If you are the presenter, it is better to be at least as conservatively dressed as the key members of the audience.

Another useful guideline is to assume the standard dress for business presentations. For men, it is a business suit of a conservative fabric, style, color and pattern, and fit (level 1 in Figure 10-4). Variations from this can be suitable for certain situations, and they should be consciously made. In other words give some thought before choosing a sport coat (level 3) over the suit (level 1 or 2).

For women, a similar hierarchy of conservative to casual exists, again starting with a basic suit (Figure 10-5). Specific examples of different wardrobe levels for men's and women's wardrobe are shown in Figure 10-6.

The role of women in business is an evolving one. Many areas that have been traditionally all male are increasingly seeing larger numbers of women in them. Yet we are still far from a state in which men and women in business are viewed the same and strictly on their merits. If a male professional dresses casually, no one takes him for the janitor. If a woman does the same, many people automatically assume she is a clerk (and I'm not knocking clerks—some of them dress better than the professionals). If she dresses in a "cutesy" way, older men might be reminded of their teenaged daughters or granddaughters. If she dresses seductively, people may assume she's advertising.

3. *Be yourself.* I watched a group of businessmen departing from a conference. All wore the approved plain gray or dark-blue suits. It was depressing. A colleague attended a meeting of women executives. She said that all the women

Figure 10-4. Men's wardrobe choices for business presentations vary.

> **Level 1—a conservative business suit:**
> *Style:* Current and yet traditional. Two- or three-button. Natural shoulder (little padding), probably single-breasted and center vent. Avoid western cut, patch pockets, back belts, contrasting thread, ornate buttons, or leisure look.
> *Fabric:* All wool or wool blend. Gabardine.
> *Pattern:* Plain, subtle or muted plaid stripes or checks, or herringbone.
> *Color:* Navy, gray, brown, all leaning toward the darker side, and in shades flattering to you.
> **Level 2—a more casual business suit:**
> Poplin (dacron/cotton) or corduroy suits. Lighter colors, slightly bolder patterns and less traditional styles in wool, wool blend, or quality synthetics.
> **Level 3—conservative sport coat/pants:**
> A dark blazer with matching plain or subtly patterned pants, all in wool or wool blend. A herringbone or quiet plaid or check sport coat with plain pants. Coats traditionally cut, without fancy buttons.
> **Level 4—more casual sport coat/pants (know your audience):**
> Lighter-colored blazers, more brightly patterned pants. Sport coats with livelier patterns or styles. Blazers with fancier buttons or cuts. Corduroys, tweeds, leathers. Turtlenecks.

Figure 10-5. Women's choices cover a conservative-to-casual hierarchy.

Level 1—basic conservative business suit:
Two-piece, with simple blouse, with or without scarf or kerchief (but *not* with a man's tie). Women can be bolder than men in colors, fabrics, patterns, and styles, but they should avoid bright colors, and flamboyance in general. Length and style in fashion but nonprovocative.

Level 2—jacket/dress combinations:
Blazer with matching skirt. Shirtdress of simple design with matching jacket or blazer. Simple blouse/kerchief or turtleneck. A bit more casual on the accessories than with the suit, but still business-oriented. No frilly skirts, flowery or busy patterns, waist-length scarves, or cutesy collars or cuffs.

Level 3—nonjacketed look:
Shirtdress or skirt and blouse, with or without kerchief. Same guidelines as above.

Level 4—pants outfit (know your audience):
Stick to a conservative, but definitely feminine, look. Pantsuit or blazer/slacks.

wore variations of the men's suits, vests, and ties, and all looked nice but a bit boring.

We don't have to all become automatons, turned out from a factory so we all look alike to be acceptable in business. Every personality and shape is different, so why do the suits all have to come from the identical mold? Within the hierarchy suggested here, there is plenty of room for diversity that is still appropriate.

When buying new clothing, first do your homework. Go to a quality shop that carries traditional clothing and test out a variety of appropriate suits. Find a competent salesperson and talk to him or her at length about what might complement you best. Choosing styles and colors that are good for you and avoiding those that aren't keeps you from buying mistakes. Find the wardrobe that can add to your overall impression, not just allow you to fit in.

In enhancing your wardrobe, consider some tips from image consultant Gloria Boileau:[16]

- *Be consistent in the way you dress.* If you dress one day traditionally, the next with a European look, and the third with a casual sporting look, your associates see you as inconsistent in wardrobe and may perceive you as inconsistent in your work.
- *Add to your uniqueness.* Accenting your outfit with a distinctive signature piece—a pin, tie, even eyeglass frame—lets you express your individuality. When you get to express who you are in your wardrobe, you can express that better in the work you do.
- *Put the whole package together.* A common mistake is "getting your colors done," and heading to the store. Color is just one part of deciding what is right for you. An equally important consideration is knowing your body

Figure 10-6. Conservative business suits (level 1, left) are standard clothing for business presentations, though less formal dress (such as level 3, right) may be acceptable for more relaxed settings. For other examples, check the photos of executives interviewed in *Business Week, Forbes, Fortune, Industry Week,* or *Savvy*.

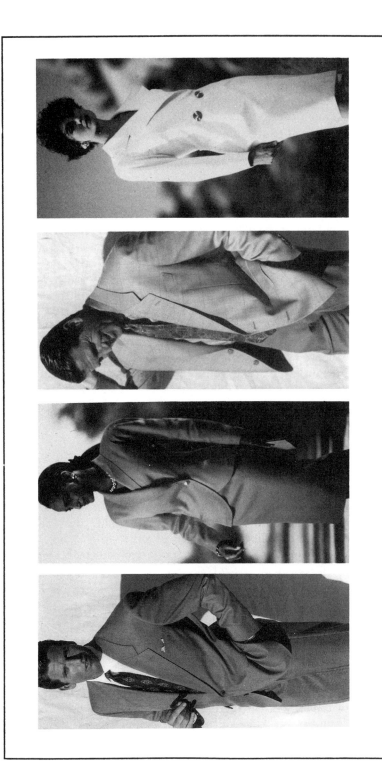

Source: Men's photos courtesy of Hartmarx, Inc. Women's courtesy of Barrie Pace Ltd.

proportion and how you can dress to enhance quality areas and diminish less desirable ones.

■ *Have a written plan before heading to the store.* Stick with that plan so when you get back home, you'll have only what you need and won't waste money.

Completing the Package. Proper fit of clothing and well-selected accessories complete the image of professionalism. A fine suit is diminished by a poor fit or inappropriate tie. Clashing colors can focus attention the wrong way. Charlie Chaplin as the Little Tramp made us laugh in part because of his wardrobe. Let's make sure that doesn't happen when we go onstage.

I was in the audience of 300 for a presentation that represented an important exposure for the speaker and his organization. The audience was high level, military and civilian, and definitely conservatively attired. The speaker wore no coat or tie and looked about right for going to a ball game, not for giving a major presentation. It was a costly mistake.

George Uhlig has seen hundreds of presentations during an active military career and as corporate executive. "It may seem phony, but when you go before the colonel, you need to dress appropriately. No question about it. For example, one fellow came to make a presentation, and he'd given no attention to what he put on. His pockets were full of pencils, and he even had different colored socks. He had a good program, but the colonel took one look and said, 'I know all I need to know,' and left. And it's not much different in the civilian world."[17]

For inexpensive guidance, follow the lead of executives pictured in *Forbes*, *Savvy* and other business magazines.

Suggestions for Men Presenters

■ *Coat,* the most important item. Many jackets are obviously ill fitting, often because the wearer recently gained or lost weight. If it obviously is under a strain when buttoned or hangs sloppily, get it to a tailor. The collar should be smooth along the neck and allow a half-inch of shirt to show. The back should be smooth, and the length should touch the cup of your hands with arms hanging. Sleeves should allow a half-inch of shirt cuff to show. *Button the coat when standing* unless you want to direct attention to your belly or be less formal.

■ *Pants.* The standard chuckle is the "high-water" look—pants 3 inches above shoes. Length, with or without cuffs, should touch shoes with a slight break. With the belt at the navel, the rear should be neither droopy nor skintight. Color should complement, not clash with, the jacket. Avoid loud patterns.

■ *Shirt.* A common problem is a collar too tight or loose; it should fit comfortably and smoothly. Sleeves (long sleeves are standard) should end at the intersection of hand and wrist. One color only for a conservative look.

■ *Tie.* The tie is the major focus of chuckles and distraction when the length is too short or too long or the pattern outrageous. The length should touch the belt. The tie should not stick out under the shirt collar. Choose colors and patterns with care, and I suggest sticking with silk. Make sure the knot is compact and straight; a Windsor or half-Windsor knot is often the best choice.

■ *Belt.* Closely match pant color, without ornate buckles or jewelry.

■ *Suspenders.* These are tempting to have fun with and get flashy, but stick with the nonobtrusive look unless you know your audience well.

■ *Shoes and socks.* Brown shoes do not go with navy blue or gray suits; black do. Brown goes with brown. Some shades of cordovan can go with either. Socks should match suit and not droop; to be safe, pick calf-length.

■ *Distractions.* An oft-repeated comment is that you can always spot an engineer because of the plastic pocket protector with six pencils in it and the calculator hooked to the belt. (In ancient times, it was a slide rule.) When up before the group, get rid of distractions (company badges, keys in pockets, "cause" buttons).

Suggestions for Women Presenters

■ *Styles.* Temper "stylish" with good business sense. Floor-length dresses, flowery and frilly blouses, and swirly skirts are best left out of the boardroom. An executive cautions, "Don't look like a stoplight. It can be too dangerous to be too 'fashionable' in a hard-core business environment."

■ *Colors.* Be aware of what's appropriate and current for your industry and profession. A woman systems specialist observed after attending a business women's dress seminar, "Magenta, fuschia, and jade may be O.K. for a bank, but they're definitely not O.K. for aerospace."

■ *Distractions.* Low-cut blouses are fine for the cocktail party but not for the conference room. Regarding skirt lengths, one woman executive said, "Make sure you can sit and not have the skirt ride up another 6 inches, especially if you're seated at the front table. When the audience members look at you as you speak, you want them looking above the table." Four-inch heels and platform shoes, bulky purses, soft sweaters, and high-fashion hats may detract from the main purpose. Flashing rings, dangling earrings, or multiple necklaces can direct attention to the wrong things and create an impression of ostentation, frivolity, or nonprofessionalism.

Personal Grooming. "Little things mean a lot," says a popular song. This is certainly true with personal grooming and cleanliness. A long-overdue haircut or overpowering body odor can prevent a sale in spite of beautiful clothes and a marvelous presentation. Many presenters handicap themselves by inattention to the little things.

Standard advice from executives is to always have hair combed and shoes shined. Hair style and grooming are high on the list of examinables. If your style is not somewhat in tune with the times, it may be commented upon. Superstylish is not the answer either—men's frizzy permanents may get as many negative comments as 1950s crewcuts. Women's flamboyant styles, waist-length hair, or plain hair may create problems. Whatever the style, it should be neatly combed and under control.

Women's makeup should enhance the appearance while creating no negative attention. Bright lipsticks, heavy eye shadow, heavy rouge, and long false eyelashes may be great for the dinner-dance but are poor for the podium. Makeup should be high-quality, understated, and applied well, with no masklike divisions (and never put on or touched up in the conference room).

Astute presenters ensure that breath and body odors don't leave the wrong lasting impression. Fragrances can cause problems, both from being too dominant or causing allergic people to react. Tobacco smoke has become a major issue, including being banned entirely in many facilities. *If you're a smoker, absolutely don't smoke when you're presenting,* and ask for permission as a meeting participant or in another's office.

LANGUAGE—THE VERBAL CHANNEL

"A few well-chosen words are worth a thousand pictures, despite what the Chinese philosopher said. I want to know what the man can do with the English language. Our great presidents were able to write well. I don't think a man can lead the nation without a grasp of the language."[18] This observation from the late news commentator Eric Sevareid fits business leaders as well as political leaders.

One of the common characteristics of successful people is their ability to use language well. The spell-binding orators, the sought-after motivational speakers, the outstanding technical presenters *may* look good, *may* have good visuals, and *may* have commanding voices, but they almost always assuredly *will* have a good command of the English language (or whatever their own language is).

Far too many professional people use language poorly, especially when speaking to nonpeer groups. It is frequently noted that many business executives, scientists, lawyers, government officials, and educators either do not know how to speak in plain language or deliberately use language to deceive.

Phillip Dunne, a movie screenwriter and director, put it this way, in an essay titled "Just Between You and I": "In particular, one may protest the misuse of our language by those who should know better: businessmen, educators, holders of high offices, and representatives of the news media. If happy illiterates can enrich a language, the pompous half-educated only succeed in impoverishing it."[19]

While language is a primary vehicle to further communication, it may also be a major interference: *inadvertent* when we misjudge an audience and use words that listeners will not understand or to which they will react negatively and *deliberate* when we use words to impress, deceive, or cover up rather than to communicate.

Language that enhances, rather than interferes with, communication is *directive, appropriate, understandable, nondistracting,* and *forceful.* Figure 10-7 summarizes some of the key points about the use of language.

Effective Language Is Directive

Speakers can use language to help direct audience attention. Combined with vocal stress and timing, directive language makes a powerful tool for the speaker. Skilled speakers become like orchestra conductors in that their word choices and emphasis strongly lead listeners to focus on key points.

Figure 10-7. Here are some tips for more effective language.

- The language you use is a major key to your success.
- Directive language helps focus audience attention where you want it.
- Before opening your mouth, check with your brain to gauge appropriateness of your words. Profanity, ethnic humor, and sexist language may turn people off.
- Acronyms and jargon are common causes of trouble. Use them sensibly.
- Audience members often will not acknowledge they don't know what you're talking about. Speak a language they can understand, and make feedback easy.
- Confusion is often the result of the speaker's ambiguity, obfuscation, and word choice.
- Language mannerism—"uh, like, y'know"—are high on the list of irritants for business audiences.
- Poor grammar, sloppy pronunciation, and misused terms create a negative impression with listeners.
- Nearly every powerful speaker is a master of forceful expression, attained in large part by words that "dance."
- Shorter words, active tense, words that spark the imagination, and dramatic phrasing help elevate language from the dreary to the powerful.
- Work to clear up language problems in all your speaking situations so you can retain your natural, enthusiastic delivery during a presentation.

Here are some good ways to direct the audience's attention:

- *Enumerate.* "The first point is . . ."
- *Emphasize.* "A particularly important factor . . ."
- *Repeat.* "Sixteen casualties. Sixteen."
- *Restate.* "Let's look at that another way."
- *Focus.* "Look at this weak area [*while pointing to a visual aid*]."
- *Bridge.* "We've seen the causes: let's examine the possible solutions."
- *Question:* "So what is the best choice?"
- *Invite.* "Put yourselves in our position."

Many presenters use verbal clueing mechanisms to good advantage. These serve two purposes: to focus audience attention organizationally and to give a memory hook to aid recall. "Follow the three P's of the platform," said a convention keynoter, "Poise, Personality, and Professionalism."

Another form of direction occurs by word choice. One word may inflame: another almost synonymous one may calm. The word *earnings* may be more positively received than *profits.* "Three of ten failed" focuses on the flops; "seven of ten worked well" focuses on the successes. Which sounds more troublesome, *revisions* or *slippages?*

Effective Language Is Appropriate

One of the fastest ways to lose an audience is to offend it. Few speakers are so foolish as to offend listeners deliberately, but many have innocently done so.

Knowing your audience is fundamental to using language wisely rather than stupidly. Here are some things to look out for.

Profanity. Be wary of telling dirty jokes, flashing pictures of naked models on the screen to wake people up, or using locker room language. I have seen this backfire on many speakers who used profanity excessively for shock effect or because they hadn't given a thought to doing otherwise. Regardless of the frequency and ease with which four-letter words are used in private conversation, movies, and literature, many people still are uncomfortable with the same words in group communication.

Now for the other side of the coin. Off-color language *can* be effective, if used in the right manner and place. Here is an example: During the 1979–1980 U.S.-Iranian crisis, in which Americans were held hostage for a long period of time, a U.S. State Department official, Henry Precht, responded with "Bullshit!" to an Iranian diplomat's statement that the hostages were under the protection of the Iranian government. This shocked the Iranian, and he stormed out, causing a minor stir. Later President Carter praised Mr. Precht, stating that the essence of good diplomatic language is "to combine conciseness, clarity, and accuracy. You have mastered this principle."[20]

Affiliation-Offensive Language. This means language that will turn off members of the audience because of who they are. It's surprisingly easy to fall into that trap. Just tell a Polish joke to an audience containing some Poles. Or start an answer to a woman questioner with "Well, honey . . ." Or make derogatory comments about the president of the United States to an audience that includes many of his supporters. Or to a Navy audience, praise the way the Air Force managed a program better than the Navy did. I didn't make any of these up. They occurred during presentations, and the predictable effects also occurred: Key members of the audience turned off or turned against the speaker. *Avoid language that will be regarded as sexist, antiminority, politically touchy, antireligious, or anti whatever the audience is.*

Occasion Insensitivity. Language that is out of place for the occasion can prove detrimental to the speaker. Wisecracks may be inappropriate for a serious event, as may total solemnity for a light event. Know the spirit of the event and the mood of the audience.

Effective Language Is Understandable

"Now as you all know, the contract had been set to be cost-plus at 150K, but we were OBE'd. Then getting a firm ETA on the RFQ has been like going through max q. We're in the same bind as on our MRQT program, where NAVFLIBTOB pulled the plug as we'd gotten the QZKT-2 on line and our realization in 257 up to viable levels." Now take out your pencils, as we're going to have a little quiz later.

The spoken word in business and government is abundant with jargon, "in" language, acronyms, abbreviations, and technical terminology that frequently baffle members of the audience. Such professional shortcuts are useful in communicating with peers but become traps when not everyone knows them. The problem is compounded when not everyone knows he or she doesn't know or when no one acts to clarify what has been said.

In interviews for this book, many top executives said they were frequently subjected by presenters to acronyms they did not know. I was on the sending end of a terminology gap that made me forever cautious about using acronyms. My report was to a half-dozen members of the company's human resources staff: ". . . and STS is proceeding well. STS is causing some overtime, but its deadlines are being met."

At about the third "STS," an audience member, the company doctor, asked me what STS meant. "Oops, sorry, Doctor," I said. "That's the Space Transportation System."

"Thank goodness," he said, "because in my business STS is well known as the Serological Test for Syphilis."

Fortunately, many presentations are interactive, so befuddled listeners have the option of asking for clarification. Listeners may do that, under some conditions, but many won't, for a variety of reasons. A risk is often associated with asking questions in general, but in particular of the type: "Maybe I'm stupid, but what does that mean?"

Retired executive vice-president Arthur Toupin commented on this problem while he was still at Bank of America.

> In our monthly management meetings, with senior officers present, junior officers won't ask questions if they don't know something. It makes it look like they don't know what they're doing. It's the same thing as when a lawyer uses legalese—it intimidates the audience. This is true with different specialities as well. For example, a person from the money side of the bank hears someone from the commercial side who uses the jargon of that field. He won't ask questions, and the result is nobody knows what's going on. This is true in most environments. People hesitate to ask questions, thinking "I should understand that. My God, how would I look if I asked a question and said to everyone I don't understand." *Perhaps the single most important thing in making a presentation is understanding of this by the person making the presentation. My own observation is that very few presenters do understand that.*[21]

Phillip Broughton devised the Systematic Buzz Phrase Projector so that anyone interested in obfuscating but without a natural talent could do it almost painlessly.[22] His system consisted of three columns of current "buzz" words (see Figure 10-8), from which the obfuscator could simply select any one from each column and instantly come up with terms that would get anyone by without being questioned—or understood. A thousand possibilities were thus instantly at the fingertips/lips of the speaker. Some samples: integrated management options, integrated reciprocal mobility, systematized organizational contingency. Don't they all sound familiar?

Figure 10-8. Broughton's "Systematic Buzz Phrase Projector" (shown in part) streamlines obfuscation. Pick any three numbers and match them to the columns (e.g., 2–9–1 = "systematized policy flexibility").

0. integrated	0. management	0. options
1. total	1. organizational	1. flexibility
2. systematized	2. monitored	2. capability
3. parallel	3. reciprocal	3. mobility
	. . .	
9. balanced	9. policy	9. contingency

Effective Language Is Nondistracting

"Uh, y'know, this stuff about, y'know, how you . . . uh . . . sound seems . . . uh . . . a bit, y'know, overdone." Not only choice of words but the way we say them can seriously affect a presentation. Effective language does not distract listeners away from the message or cause them to make negative judgments. (Figure 10-9).

The "uh" problem is a common one, universally noticed and detested by nearly everyone, except the speaker of them. People who have had considerable exposure to speech training find this one particularly distracting, as they sit and count the number of "uhs" rather than listen to the message. I counted one speaker and quit at forty-five "uhs" after only three minutes. When asked for his own estimate of the number, the speaker guessed three to four. Most speakers are unaware of problems of this type. The Toastmasters have excellent success at eliminating "uhs" quickly. They ring a bell or make some other obvious noise at every "uh," and it takes only a few short speeches for this problem to diminish drastically.

Lack of fluency with or without "uhs" can be highly irritating to listeners. False stops and starts, fragmentary sentences, uncertainties, and fillers all add up to a poor impression. According to psychologist Albert Mehrabian, these indicate anxiety and negative feelings. "They make description less effective, more difficult to understand, and generally inhibit the communication process. In this sense, the errors serve to delay what a person has to say and lead us to infer that he has at least some reservations about saying it."[23]

The "y'know" problem is the bane of this era. It may be cute in the high school classroom but is deadly in the presentation room. Roderick Nordell wondered what the Gettysburg Address would have sounded like if Abe Lincoln had the speech habits of many people of today and came up with "Like . . . fourscore and . . . you know . . . seven years ago . . . right? . . . our fathers . . . like . . . brought forth . . . I mean . . . on this continent . . . a new . . . like . . . nation . . ."[24]

Poor grammar and misuse of words have stymied advancement for several bright businesspeople, and often they don't even know the reason. We're quick to correct the grammar of children, but we seem reluctant to discuss the same

Figure 10-9. Language fillers and errors focus attention the wrong way.

problem among adults. And yet everyone else of reasonable education is fully aware of the poor language habits of the people they hear and freely discusses them with others, often saying. "Isn't it a shame? If it weren't for his language . . ." (and not referring to profanity).

In the Department of Education in Washington, employees attend a course called "Up with English." The course focuses on speech characteristics that may hold people back in their jobs or affect office relationships, such as with supervisors. Lorraine Goldman, who created the course, said that a boss unhappy about an employee's language performance is often reluctant to approach the employee about the problem. This often causes communication between the two to deteriorate and does nothing to correct the situation. When employees learned to use "acceptable" English, Goldman found, bosses quickly realized the changes and responded favorably to them. She notes that time and time again her students tell her, "I wish someone had corrected me when I was in school."[25]

Effective Language Is Forceful

The great speakers, the ones to whom we listen and by whom we are moved, almost always use language well. Martin Luther King, Douglas MacArthur, and John Kennedy were acclaimed as outstanding speakers because their ideas met the needs of their times and their messages were spoken in words and phrasing that were stirring and memorable. Their speeches were often quoted.

The business conference room is not the same as the political platform, yet the speakers discussing lasers or cash flows who are effective generally have the ability to use the language well, if not so dramatically as a Martin Luther King. Conversely, the speakers who bore us or leave us unimpressed often do so, in large part, because of the blandness of their language.

Useful advice for injecting life into language and cutting its dullness comes from veteran sports writer Fred Russell of Nashville. He advises aspiring writers to avoid "wallflower words" and to use words that "dance around the room."[26] Russell's concept of "words that dance" applies to speaking no less than to writing. Compare:

> At this point in time, and commensurate with the mitigating circumstances with which we now find ourselves, it seems advisable to interface with the really good liquid refreshments made available to us, that, I am assured by the cognizant personnel, are not too shabby. [Or, if you prefer, "Let's take a coffee break."]

> As the haughty and debonair Belgian detective Hercule Poirot, he is *formidable, merveilleux,* and a bloody delight. The black hair is pomaded scalp tight; the moustaches are waxed into elegant upturning symmetries; the eyebrows lift, the eyes roll, the gray cells can very nearly be heard to cogitate, in the low thrum of a computer. [Movie critic Charles Champlin's description of Albert Finney as Poirot in *The Orient Express.*] [27]

Both passages contain about the same number of words, but what a difference. The first is loaded with wallflower words, every one of which you have probably heard dozens of times, and which add up to little. In the second passage, Champlin expressed his opinion and described the actor's characterization using few words, but they are words that dance.

IMPROVING LANGUAGE EFFECTIVENESS

We've seen the five key factors that distinguish effective language from language that presents problems for listeners and thus for speakers. Here are some specific ways to improve the way your verbal element—language—comes across to listeners. Four basic guidelines are useful:

1. Assume that the main burden of responsibility to communicate is yours and that your duty is not to impress, baffle, or overpower your listeners but to help them understand your message.
2. Know your listeners. Determine in advance their specialties, level of involvement and interest, and familiarity with your topic.
3. Test your material in advance. A dry run with knowledgable audience members from the same background (or simulating the same back-

ground) can give you valuable feedback in advance on whether your presentation will be understood, appropriate, and interesting.

4. During the presentation, measure and respond to the audience feedback, verbal and nonverbal.

Speak to Be Understood

Several forms of confusing language were noted earlier. Here are some ways to tackle the most common problems.

- *Be careful with acronyms and abbreviations.* These shortcuts are a way of life in government and private industry. DoD, OSHA, RFQ, STS, OR, and thousands more like them are commonly used, with new ones appearing daily. These do speed up communication *if* all parties know what the terms mean and if they understand them to mean the same things. OR may mean Operating Room to a surgeon, but it means Operations Research to a practitioner of that black art (whatever that is).

Think before using an acronym. Does the audience, particularly the key members, know the term? Explain in full any acronym or abbreviation the first time it is used, unless you are certain the audience knows the term.

- *Speak a language the audience can understand.* Watch the jargon, trade lingo, and slang. For a guideline, consider how you would speak to be understood if your audience were the senior class from your local high school. Avoid inside expressions for places, people, organizations, or activities. The Pentagon in Washington is Disneyland East or the Puzzle Palace: the company president is the Gray Owl: employees work in the Spook Shop. All of these terms are fun and harmless until used with those not in the know.

- *Explain ambiguous terms.* Words and expressions do not necessarily mean the same to all people. The word *contract,* for example, comes in different forms, and when a speaker says, "We have a cost-plus contract," she may mean cost-plus-fixed-fee. A listener with a different frame of reference may interpret the comment to mean cost-plus-incentive-fee, which is definitely not the same.

Many words are commonly used, though few people are entirely clear about them. *Productivity, cash flow, disintermediation, hegemony* and *realization* fit into this category.

- *Ask for feedback to see if mutual understanding exists.* Reduce possibilities for misinterpretation by explaining words or terms, being more specific about them, or demonstrating by example. You can sometimes show illustrations, photographs, or actual objects. This would certainly have helped clarify a sign seen at a neighborhood recreation center in Hawaii: "Do Not Sit On Balls. Use For Intended Purposes Only."[28]

- *Avoid foggy phraseology.* Presenters who provide only partial or vague information risk the possibility that they will not be understood as they intend (and they may not know until later that they were misunderstood). For example: "I want ten delivered on the eighteenth." What was wanted were ten pieces delivered on the eighteenth of March. What he got were ten dozen delivered on the eighteenth of April. (Or did they go to the eighteenth green?)

"I told our new hirees to go into the shop and expose themselves to each of the machines." What a sight that must have been.

■ *Be specific.* Does "next to" mean east or west of? Is "several" three, five or fifteen? Does "50K" mean $50,000 or 50 kilometers?

■ *Distinguish assumptions from observations, probabilities from certainties, theory from established fact.* "Flight failure was due to a pyrotechnic malfunction, caused by a faulty part received from the vendor." You may be certain about the malfunction but guessing about the cause. Not making that clear could cause problems immediately or later.

■ *Clear up loose sentence connections*—improper antecedents, dangling participles, disjointed clauses. From an introduction: "Being a corporate executive and a prominent community leader as well, one might assume Miss Wilson can present us with a unique insight."

■ *Avoid scrambled metaphors.* Said the harried congressman, "We've got to stop milking that dead horse!" Metaphors and other figures of speech add color and insight to expression; they can also add confusion. If you are going to use them, make sure they are correct and complete and their logic is immediately evident.

■ *Drop the "un" and "not" garblers.* From a technical-magazine editorial: "It should not be unsatisfying to Americans to realize that the international aerospace ballgame may soon no longer be dominated by U.S. equipment." Hmmm.

Double negatives force listeners to do mental gymnastics to figure out what you mean. To call a pleasant activity "a not altogether unpleasant activity" is bad enough in writing, where the reader can go back and decipher it. It is hopeless in speaking, where the listeners don't have that luxury. George Orwell suggested that speakers could cure themselves of the "not un-" habit by memorizing this sentence: "A not unblack dog was chasing a not unsmall rabbit across a not ungreen field."[29]

■ *Fight obfuscation. Gobbledygook* or *bafflegab* means using large words, euphemisms, or indirect and lengthy phrases. This technique is often intended to impress or dodge rather than to communicate. Here are a few examples:

> *energetic disassembly* instead of *nuclear explosion*
> *reduction in force* instead of *layoff*
> *correspondence review clerk* instead of *mail sorter*
> *vertical transportation transfer agent* instead of *elevator operator*
> *attitude adjustment hour* instead of *coffee break* (they're not all bad)

An advanced form of obfuscation is patterned after the German method of combining small words to get really big ones and is called noun stacking. Perhaps the champ so far in English came from an Air Force bulletin. All supervisors were asked to report at noon for the "merit pay appraisal system research field test training session," a nine-noun term.[30]

Reduce Language Distractors

Identify and eliminate poor language habits. The first requirement is the determination to start speaking proper English in all speaking situations. Students often acknowledge that their normal language patterns are detrimental but say that they won't speak that way during a presentation. Baloney. Trying to speak correctly before a group when your normal speech habits are poor will usually come across to listeners as unnatural. Consciously trying not to use "y'knows," "uhs," and double negatives presents more problems to a speaker at a time when he or she should be concentrating on the message. My message is to start using correct speech patterns in everyday talking so that the distracting elements are gone when you stand up to speak before a group. Replace the bad habits with good ones.

Presenters can employ several methods to reduce the distractiveness of their language:

■ Read *aloud* often to improve fluency, reduce faulty grammar, and sharpen lazy English.

■ Listen to yourself as you read aloud or give presentations by using an audio or video recorder. Compare yourself to good speakers in your area, such as the top local newscasters.

■ Learn a foreign language. This helps clear up subject/verb mismatches and double negatives.

■ Have a knowledgeable friend or speaking coach listen to the way you use language in formal and informal situations, such as errors in pronunciation, grammar, and word use. Have them try the Toastmaster technique of ringing a bell when "uhs", "y'knows," or other distractions occur (in practice settings only).

■ Obtain one of the many excellent books that note common errors and proper language usage.

■ Keep a small book handy to jot down words or expressions whose uses or pronunciations are difficult. Write down the correct definition, use, or pronunciation. If certain words regularly cause you trouble, break them down to basic elements. Compare your use of language with the common language errors given in the following lists. These can be distracting to listeners and damaging to the impression you want to create.

Grammar Flaws

Double negatives	"I didn't never say that."
Subject/verb mismatches	"We wasn't told. Who done it?"
Cheap substitutes	"ain't," "warn't," "his'n."
Tense confusion	"He drunk his coffee already."
Confused pronouns	"With who am I speaking?"
Adjective/adverb confusion	"She spoke good."
Verb confusion	"I'll learn you."

Pronunciation Flaws

Extra consonant	"staStistics," "colYumn."
Extra vowel	"athAlete," "grievIous."
Confused letters	"substantUate," "eKcetera."
Misplaced syllable	"DIrect your attention."
Vowel mispronunciation (often a provincialism)	"Ārab," Eyetalian," "theĀter."
Erroneously sounded silent letter	"poiGnant," "suBtle," "ofTen."
Erroneous consonant sound	"gesture" (with hard *g*).
Foreign misexpressions	"coop day grass."

Selection or Usage Confusion

Confused words	"irreverant data," "effluent society," "jet entrails."
Nonexistent words	"irregardless."
Singular/plural confusion	"the first criteria," "a rare phenomena."

Mannerisms

Lazy imitations	"yeah," "ya," "yep," "nope," "uh huh," "huh?"
Overused expressions	"for sure," "fantastic," "wow," "oh man, hey," "Not!"
Insidious fillers	"like," "y'know," "I mean," "right," "uh," "okay."
Runtogethers	"trynago," "woncha," "hadda."

Put Zest Into Your Language

Here are some ideas to turn dull language into forceful, colorful expression that is more likely to be listened to, understood, and recalled.

- *Start with a subject you are excited about and want to communicate.* Sparkling language will rarely be present if conviction is absent. Learning how to use language better starts with the intense desire to communicate better.
- *Have something worthwhile to say.* Many people can use colorful and convincing language with little of substance behind it, and with great success. But the time comes (not always) when people stop listening to that kind of speaker. John Locke said it more than three centuries ago: The first and most palpable abuse (in communication) is using words without clear and distinct ideas.[31]
- *Keep meaning in mind.* "What is above all needed is to let the meaning choose the word and not the other way around," wrote George Orwell in a classic article on the use of language.[32]

Here also are some specific ways to spice your expression with more "dancing" words and to reduce the drabness by dumping the "wallflowers."

- *Avoid clichés . . . like the plague* such as:

"Not too shabby, really, for me."   Spoken with rare insight.

"Unaccustomed as I am to public speaking."	Well, we don't want to impose on you, so sit down.
"This whole subject blows my mind."	It certainly doesn't strain it.
"We've got to get our act together, bite the bullet, pull out all the stops, get with the program, Charlie, and win one for the Gipper."	Could you be a wee bit more specific?

■ *Minimize use of "in" terminology (vogue words).* When business people verbalize, it seems imperative that they legitimize their words, messagewise, by optimizing the application of current buzz words, lexiconwise. Thus, they *facilitize* instead of *build, strategize* instead of *plan, grow peoplewise* instead *of add jobs.*

■ *Delete and cut unnecessary redundancies.* Go after words or expressions that add nothing to the meaning, except more words:

"Personally, I think . . ."	Consider the alternatives: "Impersonally, I think . . ." "Personally, he thinks . . ." "Personally, I don't think . . ."
"Full to capacity."	Repeat the exercise above.
"At this point in time."	Now.
"Obviously . . ."	Not to me. And if it is, why say it?
"Approximately 6.431 inches."	How much closer can you get?
"Consensus of opinion."	Is there any other form of consensus?
"A somewhat unique proposal."	It's either unique or it isn't.

■ *Don't use qualifiers very much, hopefully:* "Real good." "Pretty complicated system." "Highly sophisticated." "A great effort, by a great team of great talents." Stronger speech results if the qualifiers are omitted or reduced.

■ *Use the simple word rather than the pretentious.* George Orwell was firm about it: never use a long word where a short one will do.[33]

utilize	or	*use*
terminate	or	*end*
fabricate	or	*make*

■ *Make use of verbs in their simplest forms.* Three categories present the greatest possibilities:

Single Verb Over Equivalent Phrase

"render inoperative"	"shut off"
"conduct an investigation of"	"investigate," "check"
"take into consideration"	"consider"
"exhibits a tendency"	"tends"

Active Tense Over Passive

"Inflation is increased by oil imports."   "Oil imports increase inflation."

"Programs were reviewed."   "We reviewed programs."

A Verb Other Than "Is" or "Are"

"There are three surviving bidders."   "Three bidders survive."

"Helen is a good leader."   "Helen leads well."

■ *Choose words that stir the senses.* These are words with bite, color, pungency, flavor, and snap. One of the best ways to get people to listen intently is to use language that stimulates their active mental or sensory participation. Three ways help do this.

The first is to choose the *concrete* over the *abstract.* Abstract terms are hard to relate to and are often ambiguous. The more specific the example, the clearer the concept becomes and the more strongly listeners identify with it, assuming they are familiar with the specific example. Adding detail increases the association. Which is more distinctive:

an automobile or *a 1936 silver Dusenberg?*

injuries   or *a punctured eyeball?*

Communism   or *Hungary 1956, Czechoslovakia 1968, Afghanistan 1980?*

Choose the *vivid* over the *bland.* Which has more spark and accuracy?

move   or *shake, tingle, quiver, vibrate?*

speak   or *hiss, bellow, drawl?*

good   or *splendid, savory, impeccable?*

bad   or *naughty, wanton, lubricious, licentious?*

happiness or *euphoria, ecstasy, delight?*

smell(y)   or *stench, pungent, musky?*

Choose the *imaginative* over the *commonplace.* Speakers who use metaphors and other figures of speech, colorful expressions, and unusual word arrangements well have powerful tools at their command, as these examples show:

■ From Martin Luther King's "I have a dream" speech in 1964: "America has given the Negro people a bad check—a check that has come back marked 'insufficient funds.' "
■ A corporate lawyer, referring to two corporations trying to do business with each other while suing each other: "There's an old saying in the legal profession: thou shalt not litigate by day, and copulate by night."
■ Because of funding cuts, personnel at Goddard Space Flight Center were hard pressed to keep their programs alive. One director said: "We have one foot over the cliff, the other on a banana peel."[34]

- *Let phrasing be dramatic and varied.* Good speakers use phrasing well, short sentences, even dramatic single words, repeated themes, occasional rhetorical and hypothetical questions to invoke a different listening process. Some examples:

  - John F. Kennedy's 1963 inaugural speech: "Ask not what your country can do for you; ask what you can do for your country."[35]
  - Martin Luther King: "I have a dream that one day this nation . . . I have a dream that one day on the red hills of Georgia . . . I have a dream that my four little children . . ."[36]
  - Patrick Henry: "Has Great Britain any enemy, in this quarter of the world, to call for all this accumulation of navies and armies? No sir, she has none. They are meant for us . . . Shall we try argument? Sir, we have been trying that for years . . . Shall we resort to entreaty and humble supplication?"[37]

TRANSMISSION OF LANGUAGE—THE VOICE

A good speaking voice is a valuable asset to a speaker. Franklin Delano Roosevelt, Martin Luther King, and Ann Richards come to mind as people whose voices help make them powerful speakers. The voice of James Earl Jones adds unforgettable touches to *Othello,* TV voice-overs, and *Star Wars'* Darth Vader.

We have all heard speakers whom we dislike, are amused by, or distrust, mostly because of the way they sound rather than what they say. The fender-pounding used-car salesman, the arrogant government official, the shifty personnel manager: all create negative impressions on a number of their listeners by their voices.

These intuitive observations are backed up by research. Psychologist Albert Mehrabian has shown that we are five times as likely to be influenced by the vocal tone than by the spoken words in developing our feelings and attitudes toward a speaker.[38] We are often more inclined to go by *how* something is said rather than by *what* is said. Thus both intuition and research indicate the wisdom of developing our ability to use our voices well.

The voice is a key part of a presenter's tool kit, yet seldom, if ever, does the average presenter do anything to develop its capability. An executive may spend an hour each day keeping his or her body in shape yet spend no time exercising the voice. In fact, the typical executive engages in several practices—smoking, drinking, screaming "kill the umpire"—that are abusive to the vocal system.

Speakers can do several simple things that will assist the vocal system in doing its best (see also Figure 10-10):

- Speak conversationally. Thundering oration and dramatic whispering aren't part of business presentations. A speaker doesn't need to shout, e-nun-ci-ate, or use theatrical effects to be effective. In general, speak as though you were talking to one person, in a natural, easy manner.
- Speak extemporaneously. The average nonprofessional speaker is terrible at reading material aloud. Use of a manuscript or detailed notes or

Figure 10-10.   Proper vocal use can add much to presentation success.

- Start with a subject that you are excited about and truly want to communicate to others; then many of the common vocal problems will be alleviated.
- Practice to increase vocal capability and fluency.
- Speak extemporaneously, relying as little as possible on notes or written material, to maintain a natural vocal manner.
- Speak conversationally, to one person at a time.
- Make sure you are heard comfortably by all listeners. Don't allow falloff when speaking at a screen, using a microphone, or responding to questions.
- Speak so you can be understood easily, with appropriate pace and articulation.
- Vary rate, pitch, and volume to keep interest and to place emphasis on key material.
- Work on troublesome words so you can pronounce them easily and correctly.
- Read aloud often and get feedback to improve vocal capability.
- If you are an excessively restrained speaker, make sure your visual aids are arresting and that you are well prepared and well tested.
- Work for a pleasing vocal quality to create a positive reaction in listeners and to maintain vocal capability over extended use.
- Work on posture, breathing, and tension-free throat and jaw to improve vocal quality and capability.
- Don't smoke or drink heavily.

verbatim reading of busy "word charts" will almost always be accompanied by a monotonic, boring voice.

- Give yourself good material. If you are not enthused about your subject, lack confidence in your findings or ideas, or have a presentation that is poorly organized, with visual aids that are dull and cluttered, you will find it almost impossible to come across as a forceful, exciting speaker.
- Rehearse. The words and the way they are spoken benefit enormously from a dry run. Confidence, better choice of words, and fluency are achieved by practice.
- Exercise and develop the system. Achieving a better tennis serve or speaking voice comes from learning good techniques and then developing them through practice. Speak often, read aloud, sing, stretch, and strengthen your voice.

First, You Must Be Heard

Several factors are involved. The first is awareness. Generally, the low-volume speakers are surprised when told they are not speaking loudly enough. "Really? I thought I was shouting," is a standard reply.

A second factor is projection or focus, which is not degree of loudness but placement. Many speakers keep their words inside or muffle their words. Pretend you are a stuffy, upper-class Englishman speaking. Probably you'll imitate someone who swallows his words, like Santa Claus when he says "Ho, ho, ho!" A speaker with this voice characteristic can increase the ability to be heard by focusing the voice toward the back of the room while maintaining the same loudness. To develop sensitivity to this, start with the Santa Claus "Ho, ho, ho"; then focus on a listener in a seat 3 feet away, then 10, and then 20. It works.

An irritating demonstration of focus, combined with insensitivity to adequate loudness, occurs when a speaker directs comments to one audience member, perhaps in response to a question. The result is that the other audience members cannot hear. The same results occur with large audiences when the speaker responds to a question many in the audience did not hear and immediately is greeted with shouts of "Please repeat the question."

Another factor is occasional dropout or falloff. Many speakers let their sentences trail off at the ends, so audiences miss those parts. Others fail to emphasize key words; these may be heard but not absorbed as significant.

Be Understood

Many speakers talk loudly enough, but their message fails to get across because they are hard to understand. "Wadizzitchurtrynagit ucross? Thas th'prolemwitmosofyou expurts—youspeckmirculs."

It is a rare speaker who cannot stand *some* degree of improvement in making speech more understandable. Perhaps one-third of the professional people who participate in my seminars need *substantial* improvement in this area. Their ability to get their ideas across rapidly and accurately is seriously hampered by the lack of clarity in their speech.

Some speakers are hard to understand because they speak too rapidly. Others talk at the same rate as the motormouth but can be clearly understood. The reason is that their diction is clearer. Lyle Mayer, in *Fundamentals of Voice and Diction,* says that 140–180 words per minute is generally regarded as satisfactory for reading and speaking, with the desirable rate dependent on the type of material being presented.[39] A National Aeronautics and Space Administration observer has found 100 words per minute to be a good pace for technical presentations.[40]

Speakers who barely move their lips are also often difficult to understand. Listeners will also be inclined to make judgments that the speaker is close-mouthed and trying to hide something.

Sloppy, hard-to-understand English creates negative impressions in the minds of the audience. Mayer notes that distinctness of speech is often a "rather reliable indication of the mental and physical alertness of the individual."

How widespread is sloppy English? Mayer quotes and agrees with a survey that found that more than one-third of speakers talk so indistinctly that they are in need of special help. He adds: *"Of all the problems involved with voice and speech, poor articulation is the most common."*[41]

Be Expressive

Mayer defines expressiveness as vocal variety: "The pitch level at which we speak, our vocal movements from pitch to pitch, our rate of speaking, phrasing, emphasis." This is the life—vitality, spark, interest—we put into our speaking.

Presenters may speak loudly enough, be clearly understood, and speak properly yet wonder why people don't listen to them. The audiences fall asleep, their eyeballs glaze over, or they keep asking dumb questions, indicating that the clearly delivered message isn't getting through. One of the most common reasons for these results is poor expressiveness. In my experience, few speakers are using their verbal tools as effectively as they might, and most speakers can be helped substantially by improving their expressiveness.

Richard Borden pointed out that the key technique of hypnotists is absence of pitch variation, which induces sleep "through the progressive paralysis of conscious attention."[42] Perhaps you have experienced that same reaction in some of your college classes, sermons you have slept through, or, heaven forbid, business presentations you have been the victim of.

It is fascinating to watch a dull speaker view himself or herself for the first time on video playback. Often he can't stand to watch himself and comments, as did one speaker, "Oh, that's so boring! I'm putting myself to sleep." The ultimate evaluation.

The first key to expressiveness is the personality and attitude of the presenter. If he feels good about himself, is excited about the work, and is truly interested in sharing the ideas or results with the audience, much of the work is done. If he feels insecure, has a low regard for his performance or material, and dislikes the whole idea of giving a presentation, it will be extremely difficult for him to put much spirit into his delivery.

Speakers with strong convictions rarely lack vocal expressiveness. Listen to Tom Peters speak about excellence, and you will hear an expressive speaker. Poet Carl Sandburg loved to speak about his country, and his vocal expressiveness was as remarkable as his poetry. Jesse Jackson's vocal style is a key reason for his ability to move audiences. On the other hand there's Henry Kissinger.

But shouldn't business professionals—such as engineers and financial experts—stay aloof and present their ideas dispassionately, letting the material speak for itself? Many think that, and make some of the dullest presentations seen anywhere.

Presenters who have a high degree of vocal expressiveness are better able to get their messages across than those who don't. Part of the reason is that audiences are more awake to start with. Dynamism in the presenter is also one of the three characteristics regarded as most important for speaker credibility.

The effective speaker knows that key points must be emphasized to receive proper notice, that listeners need some time to let complex or significant points sink in, that attention needs constantly to be revived. This person uses his or her voice like a hammer to punch home key points, with an awareness that the voice can be more effective than a fist hitting the lectern.

Expressive speakers tend to be more entertaining than nonexpressive speakers. Communications consultant Gloria Goforth, whose specialty is training businesspeople to become better listeners, pointed out that listening and learning are greatly enhanced when the audience enjoys listening to the speaker.[43]

Pitch Selection. The droning or monotone speaker has little change in pitch. (Mayer notes that the drone characteristically uses a range of two to four tones and that effective speakers can use a range of twelve to fourteen tones.[44])

Impact and drama can be added to expression through *pitch changes* or inflections. Consider a speaker who says, "We will meet your schedule," with a rising inflection, compared to a person who uses a falling inflection for the same sentence. The latter imparts a stronger feeling of certainty, leading to greater confidence in what the speaker is saying.

Say aloud, "Of the people, by the people, for the people" all at the same pitch and see how little sense it makes. "We are the best contractor to build your nuclear reactor for three reasons: our design is better, our technology is sound, and our production capability is proven." Would you give the business to the presenter who delivered this message in a monotone?

Rate or Pace Selection. Good speakers are particularly distinguished by their extensive use of changes in delivery rate. By contrast, little rate variation is an extremely common deficiency in mediocre speakers.

Mark Twain was a famed lecturer as well as a writer. He knew well the power of the pause: "That impressive silence, that eloquent silence, that geometrically progressive silence which often achieves a desired effect where no combination of words howsoever felicitous could accomplish it."[45]

John Barrymore, one of the great stage actors of his day, was also one of the great tipplers of his day. The story is told that following one long night on the town, he was onstage playing Hamlet. He came to the classic line, "To be or not to be . . ." and blacked out. After a lengthy pause, his brain clicked back in and he continued ". . . that is the question." In the next day's reviews a critic wrote he had never seen such a memorable portrayal.

Problems due to speaking rate surface as:

- The motormouth, speaking so fast people can't absorb the information. This is especially detrimental when speaking to general or foreign audiences.
- The drawler, speaking so-o-o de-lib-er-ate-ly audiences want to use a cattle prod on the speaker.
- The syncopator, who speaks five words, pauses, speaks five words, pauses . . . This one quickly drives audiences out of the room.

Volume Selection. The story is told of a preacher who wrote notes to himself in the margins of his sermon manuscripts. One note supposedly said, "Weak point—shout."

Both louder and softer speech can let the audience know you are now saying something particularly significant or that the mood now is different from the earlier one. As an example of the use of and need for volume changes, read the following material aloud as you would truly say it to the board of directors: "We've looked at various aspects of this new business opportunity. This project does not conflict with our long-range plans. I think you will agree that the key to winning has to be cost credibility. That is our greatest strength; it is our competitor's major deficiency. Members of the board, if we are to become a viable contractor in this new field, we must bid this contract now."

A change in volume for different *syllables* determines the meaning in words (*con*flict or con*flict*, *pro*ject or pro*ject*). Emphasis on a *single word* clarifies the meaning of expressions ("That is our *greatest* strength"). Increased volume on *word groups* or *expressions* places significance on them ("cost credibility," "We must bid this contract now"). Softening of words occurs naturally and to good effect in the end of this expression: "That is our greatest strength; it is our competitor's major deficiency."

Be Pleasing to Listen To

Another factor that often acts to the detriment of presenters is the nature of the voices themselves. Audiences generally have a negative reaction to presenters whose voices are squeaky, harsh, shrill, gushy, guttural, raspy, or weak. A "good" voice either will not be noticed at all or may be acknowledged as pleasing, powerful, or rich. The "poor" voice may or may not be immediately evident to the listener as amusing, irritating, or even painful. Voice coach John Lasher noted: "The subconscious effects of the voice are not obvious. When someone says, 'I don't know why, but I just don't like that person,' it often is because he or she doesn't like the sound of the person's voice."[46]

Psychologist Albert Mehrabian has experimentally verified that the voice plays a major role in whether we like a person or, more important for presenters, we are liked by others. His results show that 38 percent of "total liking" is due to vocal tone or expression. Mehrabian's data also indicate that the voice reflects what the speaker is feeling, since we pick up so much more from *how* a speaker says something than from *what* is said.[47] And if there is a conflict between the two, we believe the voice over the words. Lasher cited as an example our reaction when we talk to someone on the telephone: "We ask 'How are you?' and they say 'Fine' in a flat voice, and we know better. The voice is the mirror of the emotions."

Some regional accents, such as the strong Bronx accent, can be detrimental to speakers. Among the heaviest uses of diction coaches are New Yawkers and good ole boys from the South, as they have often found their accents to be professional liabilities outside their native areas. Accents that come across as affectations, such as Hahvahd accents, can also alienate some listeners.

Speech expert Gloria Goforth advises: "If a musical lilt or charming brogue adds to the positive atmosphere of the conversation, keep it. If your accent hampers communication because listeners can't understand your words or develop adverse impressions due to associations your accent creates, run and get help from your nearest speech coach. Don't let an easily correctable speech problem keep your true capability from showing."[48]

The voice can also be a reliable index of character, according to Lyle Mayer.[49] An unpleasant voice can itself be distracting and lead listeners to form negative judgments, consciously or unconsciously. It behooves a presenter to become aware of voice characteristics that may be hampering the effectiveness of his or her presentations and to develop a more pleasing voice.

Many voices that come across as unpleasant are associated with improper use of the vocal mechanism, which, if not corrected, can lead to more serious problems later. A demonstration was given by one presenter whose guttural voice gave him a high degree of authority but was raspy enough to be irritating to listen to. By the end of an hour's presentation, his voice was often nearly gone.

Good sound production must begin with a good air source. Voice experts recommend abdominal or lower-chest breathing over extreme upper-chest and shoulder breathing. The latter is what many people do when told, "Now take a deep breath." This is unfortunate, because upper-chest breathing does *not* provide a deep breath, gives little power for voice production or air management, and may be accompanied by throat tension and poor voice quality.

If your shoulders heave when you breathe, you're an upper-chest/shoulders breather, and your voice capability and quality may improve by switching to abdominal breathing, which is the way most people breathe when they are lying on their backs and relaxing.

Particularly nervous presenters often have difficulty breathing as they speak. Panting, gasping, and frequent swallowing are the signs, along with a general appearance of wanting to be anywhere else. Anxiety associated with speaking before a group clearly affects many people's ability to breathe. Even experienced speakers sometimes run out of breath before they complete sentences or lose projection as their air supply gets lower.

This difficulty in breathing may be related to inadequate air supply, excessive air supply, or poor management of that supply.

To prevent fading or running out of air, the key is to ensure that you always have an adequate air supply and that you use it economically. Inhale at logical pause spots as you speak, *before* you need air. Then release your air slowly to keep from exhausting your air supply in the first few words.

Cicely Berry notes the importance of "rooting" the breath stream, opening the breathing out in the base of the ribs—the diaphragm and the stomach—"so you are able to feel where the sound starts, and you can root it down, as it were, so that the whole frame of the body is involved with and is part of the sound."[50]

Many voices unpleasant to the ear get that disagreeable quality through poor use of the mechanisms for sound production and sound shaping—amplification and modification of sound into understandable language. What goes on with all the parts involved that make a good or poor voice? Voice coach John Lasher suggested that clues can be seen in the way a person comes home at night from the office: "If you've had a good day, you go home with high spirits, smiling and singing. If you've had a lousy day, you go home growling, with a set jaw and tight throat. The differences in the voices in the same person show how important it is that there be no tension in the throat and jaw—any tension there is wrong, both voice- and healthwise—and that the voice feeling be brought high up in the head rather than kept down in the throat. This elevated arch in the mouth associated with the buoyant feeling is directly related to a pleasant sound."

ACHIEVING AN EFFECTIVE VOICE

Suggestions will be made here in reverse order to the topics discussed in the preceding section. Reason? An effective voice starts with a healthy voice, then the personality is added. Everything else follows from those.

Developing Vocal Quality

The following activities can lead to a more pleasing voice production and better use of the voice. If a serious voice or breathing problem is present, see a doctor or speech therapist.

Take Care of Your Voice. This should seem obvious, yet the ways in which people subject their vocal production systems to abuse are numerous. Learning to *use* the voice properly is fundamental. If it is *treated* badly, the voice is sure to suffer regardless. Some basic ways to treat your voice well:

- Don't smoke. This is at the top of the list of every voice expert.
- Drink moderately, if at all. Alcohol dries out the vocal cords.
- Tone down the screaming. How many hoarse throats or cases of laryngitis have you witnessed the day after the ball game?
- Heed the danger signals; don't overdo it. If you've been speaking for a long time and you sense your voice is giving out, let it rest.
- Be kind to your voice—plan ahead. If you're scheduled to lead a tour of fifty members of the local chamber of commerce through the factory, during working hours, get a portable public address system. It beats shouting and not being heard even then.
- Avoid excessive clearing of the throat. This can damage the vocal cords. A gentle cough or liquid may alleviate the catch with less potential damage. If you need to clear your throat frequently, see a doctor.
- Lubricate if needed. A sip of water can help alleviate the dry mouth problem that nervous speakers often have. Having a glass of water at the podium will be appreciated by most speakers. Hot tea with lemon and honey is a favorite of many professional singers and broadcasters.

Work on Correct Posture. A major contributor to poor vocal quality and power is poor posture. Proper alignment allows vocal mechanisms to operate properly. Poor alignment leads to straining, poor quality, and damage.

Improve Breath Management. The following techniques are helpful.

- Stand in a good posture with your hand over your abdomen. Breathe normally. Then, with an adequate air supply, exhale slowly and evenly while making a hissing sound. Your hand should feel the air slowly being pushed out. Exhale completely. Then let the air *pop* into the lungs. Your hand should feel that happen. Repeat two more times.

- Sit or stand in a good posture. Locate your pulse. With an adequate air supply, slowly and evenly count to five, using your pulse as a timer (if your pulse is erratic, just count seconds). Inhale. Repeat, adding to the number each time (five, seven, nine, eleven, and so on) as is comfortable without totally exhausting your air. Make your inhalations brief. Over a period of time, the maximum number should increase.

- Lie on your back with your head supported. Place several books on your stomach. Raise the books by inhaling; let the weight cause you to exhale slowly. This develops breathing capability and coordination.

- Purse your lips and *very lightly* exhale, being totally conscious of the long, steady exhalation. Time how long you can do this. You may be able to double or triple your capability with practice.

Free the Voice. Loosen the tightness in the throat, mouth, lips, and tongue:

- Sing often. "The best method in my experience to develop the voice per se," said NBC broadcaster Paul Taylor.[51]

- Smile. Otolaryngologist Dr. Heston Wilson suggests that as you speak, you think that you are singing. This will help with the proper placement of voice pitch for optimum efficiency. He said that speakers' voices are often more pleasant when they are smiling as they speak. "When a person smiles, his soft palate rises, which sends the air higher and results in a more pleasing sound."[52]

- Yawn-sigh. Imagine it is the end of a full and perfect day. All is well with the world, and now you're satisfyingly tired. You yawn a long "ha-h-h-h-h," starting with a high note and descending to a low one. Make it a clear, light tone, and glide down most of your vocal range. This develops freedom from tension in the larynx and coordination of the breath and sound elements. The yawn-sigh can also be used to warm up the voice or anytime the voice tends to tighten up.

- Use the aspirated "h." If you lead off a vocal exercise, for example, the alphabet, with "hay, b, c, d . . . ," you will be using the aspirated "h." This creates an initial flow of breath before the sound occurs and reduces tension in the vocal cords.

- Use muscle looseners to increase flexibility, extend range, reduce tightness in the muscles concerned, and lessen the tendency to induce tension in other parts: (1) flap your lip as a horse blowing, (2) vocalize "ooo-whyeee" as you move your lips to extreme positions, (3) say bu-bu-bu, (4) open your mouth slightly and hum while shaking your jaw from side to side.

Improving Expressibility

Start With You. If you never show your emotions, are always in tight control, or rarely get excited, you may find it hard to become expressive before a group. Many people lack expressiveness because they are watchers, not participants; because they never become informed enough to talk intelligently about pertinent topics; because they never take a stand. They become cautious, uninvolved, dull. Why should they be any different in speaking before a group? Get into some lively discussions with informed people. Take some positions and defend them. Write letters to the editor or your congressional representative.

Look at Your Material. If the topics you've been choosing don't inspire you, select ones that do. Are your visual aids all word charts? Is your support or illustrative material mostly dry statistics? Are you using notes that resemble the morning newspaper? These are all common characteristics of lowkey, lackluster speakers. The material you use can take you to its level, up or down.

Stretch That Vocal System. The following suggestions should help:

- Read aloud to your children or to yourself. Choose material with high emotional content and ham it up. Read Dr. Seuss or "Casey at the Bat" to the kids. Read story poems, such as "The Shooting of Dangerous Dan McGrew" by Robert Service, or dramatic soliloquies of Shakespeare. Voice authorities rate poetry reading as one of the most worthwhile exercises.
- Obtain an anthology of great speeches and read aloud the words of Patrick Henry, Winston Churchill, Martin Luther King, and other famed orators, or read those of contemporary speakers in *Vital Speeches of the Day.*
- Read magazine or newspaper advertisements. Imagine you are on television delivering a commercial for your favorite product.
- Speak aloud the ABCs or count to 100. Vary pitch, volume, and rate. Whisper, shout, race, slow to a crawl, speak in sonorous tones.
- Sing often, in the shower, in the car, at work around the house.
- Read aloud, with spirit, this classic from Ernest Lawrence Thayer:

CASEY AT THE BAT

It looked extremely rocky for the Mudville nine that day;
The score stood two to four, with but one inning left to play.
So, when Cooney died at second, and Burrows did the same.
A pallor wreathed the features of the patrons of the game.

A straggling few got up to go, leaving there the rest,
With that hope which springs eternal within the human breast.
For they thought: "If only Casey could get a whack at that,"
They'd put even money now, with Casey at the bat.

But Flynn preceded Casey, and likewise so did Blake,
And the former was a pudd'n and the latter was a fake.
So on that stricken multitude a deathlike silence sat;
For there seemed but little chance of Casey's getting to the bat.

But Flynn let drive a single, to the wonderment of all.
And the much-despised Blakey "tore the cover off the ball."
And when the dust had lifted, and they saw what had occurred,
There was Blakey safe at second, and Flynn a' huggin' third.

Then from the gladdened multitude went up a joyous yell—
It rumbled in the mountaintops, it rattled in the dell;
It struck upon the hillside and rebounded on the flat;
For Casey, mighty Casey, was advancing to the bat.

There was ease in Casey's manner as he stepped into his place.
There was pride in Casey's bearing and a smile on Casey's face;

And when responding to the cheers he lightly doffed his hat,
No stranger in the crowd could doubt 'twas Casey at the bat.

Ten thousand eyes were on him as he rubbed his hands with dirt,
Five thousand tongues applauded when he wiped them on his shirt;
Then when the writhing pitcher ground the ball into his hip,
Defiance glanced in Casey's eye, a sneer curled Casey's lip.

And now the leather-covered sphere came hurtling through the air,
And Casey stood a-watching it in haughty grandeur there.
Close by the sturdy batsman the ball unheeded sped;
"That ain't my style," said Casey. "Strike one," the umpire said.

From the benches, black with people, there went up a muffled roar,
Like the beating of the storm waves on the stern and distant shore.
"Kill him! kill the umpire!" shouted someone in the stand;
And it's likely they'd have killed him had not Casey raised his hand.

With a smile of Christian charity great Casey's visage shone,
He stilled the rising tumult, he made the game go on;
He signaled to the pitcher, and once more the spheroid flew;
But Casey still ignored it, and the umpire said, "Strike two."

"Fraud!" cried the maddened thousands, and the echo answered "Fraud!"
But one scornful look from Casey and the audience was awed;
They saw his face grow stern and cold, they saw his muscles strain,
And they knew that Casey wouldn't let the ball go by again.

The sneer is gone from Casey's lips, his teeth are clenched in hate,
He pounds with cruel vengeance his bat upon the plate;
And now the pitcher holds the ball, and now he lets it go,
And now the air is shattered by the force of Casey's blow.

Oh, somewhere is this favored land the sun is shining bright,
The band is playing somewhere, and somewhere hearts are light;
And somewhere men are laughing, and somewhere children shout,
But there is no joy in Mudville—mighty Casey has struck out.

Improving Clarity

How does a speaker know if he or she is hard to understand? Few people are unintelligible on purpose. Record your voice in a speaking situation and listen to it yourself. The difficulty with this, however, is that most people do not listen to their own voices critically, according to Hilda Fisher in her book *Improving Voice and Articulation*. Yet, she says, "auditory feedback is of prime importance in changing speech habits." She recommends listening extensively to other speakers, identifying what distinguishes good voices from bad, and comparing your own criticisms with those of experts so as to "awaken your hearing."[53]

Another way is to ask for an evaluation by people in your business whom you recognize for their presentation skill. Your chums may lack objectivity: "Ya soun fine—you tawk jist lak us."

Listen to your audiences. Do they frequently ask you to repeat something you just said, perhaps to the point of becoming irritating to you? (What do you think it is to them?) The acid test is to speak to someone with a limited knowledge of English. If that person can understand your peers but not you, that's a strong sign your understandability is low.

Another tip to sharpen diction is to *read aloud often*. Take advantage of every opportunity to practice sharpness in speaking aloud. An easy way is to speak the names of freeway exits or advertising slogans as you drive. To practice *sharpening your diction*, lower your voice to a bare whisper. To be understood at a distance, you will need to speak more precisely.

To work on consonants, read this aloud:

> Amidst the mists and coldest frosts,
> With barest wrists and stoutest boasts
> He thrusts his fists against the posts
> And still insists he sees the ghosts.

Or pronounce clearly:

> lecture, humanist, important, restrict, productive, facts, explicit, right, correct, most, just, had to, next week.

Try tongue twisters. They can help improve fluency, and they're fun.

Peter Piper picked a peck of pickled peppers.
Betty Botter bought a bit of better butter, but she said this butter's bitter.
Theopholis Thistle, the thistle sifter, sifted a sieve of unsifted thistles.
Round the rugged rock the ragged rascal ran.
The seething sea ceaseth seething.
Toy boat. (Say it ten times rapidly.)

Read aloud "Nephelidia" by Swinburne to improve diction:

NEPHELIDIA

From the depth of the dreamy decline of the dawn
    through a notable nimbus of nebulous noonshine,
  Pallid and pink as the palm of the flag-flower that
    flickers with fear of the flies as they float,
Are they looks of our lovers that lustrously lean from
    a marvel of mystic miraculous moonshine,
  These that we feel in the blood of our blushes that
    thicken and threaten with throbs through the throat?
Thicken and thrill as a theatre thronged at appeal of
    an actor's appalled agitation,
  Fainter with fear of the fires of the future than pale
    with the promise of pride in the past;

Flushed with the famishing fullness of fever that
    reddens with radiance of rathe recreation,
    Gaunt as the ghastliest of glimpses that gleam
    through the gloom of the gloaming when ghosts go aghast?
Nay, for the nick of the tick of the time is a tremulous
    touch on the temples of terror,
    Strained as the sinews yet strenuous with strife of
    the dead who is dumb as the dust-heaps of death:
Surely no soul is it, sweet as the spasm of erotic emo-
    tional exquisite error,
    Bathed in the balms of beautified bliss, beautific itself
    by beatitude's breath.
Surely no spirit or sense of a soul that was soft to the
    spirit and soul of our senses
    Sweetens the stress of suspiring suspicion that sobs
    in the semblance and sound of a sigh;
Only this oracle opens Olympian, in mystical moods
    and triangular tenses—
    "Life is the lust of a lamp for the light that is dark
    till the dawn of the day when we die."
Mild is the mirk and monotonous music of memory,
    melodiously mute as it may be,
    While the hope in the heart of a hero is bruised by
    the breach of men's rapiers, resigned to the rod;
Made meek as a mother whose bosom-beats bound
    with the bliss-bringing bulk of a balm-breathing baby,
    As they grope through the grave-yard of creeds,
    under skies growing green at a groan for the grimness of God.
Blank is the book of his bounty beholden of old, and
    its binding is blacker than bluer:
    Out of blue into black is the scheme of the skies,
    and their dews are the wine of the bloodshed of things;
Till the darkling desire of delight shall be free as a
    fawn that is freed from the fangs that pursue her,
    Till the heart-beats of hell shall be hushed by a
    hymn from the hunt that has harried the kennel of kings.

IN SUMMARY: SOUND IDEAS AND GOOD DELIVERY MAKE A STRONG TEAM

Delivery is the business of standing before a live audience and belting out the message, with or without the help of visuals. Remember these key points:

- *Nonverbal communication.* How you look and act can weigh more heavily than what you say. Attention to posture, body and facial expression, eye contact, behavior, and appearance is an important investment.

- *Language.* Said Emerson: "I learn immediately from any speaker how much he has already lived through the poverty or splendor of his speech."[54] In striving for splendor, use language that is directive, appropriate, clear, distraction-free, and forceful.
- *Voice.* For many presenters, the voice is a barely tapped resource. Quality, variety, fluency, and energy of the voice determine in large part what is heard, how it is heard, and if it is heard.

Interact: Between Presenter and Audience

KEY POINTS OF THIS CHAPTER

✳ Presentations are not just *sending*; a crucial part is *receiving*.
✳ Successfully handling questions and answers is as significant to success as is the formal presentation.
✳ Successful dialogue requires the ability to read the audience.
✳ Audience members can add to presentations by facilitative listening.
✳ Keeping speakers honest is another vital listener responsibility.

"In the process of winning contracts, almost all presenters want to talk and none of them want to listen. Success in presentations requires engaging listeners." This is the observation of Department of Energy executive Michael Bayer, who has been both sender and receiver for hundreds of Washington presentations.[1]

Questions and answers (Q&A) is a standard part of most business presentations. It may occur as a separate session after the presentation but more typically occurs throughout the presentation. Audience questions can throw speakers off course and damage presentations irreparably, or they can be the speaker's best friend and become the key factor in success.

A presentation joins together briefly the presenter and the receiver. What receivers do has a great effect on the presenter, for better or worse. By constant interruptions or poor listening, they can seriously disrupt the presentation and meeting productivity. As a "coaching" listener, they can greatly aid the quality of presentations and benefit themselves as well. Finally, astute listeners can keep speakers straight by ensuring that the information and techniques used meet legitimate standards of fact and ethics.

QUESTIONS AND ANSWERS: SURVIVING THE FLAK

How important is the ability to handle the Q&A? A contractor team was bidding on a major construction contract. During the customer final interview with the team, an audience member asked a question about the team's specific commitment to a specific activity. The responsible team member waffled. The questioner asked again; more indecision. With that single question, poorly answered, the team's program director believes they lost that contract.

Another person was having a poor time with the presentation. He was clearly uncomfortable speaking, especially to a high-level audience. His hands were shaking, his voice quavering, his words coming out hesitantly. Perhaps ten minutes into the presentation, one of the audience members asked him a question. The presenter paused a moment while he collected his thoughts and then answered the question smoothly. Another question followed, and now the mode had shifted from "speech" to dialogue. The presenter became much more comfortable and succeeded admirably the rest of the way, salvaging what was looking like a dreadful performance. Q&A proved to be highly beneficial for him.

For competitions, it is common practice for the source selection board to send in advance specific questions they want answered during the face-to-face presentation (called by various names—e.g., proposal orals, short list interviews). Satisfactorily answering these questions can greatly help the presenting team's cause; poor answers can damage it, perhaps fatally.

These are examples of the key role Q&A plays in presentations today. Audience input, and the speaker's handling of it, can make or break the presentation. This also distinguishes formal speeches (no Q&A during) from presentations (extensive Q&A during and possibly after).

Common questions during my training seminars or speaker coaching sessions are: "How do you handle someone who keeps interrupting?" and "What do I do if no one asks a question?" The many worries of this type reflect the difficulty numerous speakers have had with this area and their concern about their ability to handle it in the future. In this section we'll offer ideas to help you "survive the flak."

Attitude Check: Is Q&A Good or Bad?

Many presenters approach the question-and-answer part of a presentation with fear: "Oh, God, I hope they don't ask any questions!" Others view it as a contest: "I'll show those clowns!"

A presentation is not the same as a Las Vegas show—the tactics used by Don Rickles don't fit. Neither is it a court hearing at which questioners try to wipe out the other side. The fundamental difference is that, in a presentation, the audience, not the speaker, may be in charge. The other key difference is that the presentation is a cooperative, not an adversary, venture. Both sides are there to gain certain things. Some information the speaker usually wants to know includes the answers to questions such as these:

"Is my message being understood?"
"What do they think about my idea?"
"Is this what they need to hear?"
"Do they have any better information?"
"Why are they looking at me that way?"

The answers to these questions are in the heads of the *audience*, and it is generally vital to the presenter that this information be surfaced. Providing the right environment can result in a mutually beneficial interchange of ideas, information, opinions, plans, and concerns. Stifling audience input prevents the presenter from obtaining it.

As we have seen, audience interaction can be the speaker's best friend. A dialogue format can lessen anxieties, lead to better audience connection, and let the speaker's true self (and competence) come through.

Q&A thus: (1) is there whether you like it or not; (2) potentially can give you valuable information; and (3) can aid your performance significantly. It makes sense to look positively toward Q&A and make sure your skills can help you succeed.

It Can Be a Real Pain

No question about it—audiences can be tough on presenters. The twenty-minute presentation can drag on for two hours. Just as you get rolling, a question can throw you and lead to a lengthy digression. Even worse, some of the *listeners* clearly aren't; they're having their own discussions in the back of the room.

Ask people for words describing presentations, and here's often what comes out: "Feeding frenzy," "the Gong Show," of "It's butt-chewing time."

A major factor for presentations' going way over time or ending up in sniping or bickering sessions is the interchange between speaker and audience or audience and audience. We're talking potentially major disruptions and severe loss of meeting productivity if Q&A is not well done. Both speaker and listeners play roles in achieving *productive Q&A*.

Learn to Read Your Audiences

Even when listeners are not saying anything verbally, they will be saying plenty with their bodies, eyes, faces, and tones of voice. Failure to attend and respond to the listeners' nonverbal messages can lead to their communicating through another nonverbal channel—their feet, as they walk out of the room.

To pick up the messages from listeners, first look at them. A common deficiency in speakers is to focus their entire efforts on sending, leaving their receiving channels closed off. The screen, manuscript, notes, ceiling, and back wall all get the speaker's attention; the audience doesn't.

The audience serves as a feedback system for the speaker. Each listener is a reaction sensor, and by continually checking those sensors, the speaker knows how well the talk is going, *if* he or she reads the signals right.

Astute presenters have learned this vital skill. They talk *with* their audiences, looking them directly in their eyes; they engage in a sensing/checking operation to pick up and validate messages; and they use that information to improve their presentations from moment to moment. Signals to look for are shown in Figure 11-1.

Are they *interested?* Important to a speaker are the audience's answers to such questions as: "Is what I plan to talk about of interest to you?" "I think you

Figure 11-1. Here are some audience signals and what they indicate.

Audience Signals	Favorable (Maybe)	Negative (Maybe)
Interest	Animation	Yawning
	Asking questions	Silence
	Taking notes	Inaction
	Intent eye contact	Looking at ceiling
		Droopy or glazed eyelids
	Leaning forward	Leaning back
	Nodding along	Nodding off
	Tracking chart points	Tracking watch
	Current with material	Speeding you up
Comprehension	Affirmations (verbal or nonverbal)	Scrunched face
		Head scratching
	"Good" (germane, insightful) questions or comments	Puzzled expression
		Exchanged glances
		Chin rubbing
Agreement	Smiling	Tightness
	Warmth	Stoneface
	Congeniality	Curtness
	Congruence	Half-smile
	Direct eye contact	Averted eyes
	Physical closeness	Creating barriers
	Expansive gestures	Arms crossed, hands clenched
	Nodding "yes"	Shaking head "no"

want to skip the technical details and focus on the sales aspects. Am I correct?" Sometimes it's wise to ask these questions explicitly. It's also important to keep checking.

Do they *understand?* Are you getting through? Is your material at the right level, or is it too complex or too basic? Do they understand your jargon, logic, or examples? If they aren't getting it, some regrouping is in order before you lose them permanently.

Are they *convinced?* Having understood your story, are they buying it? Is there resistance? Are they likely to sign or send you back to the drawing board? When they say, "Thank you. We'll look over your material," is the door still open, or have you blown it?

In looking for and evaluating nonverbal signals, be aware of two potential pitfalls. First, signals differ widely across cultures. A hand gesture that means acceptance in one group many mean rejection in another. Learn something about your audience, don't make hasty judgments, and check your assumptions. Second, a single gesture or action may mean little. Folded arms may not mean disagreement; they may mean the folder has a stiff back. Check the whole package of nonverbal signals before drawing conclusions.

ACHIEVING PRODUCTIVE Q&A

Like many other thoughts in this book, the proposed solutions go back to basics, with key concepts summarized in Figures 11-2 and 11-3.

Do Your Homework

Planning. Many Q&A problems arise because audience analysis and approach are faulty. It's also important to understand the rules: any time constraints, whether questions are expected throughout or whether there is a separate Q&A period, and whether questions will be supplied in advance. *If they are supplied in advance and it's tied to a competitive procurement, these must be addressed or your bid may be deemed nonresponsive.*

Design. Organizational looseness is a frequent cause of audience disruption. Many questions can be averted by the simple expedient of an agenda chart, periodic summaries, and strong transitions. Tighten your organization, and prune out anything not directly contributing toward the main objective.

A common troublemaker is not allocating enough time for Q&A. What makes this difficult is uncertainty about how much time to allow and when. A wise guideline is to time the formal presentation to conclude five to ten minutes (or more) before the allocated time. Thus, for a thirty-minute presentation, come in with a twenty-minute presentation. A time plan is useful, with specific

Figure 11-2. These are key how-to's for a productive question-and-answer session.

- Assume audience input is something to look forward to, not dread.
- Do your homework. Be prepared for questions that are likely to come up.
- Be prepared in general. Start promptly, and conduct the presentation in a professional manner.
- Have an organizationally sound talk and uncluttered, to-the-point visuals.
- Have backup data or visuals ready.
- If using a microphone, repeat all questions or comments for the whole audience.
- Be a good listener as well as speaker.
- Answer all questions courteously and accurately, without sarcasm or dodging.
- Don't fool the audience. If you don't know the answer, say so and state your intention to provide the answer later.
- Watch that your nonverbal communication doesn't send a different message from your verbal.
- Keep the "big picture" perspective. Don't let yourself or others sidetrack from the presentation objectives.
- Wrap up the Q&A session with one more brief recapitulation.

Figure 11-3.   Diligent preparation and operation enhances Q&A success.

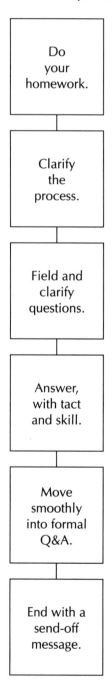

times set for Q&A at appropriate times. You may even need some extra open time as a contingency.

Support. Have solid substantiation ready to back up your claims; data should be current, complete, and accurate.

The design and content of visual aids are major factors in expediting or disrupting the presentation flow. Busy charts invite nitpicking, as has been demonstrated in many conference rooms, to the dismay of speakers who find themselves addressing in detail minor topics. They created their own disruption. Simple, readable charts with clear messages will do much to calm the potentially troubled waters.

Another key to time flexibility and responsiveness is to prepare backup charts. When a question hits, it's impressive to be able to provide a visual immediately that may quickly put the issue to rest and head off a possible ten-minute discussion.

If you are answering questions provided in advance, clearly identify these for each specific question. Leave no doubt that you have responded to their requests.

Staging. If the audience realizes you are poorly prepared, they might give you the same treatment you are giving them—cavalier. Being a professional means taking care of needed arrangements, having equipment in place and ready to go, and being clearly prepared.

Room quality, comfort, and layout can affect the meeting process; a disorderly room invites a disorderly crowd. Who they are and where they sit can help or hinder. To facilitate dialogue, reduce barriers between you and audience members. This is often a problem with computer-driven presentations, where speakers may operate from behind a computer. For these presentations, audience contact is improved by remote controllers. Avoid a totally dark room.

You may increase your success and avert trouble by some judicious advance activity with key attendees. Conference room seating that precludes potential antagonists to your cause from sitting together may be wise.

Finally, get some insurance by testing yourself and your product. Develop a list of potential questions (and suitable answers). Ask colleagues to preview your presentation and give you feedback about likely audience response and questions.

Clarify the Process

Taking care in the first few minutes can do much to set a positive pattern for the presentation:

- *Define your boundaries.* Let them know what you plan to address and what others will address.
- *Capsulize your talk at the start.* High-level listeners particularly value hearing the essence of the talk immediately.
- *Agree on procedures.* Normally, the audience will ask questions at any time,

in spite of requests to "Please hold the questions until the end." If you intend to make that request, have a good reason why, other than that you don't want to be bothered. Mutual understanding of the agenda and time will help keep questions from sidetracking the presentation.

Field and Clarify Questions

Rather than instantly blurting out an answer to a question, first figure out what the question is and the best way to handle it. (In other words, engage brain before mouth.)

- *Listen to the entire question.* A common urge is for the presenter to start answering before the questioner completes the question. Often this results in the wrong question being answered and irritation to the questioner.

- *Make sure you understand it.* Even if you listen to the total question, you may not understand it the same way the questioner does. Audience members don't necessarily put into words exactly what they mean and often don't clearly know what they want to ask. Some checking and restating may help clarify ambiguities and get at the real question.

- *If appropriate, repeat the question* so all can hear, before answering. *Always* do this if using a microphone.

- *Treat each question seriously.* Avoid verbally or nonverbally rebutting with, "Boy, is that a dumb question!" or "I just told you that." It's possible that you may not have communicated as clearly as you thought. Before answering, explore and develop the question so that you understand it. Above all, don't embarrass the questioner.

- *Resolve factual errors or misunderstandings quickly.* Often the question arises from incorrectly stated or understood facts.

- *Defuse the loaded question.* Audience members have been known to ask no-win or trick questions—the "When did you stop beating your spouse?" type. Questions asked in a way that prevents a fair answer need skilled but decisive treatment. "Is it A or B?" can be expanded to include C and D before answering. "Since oil companies caused the so-called fuel shortage, why shouldn't they be nationalized?" False premises should be challenged but not so that a sidetracking debate away from the main issue ensues. Often a simple statement of nonacceptance of the premise keeps it from being accepted implicitly.

- *Determine if you or a colleague should answer.* If the question can be better answered by someone else, direct it to her. Caution: First look at your colleagues to see if they're eager to help or have gone into hiding.

- *Give all audience members a chance to ask questions.* As the person in front, you have much control over who asks questions by where you stand and look. Listen for interruption points in a monologue to divert the discussion to another audience member who seems anxious to talk. State you would like a variety of inputs, to encourage others.

Answer with Tact and Skill

The question has been sorted out. The next key is how it gets answered.

- *Talk to the whole audience, not just the questioner.* This is a common mistake. People don't like to be left out. Eye contact is important to maintaining control and not letting side discussions develop. It may also be more important that someone other than the questioner hear the answer to the question.

- *Answer positively, without apology.* Saying, "Oh, I'm sorry, I forgot to cover that," is immaterial, time-consuming, and self-deprecating.

- *Be careful with humor, sarcasm, criticism, or arrogance.* You can make an enemy for life by making a "witty" answer to the wrong person. Innuendoes about the questioner's motivation or intelligence generally backfire. Even if the questioner's manner is negative, resist the urge to reply in kind. While you may succeed in "putting down" the questioner, you may lose other key people.

- *Hold your temper.* Often the intelligence section of the brain gets short-circuited when temper flares. Losing control can act as bait for an audience that doesn't think much of your ideas anyway.

- *Let your sense of humor show.* Speakers sometimes lose points by not loosening up and enjoying the humor that often is a part of Q&A. Humor can be an effective vehicle for breaking down barriers between presenter and audience.

- *Expand the answer if appropriate.* Elaborating may give the audience time to formulate another question on the same topic. A quick "no" may be the correct answer, but, if perceived as abrupt, it may cut off further communication. (Though, if that is a style, it may be regarded as indicative of a no-nonsense speaker.) Senator Mike Mansfield was famous for brief replies. At the press conference announcing his retirement, he was asked several questions.[2]

Q: Senator, what kind of leader have you been?
A: Average.
Q: Who will win [the presidential election] in November?
A: Carter.
Q: By how much?
A: Enough.

- *Yet, don't get carried away with your answer.* Mark Twain is reported to have observed about a rambling answer to a straightforward question, "We just heard a lot more about penguins than we really wanted to know." You may have answered the question with your first statement, then led them into a progressively deeper state of boredom with your next dozen.

- *Don't be afraid to say "I don't know."* You may want to acknowledge that you really should know, or have the right person there who does know. Let the questioner know you will get the answer.

- *Ask to defer a question that requires a lengthy answer* or that will take up more time than it's worth. It's often wise to give a capsule version of the answer and then offer to discuss it more fully later.

■ *Let the audience give you valuable input and support.* They can be a valuable resource, helping you out of sticky spots by providing information or perspectives you may be lacking. Be careful not to put people on the spot, however.

■ *Measure feedback and test for the quality of your answer.* How is your answer being received? Is the questioner obviously attempting to interrupt or shaking his head in disagreement? Has the question been answered satisfactorily?

■ *Maintain perspective.* Keep your eye on the goal and the clock. You want to let the dialogue flow freely but productively. You also want to achieve specific goals with this presentation, and questions that are excessive or of marginal usefulness, or that require detailed answers, can sidetrack from the main goals of the presentation. Limit questions, if necessary and feasible. With customers and higher management, this takes special tact and determination, yet they often will respond positively to an assertive, tactful presenter. Mutually agreed-upon goals, agenda, and time allotted are useful toward this end.

Move Smoothly Into a Formal Question Period

If a question period is planned, rather than or in addition to questions during the talk, prevent the awkward moments when people are looking at each other and wondering what's next. If you've used a projector, turn it off; the last visual or a lighted screen is distracting. Don't worry about gathering up your charts or straightening up your table. Give your full attention to the audience, and move to a position as barrier free as possible, close to the audience.

Often getting a question period started is difficult. Adopt a positive attitude that shows you truly do welcome questions. One speaker at the conclusion of his talk folded his arms, raised his chin so he could look down at the audience, turned the corners of his mouth down, and said in a flat tone, "Are there any questions." All aspects of his nonverbal message conflicted with his verbal "invitation." In that situation, listeners generally believe the nonverbal over the verbal (and usually they are right).

Choose transition statements that encourage feedback: "We've covered a lot of territory. I'll be pleased to go into detail on any points you choose" rather than "Any questions?" (often accurately interpreted as "There'd better not be").

Offer an exit opportunity for those who want to leave. Rank or protocol may deter some from leaving, so your explicit invitation may be well appreciated. This will also let people get back to doing other more productive tasks.

If they don't ask questions, here are some ways you might stimulate them:

Suggest potential topics. "One area we had to skim over was our planned test program. I'll be happy to elaborate on that, if you like."

Refer to a probable question. "A question that came up with another group was how many of these systems have we delivered. The answer is forty-two, which includes twenty to other governmental agencies."

| *Invite their contributions.* | "Something I'm interested in hearing more about is experience any of you have had with this type of program." Overhead questions can stimulate contributions without putting people on the spot. "We've suggested this new procedure. Have we overlooked anything?" |
| *Use humor.* | "Let's see. This could mean that my presentation was so outstanding it answered all your questions or else so confusing you don't know where to start." |

End the Q&A with a Final Summary

This can be an important opportunity for you to retake control of the session and drive home once more the key message of the presentation. It lends a professional touch and ends the show on a positive note. Take action to end the talk when the productivity of the Q&A session has waned rather than let it drag on while participants drift away. If the allotted time is up, call this to the attention of the group and prepare to wrap it up, unless key participants choose to extend the time. Your summary comments might go like this: "We've run out of time, and I'm pleased that so many of you are interested in further discussion. Let me summarize by saying that our proposal offers the government a low-risk, low-cost alternative that promises a major technical advance toward practical solar energy."

THE LISTENER'S ROLE IN IMPROVING PRESENTATIONS

Presenters put forth considerable effort to help listeners get the message more quickly and better.

Yet messages don't get across, interruptions abound, and much time is spent explaining and repeating material. While many of these common presentation characteristics can be attributed to the speaker, many result because most of us are lousy listeners. Few of us are willing to admit it, but we all know plenty of *others* who are poor listeners: the entire audience for our last presentations.

Studies have shown that as much as 75 percent of presentation content typically is not absorbed by listeners.[3] For presentations using visuals this may differ—better comprehension with good visuals, worse with poor—but the point is that we don't listen so well.

Success and efficiency of a presentation have almost as much to do with the audience as with the speaker. They can set a speaker at ease or be intimidating. They can be facilitative or disruptive, courteous or antagonistic. The results of a presentation are vastly different with positive or negative audience behaviors.

Companies and agencies spend lots of money and effort to upgrade the listening skills of their employees. They wouldn't be doing that if they didn't feel that a problem exists and it's worth the trouble.

Another aspect of listening concerns what we do with whatever little information we've absorbed. I think the evidence is ample to show that too often, we don't do anything with it. We don't challenge it, evaluate it, or even think about it. We just accept it. Here's a comment by Leonard A. Stevens in his important book, *The Ill-Spoken Word: The Decline of Speech in America:*

> There is unsettling evidence of speakers and listeners in positions of wealth and power who use the modern techniques of spoken language without regard to the intellectual integrity that "is one of man's necessities" in a democracy. . . . At the same time we suffer an oversupply of poor listeners who do not have the critical sense to demand good speech ethically committed to issues of importance.[4]

A key premise of Stevens's book is that a society that does not concern itself with the proper use of the spoken word is headed for trouble. He offers the example of Hitler, who rose to power in large part by skill in oratory in a country that had limited experience with orators. Since almost all their great leaders and thinkers had communicated through the written word, the German people were unsophisticated in dealing with the spoken word. Hitler recognized and used the power of speech incredibly well and mobilized a speakers' bureau of thousands of party members. Technique, enthusiasm, and careful staging were key elements, not the message that was put forth.

Unfortunately, I believe that reasoned speaking and listening have continued to decline in the ten years since the first printing of this book. Radio talk shows, TV expert panels, and confrontation interviews all seem to be talk competitions: people often talking at the same time with little true dialogue, analysis, and listening to others' viewpoints.

From my experience in many speaking situations, I think that the audiences in *most* business and technical presentations demand more of presenters than the general public does of public speakers. Top management and government proposal evaluation teams are trained in and charged with analytical thinking. They expect that presenters will be clear about propositions, have claims thoroughly investigated and backed up, and satisfactorily stand up to penetrating questions. Most business presenters are fully aware of this, and if they're smart, they will have done their homework and will expect their presentations to be worked over thoroughly.

These requirements are often not expected of, or assumed by, speakers to general audiences. Political candidates, media preachers, and, yes, businesspeople, when communicating with general groups (for example, consumers and public interest groups), often get by with messages that would be shot full of holes by the average proposal evaluation team. And surprisingly, some of those same astute technical and businesspeople, when they put on their consumer or voter hats, fail to apply the same high critical standards to speakers who promise paradise.

In an article entitled "Bafflegab Pays," J. Scott Armstrong, marketing professor at the Wharton School of Business, noting the evidence that we professionals have provided that says we are more impressed with complex communication than we are with that which is more easily understood, offered this advice: "If you can't convince them, confuse them." Armstrong was digging deeper into the celebrated "Dr. Fox" experiment done during the early 1970s, in which groups of learned people passed highly favorable judgment on presentations by Dr. Fox, who was a complete phony pitching made-up data and theories in double-talk, though in the style of the professionals. Professor Armstrong's tests, using written material with management professors, found that competence of sources was rated high if the material was harder to read than if the same material was written in simpler style. We apparently may not understand the complex stuff, but we sure seem to be more impressed by it.[5]

Let's look at listening from these two perspectives: facilitative and critical listening, summed up in Figure 11-4.

Facilitative Listening: How Audience Members Can Help Presentations

A positive approach can help the audience achieve their own needs and use their own time wisely. Audience members who have done their homework, listen well, and are courteous and constructive are valuable assets to meeting productivity. Specific suggestions include:

- *Decide to be a good meeting contributor.* Isn't it in your own best interests to have a good meeting—to get what you need from the presentation, to get your input into the discussion, and get it done efficiently?

- *Examine your style.* Are you a positive contributor or notorious for ripping speakers apart? How do others see you? How do you compare with those you rate highly? Would some style adjustments possibly be beneficial?

- *Come prepared to meetings.* A major flaw of meeting attendees is that they haven't done their homework.

- *Get there on time, and stay there.* A major aggravation and disrupter of meetings is key people coming and going or frequently having their attention diverted and then asking for an update. How about discouraging interruptions except for the urgent category?

Figure 11-4. Audience members can help presenters by applying these guidelines for good listening.

- Be prepared for meetings.
- Get there on time . . . and stay there.
- Help keep the environment safe rather than intimidating.
- Truly pay attention to what the speaker is saying.
- Be part of the dialogue, not a stoneface.
- Give the speaker a chance; don't constantly interrupt or divert your attention.
- Before asking a question, clarify *your* message.
- Be a team player; help presenters rather than humiliate them.
- Keep things in perspective, such as the big picture and the clock.
- But keep your flim flam detectors alert.

■ *Buy into the process.* What are the rules? the objectives? the timetable? If they're poorly defined, get them cleared up. If they are reasonable, commit to doing your part to see these are met. It's in both your interests to get this meeting over with expeditiously.

■ *Nudge where it matters.* Presentations are rarely perfect. Q&A plays an important role in clarifying, expanding, and redirecting.

■ *Give presenters a chance.* Increasingly executives interrupt constantly, yet the question is often addressed on the next chart. Giving speakers just a bit more leeway may return a big dividend.

■ *Balance your input.* As Ken Blanchard and Spencer Johnson said in *The One Minute Manager,* "Try and catch them doing something right."[6] Many presenters hear nothing but negatives about their presentations. An occasional pat on the back might be appreciate⌣ by your presenters, though they might look warily at something so out of character.

■ *Listen to fit the purpose.* By knowing which listening hat to wear, listeners can get more out of the presentation and properly direct their own efforts. If the presentation is supposed to be entertaining, looking for facts and logic isn't necessary. Relaxing and enjoying noncritically are. If it is to *inform,* specific points and data are important. If listeners are expected to *act* on the basis of information presented, a higher level of critical and interactive listening is called for. If it is a dry run and the primary purpose is to *improve* the presentation, listener and presenter roles are intertwined.

■ *Listen to the speaker.* Facilitative listeners practice good listening techniques, focusing on what is being said at the moment, not daydreaming. They concentrate on what the speaker is saying, rather than what they, the listeners, want to say. They keep an open mind and avoid drawing hasty conclusions, particularly if the speaker's views are different from their own. They work at listening, perhaps taking notes to better retain main points.

■ *Be a responsive listener.* Entertainers and public speakers say they perform better for a "good" audience. The worst audience is that which does nothing— no facial expression (unless a blank stare is an expression), no smiles, cheers, or even boos, no verbal response. It is disconcerting to a presenter not to know whether he or she has established satisfactory rapport or even if the audience is alive.

A facilitative listener gives the speaker appropriate nonverbal feedback in the form of eye contact, facial expression, and body movement so that the speaker can tell whether the information being presented is of interest and value to the audience. Remember, if you don't laugh at the joke, the speaker may assume you didn't understand it and tell it again.

■ *Be a team player.* Sometimes a nervous presenter needs a little help to get unstuck, especially in the early phases of the presentation. By asking a question, an audience member can gently help the presenter relax, link up with the audience, and come across more naturally and confidently.

■ *Request clarification of unclear material.* Complex concepts, special terminology and acronyms, references to events and people, and inadequately covered material offer possibilities for misunderstanding. The speaker assumes everyone is following, and often listeners sit quietly even though they are confused. No one wants to be the one to say, "I don't know what you're talking about." When someone does ask the "dumb" question, generally others are grateful, because they don't know either. The speaker wishes someone had done it ten minutes earlier to have cleared it up then rather than have wasted time talking about something half the audience didn't follow.

- *Think before asking questions or making comments, and keep your input brief and to the point.* Frequently audience members make lengthy and circuitous comments before getting to the point, if ever. Or they sidetrack, bog down, or take over the presentation. This may meet their particular needs (or be good for their egos) but probably does little to meet the needs of the other dozen people who came to hear the presentation. A facilitative listener will choose a good breaking spot rather than interrupt others, make queries or inputs that are relevant to the immediate topic, and speak loudly and clearly so all, not just the speaker, can hear.

- *Work with the speaker toward mutual understanding.* Communication snags are common in presentations. The facilitative listener helps the speaker resolve these by suggesting specific examples, paraphrasing statements, stating points in different terms, and offering insights or additional information from a different perspective.

- *Resist side conversations or other distractions.* Another severe handicap to a presentation is when six conversations go on simultaneously. The facilitative listener directs attention to the main business at hand and does not shift attention to himself or herself by chewing ice, jumping up and down, or belching.

- *Give feedback tactfully.* In the heat of the action, it's easy to come down on the speaker with "hobnailed boots," to beat him or her into the ground. Humiliating and clobbering the speaker may be momentarily satisfying but may backfire as conflicts erupt, personalities clash, issues get clouded, and other audience members turn on the caustic critic.

- *Keep the environment safe.* Group leaders particularly influence the style in which a meeting is conducted. Lower-level members or speakers maybe intimidated by the presence of higher-level members of the organization. Abrasive behavior by leaders can stifle presenters and set a pattern that others may follow. A facilitative listener of high rank ensures that all parties feel free to participate regardless of rank and without intimidation by others.

- *Listen with perspective.* Nonprofessional speakers rarely will be perfect. They may have delivery flaws, use the wrong word, and have inadequate data or visuals that could be better. While not ignoring significant omissions or errors, facilitative listeners do not get hung up on minor ones or close off speakers unfairly. They keep main ideas and priorities in mind and limit nitpicking. They are able to separate valid material from marginal and hear out a speaker rather than discount all of what is said because of minor flaws or disagreement with some part.

■ *Listen to help the speaker improve.* Facilitative listening often means listening noncritically. For many types of presentations, the best role of the listener is to be attentive, appreciative, and empathic. In other situations, such as a dry run preparing the presenter for the real thing or in actual presentations where it is useful to know then or later what is going well or badly, the facilitative listener then adds the important function of evaluative, critical listening.

Critical Listening: Shaping Up the Flimflam

As a member of the group to which the presentation is being given, you do not want to be bamboozled. As a member of the presenter's team, you want to be able to help upgrade the presentation and advance your team's cause. As a presenter you want to be able to present arguments that will stand up to critical assessment, that will not be shot down by the sharp critics who abound in the business world, especially when it is their dollars that are being spent or their business success that is at stake.

For any of these purposes, knowing what makes sense or doesn't, being able to spot the flaws or flimflam, and cutting through the razzle-dazzle to get at the crucial stuff require that attentive listening be backed up with smart listening. The sophisticated listener knows what to look for to understand and appreciate sound thinking and to challenge or discount faulty thinking.

■ *Look beyond technique to substance.* It's easy to be dazzled by flamboyant speakers, resonant voices, full-color multimedia displays. Hitler's audiences certainly were. Many listeners walk away from such shows saying "Wasn't that great!" and even fork over $10 or $20 for the snake oil. When asked what the speaker said, they're hard pressed to come up with anything. "But wasn't he beautiful, and so dynamic."

■ *Look for strength and even greatness in ideas.* Many people talk a lot and say little, following the strategy: Tell lots of stories, overwhelm them with data, stay on safe ground, and don't get into trouble. If ideas and opinions are stated, they fit into the motherhood category—rehashing of old ideas or parroting of commonly held views with little deliberation given to them.

The critical listener looks for ideas with something behind them—ideas that show reasonable thinking, insight, and imagination.

"What is the point of all this?" is a question that should be asked if the point is not becoming readily apparent. Other useful questions for pursing ideas are "What do you propose we do?" and "What are you offering that is unique or better, or has more promise, than anything else we've been hearing about?"

■ *Insist on specifics, not generalities.* If a speaker says, "I can stop inflation," the critical listener asks, "How?" Unfortunately, political campaigns are built on generalities; candidates are advised to forget issues and not to get into specifics, because that can cause trouble.

■ *Don't blindly accept clichés.* "In foreign affairs," a major candidate said, "it's time we got our act together." No more than that. And we let the person get away with that and cheer mightily. The easy clichés can be heard by the thousands during political campaigns, and few people seem to ask: "Just what do you mean by that?"

■ *Demand evidence and verify that it meets acceptable standards.* Speakers of all types often get loose with "facts." "Nuclear power plants are unsafe." "Nuclear power plants are safe." "300,000 people die every year from air pollution." "The Russians are stronger than we are."

These may or may not be "facts." The critical listener listens to the claim and says: "Prove it." That's step one, which too many listeners don't bother to take. Astute speakers are ready for that rare request, however, and out comes the "proof"—the figures, the expert witnesses, the examples. Now the critical listener applies step two, subjecting that "proof" to reasonable tests to see if it indeed backs up the claim.

■ *Scrutinize the assumptions.* Results and conclusions can be greatly influenced by the choice of ground rules. A strong case might be made for the economic sense of the space shuttle, assuming 100 launches per year and a $10 million cost per launch. If the reality is closer to 10 launches per year at a cost of $250 million per launch, the economic picture changes drastically.

■ *Make sure apples are being compared to apples, not potatoes.* The glib salesperson asserts that the Hapmobile Special is a better buy than the competition 560L because it costs less and gives better mileage ("Particularly, heh, heh, when I leave off the Hapmobile $2,000 accessories costs, and compare the Hapmobile's highway mileage to the 560L's city mileage. Just sign on the dotted line.")

■ *Be alert for sidetracking ploys.* In lieu of reasoned arguments, and particularly when their case is weak, speakers often resort to subterfuge to throw listeners off the trail. As the minister wrote on his sermon manuscript: "Weak point—shout." Here are some methods used by speakers to divert listeners' thinking.

- *Inserting a few loaded words.* A fiery young speaker calls businesspeople "bloated parasites," and the crowd roars its approval of whichever cause the speaker is touting. A politician calls for patriotism and blasts lazy bureaucrats, and the crowd roars its approval (different crowd).
- *Slinging a little mud.* This is one of the most commonly used methods to avoid discussing issues and evidence. Attacking an opponent's associations, appearance, and life-style is much simpler than legitimate debate.
- *Blowing a minor flaw out of proportion.* "This so-called expert admits he knows nothing about the Murchison Co. case, back in 1947. Obviously his case won't hold up, so we can dismiss his testimony immediately." Almost any presentation has some areas that are weaker than others. The sidetracker tries to focus all attention on those areas, aiming to discredit the entirety. The astute listener examines the weak areas but keeps them in perspective.
- *Tossing in a red herring.* This can be a subversion technique by the presenter: "We're a little vulnerable in the quality-procedures area. So let's overwhelm them with data and busy charts. They'll be either so impressed or bewildered, we should be able to slip by."

- *Bringing out the handkerchief.* When all else fails, who can help but be enchanted with the speaker who storms back and forth across the stage, delivers lines in hushed tones and exuberant shrieks, and pounds the table furiously. As the audience leaves, obviously moved, someone may say, "But he never did answer the real question."

- *Shoot holes in faulty thinking.* "On the basis of what you have heard, there should be no doubt that my proposal is the only way to go." Maybe. The critical listener looks carefully at how the presenter got from A to B to see if that path will hold up to rigorous inspection. Fallacious arguments often succeed, much as a shell game does. It all seemed so easy and logical, except that the con artist now has your money. Here are some examples.

  - "Inflation is caused entirely by excessive government spending. Therefore the cure is simple—cut government spending." The *premise* has to be examined carefully before the *conclusion is* accepted.
  - "Battleships were instrumental in winning World War II. Therefore we should go back to battleships today." Perhaps this is a valid analogy. The critical listener doesn't accept it on assertion alone but tests the validity of the first "fact," the true similarity between the two situations, and the existence of other factors that might lead to counterconclusions.

A presentation built on solid ideas and support gains from a good listener. In the words of Samuel Hoffenstein's poem "Rag Bag II," a presentation with a shaky foundation and supported mostly by flamboyance crumbles before a good listener, as:

> Little by little we subtract
> Faith and fallacy from Fact,
> The Illusory from the True,
> And starve upon the residue.

IN SUMMARY: BOTH PRESENTER AND LISTENER CONTRIBUTE

In a presentation, speaker and listener roles are largely interchangeable. Presentations more closely resemble dialogues than one-way lectures. Handling audience interruptions and questions can be a severe challenge for presenters. Ability to perform well under fire is a definite asset for a presenter.

The listener can do much to advance or disrupt a presentation. The facilitative listener is a positive force and beneficial to the speaker and meeting productivity. Then, by examining presentations with a demanding ear, eye, and brain, the critical listener keeps the speaker straight and helps maintain the discussion at a level where it truly addresses the issues at hand.

✳ ✳ ✳ 12 ✳ ✳ ✳

Follow Up

KEY POINTS OF THIS CHAPTER

✳ What goes on after the presentation may be even more important than the presentation itself.

✳ Giving further presentations, answering open questions, and integrating information gained are key tasks after the presentation.

✳ Tabulating a presentation scorecard and debriefing team members are valuable for future presentations.

The party's over. The guests have departed. The room is dark and empty. The projector has been returned. You've made your presentation. Nothing more to do.

Or is there? It may be a poor assumption to conclude that all the work is done when the presentation is completed. Consider some examples:

- You were part of an industrial contractor team that gave a presentation to key personnel at the Jet Propulsion Lab (JPL), part of the National Aeronautics and Space Administration (NASA). JPL personnel said their counterparts at the NASA center in Houston could benefit by seeing the presentation.

- The JPL program manager said he wanted to use several charts from your presentation for his own meetings with NASA headquarters officials in Washington.

- During the presentation, issue was taken with some of the conclusions stated because certain assumptions were no longer valid. No one from your team could state with certainty how the new data would affect the projections.

- This presentation had been particularly painful to develop. Many last-minute changes were required, the budget was badly overrun, and a key customer concern was never addressed.

So, is it all over? Sounds as if there is some more work yet to be done. What goes on after the presentation may be as important as the presentation itself.

The postdelivery actions and assessments conclude the current presentation and prepare for the next one.

KINDS OF FOLLOW-UP

The Next Step

The presentation may have just been a door opener or one part of an overall marketing program. The customer has indicated that a presentation elsewhere might be profitable. Perhaps others would be wise as well.

Often the key member of the audience wants to use all or part of the presentation to convince higher management of the validity of the program.

You will probably be more than willing to help by making copies of your charts available or by providing additional data.

The oral presentation may be followed by a formal written proposal or report. The work that went into making the presentation may be extremely useful in preparing the written document. Further meetings, as separate working groups or on a one-to-one basis with key people, are common.

The Loose Ends

Questions raised may require further study and feedback to audience members. Any open items or commitments made during the presentation should be followed up.

The Intelligence Function

A presentation is an excellent opportunity for picking up information of a variety of types. The audience members may offer their opinions, objections, and concerns about your approach or proposals. They may provide more recent, correct, or additional data. They may share some of their plans and concerns, as well as what your competitors have been doing.

As much information may be gleaned from what was not said, the nonverbal messages, as from what was said. These include facial expressions or other reactions to your statements, the presence or absence of key people, people coming late or leaving early, congeniality or aloofness of listeners, glances exchanged or side discussions, the tone of voice in comments or questions.

All this can be valuable information for you, but it has to be observed, documented, and evaluated to be useful. Getting the principals together afterward to process these data and incorporate them into future activities is an important postdelivery function.

Business Etiquette

Send a note of appreciation to each person who was instrumental in bringing the presentation about and helping with it. This might be the contact person who coordinated the meeting, a host who provided a tour, or team members. Don't forget them. A thank you costs almost nothing, is well appreciated, and may be conspicuous by its absence.

ASSESSMENT AND FEEDBACK

Lessons Learned

Something that happens too often in presentations is that the same mistakes keep occurring. One way to address this problem is to prepare a scorecard after the presentation. For example, why did the presentation have so many late changes, proceed with bad information and overrun the budget so badly? What can be learned from that exercise? Or, on the other side, the presentation seems to have been successful on many counts. Was that by accident? Not likely. What made it successful? It helps to know what worked, because you may want to use those things again or even make greater use of them the next time. You also want to know the deficiencies so they can be worked on and won't create problems for you again.

Feedback

Often presenters overlook feedback to the behind-the-scenes people who contributed to the presentation. Rarely do the people who helped generate data, edit material, and prepare visuals get to see the finished product or get feedback that tells them how it went. To keep getting better work, fresh ideas, and improved turnaround, it is well worth the time to conduct a debriefing.

IN SUMMARY: COMPLETE THE STAFF WORK

What goes on after a presentation may be just as important as what went on before or during. Carrying out the next step, following up the loose ends, integrating what was learned from the audience, capitalizing on strengths, and learning from mistakes are all important postdelivery functions.

* * * Part III * * *
Special Presentation Situations

$*** 13 ***$

The Team Presentation

KEY POINTS OF THIS CHAPTER

* Team presentations are common in business today and often in high-stakes situations.
* Much time and energy often are wasted in developing team presentations, due largely to inadequate management attention and support.
* The signs of a cohesive team (or its opposite) show up most readily in presentation content, visual aids, and performance.
* Effective team presentations are the result of a rigorous approach to all phases of planning, development, rehearsal, and execution.

One more opportunity was at hand for EnviroSolve, Inc. and its two subcontractors. They'd been working to land this contract for months. So had five other teams, but now only three were left. The customer had asked each team to prepare oral presentations summarizing its proposals and addressing a five-page list of customer concerns. The EnviroSolve team had one week more to develop its four-hour presentation, which would be conducted at the customer's headquarters in Chicago.

The team hove to, and, after an arduous week for all the eight speakers and an equal number of behind-the-scenes associates, it was ready to face the customer's source selection board. The next four hours went smoothly, with considerable interaction with the board members. The team felt positive about the session.

Two weeks later, EnviroSolve was awarded the contract. The presentation was one of many factors in the team's success. Later debriefing sessions revealed that the brand X competing team had put on a poor presentation, indicating to one board member, "They didn't seem to want the contract." Brand Y's performance was adequate, but EnviroSolve's outstanding performance had pulled them from an underdog position to the winner.

This is one example of the important role that team presentations play in business. They're seen in many situations:

- For a contract, a whole series of presentations will occur through the life of the contract. These go by such names as program, design, readiness,

277

and even lift-the-contract reviews and may involve a dozen speakers over one or several days.

- A company seeking backing from the financial community may take its key people into the offices of banks or venture capital firms for face-to-face interviews about their business plans, organization, and projections.
- A city's economic development board trying to persuade companies to locate their new plants in its town takes its team on the road to various corporate headquarters.

TEAM PRESENTATIONS—VARIED AND IMPORTANT

Team presentations are important; the stakes are often high. There generally has to be a significant reason to gather a diverse, highly paid, and often influential group together to hear a team of presenters. And whether the presentation involves the company president or a junior designer, the presenting team has generally put forth a great deal of time and money in getting ready, reflecting the importance an organization places on team presentations. This is often not the case in single-speaker presentations.

A related characteristic of team presentations is their use by the listeners in gauging the likely competence and future performance of the team. This is another reason for giving attention to the team presentation. Most business ventures are team efforts requiring good planning and coordination. The team presentation gives an audience a first-hand preview of the ability of this team to work together.

If the presenting team looks like a smooth, well-oiled machine, the impression gained by the audience does much to build confidence or allay fears. If the team looks more like the Marx Brothers than the Dallas Cowboys, the audience has just been given Exhibit A in favor of giving the business to someone else.

An additional set of unique problems comes with team presentations. It's difficult enough for a single presenter to plan, develop, and present material. But this person is developing a stand-alone presentation, which he or she alone organizes, creates visuals for, makes arrangements for, and delivers. The decisions and actions are basically one person's.

All this has to be done by the speaker in a team presentation, but with one very significant added constraint—the rest of the team. Decisions cannot be made without consultation and coordination with the other team members. This one constraint becomes a major complicating factor.

Team presentations are notoriously inefficient. Horror stories abound about wasted efforts, duplication, redirection or rework of material, major last-minute changes, and missed assignments. Team presentations can involve frequent meetings of highly paid talent; many iterations on themes, materials, and visuals; and lengthy dry runs with top management participation. All these add up to lots of time and money, much of it poorly spent.

DEVELOPING A GOOD TEAM PRESENTATION

A common pattern of team presentations is that many of the changes occur during the later stages of preparation, after visual aids have been made and during dry runs. This is most expensive and leaves too little time for making changes. Greater attention to the earlier stages of the preparation could often have reduced the pain and expense during their later stages. *Developing and delivering a good team presentation requires a rigorous approach to all phases, from early planning through the final summary.* Some general keys to a successful team presentation are:

- *Recognition by top management and team leadership of the importance of the presentation and the energy that will be required to put it together.* Last-minute or poorly budgeted support will cost more in the long run than adequate attention from the start.
- *Early direction and frequent review by leadership.* Too often the working troops are left to flounder in the wrong direction or in several directions. Weak or absentee leadership generally guarantees poor team spirit, massive last-minute changes, and shaky presentations.
- *Recognition of the team focus by everyone.* In sports or in business, the team efforts generally come through best. Each member of the team should understand that his or her contribution is essential and that one bad apple can indeed spoil the barrel.
- *Treatment of content that recognizes the audience is probably a team too.* Team presentations often draw audiences that are more diverse in both level and discipline than audiences for single-speaker presentations. Knowledge, interests, and mental stamina of listeners need careful consideration.
- *Careful attention to operational detail.* There is plenty that can go wrong in a single twenty-minute presentation. Add in several players and segments, and the potential problems are compounded.
- *Getting to know each other.* The keys to team cohesion may rely as much on group dynamics as on specific procedures. For proposal presentations, teams are often pulled together for the project and may be barely acquainted. Getting that vital team flavor may take some working or socializing together. I was coaching such a team and it was clear they were uptight. We scheduled a highly informal dinner. Relaxing over pizza and beer brought them close together and that came through during the presentation.

These factors seem to be consistently associated with efficiently produced and effective team presentations. Here are some specific techniques that can help bring these about (summarized in Figure 13-1).

Plan Thoroughly

Careful upfront planning gets it all started in the right direction.

- *Get management on board.* Early decisions that set the direction of the presentation should reflect the knowledge and commitment of the organization's key people. Their attention and support will be essential as priorities and team members are set.

Figure 13-1.   Apply these tips for successful team presentations.

- Determine and provide the needed priority and resources.
- Avoid wasted efforts and excessive rework with early and continuous input from top management.
- Plan thoroughly and clearly communicate directions and assignments.
- All team members should focus their segments toward the overall team theme and strategy.
- Stress organizational clarity and consistency; moving agendas and periodic summaries help the audience stay oriented.
- Storyboards from each speaker are a valuable aid to coordination, visibility, and review.
- Visuals should lean toward simplicity (for a probable mixed audience) and use interpretive concepts and titles heavily.
- Compatibility of formats and visuals adds to the image of a harmonious team.
- Make sure all participants know the procedures and assignments.
- Dry-run each segment and the complete presentation. Strengthen and prune weak areas.
- All speakers should make a special effort to adhere to the planned schedule and provide mutual support.
- A total impression of a proficient, smoothly working team is essential, with the team head clearly demonstrating effective leadership.

- *Identify audience requirements.* Foremost in planning are specific directions from the audience, whether a customer or internal management. For a contract competition, this may be explicitly stated in the request for proposal. Or the customer may provide specific topics or questions to be discussed. *Such requests must be addressed.*

- *Develop analysis and strategy.* All the analyses noted in Chapter 5 should be given careful attention. Team members, who may lack insight into the audience and overall marketing program, will request and need a clear picture of such matters from team leadership and strategists.

- *Develop a team theme.* A crucial and far too commonly absent part of planning is the definition of the team theme or overall focus. This must come from the top and be understood by all participants. Failure to establish this results in individuals heading in several directions, misdirecting their emphases, or floundering.

Contained within or noted with the overall theme is any information regarded as the presentation "party line." Every piece of the presentation should tie into and add to the credibility of the overall theme. If individual presenters are unaware of the theme, they will be unlikely to highlight the key points and possibly will play up the wrong ones.

If for an existing proposal, the theme has probably already been finely tuned. The presentation theme should closely track that, though often it will need to be streamlined. For other presentations, with no theme set, develop one early following the guidelines discussed in Chapter 5 (Plan). Some examples:

| *Persuasive* | "R-company: proven expertise for on-time delivery of quality products." The key element is addressing priority audience needs. |
| *Informational* | "Three steps to compliance with new labor law." Capture the essence of the message in one line. |

■ *Set team members and topics.* This is a first-cut organization, which will be refined as the presentation develops. This may be specifically requested or inferred from the customer's requests, or there may be considerable latitude. For proposals, the customer will want to hear from certain key individuals. Will those people be available? What are the presentation abilities of potential speakers? What strengths or deficiencies do candidates bring?

"It's awfully important that the right people be presenting," says retired executive Grant Hansen. "We took a team for proposal orals—I to show the flag, the controller, operations manager, and a couple of others. We lost the bid and were told later that the review board wanted to see not the executives but the proposed site managers. The competition brought theirs in. The review board head said if we'd done that, they'd have probably chosen us."[1]

■ *Commit resources.* Recognize this is not going to get done without the people and budgets to make it happen. This needs to be developed in detail. Besides speakers, what other people will be needed to get the job done? Graphics experts, reviewers and coaches, equipment experts, printers, shippers? Are they available when needed? What about costs and feasibility for visual aids, props, printing, and so on?

■ *Lay out a realistic schedule.* This is vital to preventing last-minute crash efforts too commonly seen. Now make sure the key milestones are actually met.

■ *Pick a presentation development coordinator.* For anything beyond simple presentations, somebody with the right experience and coordinating skills should be put in charge. I've heard program managers say, "Well, I'm going to do that myself." Sure—and land in the hospital critical care ward at the end of the job. A lot goes into keeping this team on course.

■ *Provide strong direction and clear communication.* This is the primary role of the coordinator, backed by management. Failing to do this results in overrun budgets, missed deadlines, extensive rework, and highly stressed people, the last thing your presenters need to be.

Steve Aliment helps coordinate many major presentations for the Boeing Services Division. "You must let the team know early who the actual presenters will be. For one presentation the program manager didn't identify speakers until late in development. Then they got up at our dry run and stumbled badly as they hadn't prepared the material."[2]

Get Organized

With multiple presenters, clear and coordinated organization is vital. Here are some tips.

■ *Refine the presentation structure.* This develops the theme, segments, and speakers. To be settled are the need for an executive summary or overview, roles of top management and program leaders, speaker order, and other activities, such as working group sessions, breaks, and tours.

■ *Allocate times per speaker.* Assign a target time for each section. Consider the role of audience questions carefully and how much time to allow for these and where to place the Q&A segments. This varies widely depending on the presentation nature, circumstances (is the program in trouble?), previous practice, and likely audience members. *A general rule is to put in plenty of time for questions.*

■ *Develop outlines.* All presenters should clearly identify key points for their sections, another good review opportunity. Then develop complete outlines. Shortchanging this step is tempting to many but may surface later as a bad move.

■ *Focus on organizational clarity.* Because of the likely mixed nature of the audience and multiple presentation topics, strive for clarity, simplicity, and consistency. Apply heavy use of the "tell 'em" approach: introductory previews and agendas, transitions, and interim and final summaries. Tie each segment to the overall theme and pattern conceptually and visually. A common way of doing this is to use a repeated or moving-agenda chart (Figure 13-2). This provides a good mechanism for both audience orientation and speaker transitions.

With teams, some degree of consistency is a virtue. For example, if three

Figure 13-2.   The moving agenda is much appreciated by audiences of team presentations.

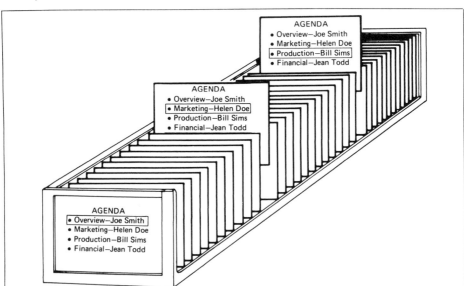

segments have summary charts and the fourth does not, it jars the sense of order and leads to lost listeners.

■ *Design in variety.* Consider the audience perspective. They'll be sitting through five to six presenters over the next several hours. So weave in some changes of pace. An example: After two presenters had spoken with heavy reliance on viewgraphs, the third stood up, shut off the projector, and opened his segment with an anecdote. The renewed audience interest was obvious.

■ *Develop storyboards.* This is a valuable step in the development sequence. Storyboards provide oral and visual overviews for each segment, give a quick sense of how well each fits the targeted time, and facilitate cross-visibility by all presenters. Computer graphics programs aid in the development of these and provide high flexibility.

The time required for the various parts of the presentation can be quickly estimated from the number of storyboard visuals. Thus, with a two-minute-per-visual average, thirty visual sketches would take about one hour. If the section's time budget is twenty minutes, there is a problem.

■ *Get management review and redirection.* This is a key time for management to give its input again. Changes beyond this point become more costly and difficult as artwork gets developed and time is shortened.

Storyboards offer an excellent vehicle for review, which can be done in several ways: by reviewing them on computer monitors or printouts, by taping paper slips to walls (Figure 13-3), or by laying them out on a table.

Build Effective Support Material

The winning presentations have a consistent style and quality.

■ *Fit the level to the likely broad-based audience.* With team presentations, audiences often represent several specialties and management levels. It's easy to get so immersed in detail that much of the audience gets left out. Consider what the audience needs to understand or be convinced. That may be less the hard data—extensive studies, voluminous statistics, detailed information—and more personal experiences, lessons learned, clear interpretations, and portrayals of data. Paramount is that any presupplied questions be answered.

■ *Put extra effort into clearer and simpler visual aids.* Again, keep in mind the general nature of the audience and the fact that it may be sitting through a series of presentations, perhaps for hours. Busy, lifeless visuals that may be palatable during one thirty-minute presentation may be dreadful to an audience that has sat through a full day already. All presenters should put forth extra effort to come up with punchy visuals whose messages can be quickly grasped. Valuable are interpretive titles, focused information, more visual aspects (pictures, graphs, relationships) than words, and color (see Figure 13-4). Words should be easily readable. Hardware, models, displays, and videotapes can provide an appreciated change of pace.

■ *Adopt a consistent visual style across all segments.* Presenters of different backgrounds and experience may have visuals of different levels of quality and

Figure 13-3. Storyboards are particularly useful for planning, interteam communications, and review of team presentations.

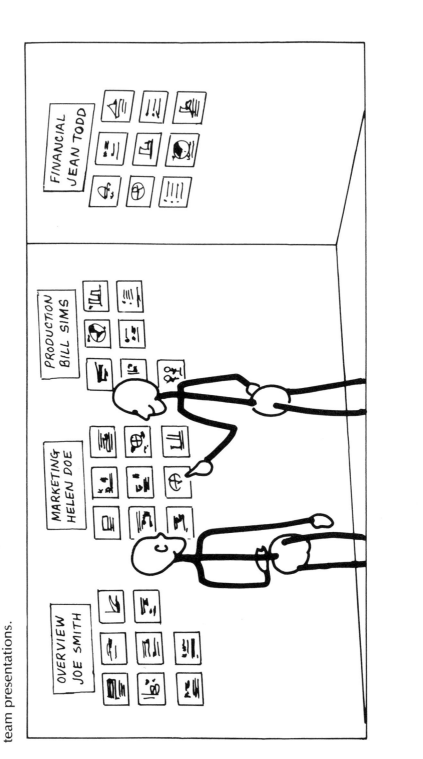

Figure 13-4. Strive for visual simplicity and easy interpretation of messages.

TOWARD THIS:

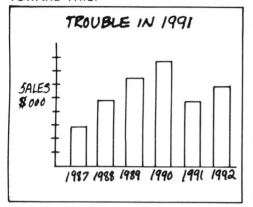

AWAY FROM THIS:

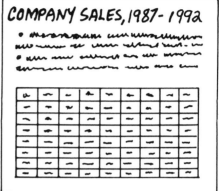

design, prepared with separate computer graphics programs. A team can take on a slapdash appearance unless extra effort is made to achieve visual compatibility. Some computer software programs can import graphics from several other programs and convert all to the same design, type styles, and sizes and colors.

All presenters should strive for roughly the same level of visual refinement. A ten-chart presentation of busy word charts and dull titles by itself might receive casual criticism, but if it follows three hard-hitting, dynamic presentations, the audience might legitimately wonder if these people had been talking to each other. Visuals should have the same style. Logos should be on all charts and in the same location. Typing and quality of art should be consistent. When more than one organization is represented in the team, visuals should still have a high degree of commonality in appearance.

■ *Have a single support-specialist contact point.* If you want to guarantee chaos, have six presenters talk directly with six artists, editors, or reproduction experts. Compatibility, quality, and priorities cannot be maintained without tight control. Single-point contact through which all input/output funnels is essential.

■ *Ensure necessary supplementary material.* In focusing on visuals, the requirements for support material such as brochures, models, or hardware often get sidetracked. These should be planned for and scheduled along with all other elements. Some material, such as visual aid brochures, will be in a revision state along with the visuals themselves, and the publication requirements must be rigorously observed if this material is to be available when required.

Stage It Carefully

Careful attention to detail and good communications are necessary.

■ *Check out the facility—early.* Horror stories abound of extensive rework required due to faulty information about the facility.

■ *Make a comprehensive checklist.* With many speakers and divided responsibilities, it's easy to have important details slip through the cracks. The best way to prevent a presentation from falling victim to Murphy's Law is a detailed checklist covering equipment, facilities, refreshments, deliveries, and transportation. Plan for contingencies and backups.

■ *Draw up a set of operational procedures, clearly communicated to participants.* To prevent the old "Who's on first?" routine from occurring, rigorously plan procedures and assignments for dry runs and actual presentations. Include travel schedules and plans, lodging, directions, on-scene times, wardrobe, protocol, clearances, operational sequences, distributions, and anything else.

■ *Arrange to aid the audience (and your chances).* For some presentations, you can improve audience receptivity by paying attention to their facility and arrangement needs: special parking spaces, streamlined entry and posted welcome, private caucus room (supplied with copier, chalkboard, coffee), personal table identifers, and others.

From Jim Dollard, president of Management Analysis Company: "Only once did we lose ground on proposal orals. We elected to have the presentation on site at a motel conference room, thinking to minimize audience travel time. Bad decision. The room was too small, overheated, not conducive to the purpose. We learned our lesson, so for a later one, we invited the review team to our facility and did a lot of things with arrangements and facilities that would make their tasks go easier. We won, and later the board expressed great appreciation."[3]

■ *Impress upon speakers the need to meet set times.* This is a constant problem yet is critical with multiple speakers and time limitations. Have speakers practice their sections with timers running. A valuable help to meeting time targets is to have presenters develop delivery scripts, with specific spoken comments matching each visual (discussed in Chapter 6).

■ *Review in steps.* Set a review program that considers the individual capabilities, deadlines, and availability of support personnel. For speakers with limited experience or high anxiety, don't throw them immediately into a full-blown dry run. Have them rehearse their sections in a low-pressure mode, with one or more coaches at hand to help improve their confidence.

The next phase is to conduct reviews for all sections. This can be time-consuming, with reviews going on for hours. Setting procedures and time limits will be helpful. I've found it more productive, for example, to let the presenters complete their sections and then conduct reviews rather than have interruptions throughout. Videotape speakers so they can review their performances.

It's important for speakers to observe presentations of their team members, especially key sections that cover overall philosophy, themes, or management approaches.

■ *Use a review team.* Select reviewers or coaches to provide a suitable variety of backgrounds. For major presentations, these "red teams," as they are often called, may include internal and external people. Other support people, such as graphics experts, will participate. Provide the review team in advance with information and guidelines so they can be prepared.

- *Simulate all aspects of the presentation.* Use actual or simulated equipment and room layouts. Try out seating and movements. Practice transitions and coordinated activities. Have speakers wear their planned clothing for at least one dry run. (Be specific about wardrobe. On several occasions, we've noted to presenters their wardrobe was not appropriate for this level of presentation. They've gone directly to buy new suits.)

- *Conduct a final complete dress rehearsal.* Run through the entire presentation exactly as it will be given.

Deliver with Precision

Individual and team competence will be sensed strongly from how this team now performs under pressure.

- *Demonstrate a cohesive team.* The presentation is a good opportunity for the program leader to show that he or she can put together and lead a cohesive team (or demonstrate the opposite). How the presentation is run will be interpreted as an indicator of how well this team is managing the program under review or proposed. The leader should thus demonstrate good leadership qualities during the presentation, and all presenters should show they can work smoothly together.

- *Adhere closely to allocated times.* The speaker who gets carried away can wreak havoc with the following speakers, who have to adjust their presentations to shorter times. (Tip: Make sure you have a time signal system.)

- *Be flexible as warranted.* Team leaders need a strong sense of perspective coupled with the ability to adjust the program where it clearly is not meeting audience needs or team objectives. Allowing more time or cutting down on time, deleting parts, rearranging the agenda—all are prerogatives of the leaders and measures of the ability of this team to perform.

- *Support each other.* Team members must recognize they are effectively all on stage during the entire presentation. They should be attentive and alert to assist other speakers and not divert attention from the current speaker. They should avoid derogatory or embarrassing comments about their own team members and maintain a professional and constructive manner, on and off stage. They should look, think, and act like a team.

A speaker was giving an important presentation to the customer's key contracting officials. Several times during the talk, the listeners' attention was jarred by a crunching sound from the rear of the room. The sound was from crushed ice in a soft drink, being chewed by the presenter's own program manager.

- *Coordinated Q&A response is vital.* A key person is the presentation principal person or program manager. Because of overall program perspective, he or she needs to serve as question manager, clarifying, transferring, or answering. Others need to be ready to pitch in when needed but should resist the urge to jump in. One program manager killed off his team's success by answering all questions himself, some of which would have been better handled by his team members.

IN SUMMARY: TEAM PRESENTATIONS ARE
TOO IMPORTANT TO TOY WITH

Team presentations, seen regularly in marketing presentations and program or management reviews, are often high-stakes events involving many people. They are important factors in determining contract decisions and a first-hand measure of likely future performance. They can absorb a lot of resources and energy in preparation. Thus, it's important that they be done right. The keys are careful planning, early top-level support, practice, and teamwork in execution.

In August 1992, the Department of Energy awarded a $2.2 billion contract for environmental cleanup to a team headed by Fluor Corporation, following "short-list" presentations by Fluor and the runner-up contractor, with two others eliminated earlier. In an article about the contract award, Assistant Energy Secretary Leo P. Duffy said Fluor made the best impression. "All the firms had capabilities, but how the team works as a team in the oral presentations is a key determining factor."*

---

*"DOE Picks Fluor for Fernald," *Engineering News Record* (August 24, 1992): 9.

✳ ✳ ✳ 14 ✳ ✳ ✳

International Presentations

KEY POINTS OF THIS CHAPTER

✳ Presentations to audiences in or from other countries are frequent in business and government today.

✳ Standard approaches used for U.S. audiences may backfire for audiences from other countries.

✳ Knowing your audience takes on an even greater importance and complexity for international presentations.

✳ Differences in culture and language can easily lead to misunderstandings and require special care to overcome.

"We really appreciate the chance to talk to you folks from Japan. We have some new ideas we want to bounce off you that we think will really blow your minds. Our new Widget has been cutting through our competitors like Franco Harris going through the line. Speaking of Franco, there's a great story about the time he played in Super Bowl X at the Orange Bowl . . . Our Widget has had great success in CONUS, especially on DoD spook programs such as HTSM and FRGM. I know you'll want to put in an order today, so we've got our sales manager here and we can get to that right after we take a coffee break. Let's take ten and hit the john."

As the world becomes smaller in the time and travel sense and more intertwined in the business sense, presenters often may find themselves speaking to audiences composed of people from other countries. Language and culture differences make this a vastly different presentation situation from speaking to people from the United States. With the stakes so high and the pitfalls so many, anyone speaking to "foreigners" needs to pay special attention to these differences.

The monologue at the start of the chapter encompasses many of the problems U.S. presenters give themselves and their foreign audiences. While it is a fictional example, it is not entirely a product of my imagination. I have heard presenters make comments that are not much different from the ones printed here in that they have been incomprehensible, confusing, and sometimes offensive to listeners. In fact, I have been chagrined on occasion to find myself as one of those presenters.

When presenting internationally, the fundamental requirement is to recognize that business as usual is dangerous business. "They" are not the same as "we." We speak different languages, even if we both speak English; we act differently; and we view things from different perspectives. All these differences set the stage for communication difficulties and potential misunderstandings.

We particularly misread messages from people of different age groups, economic levels, religious or racial backgrounds, or nations. The use of time, need for "space bubbles," and gestures all differ greatly between different groups. Sidney Jourard observed touch frequencies between people in ordinary conversation in coffee shops around the world. In Paris, people touched each other 110 times per hour. In London and the United States the numbers were 0 and 2.[1] So what happens when the Frenchman and the American get together to do business? The Frenchman keeps touching, the American keeps recoiling, and each one thinks the other one is nuts.

Anyone who has tried out college Spanish or German with real Spaniards or Germans or who has visited another country should immediately be able to understand the problems a person from another country may have listening to a presenter from the United States. As soon as we say in halting words *"Wie geht es Ihnen?"* or *"¿Donde está el baño?"* we are presented with a flow of words so fast we get lost immediately. And half the words aren't in the phrase book or even the dictionary. Then the Indians shake their heads "no" when they mean "yes," the Japanese get too close, and the Mexicans don't seem to know what "promptly at eight" means. So we get bewildered and wonder why the devil they don't act like us and learn to speak English as well.

Well, surprise. Those are exactly the same kind of problems people from other nations have when they deal with us in business or pleasure. We speak too fast, we use too many expressions only Americans could be expected to know, we smile and rush too much, and it is *they* who then look forward with relief to when they can get back home to where people act normally and can be understood.

Language and cultural differences exist when presenter and listeners are from different nationalities, whether "foreigners" are visiting the United States or the presenter is visiting another country. In the latter case, however, another set of potential problems presents itself. These deal with transporting or shipping equipment and getting it through customs on time, determining if your slide projector will work on European or South American current, and establishing if a standard conference room for twenty people and with an overhead projector means the same thing to a French hotel manager as to an American marketing manager.

The subject of communicating and doing business internationally is a full one in itself. That it is deserving of serious attention is given focus by this observation by Jean Marie Ackermann, director of transcultural training for Organizational Consultants, Inc.: "Those very behaviors that spell success at home for a U.S. businessperson may spell disaster abroad." Specifically she noted as rubbing many people wrong some of the styles U.S. businesspeople hold dear: a pragmatic approach—quickly getting to the heart of the matter; emphasis on blunt, straight talk—telling it like it is; separation of our business relationships from our family and social relationships; and our confident belief that the American way is the logical and natural, therefore superior, way of doing things.[2]

Philip Cateoria and John Hess have noted that adaptation is a key concept in international marketing, and that *willingness* to adapt is a crucial attitude.[3] This definitely applies to presentations, including the very concept. In the United States, full-blown visual aid presentations are a standard part of the way we do business. They are a valuable means to display the facts, options, pros and cons, and recommendations for action to many people in an efficient manner, and decisions are often made immediately on the basis of the presentations. We value the efficiency, the conciseness, and the completed staff work that come with presentations. Businesspeople from other countries, however, may not value that at all. Thus, presentations of the U.S. type may not even be part of the business world in countries where business proceeds in a much less structured, less rapid manner, and often on a one-to-one basis rather than in groups, as is common for our presentations.

Chris Phillipe, formerly a communications specialist in Saudi Arabia with ARAMCO, said that in the Arab world, a flashy presentation would mean little: "They're not so impressed with a great presentation. Most important is how you come across as a person. The main thing Westerners and especially Americans do is get right to business and try to close the deal quickly. You can't rush a Saudi or come on too strong. You must first let them know you understand and appreciate the finer things in life. You have to be very patient and be able to just be around."[4]

On the other hand, in Japan, presentations—and plenty of them—are expected to be given to the whole range of departments involved in decisions. Thus knowing the market is fundamental. Cateoria and Hess point out that a businessperson needs to use a soft-sell approach in Great Britain and the hard sell in Germany, to emphasize price in Mexico and quality in Venezuela. Without knowing your audience, you can easily head down the wrong track.

With that very brief background and caution about a very complex subject, here are some basic considerations for one part of the international marketing process—the presentation to non-U.S. audiences (summarized in Figure 14-1).

PLAN CAREFULLY, DRAWING ON EXPERTS AND EXPERIENCE

For presentation success across cultures and in foreign environments, the importance of careful planning cannot be overemphasized.

■ *Learn all you can about your listeners and how they do business.* Use the experts, such as the Department of Commerce, who know the specific country well. Consulates and embassies located in the United States can provide helpful background on their countries, as can U.S. government offices located overseas. AMA/International, headquartered in New York and with centers in Europe, Canada, South America, and Mexico, can be an important contact.

Identifying key things that definitely should and should not be done will

Figure 14-1. Apply these tips for winning international presentations.

- Know your audience, and consider cultural as well as business backgrounds in planning your presentation.
- Consult the experts to understand the audience better and to prevent faux pas.
- If presenting outside the United States, be aware of all the pitfalls regarding mechanics.
- Make sure both parties understand specific goals and the agenda.
- Organize your talk so it can be easily followed. Frequently provide direction and reiterate points.
- Allow for extensive two-way communication.
- Emphasize simplicity and visualization in visual aids.
- Prepare speakers to consider language and cultural problem areas and to demonstrate understanding of the audience.
- Dry-run the presentation (and presenters) with someone familiar with the audience's culture and language.
- Speak slowly and distinctly, avoiding acronyms and jargon and explaining technical terminology fully. Keep checking to ensure mutual understanding.
- Use standard international business terminology.
- Repeat and summarize often, allowing ample opportunity for feedback.
- Be careful about assumptions based on nonverbal signals.
- Make sure the spoken word closely follows the visual aids.
- Provide copies of visual aids.

aid the planning process for the presentation, though this should be regarded as only one small part of the total orientation process. The "do" list could identify protocol requirements, often more significant in other countries than in the United States; considerations related to timing and form of presentation, including giving no presentation; meeting procedures; and probable desires of the audience. Use the "no-no" list to surface taboos. Making reference to Montezuma's revenge is not the way to endear oneself to a Mexican, as President Carter discovered during his visit to that country. Referring to women or animals is not wise when speaking to Arabs. And knowing that many Asians have strong feelings about lucky and unlucky colors may prevent some serious mistakes on visuals or brochures.

■ *Give special attention to how cultural differences might affect style of presentation and strategy.* Howard Van Zandt provided this example about doing business in Japan:

> In making a presentation, it should be remembered that Japanese and Americans have different objectives in doing business. The former continually stress growth, steady jobs for their own employees, full employment in the nation as a whole, and superiority over competitors. Profit, as a motive, falls behind these needs. But U.S. executives are motivated only by profit—or, at least, that is the way Japanese businessmen see it. . . . Since the Japanese prefer a low-pressure sales approach and value sincerity so highly, Westerners are

advised to build up their case a step at a time, using modest language rather than making extravagant claims.[5]

■ *If presenting outside the United States, be rigorous and precise in your arrangements planning.* If you do not have previous experience with the country or an established, reliable base there, call in the experts *early*. Organizations specializing in international meetings or meeting managers of international hotel chains can provide valuable consulting and handle arrangements in other countries. The experience of other businesspeople in the country may be of value. Many countries today have sophisticated facilities and considerable experience in audiovisual presentations. The main thing to remember, however, is that paperwork, power requirements, terminology, equipment, and common practices may be different there.

Schedule all elements carefully, including support needs such as delivery of gadgetry or slide brochures. Do not take anything for granted that has to be provided, delivered, shipped, or carried. Customs delays can be unpredictable and often lengthy. The ability to make last-minute changes may be limited. Taking equipment into a country can be difficult; taking visual aids is generally smoothly accomplished. Check first.

■ *Discuss fully with the key contact person at the other end the main aspects of the meeting*—purpose, desires of both parties, incidentals such as arrival times and hotels, agenda for the day, such as tours or private visits—and the presentation itself. Identify as fully as possible the exact names, titles, and backgrounds of the audience members. Obtain phonetic spellings of the names. Maintain a dialogue with your key contact to stay abreast of current information and to ensure that both parties are clear and in agreement on the purpose of the meeting and the presentations. Even with constant and close attention to mutual understanding, achievement of that goal will be a major challenge.

■ *Provide as much assistance and information as possible* to smooth the way for the other parties as well. If they are in your environment, it will be strange to them, and they will probably appreciate any help to make them comfortable and to avert gaffes. They will have as much trouble with your names as you will have with theirs. You may want to provide a list of attendees' names (speakers plus audience) and their titles, which are often used, as well as name place markers.

■ *Consider differences in hospitality.* Do not overlook the simple things, such as refreshments during breaks or lunch. Standard U.S. sweet rolls may be regarded as unpalatable and even uncivilized by Europeans. Typical U.S. coffee breaks with paper cups may look pretty basic to European businesspeople accustomed to china.

■ *In planning agendas and facilities, consider that the audience may wish some time and private space to meet separately.*

■ *Select your speakers carefully.* Be aware of potential problems certain types of speakers may present for certain audiences. A hard-charging, fender-slapping salesperson may not go over well with some audiences. A person with a few too many rough edges may create a poor impression with sophisticated listeners. If the listeners have a limited knowledge of English, it may be wise to screen out speakers who are hard to understand.

■ *Prepare your speakers.* They should know how to pronounce any foreign names that are in the presentation. If you're trying to get business in Saudi Arabia, all your team members should know where Riyadh is located, that it is the capital city, and how to pronounce it. They should know key people and agencies involved. Whatever their backgrounds, people are more favorably disposed to those who have taken the time to become familiar with the people and culture of the other country.

■ *Orient presenters to audience culture and style.* Many speakers are heading into an environment with which they have little experience. Advance education can be invaluable. Jay Carson has had many technical and managerial assignments in several mid-East countries. For one program, he said the U.S. prime contractor hurt itself badly on customer presentations in Saudi Arabia: "They would come in with arrogant attitudes, assuming they were experts. They'd want to get right to the heart of the matter and tell them what to do versus persuade them. After they left, they would be cut apart within an hour. Over there, if you're prideful and arrogant, you won't get anywhere."[6]

■ *Try to find nuances.* Somers White, as a business executive and professional speaker, has spoken to audiences on all continents (except Antarctica). He says it can be valuable to learn about local events and interests, such as government, the makeup of the population, policies, and local hot issues. "In the Philippines, I spoke to a group about various financial topics. A man asked a question about investing in Philippine art. I was able to answer knowledgeably about the current status of why Philippine art has not been a good investment for the last six months. What did that do for my credibility?"[7]

■ *Consider how other attendees can be of help.* SDC Systems Group often has SDC employees who are natives of the audience country attend its international presentations. Being familiar with both the company and the visitor's country and language, they have helped make the audience comfortable as well as assisted with explanations.[8]

DEVELOP MATERIAL STRESSING CLARITY AND SIMPLICITY

Information and adaptation provide the basis for developing presentation content.

■ *Plan to cover less material.* The audience familiarity with the English language and the style of meetings may differ considerably from typical U.S. audiences. A consistent lesson learned is the need to cut material.

■ *Aim toward greater organizational simplicity* than for standard presentations, with plenty of direction signs and reiterations. Support material should be examined to make sure it is relevant to the audience. That means eliminating references that will mean little to non-Americans, such as game plans, "Sixty Minutes," and Lone Star Beer (unless you're selling Lone Star Beer).

The value of an initial summary when speaking to top-level U.S. audiences has been noted. It is even more important when speaking to non-U.S. audiences, as it enables both parties to see at the start just what the objectives and essence of this presentation are.

Allow plenty of time for questions, comments, and repetition.

- *Visual aids make up a major part of the presentation,* because they can greatly assist the communication process beyond the spoken word. Visuals should lean heavily in the direction of simplicity, with photographs, animation, and other graphic forms stressed over busy word charts. Make sure all print is large enough to be read easily—small print compounds the difficulty of trying to read in an unfamiliar language. Hold acronyms to a minimum, and spell out those that you do use. Use headline titles profusely to increase the ease of grasping the message of each chart. Provide moving agenda charts to introduce each section, with names of all speakers spelled out in full. Summarize frequently.

What about translation of visual aids? Since English is widely used internationally, this may not be necessary. Where the audience is not familiar with English, this may be wise, and many corporations do translate their visuals (Figure 14-2).

Translating written material or graphics is tricky business. In the same language, many terms differ across dialects (Madrid Spanish versus Guadalara Spanish; Hong Kong Cantonese versus Beijing Mandarin). Graphics layouts may need to be changed. English-language graph axes and flowcharts don't directly transform into Arabic, which moves from right to left.

Native speakers may be of some help, but problem opportunities abound. A Puerto Rican doing a Spanish translation for an audience in Caracas may make serious mistakes (and vice versa). A person away from his or her native country for more than a few years can quickly lose touch with the language. A native speaker may be fluent in everyday but not technical language.

Some words don't translate so well. Boeing discovered that its slogan for the 747—the Queen of the Sky—was precluded from use in several languages because it translated as the Virgin Mary.[9] Also be wary of terms that seem to be the same but have different meanings. "Short-term debt" is defined differently in the United States and Germany, so translating the term might create more confusion. If it is left in English, the Germans probably will know which definition to apply.[10]

- *Allow time to meet with interpreters.* Often interpreters are essential to conducting international business. Advertising executive Robert Smith has had ample experience with interpreters both in international marketing and as a conference leader for AMA/International. "The important thing is to go over the presentation in advance with the interpreter. Review the handouts, visuals, and anecdotes. Then remember to pace yourself so the interpreter can do his job, so the two of you can work as a team. This is especially critical for simultaneous translations."[11]

- *Hard copies of visuals are particularly useful for an international presentation.*

Figure 14-2. Visuals are often translated into the language of the audience.

EQUIPOS DE APOYO TERRESTRE

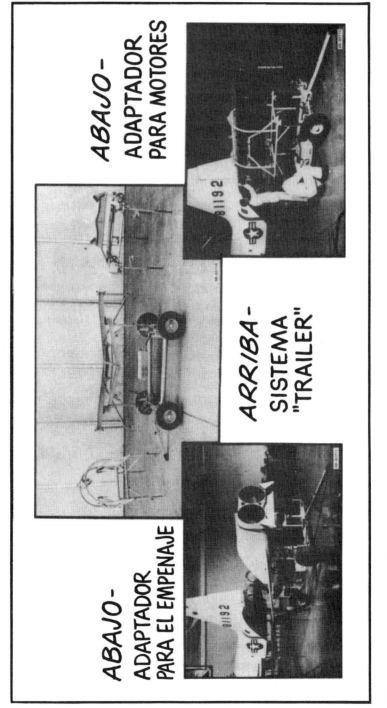

ABAJO –
ADAPTADOR
PARA MOTORES

ARRIBA –
SISTEMA
"TRAILER"

ABAJO –
ADAPTADOR
PARA EL EMPENAJE

While generally not recommended because of the problem of diverting attention, it often may be useful to distribute copies of the visuals for use *during* the presentation. Electronics executive Thomas Kurtz has given many international presentations. "I always gave them copies of my slides at the start so they could make notes on them in their own language as I talked. This worked out very well."[12]

Howard Van Zandt recommends distributing copies of presentation material in Japan, because this provides a test of sincerity, which the Japanese value highly. "They feel that when a man is willing to put his case in print, where all may challenge what he has said, it is likely that he will be accurate so as not to lose face." He also advises this because oral statements are often misunderstood due to the heavy use of homonyms (words that sound the same but don't mean the same) in Japanese. He also suggests that presenters in Japan lend copies of visual aids to the Japanese for their use with other groups.[13]

- *Test out your presentation and all your speakers,* preferably with listeners who are knowledgeable about the country of the real audience. Screen both content and speakers (using the guidelines for delivery to follow). John Frank, group director for civil marketing for the Computer Science Corporation, said this was paticularly valuable: "We have the translator or adviser sit through the dry run. He catches the clichés and jargon and tells us to stop. This forces us to use terminology that can be understood."[14]

- *Learn a few words of the language.* Cross-cultural expert Dr. Sondra Thiederman says nothing else will win trust more. "And don't worry about doing it right—do the best you can. You show a certain leveling and vulnerability by trying to pronounce a few Japanese words and sort of floundering. As long as you're not arrogant about it. You might also learn 'That's all I know' in case they come rushing up and start to talk to you."[15]

DELIVER WITH COURTESY AND CAUTION

Careful preparation and rehearsal should have already surfaced and corrected typical delivery problems. Some further tips follow.

- *When in Rome . . . know what to expect.* Your cultural training should have prepared you for your Saudi conference room, with many people possibly reclining around the room. You should know about a more formal flavor in Munich or Osaka, with orderly introductions with titles and perhaps passing of business cards and gifts.

- *Speak slowly and clearly* if you are speaking to people whose native language is not English. Make sure you can be heard easily.

- *Speak in simple, single-clause sentences* as much as possible.

- *Do not use slang, colloquialisms, clichés, metaphors, and other expressions that mean nothing to the listeners.*

- *Limit the use of acronyms and jargon* to what is necessary. Then explain fully all acronyms or jargon you do use, with lots of checks to ensure mutual understanding. "This was one of our biggest problems," said international businessman Meredith Goodwin, who himself speaks English. "As soon as the speakers lapsed into their technical jargon and mnemonics, they lost us. This can be a potentially very serious problem, for example, when terms are not fully explained. In one business relationship, it was months before we realized that when the representatives of the U.S. company said 'cost-plus' and we said 'cost-plus,' we weren't talking about the same thing."[16] To prevent such potentially expensive misunderstandings, use the accepted international business terms.

■ *Be careful with jokes or humor.* They often don't translate well and sometimes make a puzzled listener feel he or she is either stupid or being made fun of. On the other hand, humor that is appropriate can be well received. Eric Herz, general manager of the Institute of Electrical and Electronics Engineers, mentioned positive feedback he had received from a presentation to multicountry groups in Malaysia: "After I came back, the guys from India said, 'We listened to your presentation, and you made us laugh. When we first saw you, we thought you were a very serious person.' I simply like, if I want to get a message across, to not be a total deadpan if I can avoid it."[17]

■ *Tie your words closely to the visual aids.* Lead your listeners through the aids, using a pointer to help them track you.

■ *Repeat and summarize often.* Explain key concepts or data in several ways and allow ample "soak-in" time.

Other factors include the following nonverbal items:

■ *Be expressive.* It is generally easier to understand a person who uses gestures, facial expression, and vocal emphasis to add to words. Monotonic, immobile speakers are harder to understand.

■ *Establish and maintain an open environment.* If you know the audience views feedback positively, make it clear at the start that you welcome questions or comments, and maintain a dialogue format rather than a strictly one-way presentation. Be careful not to place anyone in an embarrassing position. Provide ample opportunities for easy audience input, even asking such questions of your own as, "Does this provide the kind of information you were looking for?" or "Have I explained that fully?" For an audience not oriented toward questions, little feedback is likely, and overt invitations to respond are better tentatively expressed or left out.

■ *Listen intently to their questions and comments.* Paraphrase them back before responding to make sure that the question is understood correctly. Be patient if it takes a while to comprehend your message.

■ *Be aware that their (and your) nonverbal messages may mean different things from what you think.* Facial expression, eye contact, hand movements, touching, use of space and time are all ripe areas for misinterpretation and irritation. Be slow in making assumptions on the basis of nonverbal messages. Keep checking, and be patient—they can't figure you out either.

■ *Be respectful of their customs, clothing, facilities, history, and world status, and be careful about playing up the United States.* Inadvertent insults can creep in easily and can be costly. Conducting a seminar in Canada, I once used the example of the great patriot Patrick Henry's famous "Give me liberty or give me death!" speech to demonstrate ways of holding the interest of an audience. One of the listeners later gently reminded me that while Patrick Henry may be a hero in the United States, he was regarded as a traitor in Canada.

■ *Be cautious about the hard sell,* pushing hard for commitment or action, or heavy chest thumping. These great U.S. standbys may backfire overseas.

■ *Recognize that the audience may be observing much more than the presentation.* Acting like a clod during the coffee break or lunch may destroy your finely delivered presentation.

■ *In spite of all the previous cautions, be yourself.* If you truly want to communicate and you recognize that differences exist which can interfere with that process, you will be well along toward communicating successfully with an audience from another background.

IN SUMMARY: PRESENTING TO INTERNATIONAL AUDIENCES IS NOT BUSINESS AS USUAL

It is difficult enough to try to communicate with someone from our own background. Presentations to international audiences are made even more difficult because of differences in culture, language, and business practices. Knowing your audiences takes on added significance. Some key points:

■ U.S. style and procedures may be counterproductive.
■ When you're crossing borders, arrangements need extra care.
■ Misunderstandings can easily occur because of nonverbal confusion, overspecific terminology, and inability to catch what is said.
■ Visuals may benefit from translation, though that can be tricky.
■ All visuals should be easily read and tend toward simplicity.

Closing ceremonies of the 1984 Olympics in Los Angeles included lavish salutes to all the previous Olympic cities. While watching it, I was amazed to see the tribute to Mexico City accompanied with a stirring rendition of "Granada." So was the Mexican consul general, who protested the "unjustifiable ignorance" the hosts displayed by not knowing "Granada" is a fine song of Spain, not Mexico.[18]

* * * 15 * * *

Speaking from a Manuscript

KEY POINTS OF THIS CHAPTER

* Read a speech only when absolutely necessary.
* Many good presenters are often poor manuscript speakers.
* Written speech material often doesn't speak well.
* Many read speeches are notable for wooden delivery and little audience contact.

The featured speaker at a university commencement program had been flown 3,000 miles to deliver the commencement address. Before he spoke, he was seated at the head table so all in the audience could see what he looked like. This turned out to be the last chance, because once he started speaking, all that could be seen was the top of his head and endless pages being turned as he read his speech.

Over several years, I've worked with a professional group that provides monthly forums for business speakers. Despite our strong suggestions to steer clear of manuscripts, some speakers use them. Almost without exception, audience evaluations consistently are critical of these speech readers.

Academic speakers at professional symposia say they're going to "read their papers." They mean exactly that. If there's a worse way to communicate with one's peers, I hope it never surfaces. These are generally dreadful experiences for listeners, with most succumbing to the glazed-eyeball syndrome within minutes.

Probably everyone has had similar experiences, listening to speakers drone on and on as they read from prepared manuscripts. Probably everyone in that situation wanted to be somewhere else as she tinkered with the last dregs of the after-dinner sherbet or tried to look interested because the boss was seated across the table. If asked later what was memorable about the speech, she usually was hard pressed to remember anything but wishing it would end and thinking what a fine cure for late-night insomnia a recording of the speaker would be.

Fortunately, many other speakers have learned the techniques of speaking from a manuscript, delivering a fully written speech in such a way that the audience is scarcely aware the speech is being read.

Although I strongly discourage reading a speech or paper, some situations call for material to be read verbatim:

- A prepared talk for a luncheon of community leaders.
- Reading a scripted sales presentation.
- Quoting from a test report during a failure analysis presentation.
- Speaking from a teleprompter for a major users' conference.

Two basic reasons cause most of the problems with reading written material: (1) *written* language often is poor *spoken* language, and (2) we do so little reading aloud that when we do, it comes across in a dull monotonic style, devoid of feeling and meaning. What is the result? Listeners start to yawn, their attention goes elsewhere, the reader's message never gets through.

If these are the basic causes, they must also indicate the remedies for ineffective reading. In summary (Figure 15-1), they are:

- Write a manuscript the way you talk, not the way you write.
- Practice reading aloud in general, and practice with the specific material.
- Read to convey the meaning as well as hold listeners' attention.

PREPARATION

Material may already exist (such as a policy statement or a page from a proposal). You may have to prepare it from scratch for delivery by yourself or another person. Or you may work with someone else who will write all or parts of it (for example, if you're the chief executive officer and employ a speechwriter).

Figure 15-1. Speaking from a manuscript can work—here are some principles.

- Write as you talk, using simple sentences, conversational language, and an informal, personal style.
- Try out the words aloud to see if they flow well and have good tone.
- Do not speak for more than 20 minutes.
- Have your manuscript typed with double space on one side of the page only and marked to aid you as you read it.
- Practice reading aloud to develop this skill.
- Practice with the specific material so you know it and can deliver it well.
- Read to truly communicate with your audience, particularly watching the tendency toward monotone and no eye contact.
- Talk to the audience, not the manuscript, maintaining the important nonverbal channels.

For existing material, the basic task is that of putting it into a format that is easier to read. For material that has to be created, the task is to organize and write it in full in a manner that will read well aloud. If you're working with a speechwriter, another set of factors enters, dealing with communication between you and the writer.

Getting "Talking" Material

Mark Twain wrote, "Written things are not for speech; their form is literary; they are still, inflexible and will not lend themselves to happy and effective delivery with the tongue. . . . They have to be limbered up, broken up, colloquiallized and turned into the common forms of unpremeditated talk—otherwise they will bore the house, not entertain it."[1]

The guideline for creating material is to write as you talk. What's wrong with just writing the way we do all the time? For the answer, consider this example of written material:

> "The feasibility study, undertaken at the onset of the nuclear fusion program, quickly surfaced contract ambiguities, which had to be resolved before the many real technical problems could be ascertained."

Cumbersome, right? Here's how we'd probably "talk" the same information:

> "We did the feasibility study at the start of the nuclear fusion program. Right away we got hung up on the contract technicalities. Once we got those squared away, we got to the technical problems—lots of them."

Consider the differences between these two examples:

Written	*Spoken*
Long sentences, modifying and connecting clauses	Short, even incomplete sentences
Passive voice	Active voice
Ten-dollar words	Common words, contractions
Formal tone	Conversational, punchy style

A fundamental goal is to put *you* into it and to make it sound like *you*. The public-relations firm Burson-Marstellar noted that a major failing in prepared speeches was the lack of conviction: "The words do not seem to be tailored to the individual giving the speech. Often they sound deliberately colorless and 'canned.' The listener often has the uneasy feeling that the same speech might be given by any of a half-dozen other executives in the company without loss of content. And, in truth, it often is. . . . A good speech cannot be interchangeable."[2]

The problem, then, is to get your ideas and personality into the written text. One method is to jot down the key ideas and then talk the speech into a tape recorder, rather than write out the speech. Have the tape transcribed into a written text, and you have a starting point for your speech in your own "talking" style. Resist the temptation to "tinker" too much with the expressions because they don't look "formal" enough—that is, because the result looks like poor *writing*.

Writing a Manuscript

Use conversational language. Your listeners don't have dictionaries or time to use them. If it sounds formal, academic, pretentious, and unlike you, change it toward the direction of everyday English. How often do you say, "One seldom is presented with a more fortuitous opportunity. Thus well might it behoove us to ascertain, and more importantly, to legitimize . . ."? This is not to say simple words are always better—well-chosen words or phrases, which may vary from highly informal usage, are effective parts of any presentation.

Keep the sentences simple. Throw out clauses that interrupt smooth flow: "The test results, after elimination of spurious data and normalization of the remainder, with application of standard statistical techniques, were positive." By the time the audience hears the verb, they've forgotten the subject. Simplify: "We took the test data, threw out the bad points, and normalized the rest. To analyze the results we used standard statistical methods. The results—we were delighted to see—were positive."

Repeat, emphasize, capsulize, query. Seem reasonable? "Let me try that again. One hundred billion—'b', not 'm'—is what we are spending for foreign oil. Incredible."

Be personal and use the active tense. "I think" rather than "It is thought."

Use contractions, if informality is in order. How often do you say, "I do not think so"? (Note, however, that deliberately *not* using a contraction can provide an effective dramatic touch. "Don't ask what your country can do for you" probably wouldn't have made it into as many books of quotations as "Ask not . . .")

Write so that words and expressions flow freely. This may be hard to discover until the words are read aloud. Interfering with flow are changes in pattern, interruptions in thought due to inserted words or phrases, and tag-on phrases: ". . . of the people, by the people, and, significantly enough to require its inclusion, whatever is good for the people, and this is true in other respects as well, clearly."

Finally, don't be so conversational as to be colorless. The emphasis so far has been on achieving a more effective spoken sound by reducing formality, complexity, and stiffness associated with much written material. In striving for that goal, keep an eye on another goal: affecting your audience. It is possible to be so conversational as to be boring and easily forgettable, and thus ineffective. After you have rid your material of the burdens of heavy writing, spend some time polishing it. The right word or combination of words, a well-turned phrase, an expression with a special touch can make the difference between excitement and blandness. Martin Luther King, John Kennedy, and Douglas MacArthur selected and refined their words with great care, and they moved audiences.

"Why do so many executives make dull speeches?" asked top business and political writer Daniel Lynch. He answered in part with this observation:

> We humble mortals must admit that a genuinely new idea is rare; therefore, it is more often the way a speaker says things than what he says that is significant. In other words, a good speech must have tone: the order and consistency of texture found in a work of art. Nothing in a speech is more important for success or failure than appropriate tone—what we writers call "felicity of phrasing."[3]

Working With a Speechwriter

Plan to spend ample time with the writer and on the speech. William Lovell, top speechwriter for General Motors, said the number one problem for that company's writers was availability—getting enough time with the speakers.[4] Remember, the writer will need time for research and preparation. You'll need time to review, rewrite, and rediscuss. Don't expect miracles to occur overnight and with little effort.

From the Burson-Marstellar report: "All too often the chief executive expects a speech to appear magically on his desk without any contribution on his part. He feels too busy to give the speech the attention it deserves. In the end he becomes the victim of his own neglect. He stumbles through a speech which, from start to finish, sounds contrived. And then he wonders why nobody listened to what he said."[5]

Do your own homework before meeting with the writer. It's your subject and your speech. Don't expect the writer to read your mind or come up with the main ideas. That's your bailiwick.

Meet personally with the writer. You are placing a severe handicap on the writer who has to get information about your ideas and wants through a third party. Give the writer the full picture. If you hold back key information about the occasion, audience, or related factors, he or she may spend unnecessary time going down the wrong road.

Work *with* the writer, as a team. The writer is trained in how to communicate effectively. Listen to her or his ideas and assessments of your ideas and plans. Speechwriter Lynch said that an important role is played by the writer "who is not afraid to tell him [the speaker] that his ideas are lousy, and who insists that the speech bear the clear stamp of one voice—the speaker's—not a chorus of discordant notes and sounds."[6]

Let the writer know you and your world. If you keep the writer off in an isolated corner of the organization, uninformed about the business activities and knowing little about your way of thinking, it's doubtful she'll be able to capture your style or know what is significant or current.

Preparing and Testing the Manuscript

Few people can read "cold" material well. It takes one or more readings for even experienced people to grasp the meaning, to determine which words or syllables to emphasize, to note where to put the pauses and where to move quickly.

The purpose of manuscript preparation is to put the material into a format that helps the speaker do a more effective job of reading it. This involves both interpretation and mechanics of the material. Here are some suggestions:

■ Have the material typed, double- or triple-spaced. Single-spaced typing, newspaper or magazine printing, and handwriting are all harder to read and often result in the speaker's losing the place.

■ Type on one side of the paper only and number the pages.

■ Do not carry a sentence over to another page. It's hard to capture the meaning of a phrase if you have to flip the page in the middle.

■ If you must coordinate the manuscript with slides, events, or times, prepare it in storyboard form (visual identifier in box on left, matching spoken words on right) or insert easily read indicators to keep you on course.

■ Assemble the pages loosely so that you can slide each page to the side as you finish it. Do not staple the pages or place them in a binder, as this creates a distraction each time you flip the pages.

■ Read the material aloud and identify points of emphasis, pauses, continued movement, or changes in thought. The tape recorder can be a valuable tool. Speechwriting authority Jerry Tarver advises, "Possibly the best single strategy would be for you to read a draft of your manuscript into a tape recorder. Play it back and *edit for the ear* [my emphasis]."[7]

■ Practice aloud so that any troublesome words surface and are dealt with or eliminated. It is extremely embarrassing to stumble through a reading or mangle pronunciations. Phonetically spell out words with which you are unfamiliar.

■ Mark the manuscript to give yourself signals as to how you want to read it. Marking systems vary: symbols directly on the copy, notes in margins, and color highlighting have all been used successfully. Use whatever system you are comfortable with and stick with that system. Here's an example using the system from the *Encyclopedia of Radio and Television Broadcasting*, which is specifically intended for newscasters but applies well to speech reading: slash (/), pause; dash (—), run together; squiggly line under, all one thought; one to three underlines, emphasis; paragraph mark (¶), change thought; parentheses ( ), lower voice.[8]

"That we here highly resolve that these dead shall <u>not</u> have died in vain; / that this nation, / under (God,) / shall have a new birth—of—freedom, and that government of the people, by the people, and for the people shall <u>not</u> perish from the earth."

■ For a carefully timed speech, mark time targets in the margin.

DELIVERY

Item from the *San Diego Tribune*: "When [Vice President Dan] Quayle arrived later at General Dynamics, he was speechless. Aides faxed the speech he'd left in his Marriott hotel room."[9] The governors of California and Georgia have both found themselves in the same circumstances for their State of the State addresses. The first need is to remember to take the speech with you.

As for any presentation, checking the facility is vital, especially the lectern and sound system (see Chapter 8). Since many lecterns are badly designed for speakers' notes, check carefully as to where you'll keep your manuscript. A device that has proven valuable is the Script-Master, a folder in which to carry your speech or notes to keep them from slipping off the lectern.

When speaking, above all convey the *meaning* of the message. Meaning is determined at least as much by the *way* it is read as by *what* is read. Listeners reply on changes in tone, pitch, rate, and volume to determine the true message. These also are critical in maintaining interest. With the most common reading pattern—a monotone—the audience loses essential clues to meaning and soon goes to sleep as well.

A variety of other nonverbal clues help convey the message. Eye contact, facial expression, gestures, and body movement often are stifled when speakers read material. Good speakers are able to keep these nonverbal avenues operating even when they read material, and this is the main reason listeners hardly are aware the speaker is reading. Poor speakers show only the tops of their heads: "One of the most serious lapses that I have observed in executives making presentations is their seeming inability to look their audience square in the eye," said Robert Levinson, in an article on executive communication in *Dun's Review*. "To me this is a sine qua non of speechmaking. Yet many a manager rarely even lifts his eyes from the prepared text. You have got to look people in the eye or you are not going to communicate."[10]

With a manuscript that you have practiced with and marked well, you can free yourself from total attention to the typed page and truly talk to your audience. Here are some ways to help do this:

- Think in terms of ideas rather than individual words. Many ideas flow comfortably, thus providing opportunities to look directly at the audience as you say them. Is it necessary to keep your eyes glued to the paper as you read ". . . of the people, by the people, for the people"?
- Use natural change points—major pauses, transitions, summaries, questions—as times to look directly at the audience.
- As you are completing a phrase, glance back down to the page to pick up the next phrase. You may want to keep track of your place by placing a finger at the right spot in the margin. Gesture as you like with the other hand.
- Insert ad libs carefully. These can add personal touches and informality but may disrupt a carefully scripted message design. Experienced speakers use these well, but ad libs have a nasty habit of coming back to haunt the careless.

IN SUMMARY: IF YOU HAVE TO READ IT, DO IT RIGHT

Adlai Stevenson was about to speak to an audience next to Lake Michigan in Chicago—the Windy City. As he placed his manuscript on the lectern, a sudden gust of wind caught it and blew it away. Said Stevenson, "My loss, your gain."

* * * 16 * * *

The Presenter as Emcee

Key Points of This Chapter

* Professionals often are called upon to give introductions, be the toast-master at an event, or serve as chairperson or moderator.
* Good emcees add much to meetings, but inept ones are common.
* Successful emceeing comes from thorough preparation, then applying a friendly, firm hand.

Harry Truman was once introduced this way: "Ladies and gentlemen, the President of the United States." Mr. Truman responded, "That was the shortest speech I ever heard you make in my life. I appreciate it, and I know you meant every word of it."[1]

A special situation that arises occasionally is the opportunity to serve as a master of ceremonies or emcee. These opportunities become more common when people take on more leadership roles in their organizations, though the emcee request can be made of anyone. The emcee plays an important role in the success of the event, even though he or she is not the featured attraction.

Many people duck the emcee role, assuming it means unneeded aggravation in a busy life with little reward. They've never done it before and don't want to be embarrassed in front of a group. All understandable. Yet taking on the emcee role can have a high payoff in terms of recognition, appreciation, and future assignments.

Doing it well is achieved by following the same principles of careful preparation, practice, and performance talked about all along in this book. So, when the call comes, here are some suggestions that may help (summarized in Figure 16-1).

UNDERSTAND THE JOB

For an introducer of the main speaker at a professional meeting, the basic tasks are to (1) help the audience get ready to listen; (2) help the speaker get off to a good start; and (3) do both quickly and exit.

A toastmaster conducts an event, such as a retirement party or a change-of-

Figure 16-1. Key how-to's for the presenter as emcee.

- Being an effective master of ceremonies calls for the same thorough approach as being a presenter.
- Requirements for three common types of emcee—introducer, toastmaster, and chairperson/moderator—differ greatly and need to be understood at the outset.
- The emcee should make sure that all "must-do" tasks get done.
- The emcee and all key participants should be clear on format, arrangements, and schedule.
- As emcee, know the territory in advance.
- The first and most commonly violated rule for introducing speakers is to be brief.
- The introducer's role is to set a positive tone for the speaker, not place him at a disadvantage. Do not embarrass a speaker.
- The introducer must keep in mind that the audience is there to hear the speaker, not the introduction. The emcee must not upstage the speaker by stating his views on the speaker's topic.
- The last words in the introduction should be the speaker's name, clearly and correctly spoken.
- If an interactive audience is involved, the chairperson should repeat questions and comments so all can hear.

---

command ceremony. He or she plays the lead role in establishing and maintaining the spirit of the occasion and operates as a conductor to see that activities stay on schedule.

As a chairperson or moderator of a panel of experts, the role is to introduce speakers, facilitate balanced communication among speakers, maintain order and the schedule, and process audience questions and comments.

PREPARE

Some specific steps are useful:

■ *Do your homework.* Before getting immersed in information-gathering, find out how much of your job will be done for you. Many speakers today prepare their own introductions for emcees to read. Information to know includes meeting themes; the agenda and events; time targets; speakers by name, title, and affiliation; titles of programs; key people other than the speakers; room setup; audiovisual setup and planned use; expected process: audience roles; protocol needs; group culture; and must-do's and must-avoids.

■ *Communicate with all key players.* Make sure everybody is clear about the format, procedures, and schedule.

■ *Make a written to-do list.* It's easy to overlook important items, both before and during meetings.

■ *Research and develop your material.* Key information will tie in the group, event, and speakers. Why is this topic of interest to this group? Why are these good speakers for us to listen to about this topic? What connections do these speakers have to our organization, industry, or current activities? What do you know about any of this that can spark interest, stir after-dinner lethargy, or provide a tantalizing hook? Look for ways to add personal touches about the speakers—anecdotes, incidents, relationships.

■ *Prepare your delivery material.* Either make note cards or write out your comments in full. Make them easily readable, typed double space. Key parts to an introduction include:

- State the topic and why it's relevant to the audience
- Note the speakers and what key background (very briefly) they bring
- Relate an incident that captures the speaker in a personal, positive light
- Close with the speech title and the speaker's name

■ *As appropriate, see humor liberally and wisely.* It's a particularly useful tool for loosening up a group and providing an atmosphere conducive to group interaction. "Humor is a social lubricant," said Robert Orben, editor of a humor service for public speakers. "That is its principal value to the businessmen. It helps put him on the same plane as the people he is talking to."[2] However, humor can easily backfire or fall flat, so use it with care.

■ *Remember to keep your part short.* You're not the primary speaker, nor do you want to upstage them.

■ *Make sure all of the mechanics are being taken care of.* This includes where people sit, paths for speakers getting to the lectern, microphone setups, and operations.

■ *Visit the facility in advance and check layout and all equipment you will be using.*

■ *List all events, speakers, time targets, and essential acknowledgments or announcements.* Be accurate and complete. I thought I was doing the right thing after a talk by thanking key committee people, except I left off a couple of key names. Bad mistake.

PRACTICE

Try out your material—introductions, anecdotes, closing, and any other comments—to smooth them out and increase your comfort level. Time yourself. If you will be reading material, practice to convey meaning and connect with your audience.

PERFORM

Here are some general guidelines.

■ Get there early and check again the layout, the sound system, and anything else you'll be using. Have a crony check your use of the mike from various parts of the room. Do not test a mike by blowing into it; either talk or lightly tap it.

■ Meet the speakers. If they're strangers to your world, be a good host. Ask what you can do to help them or if they have any changes you should know about. Show them their assigned places, review procedures, and test the setup with them.

■ Bring the meeting to order. Your action in taking the podium may do the job, but for a lively crowd, you'll need to be assertive and tell them it's time to begin. If they still haven't settled down, banging the gavel or tapping a glass are standard attention devices. When attention has been gained, begin.

■ Know that you're being heard. Project. Speak clearly. Use the mike properly. Make sure everyone in the audience can hear you easily.

■ If it hasn't been done by someone else, identify yourself and note your affiliation with the group or event, or any other reason for being the emcee. A common question asked during meetings as the emcee is talking is "Who is this person?"

■ Set the tone. You're a combination of conductor, cheerleader, and referee.

■ Be personal. Good emcees bring their personalities to the lectern. Others exercise their roles so woodenly, you can't wait for them to finish. Reading material in a monotone is a major culprit. Follow the advice of James Humes: "In making introductions, get the name straight, then put the resume away and talk from your heart: what he does, how you met him, why you like him."[3]

■ When introducing a speaker, build to a wrap-up statement that makes it clear it's time for transition and applause. State the program title and the speaker's name. Not "Here then is Jean Wilson, speaking to us about business and taxation, so let's welcome her aboard our program today," but "Thus today's program, '*Taxation With or Without Representation*, is particularly relevant. Join me in welcoming our speaker, *Jean Wilson*." (Once more, pronounce names accurately and distinctly. Any experienced speaker can relate the many emcees who blew his or her name.)

■ Be a good listener and observer. You're part of the speaker's team and highly visible. Don't create distractions by talking to others, fumbling papers, or gesturing to audience members. If they need a hand, be there to help out with such tasks as distributing materials, helping pick up dropped notes, and even being a good foil.

■ Keep an eye on the clock and the meeting environment. Alert speakers if hook time is near or a program shift seems wise. If you're the moderator or toastmaster, this is one of your key roles.

■ If your role includes managing audience questions, the first rule is always repeat the question. You may need to prime the pump with a question or two, clarify or paraphrase questions, and tactfully keep the Q&A productive.

■ If it is part of your role, conclude the program with a brief summary, extend appreciation to the speaker, and lead the applause. Don't try to top the speaker by adding on your own lengthy commentary. Complete remaining closing tasks, such as asking for program and speaker evaluations.

■ *Moderator-specific.* Your role includes acting as introducer, meeting leader, stimulator, clarifier, and referee. Make sure everyone understands the agreed-upon rules (perhaps give a quick review of *Robert's Rules of Order*), process, and schedule. Time control is essential, as speakers late on the agenda often get shortchanged. See to it that fairness reigns and that all are allowed to contribute. Keep speakers straight—if "facts" are questionable, insist on sources and specifics.

■ *Toastmaster-specific.* If people are being honored, your job is to see that they are properly recognized and fully enjoy the event. Honor their wishes; if they don't want to give a speech, don't place them in an awkward position. Sense the group's mood and change pace or style as warranted to keep the program moving and the proper spirit maintained.

Notes

CHAPTER 1

1. Lee Iacocca, *Iacocca, an Autobiography* (Toronto: Bantam, 1984), pp. 16, 54.
2. Martha Rader and Alan Wunsch, *Journal of Business Communication* (Summer 1980): 35.
3. Interview, October 14, 1991.
4. Interview, October 3, 1991.
5. Interview, October 12, 1979.
6. *Los Angeles Times*, December 18, 1989, p. D7.
7. *San Diego Union*, December 9, 1991.
8. Interview, July 31, 1979.
9. William R. Kimel and Melford E. Monsees, "Engineering Graduates: How Good Are They?" *Engineering Education*, November 1979, pp. 210–212.
10. Interview, September 19, 1979.
11. "Presenter's Guide," U.S. Air Force document 27-3-72/3000.
12. Robert Levinson, "Executives Can't Communicate," *Dun's Review* (December 1972): 119.

CHAPTER 2

1. All quotes are from personal interviews unless otherwise noted.
2. *Boston Globe*, October 23, 1990.

CHAPTER 3

1. Dwight Kirkpatrick and Alan Berg, "Fears of a Heterogeneous Nonpsychiatric Sample: A Factor Analytic Study" (paper delivered at 89th annual meeting of the American Psychological Association, Los Angeles, 1981).
2. *San Diego Union*, April 21, 1988.
3. Philip Zimbardo, *Shyness: What It Is, What to Do About It* (Reading, Mass.: Addison-Wesley, 1977), p. 37.
4. Steve North, United Stations Radio Network, quoted in *Readers Digest*.
5. Lee Iacocca, *Iacocca, an Autobiography*. (Toronto: Bantam, 1984), pp. 16, 53.
6. Interview, September 9, 1979.
7. Interview, July 5, 1991.
8. Mike Silverman, "Cagney Says 'Good Morning,' " *San Diego Union*, February 13, 1979.
9. Joe Edwards, "Faron Young Still Gets Butterflies," *San Diego Union*, May 26, 1979.
10. Wayne Dyer, *Your Erroneous Zones* (New York: Funk & Wagnalls, 1976), p. 83.

11. Wendell Johnson, *People in Quandaries* (New York: Harper Brothers, 1946).
12. Zimbardo, *Shyness*, p. 29.
13. Tom Wolfe, *The Right Stuff* (New York: Farrar, Straus & Giroux, 1979), p. 148.

CHAPTER 4

1. Interview, December 13, 1991.

CHAPTER 5

1. *San Diego Union*, February 7, 1978.
2. Interview, July 31, 1979.
3. Author's notes from television coverage.
4. Interview, May 19, 1992.
5. George Condon, "For Glenn, It's Quite a Fall," *San Diego Union*, March 17, 1984, p. A-8.
6. Gerald M. Phillips and J. Jerome Zolten, *Structuring Speech* (Indianapolis: Bobbs-Merrill, 1976), p. 70.
7. James Beveridge and Edward J. Velton, *Creating Superior Proposals* (Talent, Oregon: JM Beveridge & Associates, 1978), p. 2-1.
8. Phillips and Zolten, *Structuring Speech*, p. 76.
9. *Los Angeles Times,* October 8, 1988, p. 17.
10. Henry Boettinger, *Moving Mountains* (New York: Collier, 1969), p. 94.
11. Paul Holtzman, *The Psychology of Speakers' Audiences* (Glenview, Ill.: Scott, Foresman and Co., 1970), p. 42.
12. Interview, September 27, 1979.
13. Interview, October 12, 1979.
14. Interview, July 22, 1991.
15. Interview, September 27, 1979.
16. Interview, January 25, 1980.
17. Beveridge and Velton, *Creating Superior Proposals*, p. 2-2.
18. Interview, September 27, 1979.
19. *ENR*, November 25, 1991, p. 24.
20. Robert E. Miller and Stephen E. Heiman, *Strategic Selling* (New York: Warner Books, 1985), p. 61.
21. Interview, January 15, 1992.
22. Holtzman, *Psychology.*
23. James Cathcart, *Relationship Selling* (New York: Perigee Books, 1990).
24. *Los Angeles Times*, October 13, 1989, p. D3.
25. Theodore Clevenger, *Audience Analysis* (Indianapolis: Bobbs-Merrill, 1966), p. 111.
26. Ibid., pp. 110–111, contains a detailed discussion of these changes.
27. Abraham Maslow, *Motivation and Personality*, 2d ed. (New York: Harper & Row, 1970).

CHAPTER 6

1. Interview, October 14, 1991.
2. Cited in Wayne C. Minnick, *The Art of Persuasion*, 2d ed. (Cambridge, Mass.: Riverside Press, 1968), p. 262.
3. Interview, October 31, 1991.
4. Interview, October 31, 1991.
5. Larry A. Samovar and Jack Mills, *Oral Communication, Message, and Response*, 4th ed. (Dubuque, Iowa: William C. Brown, 1980), pp. 105–106.

6. Richard Borden, *Public Speaking as Listeners Like It* (New York: Harper Brothers, 1935), p. 3.
7. *Los Angeles Times*, August 13, 1980.
8. Interview, January 11, 1980.
9. Barney Oldfield, "How to Succeed in Public Relations by Really Trying," *Vital Speeches of the Day*, September 15, 1974, p. 726.
10. Interview, October 12, 1979.
11. Interview, July 22, 1991.
12. Interview, September 19, 1979.
13. George A. Miller, *The Psychology of Communication* (New York: Basic Books, 1967), pp. 14–43.
14. Ross Smythe, "Humour (or Humor) in Public Speaking," *Vital Speeches of the Day*, September 1, 1974, pp. 690–693.
15. Allen Monroe and Douglas Ehninger, *Principles of Speech Communication*, 6th ed. (Glenview, Ill.: Scott, Foresman and Co., 1969), p. 258.
16. Ralph Smedley, *Basic Training for Toastmasters* (Santa Ana, Calif.: Toastmasters International, 1964), p. 30.
17. Borden, *Public Speaking as Listeners Like It*, p. 3
18. Dale Carnegie, *The Quick and Easy Way to Effective Speaking* (New York: Pocket Books, 1977), p. 104.
19. June Guncheon, "To Make People Listen," *Nation's Business* (October 1967): 96–102.
20. Inteview, January 15, 1992.
21. Interview, July 5, 1991.
22. Speech Communication Association 66th Annual Meeting, November 1980.
23. *Los Angeles Times*, June 22, 1980.
24. Interview, May 20, 1992.
25. "Audience Moved by Mother's Letter to Reagan," *Los Angeles Times*, September 19, 1981, p. I-27.

CHAPTER 7

1. *Los Angeles Times*, March 2, 1988, p. 20.
2. *New York Times*, November 24, 1991, p. F9.
3. Robert Alberti and Michael Emmons, *Your Perfect Right: A Guide to Assertive Behavior* (San Luis Obispo, Calif.: Impact Pubs. 1990).
4. Steve Bell, ABC-TV, November 20, 1985.
5. Joseph Flannery, "Government Regulation, the Classic Growth Industry," *Vital Speeches of the Day*, October 1, 1978, p. 749.
6. Wes Magnuson, "Success Is" (videotape presentation given at General Dynamics Convair Management Association, San Diego, Calif.: February 15, 1975).
7. Jerry Tarver, "The First of the Big Shots," supplement to *Los Angeles Times*, undated.
8. Arthur Doerr, "The Bounds of Earth," *Vital Speeches of the Day*, February 1, 1974, pp. 229–231.
9. *Los Angeles Times*, August 14, 1974.
10. *San Jose Mercury News*, March 2, 1989, p. 12A.
11. *Nation's Business*, July 1977, p. 61.
12. Flannery, "Government Regulation, the Classic Growth Industry."
13. *Los Angeles Times*, October 6, 1980.
14. *Aeronautics & Astronautics*, American Institute of Astronautics & Aeronautics, February 1976, p. 8.
15. Peter Lewis, *New York Times*, November 27, 1992, p. F9.
16. "Congressional Leadership," *Vital Speeches of the Day*, November 1, 1976, p. 52.
17. Amitai Etioni, "Future Angst, Nine Rules for Stumbling Into the Future," *Next* (July–August 1980): 69.

18. *San Diego Union,* June 19, 1989, p. A8.
19. Correspondence, May 20, 1980.
20. Author's notes from television broadcast, September 24, 1984.
21. Tarver, "The First of the Big Shots."
22. Ross Smythe, "Humour (or Humor) in Public Speaking," *Vital Speeches of the Day,* September 1, 1974, pp. 690–693.
23. Interview, October 14, 1991.
24. Pat Taylor, "The Relationship Between Humor and Retention," Speech Communication Association, 1972.
25. *Public Relations Journal* 35, no. 5 (May 1979): 6.
26. Malcolm Kushner, *The Light Touch* (New York: Simon & Schuster, 1990), p. 92.
27. Interview, December 18, 1991.
28. Walter Beran, "How to Be Ethical in an Unethical World," *Vital Speeches of the Day,* July 15, 1976, p. 32.
29. Interview, September 6, 1991.
30. *Los Angeles Times,* May 29, 1980.
31. Elbert R. Bowen et al., *Communicative Reading,* 4th ed. (New York: Macmillan, 1978), p. 36.
32. J. Myers and W. Reynolds, *Consumer Behavior and Marketing Management* (Boston: Houghton Mifflin, 1967), p. 60.
33. Joe Griffith, *Speaker's Library of Business Stories, Anecdotes and Humor* (Englewood Cliffs, N.J.: Prentice-Hall, 1990), p. x.

CHAPTER 8

1. Hower J. Hsia, "On Channel Effectiveness," *AV Communication Review* (Fall 1968): 248–250.
2. "A Study of the Effects of Overhead Transparencies on Business Meetings . . ." cited in *How to Run Better Business Meetings,* 3M Meeting Management Team (New York: McGraw-Hill, 1987).
3. R. Hubbard, "Telemation: AV Automatically Controlled," *Audiovisual Instructor* 6, no. 9 (1961): 438.
4. Interview, October 3, 1991.
5. Interview, October 5, 1979.
6. Robert McKim, *Experiences in Visual Thinking* (Belmont, Calif.: Wadsworth, 1972), p. 24.
7. "Priestly Prayer Triggers Plea to Turn in Guns," *Los Angeles Times,* April 10, 1982.
8. *San Diego Union,* April 25, 1979.
9. Jane Applegate, "Entrepreneurs Discover Value of Working Model," *Los Angeles Times,* December 1, 1989, p. D3.
10. Interview, July 22, 1991.
11. Author/Speaker Manual (El Segundo, Calif.: Electronic Conventions, Inc.), p. 6.
12. Carl Hovland, Irving Janis, and Harold Kelley, *Communication and Persuasion* (New Haven, Conn.: Yale University Press, 1953), p. 99.
13. George A. Miller, *The Psychology of Communication* (New York: Basic Books, 1967), pp. 14–43.
14. Margaret Rabb, *Presentation Design Book* (Chapel Hill, N.C.: Ventana Press, 1990), p. 66.
15. Jan V. White, *Graphic Design for the Electronic Age* (New York: Watson-Guptill, 1988), p. 31.
16. Jerrold E. Kemp, *Planning and Producing Audiovisual Materials,* 3d ed. (New York: Thomas Y. Crowell, 1975), p. 121.
17. Michael MacDonald-Ross, "How Numbers Are Shown," *AV Communication Review* (Winter 1977): 376.
18. James W. Brown, Richard B. Lewis, and Fred Harcleroad, eds., *Audio-Visual Instruction: Technology, Media and Methods* (New York: McGraw-Hill, 1977), p. 96.

19. Cited in Ronald E. Green, "Communications with Color," *Audio-Visual Communications* (November 1978): 14.
20. Brown, Lewis, and Harcleroad, *Audio-Visual Instruction*, p. 96.
21. Kathi Gabriel-Karen, Genigraphics, San Diego, memo, January 30, 1992.
22. "Legibility—Artwork to Screen," Kodak publication S-24.
23. Ibid., p. 7.
24. John Brooks, *Business Adventures* (New York: Weybright and Talley, 1969), p. 49.

CHAPTER 9

1. "Practice for Slide and Filmstrip Projection," Publication No. ANSI PH3.41-1972 (New York: National Standards Institute, 1972), p. 9.
2. Ibid., p. 8.
3. Interview with Carolyn DeVinny, media manager for General Telephone Company of California, November 5, 1980.

CHAPTER 10

1. Robert E. Levinson, "Executives Can't Communicate," *Dun's Review* (December 1972): 102.
2. William Luce, *The Belle of Amherst* (Boston: Houghton Mifflin, 1976), p. 8.
3. Cited in Larry Samovar and Jack Mills, *Oral Communication: Message and Response*, 5th ed. (Dubuque, Iowa: William C. Brown, 1989), p. 222.
4. Louis Nizer, *My Life in Court* (New York: Jove, 1978), p. 269.
5. Interview, June 27, 1991.
6. Interview, November 8, 1991.
7. Interview, October 14, 1991.
8. Ibid.
9. Interview, October 3, 1991.
10. Interview, June 25, 1991.
11. Interview, September 27, 1979.
12. Interview, September 19, 1979.
13. Albert Mehrabian, *Silent Messages* (Belmont, CA: Wadsworth, 1971), p. 43.
14. Interview, July 31, 1979.
15. Interview, October 14, 1991.
16. Interview, December 16, 1991.
17. Interview, November 3, 1991.
18. *San Diego Union*, July 19, 1976.
19. *Newsweek*, February 13, 1978, p. 15.
20. *San Deigo Union*, April 10, 1980.
21. Interview, October 12, 1979.
22. *Times Magazine*, supplement to *Army/Navy/Air Force Times*, February 9, 1976, p. 27.
23. Mehrabian, *Silent Messages*, p. 92.
24. *Christian Science Monitor*, March 16, 1972.
25. *Los Angeles Times*, July 3, 1980.
26. *San Diego Union*, May 15, 1977.
27. *Los Angeles Times*, December 22, 1974.
28. *Verbatim—The Language Quarterly* (Winter 1979–1980): 7.
29. George Orwell, "Politics and the English Language," in Robert L. Scott and Douglas W. Ehninger, *The Speaker's Reader: Concepts in Communication* (Glenview, Ill.: Scott, Foresman, 1969), p. 168.
30. *Verbatim*, op. cit.
31. John Locke, "Language and Its Proper Use," in Sterling P. Lamprecht, ed., *Locke Selections* (New York: Charles Scribner's Sons, 1928), p. 33.

32. Orwell, "Politics and the English Language."
33. Ibid., p. 169.
34. *Aviation Week*, October 31, 1977, p. 15.
35. Houston Peterson, ed., *A Treasury of the World's Great Speeches* (New York: Simon & Schuster, 1965), p. 385.
36. Ibid., p. 837.
37. Ibid., p. 141.
38. Mehrabian, *Silent Messages*.
39. Lyle Mayer, *Fundamentals of Voice and Diction* (Dubuque, Ia.: William C. Brown, 1974), p. 110.
40. Harvey H. Hubbard, "Guidelines for the Planning and Preparation of Illustrated Technical Talks," NASA Technical Memorandum X-72783, November 1975, p. 3.
41. Mayer, *Fundamentals of Voice and Diction*, pp. 4, 131.
42. Richard Borden, *Public Speaking as Listeners Like It* (New York: Harper Brothers, 1935), p. 104.
43. Interview, October 18, 1979.
44. Mayer, *Fundamentals of Voice and Diction*, p. 92.
45. *The Autobiography of Mark Twain* (New York: Harper Brothers, 1959), p. 198.
46. Interview, November 5, 1979.
47. Mehrabian, *Silent Messages*.
48. Gloria Axelrod, "Help Yourself to Clear Speech," unpublished manuscript.
49. Mayer, *Fundamentals of Voice and Diction*, p. 29.
50. Cicely Berry, *Voice and the Actor* (New York: Macmillan, 1973), p. 16.
51. In *A Guide to Better Technical Presentations* (New York: IEEE Press, 1975), p. 157.
52. Interview, October 12, 1979.
53. Hilda Fisher, *Improving Voice and Articulation* (Boston: Houghton Mifflin, 1966), p. 53.
54. Ralph Waldo Emerson, "The American Scholar," in *The Works of Emerson* (Roslyn, N.Y.: Black's Reader's Service), p. 561.

CHAPTER 11

1. Interview, October, 31, 1991.
2. Robert P. Griffin, "Congressional Leadership," *Vital Speeches of the Day*, November 1, 1975, p. 53.
3. Ralph Nichols, "Listening Is a 10-Part Skill," *Nation's Business* (July 1957).
4. Leonard A. Stevens, *The Ill-Spoken Word: The Decline of Speech in America* (New York: McGraw-Hill, 1966), p. 131.
5. J. Scott Armstrong, "Bafflegab Pays," *Psychology Today* (May 1980): 12.
6. Kenneth Blanchard and Spencer Johnson, *The One Minute Manager* (New York: Berkley Books, 1981), p. 39.

CHAPTER 13

1. Interview, June 25, 1991.
2. Interview, October 14, 1991.
3. Interview, January 15, 1992.

CHAPTER 14

1. Sidney Jourard, *Disclosing Man to Himself* (Princeton, N.J.: Van Nostrand, 1968).
2. Jean Marie Ackermann, "Skill Training for Foreign Assignment," in Larry

Samovar and Richard E. Porter, *Intercultural Communication: A Reader,* 2d ed. (Belmont, Calif.: Wadsworth, 1976), p. 300.
3. Philip Cateoria and John Hess, *International Marketing,* 3d ed. (Homewood, Ill.: Irwin, 1975), p. 178.
4. Interview, June 2, 1980.
5. Howard Van Zandt, "How to Negotiate in Japan," in Samovar and Porter, *Intercultural Communication,* p. 315.
6. Interview, November 4, 1991.
7. Interview with Hugh Williams, manager of public relations, SDC Systems Group, July 31, 1979.
8. Interview, December 15, 1979.
9. *Fortune,* September 1978, p. 135.
10. Ibid., p. 125.
11. Interview, April 21, 1981.
12. Interview, December 19, 1979.
13. Van Zandt, "How to Negotiate in Japan."
14. Interview, October 8, 1980.
15. Sondra Thiederman, "The Speaker and Diversity: Tips on Presenting to the Culturally Diverse Audience" (audio cassette), National Speakers Association, 1991.
16. Interview, December 15, 1979.
17. Interview, September 19, 1979.
18. "Mexico's Consul General Protests 'Granada' Salute," *San Diego Tribune,* August 16, 1984, p. A-24.

CHAPTER 15

1. *The Autobiography of Mark Twain* (New York: Harper Brothers, 1959).
2. *Wall Street Journal,* June 13, 1975.
3. Daniel Lynch, "Confessions of a Speechwriter," *Dun's Review* (November 1965): 42.
4. Interview, July 12, 1979.
5. *Wall Street Journal,* June 13, 1975.
6. Lynch, "Confessions of a Speechwriter."
7. Jerry Tarver, "Edit Speeches for the Ear," *Dateline* (Publicity Club of Chicago) (February 1978).
8. Robert St. John, 2d ed., *Encyclopedia of Radio and Television Broadcasting* (Milwaukee: Cathedral Square Publishing, 1968), p. 199.
9. *San Diego Tribune,* July 19, 1989, p. B1.
10. Robert Levinson, "Executives Can't Communicate," *Dun's Review* (December 1972): 119.

CHAPTER 16

1. George S. Caldwell, ed., *The Wit and Wisdom of Harry S. Truman* (New York: Stein and Day, 1973), p. 49.
2. John Costello, "Jests Can Do Justice to Your Speeches," *Nation's Business* (January 1978): 37.
3. James Humes, *Roles Speakers Play: How to Prepare a Speech for Any Occasion* (New York: Harper & Row, 1976), p. 74.

Glossary

Acronym   Shortcut terminology made up of initial letters but pronounced as a word; for example, GIGO—Garbage In, Garbage Out.

Action (title)   On visuals, a full-meaning title that concisely explains the essence of the chart. Also called *interpretive message* or *headline title*.

Agenda   The list of topics the presentation covers, often an early chart. The "moving agenda" is shown before each section.

Arrange   Preparation activities that consider facilities, equipment, and incidentals.

Artist's aid   Ready-made illustration and lettering form for making visual art.

Audience analysis   Identification of the audience as a group or key individuals and assessment of how to shape the presentation for the audience.

Audiovisual   Communication which addresses hearing and vision.

Background   In the introduction, a quick update of the program or precipitating activities.

Body   The middle and largest part of the presentation.

Briefing   Military term for presentation.

Bullets   On visuals, highlighting dots before key points.

Camcorder   Compact video-recorder/camera.

Cassette   Self-contained (winding/rewinding) audio- or videotape or film case.

CD-ROM   Compact disk, read-only memory. Used in interactive or multimedia presentations for high-quantity information storage.

Chalkboard   Surface used with chalk or markers.

Chart   Term commonly applied to any two-dimensional visual. More specifically refers to flip charts or poster charts.

Clamp   On an easel, the part that holds the flip charts.

Class A   A presentation given top-quality visual treatment.

Classification   The security level of the meeting or the visuals.

Clip art   Illustrations pulled in from a collection, either printed or on a computer.

Compatible   Audiovisual elements that work correctly together.

Computer graphics   Visual aids prepared with a computer.

Connection   Eye contact or mental linkage between the speaker and an audience member.

Controller   A device, wired or wireless, which advances computer images or initiates events on the screen while at a distance from the computer.

Delivery   Term used in this book to describe the actual giving or conducting of a presentation.

Delivery script   Preparation tool that matches spoken words or key points to each visual.

Demonstration   Showing how something works.

Diaphragm   Muscular membrane between lungs and stomach area. Diaphragm breathing employs lower chest and stomach rather than upper chest.
Display system   Method of showing material using boards such as magnetic, flannel, and Velcro to hold items.
Dissolve   Smooth blending in and out of two images.
Dry run   Practice.

Easel   Gadget which holds flip charts or posters.
Electronic chalkboard   Large board for manual printing with markers, combined with electronic printout and storage.
End product   Desired result of the presentation.
Executive summary   Concise summary of the presentation, given at the start.
Explanation   Material that provides description, definition, and ground rules.
Extemporaneous   Speaking that is prepared (organized and developed) but not fully written out or memorized. Occasionally used to mean impromptu (unprepared) speaking.
Eye contact   Refers to the presenter's looking directly at the audience.

Facing page   In a brochure, the written description of the visual shown.
Filmstrip   A series of pictures on 16mm or 8mm film, viewed one picture at a time. Often with a soundtrack.
Finished (visuals)   Final artwork completed.
Flip chart   Paper used with an easel.
Focus   Sharpness of visual image.
Foil   Another term for *viewgraph* or *overhead transparency*.
Frame   Plastic or cardboard mount for viewgraphs.

Handout   Expression referring to material distributed.
Hands-on   Demonstration in which audience members operate equipment.
Hard copy   Reproduced copies of visuals.
Hardware   Physical equipment, such as a computer or printer.
Headline title   Visual aid title that has a complete message, also called action or interpretive title.

Impromptu   Speaking with little advance notice or preparation.
Initialism   Initial letters of a term verbalized letter by letter (such as C.O.D.).
Introduction   The first part of the presentation, or the lead-in comments by the program chairperson.

Keystone effect   Image distortion caused by overhead projection, with the top wider than the bottom.

Lantern slide   A photographic transparency for projecting images, with image area of 3 in. by 2 in. rather than the standard 35 mm.
Larynx   Area containing the vocal cords.
LCD   Liquid crystal display. A device used to show or project computer images.
Lectern   Stand or desk behind which speaker stands, and on which are placed notes or manuscript. Often contains a microphone.
Live (presentation)   One personally delivered, as distinct from one with a taped sound track.

Mannerisms   Unconscious, repeated, and often distracting movements or sounds made by presenter.
Manuscript   Fully typed text of speech.
Marker   Ink pen or crayon for writing on visuals or boards.
Microphone (fixed)   Microphone mounted to a stand and not movable.

Microphone (hand-held)   Microphone held near the mouth by hand and movable.

Microphone (lavaliere)   Microphone hung around the neck.

Microphone (wireless)   Microphone with electronic, nonwired connection to the amplifier.

Mike   Microphone.

Mixed media   Presentation using more than one medium, for example, slides plus videotape.

Model   A full-size or scaled replica. A working model has moving parts. Also, a person who helps show the product.

Modem   System that links computer to another location via phone lines, such as for sending computer graphics to a service bureau.

Monitor   A display screen for videotape, a computer, or some other instrument.

Monotone   Voice of nearly constant pitch.

Multi-image   Two or more visual images shown simultaneously.

Multimedia   Computer-based presentation that combines still images, video, animation, sound, and interactive participation.

Murphy's Law   "Whatever can go wrong, will."

Notes   Key words or material referred to by the speaker. Often on cards.

Outline   Planning tool showing organization of talk and key points.

Output device   The mechanism that displays, transmits, or prints computer graphics.

Overhead transparency   See *viewgraph*.

P.A.   Public address (sound) system.

Pitch   Slang expression for a presentation. Also refers to vocal tone or scale.

Planning   First phase of developing a presentation: information gathering, analyzing, and developing the approach.

Podium   A specific place or raised platform for the speaker to stand on. Also often used to mean lectern.

Point (main, sub)   A key idea in a presentation.

Pointer   Instrument used by presenter to direct audience attention to a specific part of a visual. May be a physical or electronic (light) pointer.

Post-delivery   In this book, the follow-up activities after the presentation.

Poster   Visual aid, usually cardboard, which sits on an easel or other mounting system.

Presentation   An oral and often visual communication, generally given by a live speaker to an interactive audience.

Printer   Device that copies computer output onto paper or transparencies. A laser printer produces high-quality print with laser technology. A dot matrix printer uses contact pins. Paint or inkjet printers use spray technology. Thermal printers apply heat to temperature sensitive inks.

Programmer   A device which controls sequencing of visuals and multiple pieces of equipment. Primarily used in multi-image presentations.

Progressive disclosure   Also called revelation. Showing only one part of a visual at a time and building up to the complete visual.

Projection (voice)   Carrying power of the presenter's voice.

Projector   Machine which uses light to throw an image onto a screen. Standard types include motion picture, slide, overhead, opaque, and filmstrip.

Purpose   The objective of the presentation.

Q&A period   Question-and-answer period.

Rear screen   Projection that comes from behind the screen, rather than from in front of it.

Reel-to-reel   Audio- or videotape with physically separate lead and take-up reels.

Remote control   Control of audiovisual equipment at a distance from it.

Reverse image A projected visual with content and background displayed opposite from standard projection.

Review Examining the presentation before it is actually given. A dry run. May have priority designations such as pink-team (preliminary) or red-team (final) reviews.

Role play Participants assuming and acting out characters other than their own.

Rough Preliminary material.

Screen Material onto which an image is projected. Also, the process of reviewing and selecting material.

Simulation A demonstration intended to portray an actual activity. A presentation dry run with all events done with a substitute audience (simulators).

Situation analysis In the planning phase, assessing the effects of the setting and related events on the upcoming presentation.

Slide Photographic transparency made for projection. Most common size is 35mm, but larger *lantern slides* are also used.

Slide service A company that makes visuals (for example, slides) from computer inputs sent to them or creates original visual art.

Software Computer program used to create presentation graphics or other materials.

Speaker The presenter or a sound system output device.

Staging Preparation phase for making ready the mechanics of presentation: arrangements, facilities, equipment, practice.

Stick figures Simple drawings of figures.

Storyboard Planning method which shows visual ideas and key verbal points in preliminary form.

Summary Final part of the talk.

Support Material such as statistics, examples, and testimony which backs up the main proposition.

Systems approach In this book, the comprehensive and rigorous process of developing and conducting a presentation.

Team presentation Presentation with two or more presenters.

Teleconference Meeting with participants in different sites communicating through electronic systems.

Theme (main) The single sentence which states the essence of the presentation.

Transition Statement or visual that bridges sections.

Transparency A picture you can see through, for projection, such as a 35mm slide. Common term for visuals for overhead projection. Also called *viewgraph*.

Videoconference Meeting or presentation between two or more sites linked by video.

Videodisk Video system which uses disks rather than tapes.

Video monitor Screen used for showing video pictures.

Video player Component which plays recorded tapes.

Video recorder Component which records video images from a wired or transmitted signal. May include the player.

Videotape Video system using cassette or reel-to-reel tape. Popular systems include U-matic (¾"), VHS or Betamax (½"), and Technicolor (¼").

Viewgraph Transparent visual shown by overhead projector.

Word chart Visual consisting only of words, containing no drawings or pictures.

Suggestions for Further Reading

GENERAL COVERAGE OF PRESENTATIONS

Books

Ailes, Roger. *You Are the Message.* New York: Doubleday, 1976.

Carnegie, Dale. *The Quick & Easy Way to Effective Speaking.* New York: Pocket Books, 1977.

Close, E. Burt. *How to Create Super DeskTop Presentations.* Ft. Myers, Fla.: Touche, 1990.

Gronbeck, Bruce, Kathleen German, Douglas Enninger, and Alan Monroe. *Principles of Speech Communication.* New York: Harper Collins, 1992. One of the classic college texts.

Howell, William S., and Ernest G. Bormann. *The Process of Presentational Speaking,* 2nd ed. New York: Harper Collins, 1987.

Humes, James. *The Sir Winston Method: 5 Secrets of Speaking the Language of Leadership.* New York: Morrow, 1991. Churchill examples and stories.

Jeffries, James R., and Jefferson Bates. *The Executive's Guide to Meetings, Conferences & Audiovisual Presentations.* New York: McGraw-Hill, 1983.

Logue, Cal M., Dwight Freshley, Charles Gruner, and Richard Huseman. *Briefly Speaking: A Guide to Public Speaking in College & Career.* Needham Heights, Mass.: Adlyn & Bacon, 1992.

Lustberg, Art. *Building Podium Power.* Washington, D.C.: U.S. Chamber of Commerce, 1988.

Mambert, William A. *Presenting Technical Ideas.* New York: Wiley, 1968. Strong theoretical background combined with many applications. Highly recommended.

———. *Effective Presentation: A Short Course for Professionals,* 2nd ed. New York: Wiley, 1985.

Morrisey, George L. *Effective Business and Technical Presentations,* 2nd ed. Reading, Mass.: Addison-Wesley, 1968, 1975.

Pike, Robert. *Creative Training Techniques Handbook.* Minneapolis, Minn.: Lakeland, 1989.

Samovar, Larry A., and Jack Mills. *Oral Communication, Message, and Response,* 7th ed. Dubuque, Ia.: William C. Brown, 1989. Widely used basic college text.

Simon, Herbert W. *Persuasion: Understanding, Practice, and Analysis,* 2nd ed. New York: McGraw-Hill, 1986. Strong on organization and logic.

The 3M Management Team. *How to Run Better Business Meetings.* New York: McGraw-Hill, 1987.

Vardaman, George T. *Making Successful Presentations.* New York: AMACOM, 1984.

Verderber, Rudolph. *The Challenge of Effective Speaking,* 8th ed. Belmont, Calif.: Wadsworth, 1991. Widely used college text, strong on examples and analysis.

Wilder, Claudyne. *The Presentations Kit.* New York: John Wiley, 1990.

Woelfle, Robert M. (ed.). *New Guide for Better Technical Presentations.* New York: IEEE Press, 1992. Compilation of articles related to technical presentations.

Periodicals

Communications Monographs (formerly *Speech Monographs*). Falls Church, Va.: Speech Communication Association. Quarterly. Research emphasis.

Educational Communication and Technology Journal. Washington, D.C.: Association for Educational Communications and Technology. Quarterly.

Practical Presentations Newsletter. Mammoth Lakes, Calif.: C&M Communications. Monthly.

Presentations Products Magazine. Malibu, Calif.: Pacific Magazine Group. Monthly.

Quarterly Journal of Speech. Falls Church, Va.: Speech Communication Association. Quarterly. Scholarly.

Technical Communication. Washington, D.C.: Society for Technical Communication. Quarterly.

The Toastmaster. Mission Viejo, Calif.: Toastmasters International. Monthly.

Vital Speeches of the Day. Southold, N.Y.: City News Publishing Company. Twice a month. Full texts of current speeches by business, government, and foreign speakers.

Videos

"Be Prepared to Speak: The Step-by-Step Video Guide to Public Speaking." San Francisco: Kantola Productions. Distributed by Toastmasters International. Useful; modest price.

"Bravo! What a Presentation!" New York: American Management Association.

"Presentation Excellence." Chicago: Video Publishing House, Inc. With clips from famed speakers.

Public Affairs Video Archives. Lafayette, Ind.: Purdue University. Videos of contemporary speeches from C-Span.

CHAPTER 3   BECOMING A WINNING PRESENTER

"Coping With Fear of Public Speaking." Pullman, Wash.: Communications Video. Modest price.

Marshall, W. L., and W. R. Andrews. *Public Speaking Anxiety.* Kingston, Canada: Queen's University, 1979. A self-help manual using desensitization.

Nelson, Robert. *Louder & Funnier: Practical Guide for Overcoming Stagefright.* Berkeley, Calif.: Ten Speed Press, 1985.

Sharing Ideas. Glendora, Calif.: Royal Publishing. Bi-monthly. A plethora of tips about professional speaking.

Walters, Dottie, and Lilly Walters. *Speak and Grow Rich.* Englewood Cliffs, N.J.: Prentice-Hall, 1989. Valuable for those wanting to become professional speakers.

CHAPTER 5   PLAN

Alessandra, Anthony J. *Non-Manipulative Selling.* Englewood Cliffs, N.J.: Prentice-Hall, 1987. Responding to different receiver styles.

Bandura, Albert. *Social Learning Theory.* Englewood Cliffs, N.J.: Prentice-Hall, 1977.

Beveridge, James N., and Edward J. Velton. *Positioning to Win.* Radner, Pa.: Chilton, 1982. Proposal strategy and primary message focus.

Clevenger, Theodore. *Audience Analysis.* Indianapolis, Ind.: Bobbs-Merrill, 1966.

Cronkhite, Gary. *Persuasion, Speech, and Behavioral Change.* New York: Macmillan, 1969. Survey of receiver response and speaker strategies.

Holtsman, Paul D. *The Psychology of Speaker's Audiences.* Glenview, Ill.: Scott, Foresman, 1970. Analyzes audience factors and their significance for speakers' strategies.

Karlins, Marvin, and Herbert Abelson. *Persuasion: How Opinions and Attitudes Are Changed,* 2nd ed. New York: Springer, 1970. A summary of experimental research on receiver response.

Mager, Robert F. *Preparing Instructional Objectives.* Belmont, Calif.: Fearon Publishers, 1962.

Miller, Robert, and Stephen Heiman. *Strategic Selling.* New York: Warner, 1985.

Minnick, Wayne C. *The Art of Persuasion,* 2nd ed. Cambridge, Mass.: Riverside Press, 1968.

Smith, Craig, and David M. Hunsaker. *The Bases of Argument: Ideas in Conflict.* New York: Macmillan, 1972.

Thompson, Wayne N. *Quantitative Research in Public Address and Communication.* New York: Random House, 1967. Thorough summary of experimental findings in many categories.

———. *The Process of Persuasion: Principles and Readings.* New York: Harper & Row, 1975.

Velton, E. C., C. E. Grubbs, Jack Dean, T. C. Boren, and Thomas Leech. *The Nine Keys to Winning Proposals.* La Mesa, Calif.: Positioning to Win, 1988.

CHAPTER 6   ORGANIZE

Audio-Visual Planning Equipment. Kodak publication S-11.

Bettinghaus, Erwin. *The Nature of Proof.* New York: Macmillan, 1972.

Phillips, Gerald M., and J. Jerome Zolten. *Structuring Speech: A How-to-Do-It Book About Public Speaking.* Indianapolis, Ind.: Bobbs-Merrill, 1976.

Toulmin, Steven, Richard Rieke, and Allan Janik. *An Introduction to Reasoning,* 2nd ed. New York: Macmillan, 1984.

Zelko, Harold P., and Marjorie E. Zelko. *How to Make Speeches for All Occasions.* New York: Doubleday, 1979. Many examples of outlines for speeches of various types.

CHAPTER 7   SUPPORT, PART I: REINFORCEMENT

Bartlett's Familiar Quotations. Boston: Little, Brown & Co., 1980.

Bits & Pieces. Fairfield, N.J.: Economics Press. Monthly. Anecdotes and tidbits.

*Brussel, Eugene. *Webster's New World Dictionary of Quotable Definitions.* Englewood Cliffs, N.J.: Prentice-Hall, 1988.

Cerf, Christopher, and Victor Navasky. *The Experts Speak.* New York: Pantheon, 1984.

Computer Speech Writer. Champlain, N.Y.: Pageant. Computer diskette with a variety of forms of speech support.

Correct Quotes. Wordstar, International.

*Griffith, Joe. *Speaker's Library of Business Stories, Anecdotes & Humor.* Englewood Cliffs, N.J.: Prentice-Hall, 1990.

*Henry, Robert, Joe Griffith, Jeanne Robertson, and Doc Blakely. *How the Pros Keep Them Laughing.* Houston: Rich Publishing, 1987.

Humor Processor. Berkeley, Calif.: Responsive Software. Computer software for adding humor to presentations.

*Sources of material—anecdotes, quotations, one-liners.

*Humes, James C. *Podium Humor: A Raconteur's Treasury of Witty and Humorous Stories.* New York: Harper & Row, 1975.

*———. *A Speaker's Treasury of Anecdotes About the Famous.* New York: Harper & Row, 1978.

Kimble, Gregory R. *How to Use and Misuse Statistics.* Englewood Cliffs, N.J.: Prentice-Hall, 1978.

Kushner, Malcolm. *The Light Touch: How to Use Humor for Business Success.* New York: Fireside Books, 1990.

*Orben's Current Comedy. Wilmington, Del.: Comedy Center. Humor service for speakers.

Peter, Laurence J., and Bill Dana. *The Laughter Prescription.* New York: Ballantine, 1982.

*Peter, Laurence J. *Peter's Quotations, Ideas for Our Time.* New York: Morrow, 1977.

QUOTEMASTER.™ Houston: Penn Comp. Over 3,000 quotes in this computer database.

*Seldes, George. *The Great Quotations.* New York: Pocket Books, 1967.

Smith, Craig R., and David M. Hunsaker. *Bases of Argument.* New York: Macmillan, 1972. Covers evidence types and how to attack and defend them.

The Laugh Connection. San Diego: Bob Ross Associates. Quarterly newsletter.

CHAPTER 8   SUPPORT, PART II: VISUAL AIDS

Anderson, Ronald. *Selecting and Developing Media for Instruction.* New York: Van Nostrand Reinhold, 1976.

Arnheim, Rudolf. *Visual Thinking.* Berkeley: University of California Press, 1980.

Audio-Visual Communications. Melville, N.Y.: PTN Publishing. Monthly.

Bullough, Robert. *Creating Instructional Materials,* 3rd ed. New York: Macmillan, 1988.

Computer Graphics World. Westford, Mass.: PennWell. Monthly.

Effective Lecture Slides. Kodak publication S-22.

Guth, Chester, and Stanley Shaw. *How to Put on Dynamic Meetings.* Reston, VA: Reston, 1980.

"Illustrations for Publication and Projection." (American National Standard.) New York: The American Society of Mechanical Engineers Publication No. ANSI 15.1 M, 1979.

Kemp, Jerrold E. *Planning, Producing and Using Instructional Media,* 6th ed. New York: Harper-Collins, 1989.

*Sources of material—anecdotes, quotations, one-liners.

Legibility—Artwork to Screen. Kodak publication S-24. 1986.

Materials for Visual Presentations—Planning and Preparation. Kodak publication S-13.

McKim, Robert H. *Experiences in Visual Thinking,* 2nd ed. Monterey, Calif.: Brooks-Cole, 1980. An excellent book to stimulate thinking about visual opportunities.

———. *Thinking Visually: A Strategy Manual for Problem-Solving.* New York: Van Nostrand Reinhold, 1981.

Media and Methods. Philadelphia: American Society of Educators. Bi-monthly.

Meilach, Dona. *Dynamics of Presentations Graphics.* Homewood, Ill.: Dow Jones-Irwin, 1986.

Minor, Edward O. *Handbook for Preparing Visual Media,* 2nd ed. New York: McGraw-Hill, 1978.

Mosvick, Roger, and Robert Nelson. *We've Got to Start Meeting Like This.* Glenview, Ill.: Scott, Foresman, 1987.

New Media Products. Los Altos, Calif.: New Media Research. Monthly.

Pavey, Donald. *Color.* Culver City, Calif.: Knapp Press, 1980. Profusely illustrated discussion of color use and psychology.

Rabb, Margaret, ed. *Presentation Design Book.* Chapel Hill, N.C.: Ventana, 1990.

Slides—Planning and Producing Slide Programs. Kodak publication S-30.

Snowberg, Richard Lee. "Bases for the Selection of Background Colors for Transparencies." *AV Communication Review,* Summer 1973, pp. 191–207.

Speechmaking . . . More Than Words Alone. Kodak publication S-25.

Tufte, Edward. *The Visual Display of Quantitative Information.* Graphics Press, 1983.

Zelazny, Gene. *Say It With Charts,* 2nd ed. Homewood, Ill.: Business One Irwin, 1991. In-depth.

CHAPTER 9   STAGE

The Audio-Visual Equipment Directory. Fairfax, Va.: International Communications Industries Association. Annual.

Audiovisual Projection. Kodak publication S-3.

D'Arcy, Jan. *Dr. Jack's Adventure in Videoconferencing Land.* Bellevue, Wash.: Jan D'Arcy, 1990. Concise, nontechnical tips for speakers.

Kodak Projection Calculator and Setting Guide for Single and Multi-Image Presentations. Kodak publication S-16.

"Lens-Projection Screen Calculator." Warsaw, Ind.: Daylite Screen Company.

Marlow, Eugene. *Managing Corporate Media,* 2nd ed. White Plains, N.Y.: Knowledge Industry Publications, 1989.

Meetings and Conventions. Secaucus, N.J.: The Travel Group. Monthly.

Official Meeting Facilities Guide. New York: Ziff-Davis. Annual guide to hotels and convention centers, including conference and audiovisual capabilities.

"Practice for Slide and Filmstrip Projection." New York: National Standards Institute, Publication No. ANSI PH3.41-1972.

Presenting Yourself. Kodak publication S-60.

CHAPTER 10 DELIVER: SHOW TIME!

Nonverbal

Bixler, Susan. *Professional Presence.* New York: G. P. Putnam, 1991.

Cho, Emily, and Linda Grover. *Looking Terrific.* New York: Ballantine, 1986.

Delmar, Ken. *Winning Moves: The Body Language of Selling.* New York: Warner, 1985.

Knapp, Mark. *Nonverbal Communication in Human Interaction.* New York: Holt, Rinehart and Winston, 1972. A good summary of all aspects of the field.

Molloy, John T. *New Dress for Success.* New York: Warner Books, 1988.

———. *The Woman's Dress for Success Book.* Chicago: Follett, 1984.

Segerstrom, Jane. *Style Strategy: Winning the Appearance Game.* Houston: Triad, 1988.

Thompson, Jacqueline. *Directory of Personal Image Consultants.* New York: Editorial Services Co., 1991.

Thompson, Jacqueline, ed. *Image Impact for Men.* New York: A&W Publishing, 1983. Wardrobe plus.

Thourlby, William. *You Are What You Wear.* New York: Forbes, Whittenburg & Brown, 1980.

Von Furstenberg, Egon. *The Power Look.* New York: Fawcett, 1979.

Language

Angione, Howard, ed. *The Associated Press Style Book.* New York: Associated Press, 1977.

Bernstein, Theodore M. *Watch Your Language.* Great Neck, N.Y.: Macmillan, 1976. Compendium of language goofs.

ETC.—A Review of General Semantics. Concord, Calif.: International Society for General Semantics. Quarterly.

Follett, Wilson. *Modern American Usage.* New York: Warner, 1966. A standard reference to prevent errors in speaking or writing.

Michaels, Leonard, and Christopher Ricks, eds. *The State of the Language.* Berkeley: University of California Press, 1979. Recent writings on language.

Newman, Edwin. *Strictly Speaking.* New York: Warner, 1975. Popular, witty look at how we cloud our communication with language.

Quarterly Review of Doublespeak. Urbana, Ill.: National Council of Teachers of English. Quarterly.

Strunk, William, Jr., and E. B. White. *The Elements of Style,* 3rd ed. New York: Macmillan, 1978. Concise; as necessary as a dictionary.

Urdang, Laurence. *The New York Times Dictionary of Misunderstood, Misused, Mispronounced Words.* New York: Times Books, 1987.

Voice

Bowen, Elbert R., Otis J. Aggertt, and William Rickert. *Communicative Reading,* 4th ed. New York: Macmillan, 1978. Suggestions and demonstrations with prose and poetry for reading aloud.

Cooper, Morton. *Change Your Voice, Change Your Life.* New York: Macmillan, 1984.

Eisenson, Jon. *Voice and Diction,* 5th ed. New York: Macmillan, 1985. Many exercises and examples.

Fisher, Hilda B. *Improving Voice and Articulation,* 2nd ed. Boston: Houghton Mifflin, 1975. Thorough, readable, and easy-to-use text.

Glass, Lillian. *Talk to Win: Six Steps to a Successful Vocal Image.* New York: Perigee, 1987.

Mayer, Lyle V. *Fundamentals of Voice and Diction,* 8th ed. Dubuque, Iowa: William C. Brown, 1988. Especially strong on correctives for specific diction problems.

Sarnoff, Dorothy. *Speech Can Change Your Life.* Garden City, N.Y.: Doubleday, 1970. Strong on vocal correctives.

CHAPTER 11   INTERACT: BETWEEN PRESENTER AND AUDIENCE

Beardsley, Monroe C. *Thinking Straight: Principles of Reasoning for Readers and Writers,* 3rd ed. Englewood Cliffs, N.J.: Prentice-Hall, 1966.

Cronkhite, Gary. *Public Speaking and Critical Listening.* Menlo Park, Calif.: Benjamin-Cummings, 1978.

Haakenson, R. "How to Handle the Q&A." In *A Guide for Better Technical Presentations.* New York: IEEE Press, 1975, pp. 158–170.

Johnson, Wendell. *People in Quandaries.* San Francisco: International Society for General Semantics, 1980.

Kahane, Howard. *Logic and Contemporary Rhetoric,* 3rd ed. Belmont, Calif.: Wadsworth, 1976.

Kimble, Gregory R. *How to Use and Misuse Statistics.* Englewood Cliffs, N.J.: Prentice-Hall, 1978.

St. Aubyn, Giles. *The Art of Argument.* Buchanan, N.Y.: Emerson Books, 1979.

CHAPTER 14   INTERNATIONAL PRESENTATIONS

The Bridge: A Review of Cross-Cultural Affairs and International Training. Denver, Col.: Systran. Quarterly.

Culturgram Communication Aids. Provo, Utah: Brigham Young University, Center for International and Area Studies, 1980–1981. Series of pamphlets giving brief introductions to 75 countries.

Doing Business in [16 countries in series]. Menlo Park, Calif.: SRI International, 1978–1980.

Glossary of International Economic Organizations and Terms. New York: U.S. Council of the International Chamber of Commerce, 1980.

Hall, Edward. *The Silent Language.* New York: Greenwood, 1980. A classic on nonverbal communication across cultures.

Harris, Philip R., and Robert T. Moran. *Managing Cultural Differences,* 3rd ed. Houston: Gulf Publishing, 1990.

Incoterms. New York: International Chamber of Commerce, 1980.

Intercultural Communicating, 2nd ed. Provo, Utah: Brigham Young University, Center for International and Area Studies, 1981. Good introduction to the subject.

The Multilingual Commercial Dictionary. New York: Facts on File, 1980. Gives key business terms in six languages.

Survival Kit for Overseas Living. Chicago: Intercultural Press Network, 1979. By the director of training of the United States International Communications Agency.

Thiederman, Sondra. *Bridging Cultural Barriers for Corporate Success.* New York: Lexington Books, 1991.

CHAPTER 15   SPEAKING FROM A MANUSCRIPT

Booher, Diana. *Executive's Portfolio of Model Speeches for All Occasions.* Englewood Cliffs, N.J.: Prentice-Hall, 1991. 180 ready-to-deliver speeches, plus many speeches that have actually been given.

Bowen, Elbert R., Otis J. Aggertt, and William Rickert. *Communicative Reading,* 4th ed. New York: Macmillan, 1978.

The Executive Speechmaker: A Systems Approach. New York: Foundation for Public Relations Research and Education, 1980.

The Executive Speechwriter Newsletter. St. Johnsbury, Vt.: Words, Inc. Bi-monthly. Also provides reports on specific topics.

Hakitt, Harold O., Jr. "When Speaking From Manuscript, Say It and Mean It." *Personnel Journal,* February 1972, pp. 108–112.

Index